The Values Connection

The Values Connection

A. James Reichley

ROWMAN & LITTLEFIELD PUBLISHERS, INC.
Lanham • Boulder • New York • Oxford

ROWMAN & LITTLEFIELD PUBLISHERS, INC.

Published in the United States of America
by Rowman & Littlefield Publishers, Inc.
4720 Boston Way, Lanham, Maryland 20706
http://www.rowmanlittlefield.com

12 Hid's Copse Road
Cumnor Hill, Oxford OX2 9JJ, England

British Library Cataloguing in Publication Information Available

Library of Congress Cataloging-in-Publication Data

Reichley, James.
　　The values connection / A. James Reichley.
　　　　p.　cm.
　　Includes bibliographical references and index.
　　ISBN 0–7425–0915–X (alk. paper)
　　I. Title.
HM681.R45　2001
303.3'72—dc21　　　　　　　　　　00–062637

Printed in the United States of America

♾ ™ The paper used in this publication meets the minimum requirements of
American National Standard for Information Sciences—Permanence of Paper for
Printed Library Materials, ANSI/NISO Z39.48–1992.

For Tony Downs

Contents

Acknowledgments

This book is the product of many years of experience, reading, and thought. Its development has also been guided by insightful advice and criticism from many colleagues and friends who have steered me away from pitfalls, corrected errors, and suggested fresh tracks of research. Among these, I wish particularly to thank Martha Bayles, Colin Campbell, John S. Coolidge, Anthony Downs, Ernest Evans, Jurgen Herbst, Stephen Hess, Norman Van Hollen, Robert A. Katzmann, Maurice Kramer, O. Thomas Miles, Richard John Neuhaus, Gillian Peel, Paul Quirk, Bruce Smith, Gilbert Y. Steiner, Kerry Stoltzfus, Glenn Tinder, Dewey Wallace, and John Kenneth White. The title was suggested by John White. Over several years, I tested my ideas on and received useful suggestions from my patient students in the political philosophy seminar of the Graduate Public Policy Institute at Georgetown University. I also thank the wise and helpful librarians of the Lauinger Library and the Woodstock Theological Center Library, both at Georgetown.

Jennifer Knerr, my editor at Rowman & Littlefield, greatly enriched both the structure and the content of the book. Ann Beardsley did a first-rate job of copyediting. Lynn Weber expertly saw the manuscript through production.

As always, I especially thank my wife, Mary, for many years of putting up with too many of the trials and tribulations that only the spouses of writers can fully appreciate.

1

Moral Foundations of a Free Society

A society can neither create nor recreate itself without, by the same stroke, creating something of the ideal.

—Emile Durkheim

Free societies do not just happen. More societies in human history have been ruled through force by tiny elites than have been governed democratically under constitutions protecting personal liberties. Even at the beginning of the twenty-first century, after several decades of unprecedented spread of freedom across the globe, more than sixty percent of the world's people, including inhabitants of China, the most populous nation on earth, still live under polities in which, according to the Freedom House Survey, "basic civil liberties are not respected."[1] In some places where democracy at the beginning of the 1990s seemed to be taking hold, such as successor states of the Soviet Union and some developing countries in Africa and Asia, governmental corruption has become so widespread and demoralizing that free institutions appear to be crumbling.

Perhaps even more unsettling, many Western democracies, where freedom has the longest record and is most firmly established, have recently been suffering social troubles that are causing deep and pervasive public anxiety and anger. Among the more visible of these problems are historically high levels of crime and illicit drug use, horrendous acts of violence and terrorism such as the Oklahoma City bombing in 1995 and the Columbine High School shootings in 1999, high rates of divorce (almost 50 percent in the United States), skyrocketing rates of babies born out of wedlock (more than one-third in the United States—the rate among African Americans in the 1960s that Daniel Patrick Moynihan warned would lead to disaster—and more than half in Sweden),[2] repeated scandals of public and pri-

1

vate corruption that in some nations have become epidemic, and generally recognized increases in incivility and alienation at all social levels.[3] Near the end of the 1990s, after several years of booming economic prosperity, a national poll found that 77 percent of Americans believed the country was "morally on the wrong track."[4] Disillusion and cynicism among voters are reflected in loss of trust in government and declining participation in elections.

During the 1990s, some of these negative trends in the West seemed to stabilize or even reverse. But at the end of the decade, most indices of social malfunction remained far higher than they had been thirty or forty years before; and such improvements as had occurred were won at costs that may not be sustainable. Reduced crime rates in the United States, for example, were partly achieved through huge increases in prison populations—more than tripling from 1980 to 1998.[5]

Polls show that most people in Western democracies maintain confidence in republican government and other major social and economic institutions. But widely held moral dissatisfaction with the quality of social life creates a situation in which serious economic or external military challenges could critically undermine public will, without which a free society cannot endure.

CORE VALUES

What do we mean by a free society? Definitions of course will vary, and any definition is subject to extended debate. At various points in this book, I will take up what freedom has meant in different times and places, and what it means to us now. For our purposes here, we can employ a broad definition that will serve as basis for discussion: A free society is one in which individuals are at liberty to pursue their own life-plans without government interference, so long as they do not infringe on the life, safety, or liberties of others, within a context of necessary protections and services supplied through free exchange, volunteer aid, or democratically elected governments. Almost every word in this definition may reasonably be questioned and criticized. Some will think it includes too much and others not enough. Should not "social groups" be designated as subjects along with "individuals"? What is meant by "life-plans"? Do protected "others" include the unborn? How about animals? What is covered by "safety"? By "liberties"? What are "necessary protections and services"? Does "democratically elected" mean pluralities or absolute majorities, and might super-majorities be required for some purposes? What qualifications can legitimately be placed on voting? And so on and on.

These questions, and many others like them, are fair and valid, but they do not have to be dealt with here—some could be (and have been) topics for entire books. As we go forward, definitions will be modified and elaborated as the subject comes more clearly into view. We shall consider the possibility that the concept of a free society on which this definition is based is entirely mistaken, as some commentators, now and in the past, have argued.

How is such a society achieved and maintained? Through dedicated and enlightened political leadership, and conscientious participation by the mass of citizens. Beyond that, through well-established institutions: legislatures, laws, courts, probably political parties, free forums for expression and exchange of ideas, primarily market economies, trade unions, adequate social services, schools . . . and perhaps most of all, families and communities. Constitutions, written or unwritten. Probably enough economic affluence, reasonably shared, to discourage bitter conflict among social classes. A substantial degree of security against internal uprisings or attacks by foreign adversaries.

Beyond all of that, some consensus among the mass of citizens on a core body of shared *values*. What are values? They are underlying directives to behavior; assumptions on which constitutions, laws, and social mores are based; the "goods" for which humans strive or to which they owe allegiance. What are "goods"? Motivating forces that are intrinsic to human nature or to humanity's place in existence.

Some writers have contended that a free society does not need a consensus on values—that, as Immanuel Kant claimed, "the problem of establishing a state is soluble even for a nation of devils."[6] But Kant believed that his devils would regulate their deviltry through reason. And this formulation in any case reflects a kind of consensus on motivating forces in human nature, even if malevolent. Still, we will consider the possibility of value-free social collaboration when we consider one category of principles or ideas around which a free society might be built. Assuming that a free society requires values, what value or values are basic? Some maintain that the entire structure may rest on a single value, such as freedom itself, or utility, or self-interest. These, too, are possibilities we will consider. But the primacy of a single value seems to me to overlook, or overwhelm, the complexity and variety of actual societies—to twist human nature as we know it out of shape, and to threaten the richness and fullness of a life that most of us would find worthwhile.

If a free society is based on more than a single value, what combination of values is needed? Obviously, there will be disagreements. Lists will vary. Provisionally, I will suggest the following ten—ten being a good round number, large enough to include most of what seems essential, while sufficiently limited to avoid descent into excess verbiage. I have tried to confine the list to values that may be regarded as good in themselves, rather than only useful (instrumental) in achieving some higher good.

1. The *unique value and significance of each human life*—without taking

up at this point the thorny questions of what constitutes a distinct life, or whether individual lives may under some circumstances be sacrificed for the sake of the larger whole—the concept that each life, regardless of age, race, gender, or physical or intellectual capacities, has unique worth that must be honored by any state or society that claims to be truly free. On this value are founded both personal liberties and individual property rights.

2. Civil *order through the rule of law*, the alternative to rule by brute force. Though not limited to free societies, this value is particularly essential to societies in which individuals are given broad scope to pursue self-chosen goals. Even if government is no more than the minimal "night watchman state" cherished by libertarians, it will be needed to prevent collision and chaos among varying life-plans. For most people, social order and lawful behavior are considerably more than that—blessings in themselves, framing and enhancing other components of the good life. If the value of order is given too high a priority, of course, it infringes on freedom and other essential values of a free society.

3. *Continuity*, a value that includes, but is not limited to, the concept of "community" currently heralded by secular and religious communitarians. Continuity gives meaning and purpose to life by relating individual lives to larger patterns in time and nature. It is essential to a free society as the binding web that holds together singular wills, and as a source of support that transcends particular desires.

4. *Moral equality*, derived from the conviction that each human life by some objective standard is not only unique but also worth as much as every other human life. This value underlies the principles of equality before the law and equality of opportunity, in the sense of unimpeded access to arenas of economic, social, and political participation. It is not the same thing as imposition of approximately equal distributions of economic goods and status as an end result. This latter concept, I will argue in discussion of some equalitarian value systems, is so contrary to the rich variety of individual human natures, capacities, and behaviors that it could be achieved, or even aimed at, only through extreme concentration of social power—in other words, at the expense of freedom.

5. *Justice*, related to law, but a distinct value in its own right. In some instances, law, the rules governing society at a given time, may clash with justice, what is objectively fair by some underlying or transcendent moral standard. When this happens, as it did in the civil rights struggle of the 1960s, those claiming to pursue justice may sometimes feel impelled to break what they regard as unjust laws, but should be prepared to accept the consequences if the laws they violate are constitutionally enacted. In a free society, law should be guided toward justice but an independent sense of justice is still needed as a norm for moral equity.

6. *Popular sovereignty*. Since the time of the ancient Greeks, some writers

have argued that freedom is separable from democracy—that the former can be enjoyed under more or less authoritarian political systems. This claim has recently been pressed most assertively by some politicians and social theorists in East Asia, and now once again in Russia. Experience, ancient and modern, demonstrates, however, that without some form of majority rule, with rights to democratic participation broadly defined, freedom soon perishes.

7. *Tolerance*, openness to free expression of diverse opinions on public issues, and differences in public and private behavior. Tolerance does not require acceptance of moral relativism or an attitude of "anything goes." (Moral relativists are often distinctly *intolerant* of dissent against their own shibboleths.) But it does require recognition of the common humanity and citizenship rights of all persons, regardless of race, religion, sex, ethnic origin, class, physical condition, or political persuasion.

8. *Honor*, sometimes held to be an essentially aristocratic or military value, with little place in a democratic or civilian culture. As I use the term, however, it is close to Aristotle's idea of "virtue" as a basis for good citizenship. Francis Fukuyama and others have argued persuasively that trust is a factor that most economically and politically successful societies in history have held in common.[7] Without a widely respected sense of personal honor, general trust among citizens becomes impossible. Honor is the basis for ordinary good manners and truth-telling.

9. *Compassion*, an acted upon sentiment of concern and responsibility for persons in need or trouble beyond one's immediate social group. Without compassion, a free society inevitably descends into a cauldron of warring self-interests, with resulting political insecurity, and coarsening of individual spirits. Compassion motivates caring behavior—by no means only, or mainly, carried out through government.

10. *Realism*, a moral imperative as well as a prudential guide to economic and political action. Moral realism springs from recognition of the inherent limitations of human nature and the necessary imperfection of all human institutions and knowledge. It teaches that all schemes for achieving finished social utopias are cruel political hoaxes and that deliberate movement toward a somewhat better world is the legitimate goal for enlightened social policy.

Most readers will find this list to some extent inadequate. Many would include other values which they regard as no less vital: for instance, willingness to compromise, decentralization of social authority to the lowest level of effective administration, a work ethic, patriotism, cultural diversity, pursuit of excellence, rational administration, no doubt some others. These qualities are characteristic of most actual free societies but are less basic than those on my list. Many are a means to achieve some higher end rather than objective goods in themselves. In any case, the values on my list, or a list pretty much like it, provide at least a minimum foundation for a functioning free society.

VALUE SYSTEMS

Where do such values come from? Where do *any* values come from? I have concluded after a good deal of analysis and reflection that primary sources of value in human life can be limited to three: the *self*; *society*, beginning with the family and the gang, and rising to include whole civilizations; and *transcendent being*, which in the Western tradition we usually call God. Each of these terms will be explained more fully in the following chapters dealing with value systems based on one or more of these primary sources.

Other possible value sources, such as reason, nature, natural law, technology, and nontheistic religions, will occur to readers. It can be shown that all of these are ultimately reducible to the basic three, and I will so argue in the course of this book. For now, though, I ask only that the structure of the three primary value sources be accepted as a device, like a clock or a yardstick, through which value systems can be arranged and analyzed.

Using the three primary value sources, alone or in combination, value systems can be classified into seven categories or families of value systems, depending on which sources are regarded as fundamental. These categories, with appropriate titles, are:

- *Egoism,* based on the self as the only legitimate value source
- *Collectivism,* based on society alone
- *Monism,* based on transcendence alone
- *Absolutism,* based on both transcendence and society
- *Ecstasism,* based on the self and transcendence
- *Civil humanism,* based on the self and society
- *Transcendent idealism,* based on all three sources—transcendence, the self, and society

Although each of these titles in general usage has many different meanings, I will explain in the chapters on each why I have chosen those specific titles and will limit my discussion to the assigned definitions.

There is a further possibility not covered by this list: that *no* value source exercises genuine moral authority over human life. This is the possibility of *nihilism,* the belief that life is essentially without value, as I am using the term. I prefer to classify this as a non-system—what is left if all values fail. It is a view that is harder to maintain seriously than is often imagined.

In chapters examining the origins and development of each of the value system categories, preliminary consideration is given to the capacity to generate the values on which a free society depends. In a final chapter, these findings are summarized, and I will attempt judgment on which system or systems, alone or in combination, provide sufficient moral foundation for a free society to endure over a considerable time.

Some readers will argue that if certain values are accepted as needed to sustain a free society, belief in a free society is itself sufficient source to maintain them. This is conceivable but by no means obvious. Experience shows that some persons genuinely attracted to a free society are prepared in practice to subordinate this attraction to other values, such as self-interest, tribal loyalty, or ideological commitment. The possibility that support for a free society may itself generate the values on which it is based will also be considered.

During some periods in history, particular value systems have dominated entire civilizations. In some parts of the world, this remains to some extent true even today. In most of the West, however, and increasingly throughout the world, value systems compete within nations and civilizations, with none truly dominant. In the United States, all seven families of value systems are now active, though with varying degrees of vitality and influence.

Samuel Huntington has cogently argued—though with thoughtful criticism from many—that true competition and potential conflict in the modern world is now among whole civilizations rather than among nations. He identifies nine major civilizations currently on the world scene.[8] Huntington's analysis provides some useful insights, but the deeper and more significant competition in the world now is not among geographically separated civilizations but among value systems that cross civilizations as well as nations.

This concept of value systems may seem to present an even more complicated picture than Huntington's, but in a way it offers a more hopeful outlook. Value systems are less likely than civilizations to be frozen along national lines that may give rise to military conflict, in conditions created by modern technology potentially lethal to all human life. Interacting with each other, value systems offer possibilities for conversion, accommodation, and peaceful change. Though it is unlikely—and perhaps unappealing—that any one value system, or even family of value systems, will any time soon become dominant in the United States or the West, let alone the world community, the possibility of moving toward a general core of shared values on which a more peaceful and enlightened world might be based seems to me at least conceivable.

If a widely held body of core values is essential to the endurance of a free society, how to maintain such values is of considerable urgency to all believers in freedom. This book obviously goes only a small way toward clarifying the issues at stake, but I hope it may make some contribution to studies of fundamental value questions that are now underway in many parts of the world.

My method of study and presentation will separately trace the origins and development, as well as current manifestations, of each of the seven value system families. Some major events, such as the rise and fall of Periclean Athens, the origins of biblical Judaism and Christianity, the Renaissance and the Reformation, and the American and French Revolutions, appear in more than one of these accounts, producing at times a kind of *Rashomon* effect in which the same actions are seen from varying perspectives. Some thinkers, such as Plato, Rousseau, and Nietzsche, also appear in more than one account.

I will conclude this introductory chapter with a reminder that even so important a work as maintaining a free society is not the paramount concern of most of the religions that form the bases of many value systems. Nor should it be. As H. Richard Niebuhr wrote, "The instrumental value of faith for society is dependent upon faith's conviction that it has more than instrumental value. Faith could not defend us if it believed that defense was its meaning."[9] Faith for the faithful has goals and visions that transcend the future of human political systems, including republican government and democracy.

This being said, the social and political consequences that are shaped by underlying systems of value are of vital importance to most of us. Let us then proceed to consideration of the first of the value system families.

2

<del>◇━━━◇</del>

Egoism:
Whatever Turns You On

In the first place, I put for a general inclination of all mankind, a perpetual and restless desire of power after power, that ceaseth only in death.

—Thomas Hobbes

E *goism*, the category of value system that gives primacy to the self as a legitimate source of values, would seem to have natural advantages as a sufficient foundation for social, political, economic, and cultural freedoms. If maintenance of individual rights is the chief criterion of a free society, what more is needed to validate freedom than the drives, tastes, or appetites of the self?

Before the advent of modernity, egoism was not usually articulated or defended as an unambiguous system for rendering value judgments. Since the eighteenth century, however, it has increasingly been advanced, without subterfuge or apology, as a guide to liberation and enlightenment.

DISCOVERY OF THE SELF

Consciousness of self, though not in isolation, may reasonably be identified as the defining characteristic that distinguishes humans from all other known forms of life. Bipedality, increased brain size, the capacity to create language, and the ability to make tools are all important landmarks on the march toward humanness. But it was the discovery of "I," the conscious differentiation of the self from everything else, that marked the real breakthrough, the point of no return—a tragic moment, too, but the proximate source from which much that is uniquely human was to follow.

Prior to the conception of *I* in my mind, I do not as myself fully exist.

9

What is to become myself, as a natural being, is a bundle of instinctual drives conditioned by environmental pressures and restraints. With the recognition of *I*, there is a point of reference, a means for organizing activity beyond the capacity of any other known creature.

Even more important may be the discovery of *me*—progress from the subjective *I*, a way of viewing, to the objective *me*, a way of conceiving myself as a particular actor in the experienced world, inseparably linked with the viewing self. It may be, as Jurgen Habermas and others have contended, that recognition of *me* already implies conscious identification with a social group—a *we*. But awareness of the objective *me*, however achieved, provides an indispensable confirmation of the existence of self.

With knowledge of *I* and *me*, humans are able to make all sorts of calculations formerly out of reach, equipped to develop plans over time—on their way to at least fragile preeminence among the world of things. Discovery of the "Inner I," the psychologist Nicholas Humphrey wrote, enabled "our first ancestors . . . to make realistic guesses about the inner life of their rivals, to picture what another was thinking about and planning, to read the minds of others by reading their own." John Jaynes observed that, at a somewhat later stage in human development, "capacities for self-exhortation and self-reminding are a prerequisite for the sorts of elaborated and long-term bouts of self-control without which agriculture, building projects, and other civilized and civilizing activities could not be organized."[1]

The rewards of self-awareness go beyond an advantage in competition for material goods. Emotional satisfaction in personal mastery, once experienced, is itself a powerful motivator for further experiment, as anyone who has ever acquired skill at a game or a trade knows.

The philosopher Daniel Dennett, though hotly scornful of any distinction between human "mind" and "body," does not doubt the significance of the self: "The strangest and most wonderful constructions in the whole animal world are the amazing, intricate constructions made by the primate, *Homo sapiens*. Each normal individual of this species makes a *self*." Approaching the subject from the standpoint of sociobiology, Edward O. Wilson concludes: "The self is the leading actor" in the "neural drama" through which the human brain interprets sense experience. "The emotional centers of the lower brain are programmed to pull the puppeteer's strings more carefully whenever the self steps onto the stage."[2]

Opinions vary about the degree to which humans are genetically inclined to be cooperative, communal, or even altruistic. What is not in dispute is that every normal human individual from a very early age is able to recognize a definable self-interest. So it has always been. The intellectual historian and philosopher Charles Taylor writes that members of a Paleolithic hunting group confronting a charging mammoth "must have had very much the same sense we would have had in their place: here is one person, and there is another, and which one survives/flourishes depends on which person/body is run over by that mammoth."[3]

With discovery of the mortal self and its interests comes recognition that the life of the individual, at least in this world, must end; that the individual's most cherished interests, including interests in the welfare of others, must in the long run be frustrated; that pleasure is fleeting; and that many desires cannot possibly be fulfilled. At an early stage, therefore, a certain sadness seems to have entered human consciousness. Cave paintings at Lascaux in southern France, composed about 20,000 years ago, convey a brooding sense of human finiteness. "Celebrate the glad day," wrote an unknown Egyptian poet around 2200 BC, "be not weary therein. Lo, no man takes his goods with him; Yea none returns again that is gone thither."

WHAT'S IN IT FOR PROTAGORAS?

Class rule, representing the self-interests of particularly enterprising or fortunate warriors, characterized the military chiefdoms that developed in the Middle East about 7,000 years ago. In the first states, founded in Egypt and Mesopotamia toward the end of the fourth millennium BC, wrote V. Gordon Childe, society was divided into a "tiny ruling class, who annexed the bulk of the social surplus," and "the vast majority who were left with a bare subsistence and effectively excluded from the spiritual benefits of civilization." Merchant classes that began to appear in states, particularly Phoenicia, during the first millennium BC functioned through calculation of material self-interest.

Literary records coming down from the ancient world include occasional celebrations of the self as an independent source of values. Some passages of the Babylonian *Epic of Gilgamesh*, a myth of the quester-hero based on sources that go back to around 2000 BC, advocate unrestrained satisfaction of the self's sensual appetites.

> When the gods created men,
> upon men did they also impose death. . . .
> Thou, O Gilgamesh, gratify thy flesh;
> Enjoy thyself by day and night;
> Make a feast of joy every day;
> Day and night be wanton and happy.[4]

The Indian epic the *Ramayana*, created by itinerant storytellers from the third century BC to the second century AD, counsels: "There is no hereafter, Rama, vain the hope and creed of men; Seek the pleasures of the present, spurn illusions poor and vain." Even an atypical passage of the Hebrew

Bible conveys essentially egoistic values, as in Ecclesiastes 9:4–7: "A living dog is better than a dead lion. For the living know that they shall die: but the dead know not any thing, neither have they any more a reward. . . . Go thy way, eat thy bread with joy, and drink thy wine with a merry heart."

The Homeric epics the *Iliad* and the *Odyssey,* composed in Greece around 750 BC, express a value system with some individualistic tendencies. The most important Homeric injunction, Alasdair MacIntyre points out, is: "Always to be the best and most prominent among others." This standard requires social recognition for fulfillment, but instills values that are inherently individualistic. However, some classical scholars maintain that the idea of the self as a conscious focus of value is not fully developed in Homer.[5]

During the centuries after Homer, Greek poets and writers began to express a more clearly defined concept of self. The middle class that developed after the introduction of coinage and formation of a market economy in the seventh century "pugnaciously asserted the self-sufficiency of the individual household." Hesiod, the farmer–poet who wrote in Boeotia shortly after 700 BC, celebrated the beneficial effects of competitive economic individualism. "If a person without work in hand sees another, a wealthy man who hurries to plow and plant to put his household in good order, then that neighbor envies his neighbor who hurries after riches. This is the good strife for mortals." Carried too far, however, Hesiod warned, individualism might lead to disintegration of social order. "The evil man will hurt the superior man by speaking with crooked words and will swear an oath on them. Envy, foul-mouthed, evil-rejoicing, and ugly-faced, will accompany all pitiful people."[6]

On another track, Greek poets of the seventh and sixth centuries gave voice to the passions and anxieties of the subjective self. "Take your joy when life is joyful," urges Archilochus, "and in sorrow do not mind / Overmuch but know what ups and downs belong to humankind." The Aeolian lyric poet Alcaeus advises: "Now is the moment, now / To take what happiness the gods allow." Sappho of Lesbos places the passionate self at the center of consciousness in poems she wrote for the adolescent girls who were her students:

> When I even see you, my voice stops,
> My tongue is broken, a thin flame runs beneath my skin,
> My eyes are blinded, there is thunder in my ears,
> The sweat pours from me, I tremble
> Through and through, I am paler than grass
> And I seem almost like one dead.[7]

Tendencies toward economic individualism and aesthetic subjectivism came together in fifth-century Athens, the Athens of Pericles, to help produce the extraordinary cultural flowering of classical Greece. While the architectural masterpieces of Periclean Athens were rising on the Acropolis, teachers of rhetoric down below in the marketplace, the *agora*, were probing reality through the faculty of reason. These teachers, whom we know collectively as Sophists, at first offered moral training for upper-class youth through instruction in models of literature. But they soon began teaching skills in argument that enabled their customers to trip up opponents in the law courts and the recently founded Athenian assembly.

Socrates, Nietzsche claimed, was "the first and supreme *Sophist*, the mirror and epitome of all sophistical tendencies."[8] But Socrates, in the course of his career as teacher and intellectual gadfly, went beyond Sophism. Rational speculation, he concluded, is but a technique for discovering objective absolute truths, moral as well as mathematical and physical. This conclusion brought him into conflict with some of the professionally successful Sophists, who believed that appeal to self-interest, which was bringing them celebrity and good livings, provided standard enough. Refutation of Sophism became part of his life's work—carried on with relentless intensity by his most famous pupil, Plato.

According to MacIntyre, the main body of Sophists assumed that "social life [is] an arena in which each individual and each group of individuals seeks to maximize the satisfaction of his or her own wants and needs."[9] Building on this assumption, they constructed the first, at least in the West, exposition of egoism as a more or less coherent and consistent moral belief system. "Man is the measure of all things," declared Protagoras, "of existing things that they exist and of non-existing things that they exist not"— the existential assumption on which all moral egoism is based.

"Man is the measure of all things" simply rules out transcendence as a source of truth and, by implication, value. This formulation can accommodate civil humanism and even secular collectivism. Other Sophists made clear their belief in the sole authority of self-interest. "Justice," Plato quotes Thrasymachus as saying in *The Republic*, "is nothing else than the interest of the stronger." Callicles argues, in another of Plato's dialogues, that "both among animals and in entire states and races . . . right is recognized to be the sovereignty and advantage of the stronger over the weaker."[10] Though the Greeks had no word that exactly corresponds to the modern Western idea of the self, as formulated by Descartes and others, the concept of the primacy of self-interest underlies much of the Sophists' view of life and morality.

Egoism was not a mere academic theory expounded by Athenian intellectuals during all-night drinking bouts. After Pericles, it exerted strong influence among Athens's democratic politicians. Pericles himself, leader of the Athenian state at its zenith, attempted to maintain a moral bridge between self-interest and civic duty. But his successors, Thucydides reports, "pursued their own profit rather than that of the city."[11]

While the Sophists formed a philosophic basis for egoism in the lanes of the *agora*, Euripides, on the other side of the Acropolis in the Theatre of Dionysus, explored through drama the moral consequences of a belief system devoted to self. Euripides is generally critical of the effects of egoistic drives on social intercourse, but on occasion he expresses the passions of the subjective self with an intensity that rivals Sappho, as in *The Bacchae*:

> When shall I dance once more
> with bare feet the all-night dances,
> tossing my head for joy
> in the damp air, in the dew,
> as a running fawn might frisk
> for the green joy of the wide fields.[12]

Living on into the period of post-Periclean decline, Euripides deplored the self-aggrandizement of petty democratic politicians:

> O gods, spare me the sight
> of this thankless breed, these politicians
> who cringe for favors from a screaming mob
> and do not care what harm they do their friends
> providing they can please a crowd![13]

He mourned the collapse of the old civic virtues: "Good faith has gone, and no more remains in great Greece a sense of shame." But unlike his two fellows in the great triad of Greek tragedians, Aeschylus and Sophocles, he offered no compelling alternative to egoist values: "The man who sticks it out against his fate / shows spirit, but the spirit of a fool."[14]

The role of egoism in the decline of Athens and its eventual conquest in 335 BC by Macedonia is debatable. Certainly there were other causes, perhaps beyond the control of any social system. But Demosthenes, who led the city–state in its final defense against the Macedonians, put much of the blame on a social atmosphere in which "politics has become the path to riches, and individuals no longer place the state before themselves, but rather see the state as a means for promoting their own personal welfare."[15]

Euripides had already, in words he gave to Electra, composed the epitaph of Athens's golden age: "Look, look at this light, this gleaming / we shall never see again!"[16]

Writing in the next century, during the long Hellenistic twilight that followed Alexander the Great's whirlwind conquest of most of the ancient world, Epicurus spelled out the ethical implications of egoism for a people who had lost political vigor but retained economic and social privilege. Justice, Epicurus taught, is completely relative: "Justice is never anything in itself. It is a kind of agreement not to harm or be harmed." Morality is what brings pleasure to the individual: "Every good and evil lies in sensation." The rational man's sole objective in life is "freedom from pain in the body and from trouble in the mind." In pursuit of this goal, moral or civic responsibility is to be avoided: "We must get out of the prisonhouse of routine duties and politics." With Epicurus, egoism became the creed of socially detached pleasure-seekers and dilettantes.[17]

In the Roman Empire that inherited Hellenistic culture, egoism remained popular among courtiers and poets. Certainly many Roman politicians single-mindedly, and often unscrupulously, pursued self-interest in their careers. But the Roman mind, while receptive to some forms of egoism and humanism, was shaped by the ethos of the military camp, and remained in its essential nature collectivist and authoritarian. Egoism took refuge in the practice of subterranean vices.

THE MACHIAVELLIAN MOMENT

With establishment of Christianity as the official religion of the empire near the end of the fourth century AD, egoism suffered further loss of public prestige. During the long centuries of the Dark and Middle Ages that followed the fall of Rome to the Goths in 410, Christian doctrine, variously interpreted, promoted the service of values beyond the self. Egoism no doubt remained the personal standard of many individuals, directing practical behavior in both public and private life, but most people felt obliged to give at least lip-service to the values ordained by church and civil authorities.

It was not until the Renaissance began to rise in Italy during the fourteenth century, restoring human confidence and renewing interest in the models of antiquity, that the self (though not yet full-fledged egoism) once more strode without disguise on the public stage. "This is the culminating gift of God," wrote Giovanni Pico Della Mirandolla in fifteenth-century Florence, "this is the supreme and marvelous felicity of man . . . that he can be what he wills to be." Leon Battista Alberti, another Florentine, agreed: "A man can do all things if he will." Renaissance artists began painting from the three-dimensional perspective of the observing individual and going outside religious subject matter to produce highly personalized portraits of contemporary wielders of social power or pagan gods and goddesses. "In the Middle Ages," wrote the nineteenth-century cultural historian Jakob Burckhardt, "man was conscious of himself only as a member of a race, people, party, family, or corporation—only through some general category. In Italy this veil first melted into air . . . man became a spiritual individual, and recognized himself as such."[18]

The Renaissance self was more humanist than egoist. Scholars and artists for the most part associated the value of the individual with surrounding civic or transcendent values. But the egoist self, requiring no external sanction, begins, in the tight-lipped aristocrats of Bronzino, the hard-eyed grandees of Titian, and the smugly sybaritic *Bacchus* of Caravaggio, to break through the wrappings of piety and convention.

Niccolo Machiavelli, the inventor of modern political science, was by intent a civic patriot. He wrote to assure the survival of the Florentine republic, which he served as courtier and diplomat. As J. G. A. Pocock has observed, Machiavelli distrusted Christianity, not because it limited the individual, but "because it taught men to give themselves to ends other than the city's and to love their own souls more than the fatherland."[19] His avowed values and principles were predominantly civil humanist, picked up from the spirit of the time (the early sixteenth century). But by writing with cold realism about how men actually behaved in politics, rather than as seen through the lens of officially approved moral ideals, which he viewed as sham, he gave a kind of approval to the behavior itself, whether to serve the interest of the state, or purely for self-interest.

"When it is an absolute question of the welfare of our country," Machiavelli advised, "we must admit of no consideration of justice or injustice, of mercy or cruelty, of praise or ignominy; but putting all else aside we must adopt whatever course will save the nation's existence and liberty." But if "all else" has been put aside, why not put aside "the nation's existence and liberty" as well? Certainly not because of any respect for or confidence in the common people. "[The ruler] must be a great liar and hypocrite. Men are so simple of mind, and so much dominated by their immediate needs that a deceitful man will always find men who are ready to be deceived."[20]

La Rochefoucauld wrote that hypocrisy is the tribute that vice pays to virtue. By stripping the veil of hypocrisy from Renaissance politics, Machiavelli performed useful service for science and public candor. But he also undermined moral restraints against practices that even villains like his hero Cesare Borgia had acknowledged must be evil.

HOBBES: THE WAR OF EACH AGAINST ALL

During the next two centuries, the self, variously conceived, played a growing role in philosophical discourse, particularly among thinkers north of the Alps. Montaigne, writing in France around 1575, issued blasts of urbane skepticism against medieval scholasticism and conventional religion.[21] Descartes, half a century later, made the irreducible self ("I think, therefore I am") his foundation for reconstructing, through reason, all the old verities of truth and morality.

It was left to Thomas Hobbes, writing in seventeenth-century England, to place self-interest unequivocally at the center of the moral universe. The English had always been an unusually independent and freedom-loving people. As early as the thirteenth century, while most of Europe remained firmly under the grip of the feudal order, individual Englishmen of lowly status were successfully demanding recognition of personal rights for themselves and their families. Alan MacFarlane has shown that English farmers, unlike peasants on the European continent, were able to buy and sell land, and to bequeath property to particular offspring. By the end of the Middle Ages, English common law held "individuals rather than families . . . responsible for crimes," fostering a sense of personal responsibility.[22]

Traditional individualism was reinforced in the seventeenth century by the spirit of market capitalism that burst across northwestern Europe. "Gain is the sole and unique compass by which these people are guided," wrote a French visitor to Holland in 1648. Similar appetites blossomed among the merchant class of England, perched on the best routes to the New World.

The Protestant Reformation, which came late but with particular vitality to England, concentrated the hope of salvation on spiritual experience of the individual, and expanded both self-awareness and self-criticism. Paul Claudel's observation that "the Protestant prays alone," in contrast to Catholicism's emphasis on corporate worship, is an overstatement, but Protestantism certainly elevated the importance of the individual's direct relationship to God. As Max Weber and R. H. Tawney have argued, religious enthusiasm and discipline instilled by Protestantism helped motivate enterprising persons to improve their material lot.

The Reformation in its more radical expression divided England between those who would impose strict practice of the new faith and those who preferred only a moderately reformed Catholicism or even restoration of the old religion. In the middle years of the seventeenth century, this split helped produce civil war.

Hobbes, caught up in the bitter struggle between Royalist Cavaliers supporting Charles I and Puritan Roundheads led by Oliver Cromwell, had full opportunity to observe the crueler aspects of human nature. Taking the Royalist side, Hobbes fled to France with the future Charles II, whom he briefly served as tutor, after the Puritan triumph. Human beings, experience and reflection convinced him, are motivated entirely by self-interest. "Man, whose joy consisteth in comparing himself with other men, can relish nothing but what is eminent." Scrutiny of civil society yields "no authentical doctrines concerning right and wrong, good and evil, besides the constituted laws in each realm and government."[23]

In *The Leviathan*, published in 1651, Hobbes plunged deeply into personal consciousness to discover the wellsprings of human behavior. What he found there was nothing but pursuit of pleasure. "Whatsoever is the object of any man's appetite or desire, that is it which he for his part calleth *good*; and the object of his hate and aversion, *evil*." Desire and fear propel humans into a kind of perpetual motion, inevitably producing conflict among individuals. "If any two men desire the same thing, which nevertheless they cannot both enjoy, they become enemies; and in the way to their end, . . . endeavor to destroy, or subdue one another." Due to this inherent tendency to disorder in human affairs, Hobbes concluded, humanity's natural condition is "war . . . of every man against every man," causing "continual fear, and danger of violent death," and a life that is "solitary, poor, nasty, brutish, and short."[24]

Having stripped human nature to the bone, Hobbes perceived essential equality among men "in the faculties of body and mind." Though natural differences in physical strength and mental agility obviously exist, "when all is reckoned together, the difference between men and men is not so considerable, as that one man can therefore claim to himself any benefit, to which another may not pretend as well as he." Social and political hierarchies of the kind supported by Hobbes's royalist patrons are therefore entirely artificial, but that does not make them any the less necessary. The very equality of men requires that, to escape the war of every man against every man, they must submit, not merely to hierarchy, but to an absolute sovereign: "that great LEVIATHAN, or rather, to speak more reverently, that *mortal god*, to which we owe . . . our peace and defense." This finding must have outraged not only republican Roundheads, but also many Cavaliers who preferred to regard the king simply as first among the realm's natural God-authorized rulers.[25]

Though Hobbes acknowledges religion in his books, its inclusion seems intended for political self-protection. Some writers argue that he may have been "merely a very unorthodox believer,"[26] but the general view that he was privately an atheist is probably correct. The real source of moral authority for the political edifice he creates is nothing but self-interest, "there being nothing simply and absolutely so; nor any common rule of good and evil to be taken from the nature of the objects themselves; but from the person of man." From this uncompromising moral relativism justifying radical individualism, Hobbes derives a prescription for unrestricted authoritarian government—unless and until government threatens the very life of the individual, by which time it would probably be too late for effective resistance.[27]

ADAM SMITH: AN INVISIBLE HAND CLAPPING

Hobbes's great successor among English empirical philosophers, John Locke, writing toward the end of the seventeenth century, formulated the theoretic foundation on which much of modern individualism is based. Locke, unlike Hobbes, however, remained within the Christian tradition, and rooted his social, economic, and political individualism in Christian faith and morality. His work, discussed in chapter eleven on the ideological origins of the American Revolution, belongs morally to the family of value systems that I call transcendent idealism.

During the eighteenth century, some European intellectuals who carried on part of Locke's philosophic legacy abandoned his reliance on Christian morality. In England, the Whig publicists John Trenchard and Thomas Gordon approvingly declared human nature "restless and selfish." Sir William Blackstone, in his magisterial discourse on English common law, rejected "abstracted rules and precepts," and traced pursuit of "the rule of right [to] only our own self-love, the universal principle of action." In France in 1750, the young Turgot, among the first advocates of laissez-faire economics, hailed "self-interest, ambition, vainglory" as forces that advance society "toward greater perfection."[28]

Such ideas helped produce, and in turn were reinforced by, a social atmosphere that increasingly celebrated the rights of the self. The French social historian Roger Chartier suggests three manifestations of the "new self-consciousness": "the emergence of a new image of the child as a unique person distinct from the family or community; the prevalence of private writing in journals and diaries; and the change in the nature of literature, whose truth came to rest on exploration, exhibition, and exaltation of the self." A prime example of the last was creation of the modern novel in eighteenth-century England. In upper- and middle-class society, Chartier writes, "the rules of civility established a protected zone around each individual. . . . Table manners no longer condoned eating from a common plate."[29]

The Enlightenment, beginning in France around the middle of the eighteenth century and quickly extending through much of Europe, traced some of its origin to Locke's philosophy. But many Enlightenment writers rejected Locke's attachment to Christianity. "It is not on religion," argued Helvetius, most systematic of the *philosophes*, "but on legislation that the vices, the virtues, the power, and the felicity of the people depend." Baron d'Holbach, an avowed atheist, found "self-preservation . . . the common goal toward which all energies, forces, and human faculties seem continuously directed."[30]

Adam Smith, an absent-minded and eccentric professor of philosophy at the University of Glasgow, shared the skepticism toward religion that was common to much of the Enlightenment, but stopped well short of the outright egoism with which his work is now often associated. Smith, like many fellow participants in the eighteenth-century Scottish school of "common-sense realism," preserved a role in his system for God as a kind of benevolent overseer, but sought to make morality independent of traditional

Christianity. As Jerry Muller has commented, Smith's first book, *The Theory of Moral Sentiments*, published in 1759, "was intended in part to answer the question, Why be moral if you no longer believe in heaven or hell?"[31]

Smith's particular answer to this question was based on the hypothesis, adopted from his Scottish colleague Francis Hutcheson, that men naturally feel "moral sympathy" for one another. According to Smith, following Hutcheson, there are sentiments in man's nature "which interest him in the fortune of others, and render their happiness necessary to him, though he derives nothing from it except the happiness of seeing it." Such feelings of sympathy, Smith argued, enable each man to put himself in the other person's shoes and see himself to a considerable extent as others see him. From insights so gained, the individual can form in his own mind a disinterested third-person observer, providing the basis for objective rules of behavior that reach beyond momentary impulses of good will.[32]

Smith recognized the fragility of this mechanism in maintaining decent behavior among humans. Along with moral sympathy, he observed, men are motivated by competing self-interests. He saw a considerable role for government in protecting human beings against each other, and in nurturing their natural moral sympathies. He was far ahead of his time in promoting mass public education. But, like others in the Lockean tradition, he did not wholly trust the maintenance of social harmony and fairness to government, necessarily managed by men with limited knowledge and driven by their own self-interests.

As an alternative to government, Smith, in his best-known book, *Inquiry into the Nature and Cause of the Wealth of Nations*, published in 1776, looked to the emerging institution of the economic free market to motivate and coordinate much of the world's work. "It is not from the benevolence of the butcher, the brewer, or the baker, that we expect our dinner, but from their regard to their own interest. We address ourselves, not to their humanity but to their self-love, and never talk to them of our own necessities but of their advantages." He had no illusions about the good intentions of the merchant class. "People of the same trade seldom meet together, even for merriment and diversion, but the conversation ends in a conspiracy against the public, or in some contrivance to raise prices."[33]

Having begun with Locke, Smith had gone a considerable distance toward Hobbes. But nature itself, he believed, provides an escape from Hobbes's choice between anarchy and authoritarian government in a moral universe organized around the self. Earlier in the century, Bernard de Mandeville, a Hollander living in England, had in his *Fable of the Bees*, published in 1741, offered the daring proposition that "Private Vices" make "Publick Benefits." Smith developed this argument more systematically. Competition in the market, if left largely free of government regulation, he maintained, will naturally tend to advance the general interest of society as a whole. An individual seeking his own interest is "led by an invisible hand to promote an end which was no part of his intention. . . . By pursuing his own interest he frequently promotes that of the society more effectually than when he really intends to promote it. I have never known much good done by those who affected to trade for the public good."[34]

The question Smith does not answer is: Without moral or legal sanctions, what will prevent economically successful individuals, motivated mainly by self-interest, from using political and social power derived from wealth to rig the market in their own favor?

"NOTHING IS FORBIDDEN"

Individualism, variously based, played a major part in launching the two great political revolutions of the latter part of the eighteenth century, the American that began in 1775 and the French in 1789. American individualism grew largely from belief in transcendent sources of value, in fact to a great extent from the Christian tradition. Thomas Jefferson, Thomas Paine, and to a lesser extent, Benjamin Franklin shared the Enlightenment's skepticism about traditional Christian doctrine. But George Washington, both Adamses, Alexander Hamilton, James Madison, and most of the other leaders and participants in the patriot cause, though influenced by Enlightenment ideas, maintained the roots of their values in Christianity, as we will later see.

The French Revolution was another matter. While its complex sources include civil humanism of the kind expressed in the previous generation by Helvetius and Voltaire, and a new brand of secular collectivism formulated by Rousseau, it also drew on an emerging strain of undisguised egoism. Its opposition to trinitarian Christianity was explicit. In one of the Revolution's more exuberant moments, members of the national assembly paraded to the Cathedral of Notre Dame where a prostitute was installed on the altar to be worshipped as a goddess of Reason. Napoleon, who eventually picked up the pieces from the near anarchy that by the late 1790s was consuming the Revolution, claimed to understand its premise: "Vanity made the Revolution, liberty was only a pretext."

Beneath the Revolution's official ideology, a deeper, in some ways more profound, egoism was stirring. The Marquis de Sade, a member of the minor aristocracy who took up the cause of the Revolution after he had suffered numerous prosecutions and imprisonments for imaginative experiments in sexual depravity, wrote: "Nothing is forbidden us by nature. . . . Nothing is more immoral than nature, she has never imposed limits upon us, nor has she dictated us laws." One of Sade's twentieth-century admirers, Michel Foucault, wrote: "Sadism . . . is a massive cultural fact which appeared precisely at the end of the eighteenth century, and which constitutes one of the greatest conversions of Western imagination: unreason transformed into delirium of the heart, madness of desire, the insane dialogue of love and death in the limitless presumption of appetite."[35]

A long way from the sober meditations of Adam Smith—but no less a guide to egoism's logical moral future.

LAISSEZ-FAIRE: DEVIL TAKE THE HINDMOST

In the nineteenth century, individualism, with egoism as one of its major components, increasingly gathered steam. "Individualism," Alexis de Tocqueville wrote in 1850, "is a feeling of comfort, which allows each citizen to withdraw from the mass of his fellow men in order to keep company with his family and friends, in such a way that, having created a small society that suits him, he willingly leaves the larger society to its own devices."

Rapacious businessmen, as described in the novels of Balzac, Dickens, Zola, and Frank Norris, among others, cut their way to enormous fortunes—contributing to rapid economic growth, as Smith had predicted, but leaving widespread suffering and bitterness in their wake. Individualism lost some of the romantic sheen it had acquired during the two revolutions. Jeremy Bentham, while founding his utilitarian philosophy on the individual's interest in maximizing pleasure and minimizing pain, deplored all talk of "rights," which he described as "nonsense on stilts." Looking back on 1789, an old Frenchman told Tocqueville: "Then people had a cause, now they have only interests." The German anarchist-philosopher Max Stirner, who actually called his system egoism, also preferred self-interest to rights: "The tiger that assails me is in the right, and I who strike him down am also in the right. I defend against him not my *right,* but *myself.*"[36]

The tribe of economists who grew up in Smith's train looked mainly to the "invisible hand," manifested through the play of competing interests in the market, to organize economic and social activity. They attached little importance to the bonds of "moral sympathy" that Smith had relied on for social cohesion. Some, like John Stuart Mill (of whom more later), tried to create a synthesis of market forces and humanist values, but most found it more efficient to treat all human appetites and sentiments as simply "tastes," each to have its weight determined solely through market competition.

Charles Darwin's mid-century presentation of his theory of biological natural selection gave a further boost to egoism, first by undermining the credibility of traditional Christianity that literally interpreted the account of creation in the book of Genesis, and even more importantly by seeming to present the survival of the fittest as the determining law of organic nature.

Social Darwinists concluded that no-holds-barred competition among individuals is nature's way of perfecting the race—largely ignoring the role that communal attachments may play in evolution.

Artists and poets, increasingly disaffected from Western societies dominated by teeming industry and commerce, sometimes struck back with their own brands of pretentious vanity. "There is no sin," Oscar Wilde declared, "except stupidity." In Paris, Baudelaire heralded perversity as a means to "shock the bourgeoisie." He found "crime" everywhere: in "the newspaper, the walls, the face of man." The poet Arthur Rimbaud denounced poetry itself as good only to "cover up the leprosies of old walls."

Late in the century, Friedrich Nietzsche, though he despised vulgar egoism, which he regarded as a value system for "hair-splitters" and "philistines," dealt an additional blow against all traditional forms of social and moral restraint. "Behind your thoughts and feelings, my brother," he wrote in *Thus Spoke Zarathustra*, published in 1883, "there stands a mighty ruler, an unknown sage—whose name is self." In this vision, some turn-of-the-century business, political, and military moguls—to what surely would have been the philosopher's horror—saw their own images.[37]

LIBERTARIANISM

Modern libertarianism, based on ideas drawn among a few of its elite from Nietzsche, but mostly from Locke, Adam Smith, and Darwin, enthrones the individual's self-interest as almost the sole source of legitimate value. F. A. Hayek, the German economist whose work became a foundation of the libertarian movement, rejected all efforts to structure society around "some preconceived notion of justice," which he regarded as incompatible with the priority of individual freedom. "The principle of distributive justice," Hayek warned, "would not be fulfilled until the whole of society was organized in accordance with it. This would produce a kind of society which in all essential respects would be the opposite of a free society—a society in which authority decided what the individual was to do and how he was to do it." For Hayek, freedom is the moral value that trumps all others.[38]

Milton Friedman, the Nobel Prize-winning economist who joined Hayek in the libertarian pantheon, puts matters more bluntly. "To the free man, the country is the collection of the individuals who compose it, not something over and above them. . . . He recognizes no national purpose except as it is the consensus of the purposes for which the citizens severally strive." The business corporation is an economic surrogate for its stockholders' self-interests and as such is morally prohibited from attempting to serve any higher or larger social purpose. "There is one and only one social responsibility of business—to use its resources and engage in activities designed to increase its profits so long as it stays within the rules of the game." Rules of the game are negotiated to further mutual self-interests. Given Friedman's moral assumptions, why should individuals or firms, any more than nations, accept an obligation to continue following rules that no longer serve their selfish interests?[39]

Friedman's indifference to external moral standards is supported by a halcyon view of the market that contrasts with Smith's sardonic realism: "There is no personal rivalry in the competitive market place. There is no personal haggling."[40]

Robert Nozick, in *Anarchy, State, and Utopia*, published in 1974, provides a systematic and coherent philosophic framework for libertarian ideas, illuminated by dazzling intellectual fireworks. "The individual," he maintains, "is an end in himself, never subordinated to others." Property acquired through "just acquisition," by which Nozick appears to mean virtually any kind of acquisition except outright theft or enslavement, belongs unconditionally to the acquiring individual. Government taxation beyond that needed to support a "minimal night-watchman state . . . limited to protecting persons against murder, assault, theft, fraud, and so forth," is a form of enslavement, unjustly taking from the individual the fruit of his labor. Human life is a catch-as-catch-can struggle for advantage, governed by the principle (mocking Marx): "From each as they choose, to each as they are chosen."[41]

Nozick's system assumes a moral universe in which the will of the individual is absolutely sovereign, and in which no external moral standard is accepted as relevant. Why theft and enslavement should be prohibited in such a universe, if the individual can get away with them, is not clear. Social cooperation among individuals in a common enterprise, Nozick allows, may establish an enforceable claim for compensation. But any moral responsibility or bond based on common humanity is simply incomprehensible. In a widely cited parable, Nozick argues that "ten Robinson Crusoes," living in isolation for two years on separate islands, would have no moral claims on each other if some should prosper while others suffer hardship. It does not seem even to occur to him that such claims, at least limited, might rise from shared humanity.[42]

EGOISM OF THE LEFT

Contemporary egoism is by no means confined to libertarianism on what is conventionally regarded as the ideological right. Egoist premises, particularly since the cultural explosions of the 1960s, have also been richly represented on the conventionally defined left.

Herbert Marcuse, a favorite guru of New Left radicalism in the 1960s, preached an ethic of self-gratification: "Eros defines reason in his own terms. Reasonable is what sustains the order of gratification." Jerry Rubin in his hippie manifesto, *Do It!,* rhapsodized that the liberated individual "can do what he wants whenever he wants to do it." Timothy Leary, another left-wing guru and proselytizer for the drug culture, urged: "Turn on, tune in, drop out." Jean-Paul Sartre summed up: "Life has no meaning *a priori.* . . . It is up to you to give it a meaning, and value is nothing but the meaning that you choose."[43]

As the enthusiasms of the 1960s (which also had their idealistic side, to be discussed later) cooled, secular liberalism became more cautious and less confident in announcing its objectives. But for many on the left, the liberated self has remained the ultimate arbiter of all values. As Alasdair MacIntyre points out, modern liberalism's reasoning protagonist is "the individual *qua* individual," in contrast to the "individual *qua* citizen" assumed by classical humanism. The legal theorist Ronald Dawkins maintains: "If someone has a right to do something, then it is wrong for the government to deny it to him even though it would be in the general interest to do so." Liberal egoism's moral orientation is neatly embodied by the president of Antioch College, explaining his school's code for student sexual relationships: "The underlying philosophy asserts only one moral value: that each person has the right to have healthy human relationships and to define for himself or herself what that means." Even John Rawls, in the process of developing a social philosophy requiring a considerable amount of governmentally imposed equality, feels obliged to claim that the social arrangement he favors would be chosen behind a "veil of ignorance" by "free and rational persons concerned to further their own interests," who are, moreover, "not taking an interest in another's interest."[44]

Liberal versions of egoism assume that human nature is not inherently aggressive and selfish in the narrow sense, but rather, generous and agreeable, even altruistic. These natural traits are said to have been repressed and replaced by competitive drives through cultural conditioning, perhaps made necessary by the economic scarcity that was formerly the human lot. C. B. MacPherson argues that both Hobbes and Locke mistook the fierce competitiveness of seventeenth-century English merchants and politicians for genetically fixed human nature, when in fact it was a cultural disposition created by social and economic forces at the time. Now, the argument goes, the wonders of modern technology have at last released humankind from its ancient domination by scarcity. "Machines," wrote Charles Reich, "can produce enough food and shelter for all." According to the Belgian sociologist Ernest Mandel, "For the first time since man's appearance on earth, the insecurity and instability of material existence will vanish." Technological progress in "mature, industrial civilization," Marcuse maintained, makes possible "general automation of labor, reduction of labor time, and exchangeability of function." Human beings, therefore, are now, or soon will be, free to pursue self-fulfillment and self-expression without resort to competitive behavior or aggression.[45]

An important distinction between egoism of the left and libertarian egoism on the right is that while the latter rejects governmental controls of almost every kind, egoism of the left approves governmental intervention, at least during a transition period, to secure rights for persons who have been handicapped by social discrimination or natural causes. Egoism of the left thus positively welcomes such governmental remedies as redistribution of wealth and affirmative action—causing it to shade rather easily into egoism's natural opposite, collectivism. In a truly liberated society, Marcuse wrote, "control might well be centralized; such control would not prevent individual autonomy, but render it possible."[46]

THE CULTURE OF EGOISM

Egoism is currently a powerful force at all cultural levels in Western societies. Its influence, though not unchallenged, is almost pervasive in many sectors of the arts and entertainment.

Popular entertainment and mass advertising eagerly, and profitably, promote self-glorification. Hollywood, from Gary Cooper and John Wayne to Clint Eastwood and Bruce Willis, has always celebrated the loner hero who travels light. The loner may save a community to which he is temporarily attached, but always ends up taking off for the high country, like Alan Ladd in *Shane*, or Cooper throwing his sheriff's badge into the dust at the end of *High Noon*. Advertising has cashed in on this iconography through promotions like that for the Marlboro Man—said to have been the most effective sales campaign in advertising history.

The chivalric code that loner heroes used to follow still survives to some extent, often with touches of perversity, in such portrayals as that of *Pulp Fiction*'s crooked prizefighter played by Bruce Willis. For the most part, however, current purveyors of entertainment, competing fiercely for audiences and dollars, have plunged into an ever-deepening vortex of promiscuous sex, violence, and vulgarity, aimed at feeding the presumed cravings of the inner self, as in the rest of *Pulp Fiction* and many other films, shows, and TV specials and series. In many recent productions, including such stylishly crafted works as the movies *Boogie Nights* and *American Beauty*, and the hit Broadway musical *Chicago*, there are no good guys, even in the James Bond sense—only pathetic bad guys and brutal bad guys. Popular television sit-coms such as *Seinfeld, Frasier,* and *Ally McBeal,* present self-centered sexual promiscuity as the assumed norm for civilized human behavior.

Many viewers no doubt consume these products with large grains of salt, but numerous studies show that popular entertainment has significant impact on values and behavior, particularly among the young. A national survey of teenagers in 1996, for example, found about one-third reporting they "often want to try things they see on TV," while about two-thirds said "their contemporaries are influenced by what they see on TV."[47]

The record industry has entered this race with such ballads of sadistic narcissism as the Time-Warner label "gangsta rap" lyric: "*I am a big man (yes I am). And I have a big gun. Got me a big old cock and I, I like to have fun. Hold against your forehead. I'll make you suck it. Maybe I'll put a hole in your head.*" As the cultural historian Martha Bayles writes, "The anarchistic, nihilistic impulses of perverse modernism have been grafted onto popular music, where they have not only undermined the Afro-American tradition, but also encouraged today's cult of obscenity, brutality, and sonic abuse." Many rap records explicitly glamorize drugs. Teenagers get the message: a 1995 national survey by researchers at Columbia University found seventy-six percent of twelve to seventeen-year-olds agreeing that "pop culture encourages drug use."

Computer games, reportedly popular with the teenage killers at Columbine High School in the spring of 1999, contribute to the fun with such presentations as "Postal," a game in which "the goal is to slaughter innocent bystanders, including cheerleaders who moan for mercy." The cover of the game "Blood II" promises "over 30 screamingly fast totally immersive bloodsoaked levels! Run a savage gauntlet of multiplayer mayhem from BloodFeud to BloodBath for Maximum BloodShed."[48]

Advertising has lagged a bit behind, catering mainly to consumer longings for such mundane goods as health, status, and a beautiful body. These, however, are often reinforced through exploitation of personal anxieties or pandering enticements to self-importance, such as Cybill Sheppard's boast in television ads that she deserves an expensive hair dye because "I'm worth it." Calvin Klein's experiments with soft-core pornography probably are harbingers of a more liberated future.[49]

Highbrow intellectuals and artists preaching doctrines of "postmodernism" and "deconstructionism" may seem far removed from mass entertainment and advertising, which they scorn or patronize as pop culture. But the conclusion of these efforts at liberation has often been similar glorification of the self. "The practice of deconstruction," Peter Levine writes, "involves getting a vantage point external to culture, in order to describe—and thereby transcend—cultural biases." The locus of this vantage point almost always turns out to be some version of the primordial self. "A single stroke of paint, backed by work and a mind that understands its potency and implications," the artist Clyfford Still declared, can "restore to man the freedom lost in twenty centuries of apology and devices for subjugation." Or as Foucault, a prophet of postmodernism, put it: "Everything that morality and religion, everything that a clumsy society has stifled in man, revives in the castle of murders. There man is finely attuned to his own nature." The literary historian Robert Corrigan observes that the cult of self-expression in the arts, while often avowing fealty to "universal brotherhood," in practice has produced "grotesque dramatization of every form of brutality, cruelty, bestiality, and sensuality."[50]

WHERE EGOISM ENDS

Does it make much difference? If egoism continues to gain influence in modern societies, will that really have much effect on everyday life? Reason, experience, and common sense combine to answer emphatically: Yes.

First, egoism undermines the moral will of free societies to resist the scourge of totalitarianism that during the course of the twentieth century threatened or consumed large parts of the West. As the British philosopher Karl Popper has warned, rejection of all objective standards beyond the self "opens the floodgates to irrationalism and fanaticism." This danger may now seem remote in most of the West, but current civic apathy and alienation provide tinder that serious and prolonged economic or social troubles may easily inflame.[51]

Second, unsupported egoism cannot generate the spiritual or emotional solidarity needed to sustain civility and social order. Egoists of the right argue that unrestrained markets, through the magic of the "invisible hand," will automatically produce a fair and harmonious society. Egoists of the left believe that human beings guided by nothing but natural altruism, at least after a period of transition in which they are cleansed of culturally induced hang-ups and prejudices, will spontaneously produce a society based on justice and sharing. Evidence for either of these propositions is extremely weak.

Experience has shown that markets are by far the most efficient means to organize production and distribution of almost all material goods. But markets do not themselves judge the value of goods by any standard except economic demand. Human nature left to itself, experience also shows, creates demand for potentially harmful products: drugs, guns, cigarettes, pornography, and unlimited abortions, among others. Markets, moreover, lead to concentrations of private power that do not necessarily serve the public welfare—even if "public" is defined as nothing more than a "collection of individuals severally striving."

The assumptions about human nature held by egoists of the left are at least equally naive. There does seem to be a certain amount of natural fellow feeling, even altruism, among human beings—we probably could not have survived for so long if there were not. But drives of self-interest, which appear naturally inherent to humanity, produce competition for material goods, mates, and public acclaim. If these are not offset by some kind of moral standards or social loyalties, the results are likely to be disastrous.

The egoist is not necessarily cold, heartless, or even in the narrow sense self-centered. He or she may be warm, convivial, generous to family and friends, gregarious, and normally kind-hearted. But so long as self-interest is the sole underlying arbiter of value, these qualities are after all no more than tastes—subject to replacement by other tastes when circumstances alter.

A society governed primarily by self-interest is likely to be a varied and exciting place. Burdens and pathologies that result from social or moral restraints on emotional drives may, at least in the short run, be reduced. But there are social by-products, not necessarily for each individual but in general, that can hardly be avoided: broken families, neglected children, galloping cynicism, crime, pursuit of thrills, common rudeness, public apathy, fouled nature, shoddy art, stunted scholarship, irresponsible government—in short, the world that now sometimes seems to be coming into being among us.

Third, most human beings find that life guided by self-interest alone soon becomes stale and hollow. As the Rabbi Hillel commented: "If I am not for myself, who will be? If I am only for myself, what am I?" Creative artists like T. S. Eliot, Evelyn Waugh, John Updike, Joan Didion, David Mamet, and Martin Amis have convincingly conveyed to us that cosmic loneliness can turn the material riches of the modern world to spiritual dust and ashes. Life without purpose, at least social if not transcendent, is for most people a barren affair, only temporarily relieved by narcotics of success and indulgence. According to the German philosopher Max Horkheimer, modern man's concentration on self-fulfillment "drives subjective reason to madness, for the thought of anything that goes beyond the subjectivity of self-interest is robbed of all rationality."[52]

Finally, in a very practical sense, the self confined to its own resources tends to crumble as a point of reference for dealing with reality. In this chapter we have been treating the self as a unity—a black box. But torn from social or transcendent meaning, it is likely to become unstable and dysfunctional. The philosopher Jean Bethke Elshtain writes: "If there is no point of reference outside the self, over time what emerges is a deficiency, as, through habituation, the self is further depleted." The self standing alone loses credibility, not only as the subject of personal responsibility that lies at the core of all Western jurisprudence, but also as verifier of truth, seat of reason, and point of entry, though not ultimate destination, for all that is good and beautiful.[53]

Contemporary postmodern writers, such as Foucault and Jacques Derrida, who determinedly deconstruct and reject all conceivable objective moral standards, end with an existential soup in which the self itself disappears. "Nothing in man," Foucault writes, "not even his body, is sufficiently stable to serve as the basis for self-recognition or for understanding other men."[54]

Individualism in itself is not the problem. From a purely economic standpoint, Adam Smith was right: competition in a free market is far superior to all other known means for increasing the supply of material goods available for human consumption, and therefore has the best potential to make life healthier, more pleasant, and more interesting for most people. Beyond its economic uses, freedom is a precious human value for which countless persons have laid down their lives and fortunes. Liberation of women from economic and physical exploitation, of subjugated racial and ethnic groups from social oppression, and of most people from various forms of class discrimination, though still far from complete, has greatly enriched and empowered the lives of millions of people.

But freedom separated from any larger purpose or meaning almost inevitably becomes license—probably the first and still among the most destructive of human sins. For this reason, human beings since the Paleolithic dawn among hunter-gatherers some thirty millennia ago have experimented with belief systems supporting values beyond self-preservation and self-fulfillment.

3

◆━━━━━◆

Collectivism:
The Myth of the Hive

Each of us puts his person and all his power in common under the supreme control of the general will, and, as a body, we receive each member as an individual part of the whole.

—Jean-Jacques Rousseau

T he basic trouble with egoism as a viable source for the values needed
to sustain a free society is, of course, that while providing plenty of
motivation for "free," it gives little moral or spiritual support for
lasting "society." Egoism by itself creates few of the bonds of memory and
affection on which a sense of community depends, no vision of shared moral
purpose, and no reliable standard for social justice or ethics.

Collectivism, the category of value systems that derives all value from the
corporate authority of the social whole, meets—or claims to meet—all of
these needs. Traditionally, most champions of collectivism have forthrightly
acknowledged that their system, while bringing stability and direction to society, includes little or no place for freedom, which they regard as a subversive distraction or a cognitive illusion. Since the eighteenth century, however, some eloquent proponents of collectivism, beginning with Rousseau,
have contended that freedom rightly conceived is not only consistent with
but actually dependent on submergence of individual interests in the general
social will.

In any case, collectivism is important as a major alternative to a free society, whether or not it can itself be identified with any plausible version of
freedom. In this chapter, before taking up some past and present formulations of collectivism, a brief discussion of the role of "society" as a source
and generator of values is appropriate.

ORIGINS OF SOCIETY

Most human beings seem clearly to possess a social nature, in the sense of being drawn to association with their fellows, even apart from the biological need for physical sustenance. "A social instinct," Aristotle observed, "is implanted in all men by nature." Charles Darwin much later concluded: "Social instincts [lead the human animal] to take pleasure in the society of its fellows . . . and to perform certain services for them."[1]

Recent research shows that human infants become agitated not only when they feel hungry or in danger but also when they sense distress in others. "When they are one-and-a-half years old," James Q. Wilson writes, "they seek to do something to alleviate the other's distress; by the time they are two years old they verbally sympathize, offer toys, make suggestions, and look for help." These reactions to some extent reflect example and teaching, but small children "seem prepared to learn these things." As children develop they are naturally drawn to seek security in familiar groups.[2]

Nature draws humans to participate in society but it gives them little genetic instruction on how to behave when they get there. The *content* of social behavior, unlike that for all other animals, even the primates who are our closest animal relatives, is largely culturally formed. "There is no such thing as a human nature independent of culture. . . . The *Homo sapiens* brain, having arisen within the framework of culture, would not be viable outside of it," writes the anthropologist Clifford Geertz. Other recent social theorists have emphasized the extent to which human behavior is shaped by the socially produced medium of language.[3]

Development of institutions that could be transmitted from one generation to the next was unquestionably the key, first to relative success for the human species among its competitors, and then to a very gradual advance toward civilization. "The human achievement," E. O. Service writes, "was the creation of culture, the means by which societies tame and govern their members and create and maintain their complex social organization."[4]

FROM BAND TO STATE

The first level of social development distinguished by anthropologists is the primitive band, formed when hunter-gatherer families began pooling energies and resources to improve food supplies and provide more efficient security against rival predators. Marriage in bands, Edward O. Wilson writes, was (and in some undeveloped parts of the world still is) "arranged . . . by negotiation and ritual, and the complex kinship networks that result are objects of special classifications and strictly enforced rules."

About 10,000 years ago, as the last Ice Age was ending, some bands in and around the Tigris-Euphrates Valleys began consolidating into tribes, providing social structures required for transition to more settled agricultural communities. Tribal organizations not only made possible cultivation of land and domestication of some gregarious animals (dogs had cast their lot with humans some 2,000 years before), but also led to a period of extraordinary technological change, the Neolithic revolution, bringing with it "four staggeringly powerful new weapons . . . the bow, the sling, the dagger . . . and the mace." Agricultural tribes wrested control over fertile lands from hunter bands. Villages were formed as strongholds against understandably resentful hunters, still stuck in the Paleolithic era. By 7000 BC the first town to occupy the site of Jericho in the Jordan Valley was home to between 2,000 and 3,000 people.[5]

Around 5300 BC some particularly gifted tribal leaders began moving their societies to the next level of social development, the chiefdom. The first chiefdoms, probably organized around a charismatic individual, were apparently formed to improve the administration of social power in larger and more complex societies. Chiefs initially relied more on personality than on control of force. According to Service, "Chiefdoms have centralized direction, hereditary status arrangements with an aristocratic ethos, but no formal, legal apparatus of forceful repression."[6]

Toward the end of the fourth millennium BC, some chiefdoms in Mesopotamia and Egypt began utilizing the apparently inherent human capacity for purposeful aggression to extend their authority, subduing less successful or less aggressive rivals, and moving society to the level of the state. "In proportion as war became chronic," the historian William McNeill writes, "kingship became necessary." Around 3100 BC, a single ruler, whose name comes down to us through the mists of legend as Menes, united Lower and Upper Egypt—the Nile delta and its southern reaches—to form the Egyptian kingdom that was to last, with occasional interruptions, for almost three thousand years.[7]

In addition to states in the valleys of the Nile and the Tigris-Euphrates, others hosting cultures associated with civilization were established by 2200 BC in the Indus and Yellow River valleys of southern and eastern Asia. Similar structures developed separately in the pre-Colombian Americas around 500 BC.

KINGS HIGH

John Keegan speculates that the work of consolidating conquest may originally have been carried out, not by settled town-dwellers, but by resurgent hunters, employing their fighting skills to revenge expulsions suffered by their forebears centuries before. "The dim roots of the notion of aristocracy," writes the historian J. M. Roberts, "are to be sought in the successes (which must have been frequent) of hunter-gatherers, representatives of an older social order, in exploiting the vulnerability of the settlers, tied to their areas of civilization." Hunting rights and skills, Keegan points out, have always been associated with feudal aristocracies.[8]

Founders of states ruthlessly centralized social institutions. Rather than executing conquered peoples, as bands and tribes had commonly done, states usually enslaved them, acquiring cheap labor for further economic growth. "The moment when first the conqueror spared his victim in order permanently to exploit him in productive work," Fritz Oppenheimer observed, "was of incomparable historical importance. It gave birth to the nation and state; to . . . higher economics, with all the developments and ramifications which have grown and which hereafter will grow out of them."[9]

Domination of states by a new class of military conquerors made social unity more fragile. Samuel Noah Kramer conjectures that life in third millennium Lagash, one of the first of the Mesopotamian kingdoms, "was far from ideal, classless, and equalitarian; the slave was no doubt made to feel the lowness of his position; the strong lorded it over the weak; justice was honored largely in the breach; the orphan and the widow were at the mercy of the rich and the powerful; the woman was treated as a second class citizen who could not inherit the property of her parents, even when there was no male heir." The Code of Hammurabi, composed in Babylon near the beginning of the second millennium, prescribed social penalties assuming class distinction: "If any one strikes the body of a man higher in rank than he, he shall receive sixty blows with an ox-whip in public. If a free-born man strikes the body of another free-born man of equal rank, he shall pay one gold mina."[10]

Rulers relied increasingly on intimidation and brute force. "The gentle man perishes," laments the anonymous author of a scroll from the Egyptian Middle Kingdom, "the bold-faced goes everywhere." An ancient Chinese text, included in a compilation attributed to Confucius, complains:

> Oh! whither shall we turn?
> The thoughts in my breast make me sad.
> All the people are hostile to us;
> On whom can we rely?
> Anxieties crowd together in our hearts.[11]

Court poets warned the discontented or potentially discontented that the alternative to kingship was social chaos. "The appointment of a king is the most essential thing for a country," declares Bhisma, one of the heroes of India's second great epic from antiquity, the *Mahabharata*. "A state without a ruler becomes weak and overruled by robbers. In countries without a king, law does not become established. And the people devour each other. . . . If there were no king in the world, meting out punishment on the earth, the stronger would roast the weak on a spit, like fishes."[12]

PLATO: AUTHORITARIAN IDEALISM

Despite political manipulation by rulers and official propaganda, civil disturbances and clashes among rival factions became common in societies ruled by military kingships. In ninth century BC Greece, the legendary Lycurgus, ruler of Sparta, dealt with these divisions through constitutional reforms aimed at eliminating all resistance to an all-encompassing collectivist belief system. Lycurgus's constitution, according to Plutarch, was designed "to make the citizens accustomed to have neither the will nor the ability to lead a private life; but, like the bees, always to be organic parts of their community, to cling together around their leader, and, in an ecstasy of enthusiasm and selfless ambition, to belong wholly to their country."[13]

As we saw in the last chapter, cracks in traditional authoritarian systems elsewhere in Greece opened the way for assertions of individualism. In the fifth century BC, Athens launched the world's first experiment with democracy in a complex society. For a short time, Athenian democracy flourished, providing unprecedented civil liberties for free citizens. But democracy did not heal social divisions. Members of the oligarchic class that had formerly dominated the city-state remained disgruntled by the new distribution of wealth and power. As rivalry with Sparta turned to prolonged war, beginning in 431, the oligarchs' complaints became more bitter.

Discontent with Athenian democracy was shared and articulated by many within the city's dazzling company of intellectuals. Foremost among these was Plato, carrying on the line of argument initiated by his teacher, Socrates.

Himself a member of one of the old aristocratic families that felt threatened by democracy, Plato had ties of blood and interest to the oligarchic party within the Athenian state. His first concern, however, was not with politics, but with the health of the human soul. He initially regarded politics as an extended metaphor through which to illuminate the nature and condition of the soul. His studies of epistemology, psychology, and ethics led him to conclusions about the goals and institutions of government. He elaborated these into a comprehensive theory of politics, which has profoundly influenced political thought and practice in the West ever since.

The key to understanding the human situation, Socrates and Plato believed, is the faculty of reason, but reason is an instrument to uncover objective truth and virtue, not their ultimate source. Unlike many of the Sophists with whom they debated in all-night symposia, they rejected the idea that virtue is relative to the current appetites or situation of the individual or the practical interests of the state. Truth, goodness, and beauty are founded on objective realities in the universe, like the mathematical laws that Greek scholars at that time were uncovering. In the *Phaedo*, Socrates argues for standards of "absolute uprightness . . . absolute beauty and goodness," which are best approached "by applying pure and unadulterated thought to the pure and unadulterated object."[14]

If truth and justice are absolutes, their natures are to be determined, not through voting as in the Athenian assembly, nor by giving special weight to the opinions of the rich and powerful, but through rational inquiry "because this will be the easiest way for [the soul] to pass from becoming to truth and being." Political wisdom is not equally accessible to all human beings, no more than skill at higher mathematics. Discovery and administration of social justice are specialized responsibilities—in fact among the most specialized that humans may undertake. In the ideal state, which Plato argues is the goal set by justice, these functions, therefore, should be left to persons particularly gifted and specially trained.[15]

Like Socrates, Plato rejected democracy, which he calls "a charming form of government, full of variety and disorder, and dispensing a sort of equality to equals and unequals alike." Democracy, he believed, was bound to give way to tyranny, which he regarded as the worst form of government. He did not, however, yearn for restoration of rule by an elite who based their authority on inherited wealth and status, as his oligarchic cousins favored. Instead, he proposed a state in which philosophers themselves would be awarded power through recognition of their fitness to govern. "Until philosophers are kings," he wrote in the *Republic*, "or the kings and princes of this world have the spirit and power of philosophy, and political greatness and wisdom meet in one, and those common natures who pursue either to the exclusion of the other are compelled to stand aside, critics will never have rest from their evils—no, nor the human race as I believe—and then only will this our state have a possibility of life and behold the life of day."[16]

The philosopher-kings would not be expected personally to take care of routine administration of government or to keep the unruly masses in check. Plato recommended that these tasks should be the responsibilities of a class of "auxiliaries," which he associated with the spirited part of the soul, placed between reason and the appetites. Beneath the rulers and the auxiliaries, the great mass of human beings, corresponding to the appetites, would perform necessary labors of economic and social toil. Justice consists of every element in society carrying out its function in a manner that produces maximum benefit for society as a whole.[17]

The rulers and the auxiliaries, to keep them free of the temptations of "luxury and indolence," were to have no property. They would, however, receive compensating privileges: "Our better and braver youth, beside their other honors and rewards, might have greater facilities of intercourse with women . . . their bravery will be a reason, and such fathers ought to have as many sons as possible." Members of the worker class would be permitted some accumulation of wealth. But no citizen could own more than five times the wealth of the poorest.[18]

Recognizing the traditional family as a formidable obstacle to the kind of radical reconstruction of society he had in mind, Plato recommended that all children should be raised in common. Virtually alone among writers of antiquity, he called for complete equality between men and women. Both sexes were to strip for gymnastic exercises, symbolically removing the garments of decadent convention.

Though his entire system supposedly rested on the authority of independent reason, Plato believed that the ideal state, once formed, should take pains to mold the minds of its citizens: "The first thing will be to establish a censorship of the writers of fiction, and let the censors receive any tale of fiction which is good, and reject the bad; and we will desire mothers and nurses to tell their children the authorized ones only." Realities of politics require that the rulers "in their dealings either with enemies or with their own citizens, may be allowed to lie for the public good."[19]

Socrates, while celebrating the operation of independent reason, always accepted the traditional Greek view of the sanctity of the *polis*. Rather than flee Athens, as those who accused him of subverting the city's youth perhaps hoped and expected, he willingly carried out the state's sentence of death by drinking hemlock. Plato was even more insistent on the primacy of the state over the individual. As he grew older, and the influence of Socrates' independent spirit perhaps waned, Plato increasingly prescribed a completely collectivist frame of thought and values. Social harmony, he wrote in the *Laws*, requires "the habit of never so much as thinking to do one single act apart from one's fellows, of making life, to the very uttermost, an unbroken concert, society, and community of all with all." Remember, he warned, "you are created for the sake of the whole, and not the whole for the sake of you." As Noel O'Sullivan writes: "To destroy the sense of separation brought by individual self-consciousness was the aim of Plato, Rousseau, and Marx, who all wanted men to say 'we' and never 'I.' "[20]

Social authority itself, Plato maintained, is based on transcendent order. He almost created the idea of transcendence as a philosophic concept. His religious speculations in the *Timaeus* and the *Phaedo* deeply influenced Augustine and other Christian thinkers. Werner Jaeger went so far as to call him the founder of theology. He was therefore not truly a collectivist in the secular sense, but an absolutist, basing value on social authority reflecting transcendent will. Yet his idea of transcendence, while often poetic, is shadowy and uncharacteristically vague. He had lost confidence in the traditional gods and goddesses of Greek mythology, but never found a fully developed conception of deity to put in their place. Like Rousseau much later, he sometimes seemed more interested in the utility of religion than in its truth.[21]

Plato provided a powerful conceptual model for absolutists in all subsequent ages. But, since his idea of transcendence remained unclear and perhaps dispensable, he was also available to secular collectivists when the authority of religion began to waver in the eighteenth and nineteenth centuries. His influence in the modern world has extended, not only through the higher reaches of the church and academe, but also to the planners and propagandists of the totalitarian state.

A WARRIOR PEOPLE

Most of the founders of Greek humanism and philosophy joined Plato in disapproving democracy. The chief exceptions were Herodotus, the father of history, and Aristotle, who saw some practical merit in democracy, but only on the condition that the upper class should hold most political power.

The Romans, who succeeded the Greeks as the dominant force in the Mediterranean world, prided themselves on carrying on traditions of humanist culture and indulged privately in egoist pursuits, but always maintained the collectivist and authoritarian belief system of a warrior nation. Rome, John Keegan writes, "succeeded, by whatever means, in transforming the warrior ethos of a small city into a true military culture, an entirely novel *Weltanschauung*, one shared by the highest and the lowest levels of Roman society."[22]

Though many Romans continued to honor the pagan deities of antiquity, at least until the official establishment of Christianity in the fourth century AD, for members of the ruling class the real focus of value was the state. As Edward Gibbon wrote in his famous passage: "The various modes of worship which prevailed in the Roman world were all considered by the people as equally true, by the philosophers as equally false, and by the magistrates as equally useful."

CONFUCIANISM: GENTLE COLLECTIVISM

While collectivist belief systems, often allied with religious absolutism, dominated much of the political and intellectual life of the West, a separate and distinct—though in some ways parallel—tradition was taking hold in the valley of the Yellow River in Eastern Asia. Civilization in the form of an urban culture administered by kingship came later to the Far East than to the valleys of the Nile and the Tigris-Euphrates. But by the end of the third millennium BC, a kingdom ruled by the first of the legendary Three Dynasties, the Xia, had gained control of the area just south and west of present-day Beijing.

Chinese culture from the start was collectivist and authoritarian. "Distinctive features of Chinese life today, such as autocratic government, come down directly from prehistoric times," wrote the China scholar John Fairbank. Family structures were strictly hierarchical, with elders and males dominant. Family headship passed from father to eldest son, but family property was distributed more or less equally among all surviving sons. As a result, there was no supply of younger sons forced to find their ways through commerce, the church, or the military, as occurred in feudal Europe. Partly in consequence, strong intermediate forces between the peasant family and the state did not develop.[23]

In early Chinese religion there is no creation story of the kind found in religions stemming from the Middle East. Existence was conceived as rising through interaction between *yin* (female, dark, and passive) and *yang* (male, bright, and active). The two are complementary and necessary to each other, but *yang* is by nature dominant in everyday life."[24]

Since China at first lacked nearby civilized neighbors offering opportunities for trade or plunder, vigorous sea traffic did not develop. Chinese interests looked inward. From the third millennium BC to the unification of much of China by the Qin dynasty in 221 BC, a number of petty kingdoms competed through prolonged though not very ferocious warfare for control of territory.

Around the middle of the sixth century BC, K'ung-fu-tze—Kung the Master—whom we know as Confucius, was born in one of the warring kingdoms. According to later legend, the future philosopher and sage was delivered in a cave by his unwed mother while dragons kept watch and spirit-ladies perfumed the air. Confucius spent his long career traveling from kingdom to kingdom, teaching students and seeking a prince who would apply his theories of statecraft. Although he occasionally found a ruler receptive to his advice, he never exercised wide authority and his influence on the politics of his time was small. He left behind, however, a collection of sayings and anecdotes which, after shading and refinement by later disciples, provided a philosophic structure which has determined beliefs, attitudes, and values, not only in China, but also in much of the rest of Eastern Asia to the present time.

Through his collection of Chinese classics of an earlier age, Confucius called attention to the troubled state of his society:

> When the palace is a wild of lust,
> And the country is a wild for hunting;
> When strong beverages are liked, and music is the delight;
> When there are lofty roofs and carved walls—
> The existence of any one of these things
> Has never been but the prelude to ruin.[25]

Confucius's solution was a reinvigoration of authoritarian collectivism, China's inherited belief system. "The relation between superiors and inferiors is like that between the wind and the grass. The grass must bend when the wind blows across it." The paternalistic family, he held, should be the model for the smoothly functioning state: "There is a fundamental agreement between a loyal subject in his service of the ruler and a filial son in the service of his parents."[26]

What Confucius added to this fairly conventional formulation of traditional authoritarianism was increased emphasis on the moral responsibility of the ruler and others at the top end of the social hierarchy: "To cultivate his personal character, the ruler must use the moral law (Tao)." Irresponsible use of power, he insisted, is the ruin of the state: "Oppressive government is fiercer than a tiger." He offered a version of the Golden Rule: "When a man carries out the principles of conscientiousness and reciprocity he is not far from the moral law. What you do not wish others should do unto you, do not do unto them."[27]

Confucius did not disparage religion but he claimed no transcendent source for his own teachings. Asked by one of his students about life after death, he replied: "While you do not know life, how can you know about death?" His conclusions, he said, were derived from study of the classics: "I am a transmitter and not an originator, and one who believes in and loves the ancients."[28]

Although he attracted students and considerable honor during his lifetime, Confucius never achieved the reform of Chinese culture he believed was necessary to overcome social discord. Three centuries after his death, however, the Han dynasty, which had quickly replaced the Qin as ruler of a united China, gave official backing to Confucius's teachings as a culturally unifying force and a guide to enlightened statecraft. Han Wudi, one of the early Han emperors, shrewdly used instruction of young bureaucrats in the Confucian philosophy to build an educated class separate from the old princely families. Throughout the Han, which lasted for more than 400 years (at about the same time that Rome was dominating the West), the imperial bureaucracy trained in Confucian principles promulgated the belief that political legitimacy depends not only on force but also on moral virtue and scrupulous practice of ceremonial rituals.

Confucianism as a guiding force in society was maintained by succeeding dynasties until the early years of the twentieth century. According to Samuel Huntington, "The Confucian ethos pervading many Asian societies stressed the values of authority, hierarchy, the subordination of individual rights and interests, the importance of consensus, the avoidance of confrontation, 'saving face,' and, in general, the supremacy of the state over society and of society over the individual."[29]

From the Han on, governing bureaucrats used Confucian values to justify tight regulation of commerce and heavy taxation of business. In the fifteenth century, growing penetration of the high seas by Chinese vessels was "stopped by Confucian-trained scholar-officials who opposed trade and foreign contacts on principle." Confucian attitudes, Fairbank notes, encouraged Chinese businessmen "not to build a better mousetrap but to get the official mouse monopoly."[30]

The nationalist reformers who tried between the twentieth century's two world wars to move China in a new direction aimed to blend Western ways with traditional Confucianism. Cruel or irrational customs like foot-binding of young females were abolished, and economic development was encouraged, but strict social hierarchy was maintained.

The Communist government that took power under the leadership of Mao Zedong in 1949 decreed a far more radical break with Confucianism and all its works. During the Cultural Revolution of the mid to late 1960s, young people were incited to mock and humiliate their elders, violating the most fundamental tenet of the Confucian tradition. Mao's Red Guards systematically terrorized scholars and professional workers, as well as what was left of the middle class. Relatively moderate Communist leaders like Deng Xiaoping were ruthlessly purged and jailed. Even Mao, Fairbank argues, utilized "the dependence of the Chinese individual upon group esteem as well as the approval of authority [that was] part of the legacy from Confucianism."[31]

As poor economic performance and widespread governmental corruption after Mao's death in 1976 caused communism to lose moral authority, Confucianism staged something of a comeback. The combination of economic liberalization with political repression under the restored Deng Xiaoping led to a surge of economic growth in the 1990s but further undermined public confidence in Marxist socialism as a way of life. Chinese intellectuals and career bureaucrats report renewed interest in Confucius as a source for moral and ethical inspiration.

Elsewhere in the Far East, scholars and politicians, observing rising crime, faltering governments, and disruption of family life in the West, suggest Confucianism as an indigenous Asian model through which economic growth produced by capitalism can be combined with social harmony. Kishore Mahbubani, a leading light in the "Singapore school" writes: "The dramatic inability of either the American or European democratic systems to persuade their respective populations that the long-term interests of the nation can only be protected by painful immediate sacrifices reveals the trap that democratic systems can create. . . . The fundamental lesson that Asia can provide to the United States is that societies can be better off when some boundaries of individual freedom are limited rather than broadened."[32]

Confucianism, Thomas Metzger writes, gave China "a conventionally fixed set of social expectations to which individual behavior should conform."[33] Certainly the gentle collectivism that flowed from Confucianism raised China to a level of civilization far beyond that reached in medieval and early modern times by European states devoted to pillaging and brutalizing each other, and has proved much more enduring than any of the modern Western systems of totalitarianism.

Confucianism, on the other hand, contributed to severe limitation of individual rights and hampered economic progress. Whether in the modern world Confucianism can be anything more than a cosmetic mask for authoritarian technocrats of the kind that now run socialist China and capitalist Singapore remains to be seen.

ROUSSEAU: SERVITUDE IS FREEDOM

After Christianity became the established religion of the Roman Empire in 383 AD, the unique blend of collectivism, monism, and classical humanism maintained by the empire's old warrior aristocracy was required to share a place in the guidance of social life with more religious perspectives. During the Dark and Middle Ages, secular authoritarianism by no means vanished, finding embodiment in the codes of military orders and the behavior of frequently warring kingdoms. Christian beliefs and values, however, were officially honored and provided at least an ideal standard for actual conduct.

With the coming of the Renaissance, resurgent nationalism laid claim to human loyalties and enthusiasms. A few bold spirits like Machiavelli articulated secular collectivist ideals as an independent source of values. For most people, however, religion remained a powerful force in personal and social life.

In the turbulent social atmosphere of the eighteenth century, secular collectivism, following the path opened by its natural antagonist, egoism, at last broke free of dependence on religion. This liberation of collectivist thought and action, based on no authority but its own interests and values, was no doubt rooted in the spirit of the times, but its actual formulation was largely the work of a single inspired genius: Jean-Jacques Rousseau.

Currents of individualism, rising from the Reformation, Lockean liberalism, and the eighteenth-century Enlightenment, had swept the imagination of Europe and its overseas extensions, generating ideals of freedom and equality. Forces were in motion against which the old aristocratic order, the established church, and a social structure based on deference ultimately could not stand.

Rousseau, born in the early years of the eighteenth century in Geneva, capital of the Calvinist branch of Protestantism, imbibed the ethos of freedom, and clearly grasped that there was no going back, that many human beings already were permanently alienated against the old dogmas and the old constraints. His own lifestyle was certainly liberated, to the point of libertinism and eccentricity, modified by occasional awkward attempts at middle-class respectability. His vanity and self-indulgence left a trail of broken friendships, deserted lovers, and abandoned children strewn across the salons, bedrooms, and orphanages of Western Europe. Yet he also understood that the cold rationality of the French *philosophes* produced a vacancy and loneliness within the human soul, and that the onward march of commercial egoism was threatening traditional bonds of social and economic security. The great problem of the modern world, he wrote, was to find "some form of association . . . as a result of which the whole strength of the community will be enlisted for the protection of the person and the property of each constituent member, in such a way that each, when united to his fellows renders obedience to his own will, and remains as free as before."[34]

Rousseau attempted to solve this problem, not like Locke and the *philosophes* by trying to balance the rights of the individual against the needs of society, but by arguing that true freedom comes through active participation in the organic life of the state. There is, he claimed, no genuine tension—no need for balance. Freedom in a properly constituted state is authority, and authority is freedom. Of course, achievement of this happy condition will require considerable restructuring of society.

He began by shucking off entirely the idea that humanity's troubled condition is the result of an ingrained propensity to sin. This insight first came to him, in a characteristically traumatic moment of revelation, at the age of thirty-seven, as he walked one day in 1749 from Paris toward Vincennes to visit his friend (later critic and enemy) Diderot, editor of the great Enlightenment project, the *Encyclopedie*.

> All at once I felt myself dazzled by a thousand sparkling lights. . . . A violent palpitation oppressed me. Unable to walk for difficulty in breathing, I sank down under one of the trees by the road, and passed half an hour there in such a condition of excitement that when I rose I saw the front of my waistcoat was all wet with tears. . . . Ah, if ever I could have written a quarter of what I saw and felt under that tree, with what clarity I should have brought out all the contradictions of our social system! With what simplicity I should have demonstrated that man is by nature good, and that only our institutions have made him bad![35]

Discovery of the natural goodness of humanity put Rousseau in touch with the revolutionary spirit of liberation that was exciting the intelligentsia of Europe and touching the hearts and minds of many ordinary people, particularly among the young. It supplied the emotional drive behind all his later work. "Let us lay it down as an incontrovertible rule," he wrote in his tract on education, *Emile*, published in 1762, "that the first impulses of nature are always right. There is no original sin in the human heart." And, most memorably, at the beginning of *The Social Contract*, also published in 1762: *L'homme est ne libre, et partout il est dans les fers*— "Man is born free and he is everywhere in chains."[36]

What then had produced descent from natural liberty to enslavement? In the *Discourse on the Origin and Foundation of Inequality among Men*, published in 1755, Rousseau provided the answer: "The first man who, having fenced off a plot of land, thought of saying 'This is mine' and found people simple enough to believe him was the real founder of civil society." This departure from nature, because it caused human beings to forget that "the fruits of the earth belong to all and the earth belongs to no one," led inevitably to "how many crimes, wars, murders, how many miseries and horrors."[37]

Creation of private property, the act that John Locke and most of the *philosophes* regarded as the key to freedom, was for Rousseau, therefore, the source of human enslavement. Rousseau, however, was no anarchist. Natural collectivism once destroyed cannot be regained through a simple return to nature. Humankind must go forward, using the institutions of government and civil society to produce a rejuvenated, and even improved, form of equalitarian collectivism.

In *The Social Contract* he explained how this transformation was to be achieved. Every member of society, rich and poor, nobility and commoners, must renounce "all his rights to the whole community" through a new social contract. This commitment, which those suffering from false consciousness may perceive as a curtailment of freedom, infinitely expands true freedom. "As each gives himself to all, he gives himself to no one; and since there is no associate over whom one does not acquire the same right one grants him over oneself, one gains the equivalent of everything one loses, and more force to preserve what one has." Rousseau then takes a crucial step: the public interest is found, not by negotiating a compromise among individual interests, but rather by subordinating all to "the supreme direction of the general will."[38]

The content of the general will is initially found through democratic procedures, ideally through each citizen casting a vote on each issue of public policy. Indeed, so that the general will remains uncontaminated, citizens are "to have no communication among themselves" before voting.[39] (Rousseau would no doubt have loved the current proposal by some political theorists that public issues should be decided directly through electronic referenda by voters stationed before their television sets or the Internet.)

What Rousseau had in mind is almost the opposite of the deal making and balancing of interests that normally characterize political processes in actual democracies. For Rousseau, the purpose of elections is to *discover* the general will, which was there all the time, waiting to be revealed. Once it is found, no further negotiation is needed or even permissible. The general will is the will of all, losers as well as winners in the election. Freedom consists of participation in fulfillment of the general will. It is, therefore, a contradiction to speak of opposing the general will on the ground that it may infringe on the rights of individuals. "Anyone who refuses to obey the general will," Rousseau prescribes, "shall be compelled to do so by the entire body; this means nothing else than that he will be forced to be free."[40]

For Rousseau, the collectivist ideal of the general will is self-sufficient as a source of value: "The common good is clearly apparent everywhere, and requires only good sense to be perceived." As models, he extols the authoritarian pagan states of Sparta and Rome. Though he paid lip service to Christianity as "holy, sublime, and true," he shared Machiavelli's view that the Christian religion in practice "preaches nothing but servitude and dependence," thereby undermining the vigor of the state.[41]

Rousseau acknowledges that the mass of human beings requires the appearance of some kind of transcendent authority to motivate loyalty and obedience to the state. For this purpose he recommends the formation of "a purely civil profession of faith, the articles of which are for the sovereign to determine, not precisely as religious dogmas, but as sentiments of sociability, without which it is impossible to be a good citizen or a faithful subject."[42]

Rousseau's work is filled with seeming contradictions, ambiguities, and shifts in moral direction. His ideas are sufficiently open to conflicting interpretation to have left their mark on virtually all the major ideologies of the modern world: socialism, communism, fascism, liberalism, even conservatism. There is, however, a kind of consistency at the heart of all his writings—the unity of a dream in which humanity's natural goodness overcomes all quarrels, conquers all disputes, and combines the orgiastic moment with perpetual enjoyment of tranquility and peace. Rousseau "invented nothing," his friend Madame de Stael wrote, "but he set everything on fire."

"THE DESPOTISM OF LIBERTY"

Rousseau, who died unexpectedly in 1778, did not live to see the French Revolution. Had he done so, he would probably have been among its early victims, but before facing the guillotine he might have recognized his intellectual and spiritual progeny.

The sources of the French Revolution were complex and varied. They included several kinds of humanism and some expressions of outright egoism. Probably the dominant strain, at least by the time of the Jacobin takeover and the Terror of the early 1790s, however, was Rousseau's formulation of equalitarian collectivism.

Danton, leader of the Revolution as it moved out of its relatively moderate phase, called for a national system of education in 1792 on the grounds that children "belong to the Republic before they belong to their parents." Robespierre, Danton's more ruthless Jacobin successor, went much further. For the true patriot, Robespierre insisted, "there is no private life—private life and public life are one." Justifying the Terror, before himself going to the guillotine in 1794, Robespierre found "only two parties left in the Republic: that of good citizens, and that of the bad; in other words, the party of the French people and the party of ambitious, avid individuals." Following Rousseau's model, he related true freedom to the all-powerful state: "Is our government like despotism? Yes, as the sword that flashes in the hand of the hero of liberty is like that with which the satellites of tyranny are armed. . . . The government of the Revolution is the despotism of liberty against tyranny."[43]

The youthful Louis de Saint-Just, organizer of the Revolutionary army before his execution with Robespierre in 1794, carried Jacobinism to its logical conclusion: "The republic consists in the extermination of everything that opposes it." Chamfort, a member of the moderate Girondin party, concluded that *Liberte, Egalite,* and *Fraternite* had come to mean, "Be my brother or I'll kill you."[44]

"Gracchus" Babeuf, who survived until 1797 before going to the guillotine in his turn, concisely expressed the Jacobin social strategy, all pure Rousseau: the state should "seize upon the new-born individual, watch over his early moments, guarantee the milk and care of his mother, and bring him to the *maison nationale*, where he will acquire the virtue and enlightenment of a true citizen." The Abbe Reynal gave the endorsement of a renegade cleric to Rousseau's idea of civil religion: "The State, it seems to me, is not made for religion but religion made for the State." The French revolutionaries, unlike their American counterparts, observed the historian James Hasting Nichols, "did not want to limit the absolute powers of the monarchy; they wanted to seize them."[45]

In 1799, Napoleon Bonaparte swept aside quarreling politicians and substituted military dictatorship, but he did not abandon Revolutionary, or Rousseauian, ideology. "The law," Napoleon decreed, "takes the child at birth, provides for his education, prepares him for a profession, regulates how and under what conditions he can marry, travel, and choose a profession." Simon Schama, the Revolution's most insightful recent historian, concludes: "Militarized nationalism was not, in some accidental way, the unintended consequence of the French Revolution: it was its heart and soul."[46]

The French Revolution of course did not take place in a social vacuum. It was the repudiation of centuries—millennia—of authoritarian and frequently despotic rule by a hereditary military upper class, often backed by an established church. Unfortunately, the Revolution also helped lay the intellectual foundations for even more horrendous forms of political oppression that were not to mature fully until the twentieth century.

HEGEL: THE STATE AS DIVINE IDEA

Among those inspired by the Rousseauian vision was a mild-mannered German professor of philosophy, Immanuel Kant, who never ventured far from his home base at the University of Konigsburg in East Prussia. Rousseau, Kant said, awakened him from his "dogmatic slumbers" in ethics. So stirred, he proceeded to construct a system of ethical philosophy that remains one of the great sources of liberal humanism in the modern world. We will meet him again when we turn to civil humanism.

Kant's system derives moral authority from a categorical imperative that is the product of speculative reason. The categorical imperative exists entirely in the realm of ideas. As such, it lacks the concreteness of even Rousseau's somewhat ephemeral general will. This may not handicap it as an object for intellectual discourse, but has proven deficient in shaping the moral choices or political behavior of flesh-and-blood human beings.

This lack was cured by Georg Wilhelm Friedrich Hegel, Kant's intellectual heir and successor as leader of the idealist school of German philosophy, who held forth at the University of Berlin during the first third of the nineteenth century. Hegel developed his own highly speculative metaphysic (thesis, antithesis, synthesis), but he brought the whole thing down to earth by embodying its effects in the evolution of real world events and institutions. Though he was, like Kant, a practicing Lutheran, Hegel located operative moral authority in a generalized "world spirit," which he at first identified with the ideals of the French Revolution. Watching Napoleon ride through the streets of Jena in 1806, on the eve of one of the emperor's more spectacular triumphs, Hegel wrote that he had seen "the world spirit ride by on horseback, reaching across the world and ruling it." Subsequently losing faith in both the revolution and Napoleon, he found his ultimate choice for embodiment of the world spirit closer to home: the ascending Prussian state, which he calculated to be the final expression of the progress toward moral perfection that he claimed had driven all human history.

Hegel is currently popular with liberal intellectuals who are dissatisfied with the concentration on the rights of individuals they find in the Anglo-American tradition, rising from Locke and Adam Smith, but do not get enough spiritual charge from Kant, and regard Rousseau as intellectually woozy. Hegel, some believe, fulfills the Rousseauian mission of locating freedom *within* the community rather than *in tension with* the community. It is hard, however, to understand how any kind of liberal can feel comfortable with Hegel.

"The community," Hegel declared in *The Phenomenology of Mind*, published in 1807, "has its concrete reality in government; for in government it is an individual whole." And in *The Philosophy of Right*, published in 1821: "The State is the actuality of the ethical Idea." And in *The Philosophy of History*, published in 1832: "The State is the Idea of Spirit in the external manifestation of human Will and its Freedom. It is to the State, therefore, that change in the aspect of History indissolubly attaches itself."[47]

Fusion between the individual and the community, in Hegel's view, is promoted through the heroic experience of war. Hegel could not have foreseen such twentieth-century phenomena as trench warfare, carpet bombing of cities, poison gas, or atomic bombs, but he saw with his own eyes the devastating effects of the Napoleonic wars in Europe. He nevertheless wrote in *The Phenomenology of Mind* that "war is the spirit and form in which the essential moment of the ethical substance is manifestly confirmed and realized."[48]

Hegel always claimed to be a champion of freedom and equality, but he had none of Rousseau's belief in democracy as at least the originator of public policy. His concept of legitimate government must have been entirely agreeable to his sovereign, Frederick William of Prussia: "In the perfect form of the State in which each and every element . . . has reached its free existence, this will [of the state] is that of *one actual decreeing Individual* (not merely of a majority in which the unity of the decreeing will has no *actual* existence); it is *monarchy*." Though a university professor, he had no qualms about turning over determination of truth to the authoritarian state: "The state has, in general, . . . to make up its own mind concerning objective truth."[49]

Like Plato, Hegel was in a way an absolutist in that he regarded the ideal state as a product of transcendent will: "The State is the Divine Idea as it exists on earth. . . . We must therefore worship the State as the manifestation of the Divine on earth." But he linked transcendence so closely to the practical operations of an actual government, the Prussian state, that he was easily accessible to secular collectivists who felt no need for transcendent endorsement.[50]

A CONSUMING PASSION

Hegel bewitched the mind of the young Karl Marx. His less ambiguous descendants were the fiery nationalists who increasingly dominated politics in nineteenth-century Europe.

Nationalism in some form is very old in human history and may spring from impulses deep within the human heart: our kind, our shared past, our common language, *la patrie*, "land where our fathers died," *people like us*. But in the medieval and even early modern West, when communications were limited, and dynastic governments ruled ethnically or linguistically unrelated territories, acquired through conquest or marriage, most people found their identities in relation to their local community, or at most their region (Gascony, Yorkshire, Tuscany, Virginia), and their church. Sixteenth-century modernizing monarchs like Elizabeth I in England and Henry IV in France invoked national spirit to win supremacy over baronial oligarchies, but until the eighteenth century, the sense of a national identity in most parts of the West was slight.

The American and French Revolutions were major sources of modern nationalism. Both appealed to spirits of national unity and pride as well as to themes of universalism. Perhaps even more important, the conservative powers of the late eighteenth and early nineteenth centuries, in their response to the universalist claims of the revolutionaries, invoked national values derived from history—Burke's "rights of Englishmen"; the German nobility imploring their *volk* to throw off the domination of Napoleon; Alexander I calling for defense of "holy Russia."

In the larger world, times were changing and sometimes undermining old sources of identity. People were communicating over wider regions. Many individuals seeking economic improvement were moving from ancestral rural villages to the new industrial cities where they had no inherited bonds, or even to new lands, like the United States. The nuclear family was becoming less associated with surrounding contexts of clan and community. The hold of the churches was weakening, particularly where church establishments had dug in behind wavering feudal regimes. People began to crave new means of finding identities. The romantic movement in literature and art glamorized ties based on shared language, folk traditions, incidents of heroism and sacrifice in half-forgotten national pasts—ties based on blood. Later in the nineteenth century, expansionist governments pursuing colonial empires justified their policies in part through appeals to national patriotism—painting the map red, "manifest destiny," or taking up the white man's burden.

All of these tendencies fed into a social and cultural evolution that by the middle of the nineteenth century had made nationalism the strongest ideological force in Europe. Not all nationalists were Hegelians (some non-German nationalists cast Hegel as representative of an alien force), but Hegel offered a conceptual structure in which nationalism could thrive, particularly in his native Germany.

Toward the end of the century, Nietzsche provided fresh philosophic support for collectivist nationalism. Nietzsche's idea of the Overman was in some ways antithetical to Hegel's statist doctrine—the state, Nietzsche wrote, "is the coldest of all cold monsters," and "tells lies in all languages." But for the mass of human beings, what he called the "herd instinct" would continue to be the necessary basis for social order. "Morality is the herd instinct in the individual." And he fully shared Hegel's enthusiasm for war: "The good war hallows any cause. War and courage have accomplished more great things than love of the neighbor."[51]

The odd-couple mixture of Hegel and Nietzsche helped feed the ideological compound that burst like a consuming passion across the first half of the twentieth century. When the new century's most crucial moment of decision arrived in the summer of 1914, nationalism proved far more potent than its collectivist rival, socialism, in determining the behavior of peoples. Socialist deputies in the parliaments of all the major European powers, who had pledged never to support a war in which workers would fight against workers, voted to back military mobilization as Europe tumbled toward catastrophe.[52]

Four years of carnage served to discredit the lingering remnants of feudal autocracy that had led most countries into battle, and permanently discontinued dynastic rule in Germany, Austro-Hungary, and Russia. But, remarkably, it left the appeal of authoritarian nationalism, stripped of feudal trappings, vigorous in many minds, including some of the most acute. Thomas Mann, already a successful novelist and critic who had loyally supported the German war effort, wrote in 1918: "I don't want the trafficking of Parliaments and parties that leads to the infection of the whole nation with the virus of politics. . . . I don't want politics. I want impartiality, order, and propriety. If that is philistine, then I want to be a philistine."[53]

Postwar Germany proved unwilling to sustain the kind of old-fashioned low-key authoritarianism that Mann had in mind, and he eventually departed, a chastened humanist, for the United States. Some of his fellow German intellectuals proved less resistant to the rise of racist nationalism in its most virulent form. Martin Heidegger, perhaps the most influential European intellectual of the interwar years, greeted Hitler's ascension to power in 1933 with a Hegelian chorus: "The German University's Will to the Essence is a Will to Science; it is a Will to the historico-spiritual mission of the German Nation, as a Nation experiencing itself in its State. Science and German Destiny must attain Power, especially in the essential Will." Heidegger, too, moved away from Nazism before the end of the 1930s, but only after participating as Rektor of the University of Freiburg in the purge of Jews from the faculty and lending himself to ceremonial functions of the Nazi regime.

The Second World War, coupled with the brutal crimes of the German Nazis, Italian Fascists, and their allies, and revelation of the horrors of the Holocaust at the end of the war, did at least temporarily lance the broad attraction of the right-wing version of authoritarian nationalism. During the second half of the twentieth century neo-fascist parties have from time to time played some part in the politics of some European countries. A kind of fascism has emerged in some of the countries in Eastern Europe that were liberated from communism. But all of these have offered only pale reflections of the ravings of Hitler and Mussolini, and have not so far projected visions of hate on the scale or with the intensity of those generated by their models.

Nationalism, however, is far from dead. In its healthy form, it serves as a unifying and vitalizing force within democratic societies otherwise threatened by egoist dismemberment, apathy, and resurgent tribalism. But in harmful expression, it is used by demagogues to legitimize barriers against internal minorities. With murderous effect, it motivates clashing tribes, sometimes grouped around divisions that had seemed almost forgotten, in such places as the villages of Bosnia, the plains of central Africa, the uneasy republics of the former Soviet Union, and the terrorist-threatened cities of the Middle East. Most perpetrators of these atrocities have probably never heard of Hegel, but the old master synthesizer gave seminal formulation to the belief system that structures their warring causes.

MARXISM: THE GULAG ALTERNATIVE

As mentioned above, the young Karl Marx was among the German intellectuals who were dazzled by the idealist philosophy of Hegel during the middle years of the nineteenth century. But with the aid of the materialism taught by Ludwig Feuerbach, Marx soon rejected the idealist side of Hegelianism, and accomplished his famous feat of "standing Hegel on his head"—substituting the play of material forces for Hegel's interaction of ideas. The true driving force in history, Marx concluded, is evolution of material technology, which causes alterations in economic conditions, in turn shifting social and political structures, for which all intellectual arguments and cultural expressions are rationalizations or adornments. "It is not the consciousness of men that determines their existence," he wrote, "but, on the contrary, their social existence determines their consciousness."[54]

In his mature work, Marx praised the capitalist revolution for having vastly increased the store of the world's material goods. He was a dedicated modernizer. He maintained that "man should subjugate nature to obey history." But when he surveyed the world that capitalism had made—the "dark, satanic mills" that William Blake found in industrialized England—he could not believe that a society based on capitalist economics could be history's final destination.[55]

Marx always retained some attachment to humanist values he had inherited from the Enlightenment. His vision for the future at times seems almost an idyll of unrestricted individualism. "In communist society," he wrote in 1846 with his frequent collaborator Friedrich Engels, "where nobody has one exclusive sphere of activity but each can become accomplished in any branch he wishes, society regulates the general production and thus makes it possible for me to do one thing today and another tomorrow, to hunt in the morning, fish in the afternoon, rear cattle in the evening, criticize after dinner, just as I have a mind, without ever becoming hunter, fisherman, shepherd, or critic." This is the aspect of Marxism that has always appealed to liberal humanists.[56]

In the larger context of his work, however, Marx completely submerged the tastes of individuals in abstractions of social will. Public ownership of the means of production was not for him, as it has been for some democratic socialists, a means to serve humanist ends. Rather it was the economic application of a fundamentally collectivist belief system.

Rejecting such murky concepts as Rousseau's general will and Hegel's world spirit, Marx turned for the source of his collectivism to biology. "The perfected political state," he wrote in 1844, "is, by its nature, the *species-life* of man. . . . Human emancipation will be complete when the real, individual man has absorbed into himself the abstract citizen; then as an individual man, in his everyday life, in his work, in his relationships, he has become a *species-being*."[57]

As Hegel made the Prussian state the ultimate expression of the world spirit, so Marx predicted that the triumph of the industrial proletariat would complete the final revolution and produce the end of history. "The working class, in the course of its development, will substitute for the old civil society an association which will exclude classes and their antagonism, and there will be no more political power properly so called, since political power is precisely the official expression of antagonism in civil society." Not only religion but also that oldest of human institutions, the family, will "vanish as a matter of course."[58]

All of this, Marx acknowledged, though inevitable, will not come easily. The capitalists will not go down without a fight, so the suppressed class of workers must not shrink from inflicting violence. Transition to a stateless society, moreover, will take time. During "the period of the revolutionary transformation" there would be no nonsense about attempts at democracy. Rather, in that "political transition period" an activist state with unlimited authority will be required. And that state "can be nothing but *the revolutionary dictatorship of the proletariat*."[59]

After Marx's death in 1883, the leadership of the communist movement proved eagerly willing to scruple at nothing in service of the revolution. "If the revolution demands it," wrote Georgy Plekhanov, founder of the Communist party in Russia, "everything—democracy, liberty, the rights of the

individual—must be sacrificed to it." According to V. I. Lenin, whose Bol-
shevik faction ruthlessly crushed Plekhanov's Mensheviks after the fall of
czarism in Russia in 1917: "One must be prepared for every sacrifice, to use
if necessary every stratagem, ruse, illegal method, to be determined to con-
ceal the truth, for the sole purpose of . . . accomplishing, despite everything,
the Communist task."[60]

Lenin and his successors, beginning with Josef Stalin, imposed first on the
Soviet Union, and later on most of Eastern Europe, totalitarian regimes that
systematically suppressed civil liberties; sent dissidents to slave camps in the
Siberian Gulag; and tortured, murdered, and caused mass starvation—all in
the name of Marx's collectivist ideal. "Hang," Lenin ordered, in response
to local dissent in 1918, *"no fewer than one hundred known Kulaks, rich
men, bloodsuckers. . . . Do it in such a way that for hundreds of versts
around the people will see, tremble, know, shout: they are strangling, and
will strangle to death the bloodsucker Kulaks."*

If Marx was right, and the individual counts for nothing while the collective is the only legitimate source of political or moral authority—what, after
all, is the basis for the equalitarian side of Marx's doctrine? If only the collective matters, why bother about equality among individuals? "Equalitari-
anism," Stalin told the socialist writer Emil Ludwig, "has nothing in common with Marxian socialism."[61]

Power to the people became power to the small band of politicians, technocrats, theoreticians, and associated thugs who were able to control the
instruments of terror in the Soviet state. The dictatorship of the proletariat—in reality, dictatorship by the Communist elite—showed no signs of
withering until the Soviet system faced economic collapse in the late 1980s.

THE COLLECTIVIST FALLACY

Almost everyone agrees on the need for most human beings to live together
cooperatively in social groups. The question is whether this necessity is the
sole legitimate source for value in human life. Political systems in the twentieth century that have answered this question in the affirmative have invariably produced economic disasters and brutal social repression.

Such failures are not accidental. Collectivists argue that individual persons are mistaken in regarding themselves as having authentic interests that
are distinct from those of society conceived as an organic whole. At the
heart of collectivism is what may be called the myth of the hive: the belief
that human beings, like honeybees, are constituted by nature to serve no
other goal than the welfare of their social collective. Notions to the contrary
are the result of "false consciousness."

From what we know of human nature and the reality of social existence, this claim is simply false. Among the defining qualities of human nature—perhaps *the* defining quality, as suggested in the last chapter—is recognition of a self with interests that, while overlapping with those of other persons and the total group, are nevertheless distinct. No amount of indoctrination or brainwashing, short of biological alteration, seems finally to obliterate this sense for most people.

The record of history shows that secular elites governing complex societies organized around collectivist ideals, whether the general will, *species-being,* the world spirit, or some other essence, almost always (at least after the first ardor of revolutionary enthusiasm has passed) give priority to their own interests. By the 1950s, for example, seventy-five percent of the student body at Moscow University (the top academic institution in the Soviet Union) were children of party or government officials who made up only a small sliver of the national population.[62] Governmental corruption contributed directly to the Soviet collapse in the 1980s. Other examples from the twentieth-century histories of Nazi Germany, Fascist Italy, and Communist China, among others, will be familiar to most readers. Ordinary persons submerged in a collectivist state serve not so much the interest of society as an organic whole, as the particular interests of its ruling elite.

This does not mean that the only alternative to collectivism in the management of human society is dog-eat-dog egoism. Nor does it suggest that human nature inherently prohibits formation of a community spirit or ethic. But it does mean that some other value structure is needed to reconcile the distinct interests of the individual and society.

4

Monism:
The Indescribable Oneness
of Being

The unseen Seer, the unheard Hearer, the unthought Thinker, the unknown Knower; Brahman is thy Soul, the Ruler within, the Immortal. There is no other seer, no other hearer, no other discerner, no other knower than Brahman.

—The Upanishads

Neither the self alone nor society alone, then, can meet the value needs of a free society; perhaps the problem can be solved by finding a value system that somehow combines the two.

There is, however, at least one other possibility: that a full account of human values may require inclusion of a source that lies outside of individual human nature or social existence. Physical forces in nature profoundly affect human experience—may, in some reckonings, entirely determine it. But if we attribute *moral authority* to these forces, we seem to conceive of them as rising from some level of reality transcending physical nature as we know it through the ordinary senses, even if only Nature spelled with a capital N. All through human history, including current history, most human beings have believed that such a transcendent source of value exists—although not necessarily theistic or conceptually distinct from the natural order as a totality.

What is transcendence? All the world's religions and much of its philosophy and art have striven to answer this question. For the Hebrew Bible, it is God, "creator of heaven and earth," who spoke to Noah, Abraham, and Moses, among others, and the "still, small voice" at the heart of nature heard by the prophet Elijah. For the Christian New Testament, it is the Trinity of Father, Son, and Holy Spirit in whom "we live and move and have our being." For the Qur'an, it is Allah, "Lord of the World, the Beneficent, the Merciful, the King of the Day of Judgment." For Hinduism, it is "the root undying, whence hath sprung whatever is." For the Buddha, Nirvana, the "Universal Mind." And for the Chinese Daoist sage Lao-tzu, "the Way of Heaven."

Scholars and philosophers, both ancient and modern, have sought with limited success to give these expressions cognitive meaning. For Plato, transcendence was "absolute goodness, beauty, and greatness." For Aristotle, it was the "unmoved mover" who set the universe in motion. For St. Thomas Aquinas, "pure actuality." For Spinoza, "a being of whom all or infinite attributes are predicated." For Thomas Hobbes (mockingly?), "the power of the invisible." For Kant, "a highest principle which determines itself." And for William James, "a MORE . . . which is operative in the universe."

ORIGINS OF BELIEF

How did human beings ever come to believe in such a thing? For most primitive and even archaic peoples, the veil between natural existence and transcendent reality often seemed thin and transparent. In animistic religions, supernatural personalities are attributed to particular natural objects, with special attention given to forces that support or threaten life, such as sun, rain, volcanoes, and animals pursued in the hunt. Over many millennia these objects and forces were generalized into broader categories, such as the earth, the sky, the sea, the underworld, the hearth, the hunt, war, and erotic love. The supernatural deities representing these generalities were more distant—less likely to be encountered at twilight at the end of a village lane or in the blaze of a log fire—but still designated by the persons of multiple gods and goddesses, as in the Sumerian, Greek, Roman, and Norse pantheons. The Vedic gods of India, Bernard van Noorten writes, "originated as personifications of atmospheric and elemental phenomena and were hymned and praised with great eloquence and devotion."[1]

Primitive humans attempted to cope with nature through practical techniques developed over long periods of time, but often these devices did not carry them very far. "In spite of all his forethought and beyond all his efforts," Bronislaw Malinowski reported in his study of Trobriand Islanders, the native discovered that "there are agencies and forces [that may] bring ill luck and bad chance, pursue him from beginning till end and thwart all his most strenuous efforts and his best-founded knowledge." Faced with such obstacles, Trobriand Islanders resorted to "magic"—for them a body of exercises with purposes basically similar to those of their practical devices.[2]

Magic, Malinowski and others have pointed out, functionally has more in common with science or engineering than with the religions of more complex cultures. It operates through esoteric formulae that the magician has mastered. If the spell is done right, the spirits will respond, just as if the explosive charges are correctly placed, the building will come down as the engineer intended. For practical ends, magic employs what are thought to be practical means, though these consist of potions, incantations, and charms, instead of equations, chemical compounds, or computers.

The "this-worldly" goals of primitive magic and religion, Max Weber argued, have to a considerable extent been maintained in the religions of more complex societies. "The most elementary forms of behavior motivated by religious or magical factors are oriented to *this* world. 'That it may go well with thee . . . and that thou mayest prolong thy days upon the earth,' in Deuteronomy 4:40, expresses the reason for performance of actions enjoined by religion and magic."[3]

Yet from the beginning there seem to have been chords within the human psyche, deeper than longing for wealth or longevity, that seek emotional or spiritual resolution through contact with transcendence. Some of these are not given much recognition, or are actively rejected, by most "higher" religions.

Some anthropologists apply the findings of modern psychology and psychiatry, however murky, to trace themes in religion and mythology to traumas of infancy and childhood. Joseph Campbell linked the moment of birth itself, with its "congestion of blood and sense of suffocation," to recurring religious ideas of birth or rebirth, "from the darkness of the womb to the light of the sun." The suckling of the child at its mother's breast, with accompanying feelings of bliss but also fear of loss, has been identified with widespread worship of the Mother Goddess and her descendants. Freudians hold that the famous Oedipus and Electra complexes lead boys and girls at the age of about five to fantasize displacing the parent of their own sex, generating, among other things, the "Jack-the-Giant-Killer motif," cosmic guilt, and embodiments of the supernatural in erotic images.[4]

Whatever the exact validity of these analyses, the guilts and phobias they purport to explain seem plausible sources for many of the witches, sprites, clowns, demons, sorcerers, dragons, imps, and love gods and goddesses that flock through primitive religions, and never quite disappear in more sophisticated cultures.

Among suggested subjective sources of belief in transcendence, probably the most important is realization of mortality—knowledge of the certainty of physical death. Tocqueville's formulation that "the short space of three-score years can never content the imagination of man, nor can the imperfect joys of this world satisfy his heart," provides at least part of the explanation for our remote ancestors' conviction that there must be "something more" beyond ordinary material existence. Hope that some form of personal survival continues after physical death was supported by nocturnal dreams in which departed loved ones appeared, sometimes offering advice or complaining about bad treatment.[5]

Since earliest times, humans have marked the passage to death with religious ceremonies and burial, and have directed prayers to deceased ancestors. Graves found in the Dordogne of southern France dating from 30,000 years ago show evidence of burial with religious rites. Sir Leonard Woolley reports that contents of Egyptian tombs from around 3000 BC indicate belief in passage "from one world to another [where] service of a god on earth" will continue through service of "that same god in another sphere." Among contemporary primitive tribes of West Africa, Kwasi Wiredu relates, "the living feel not only beholden to ancestors for their help and protection, but also positively obliged to do honor to them and render service to them as appropriate."[6]

Recognition of mortality contributes to the sense of most people, modern as well as ancient, that life must have some meaning beyond personal tastes or even the welfare of the family or tribe. "If man did not believe that he must live for something," Tolstoy wrote, "he would not live at all. The idea of an infinite God, of the divinity of the soul, of the union of men's actions with God—these are ideas elaborated in the infinite secret depths of human thought."[7]

Emile Durkheim and other sociologists have argued that the chief source of belief in transcendence is society's need for validation by a higher authority of its moral rules and standards: "God is another name for society." Even kinship, Durkheim maintained, "began by being an essentially religious bond." According to Patricia Crone: "The first civilization in history was the product of religion, or in other words of imagination endowed with supreme authority."[8]

A SENSE OF DIVINITY

Most religious people, and some who are not conventionally religious, believe in transcendence, not so much because of its personal or social uses but because of evidence they find for its presence in objective reality. Many rely on sacred writings, such as the Bible or the Qur'an, and some accept rational arguments developed by philosophers and theologians. Others relate belief to answered prayers or a sense of spiritual support at times of extreme stress.

Religious thinkers like St. Augustine and John Calvin have traced belief in transcendence to a fundamental intuition that God has implanted in the human psyche as evidence of His being. This intuition, it is said, forms part of our nature whether we acknowledge it or not, and is suppressed at peril to psychological and physical as well as spiritual well-being. William James wrote: "It is as if there were in the human consciousness a *sense of reality, a feeling of objective presence, a perception* of what we may call *'something there,'* more deep and more general than any of the special and particular 'senses' by which the current psychology supposes existent realities to be originally revealed."[9] Among modern psychologists, Carl Jung and his followers have most elaborately formulated the theory of an intuition of transcendence.

Existence of a universal intuition of transcendence in human nature can never be conclusively proved, but evidence is substantial and widespread. As Tocqueville wrote, belief in transcendence seems "no less natural to the human heart than life itself." Virtually all of the indigenous tribes of North America, anthropologists report, had a word for a primordial Great Spirit, superior to the lesser animistic spirits that inhabited trees, rocks, lakes, and storms. "From Wakan-Tanka, the Great Mystery, comes all power," an old Oglala Sioux chief told a scientific investigator early in the twentieth century. Mircea Eliade found that African people troubled by "drought, excessive rain, calamity, illness, etc. [turn to a] celestial Supreme Being . . . as the last resort, when every address to gods, demons, and sorcerers to banish suffering has failed." Plutarch, surveying the Mediterranean world in the first century AD, observed: "When traveling you can find cities without walls, writings, kings, houses, property. . . . But a city without a sacred place or gods, that has no prayers, oaths, oracles, sacrifices for thanksgiving or rites to ward off misfortune, has never been or ever will be seen by any traveler."[10]

THE MOTHER GODDESS

The pattern of life in the Neolithic states that began forming in Mesopotamia and Egypt toward the end of the fourth millennium BC was cyclical, following the agricultural calendar. The relative individualism of hunter-gatherers gave way to a more structured and regimented form of existence. Seasons of planting, cultivation, and harvest proceeded with greater regularity than had the more fluctuating activities of hunters. The parade of moon and stars across the heavens was carefully charted and assumed oracular meaning.

Neolithic priests projected cyclical order into the fundamental nature of existence. Nothing happened for the first time. Everything followed a pre-ordained round of comings and goings that had always been and would always be. Religion's promise of immortality, which among the hunter-gatherers had often been for individuals, became collective. Even the tribe was portrayed as merely the temporal manifestation of a deeper cyclical process of being that filled the universe. Events were regarded as real only if they could be interpreted as reflecting underlying archetypes.[11]

Religion, focused on maintaining agricultural productivity, gave greater importance to women, who led the way from plant-gathering to plant-cultivation, and whose roles as bearers and nurturers of life seemed to correspond to the farming cycle. Even in Paleolithic times, cave dwellers had formed crude but expressively beautiful images of naked women, with large hips and breasts, such as the Venus of Lespurges, which archeologists date to around 25,000 BC. With the shift to agriculture and to a more settled existence, female deities became more prominent. According to some archeologists—though hotly disputed by others—these deities were widely conceived as aspects of a universal Mother Goddess, embodying nature's eternal rhythms.

The Mother Goddess, or at least her local archetypes, flourished through much of the Mediterranean world and across the Middle East to India from around 3500 to around 2000 BC. She took many names: Inana in Sumeria, Hathor and Isis in Egypt, Ishtar in Babylon, and Gaea in what was to become Greece, among many others. In many places her worship was associated with the moon, deity of "the waters, the womb, and the mysteries of time," and the lunar bull. In *The White Goddess* (1948), the poet Robert Graves chronicled her role as inspirer of "magical language," which he claimed "remains the language of true poetry." The Goddess, Graves wrote, "is a lovely, slender woman with a hooked nose, deathly pale face, lips red as rowan berries, startlingly blue eyes, and long fair hair." Her priestesses, he surmised, "are likely to have chalked their faces in imitation of the Moon's white disk."[12]

The Goddess was usually a benevolent deity, showering her life-giving ministrations with the kindness of mother love. She might give license for orgiastic frenzies as part of her worship, but this expressed her indulgence. In some places, however, she could show an angry face, like that of the evil Kali in Indian mythology, or the Greek goddess Demeter in her darker moods. The Mother Goddess at times demanded human sacrifices as tribute for her gift of the returning spring—probably the source, in spruced-up versions, of the myths of Osiris and Isis, Tammuz and Ishtar, Adonis and Venus, and Orpheus and Eurydice, all of which link the death of a golden youth to nature's annual renewal.

Early in the second millennium BC, the first waves of the warrior peoples who were to descend periodically from the Eurasian steppe for the next four thousand years began sweeping into Europe, the Middle East, and India. They brought with them warrior deities, embodying male authority and military ethos. The Mother Goddess lost some of her eminence; her shrines were often taken over by male successors. At the famous oracle of Delphi, for instance, Gaea was supplanted by Apollo—though still with a female priestess hovering above the boiling springs to announce the god's instructions. The moon was subordinated in mythic terms to the sun, and "the brave moon-bull with its crescent horns [was] slain by the solar blade of the sparkling matador."[13] Sometimes the Goddess, as Hera, Aphrodite, and Artemis, or Juno, Venus, and Diana, found her way into the conquerors' pantheon, where she presided over hearth, erotic love, and, surprisingly, the hunt. But often she—as Clytemnestra, Medea, Ariadne, or Phaedra— remained a vengeful spirit, wreaking terrible retribution on male warrior heroes who, after accepting her embraces, spurned her love.

MONISM AND THEISM

During her long reign the Mother Goddess did more than embody another of the natural forces that primitive humans expressed as animistic spirits. Through identification, however vague, with the whole of reality, she provided perhaps the first formulation of a general concept of transcendence that goes beyond formless mystery or manipulative magic. She at least pointed the way toward a metaphysics in which transcendence is regarded, not only as the sole source of value, but also as being identical with all existence when viewed from the perspective of pure enlightenment. I call this metaphysics and the family of value systems based on this metaphysics, *monism.*

Monism is not the only generalized and systematically formulated concept of transcendence. Its main alternative is *theism,* of which there are several varieties. Theism holds that transcendence is the source, creator, and ultimate ruler of the natural world. Under theism, however, transcendence originates *outside* the natural world known through the ordinary senses. The created world, in this formulation, is not identical with the creator.

Many writers use the term transcendence to cover only what here is called theism. They designate the idea that deity embraces all of nature by the terms pantheism or immanence. Monism is preferred here for the latter idea because it seems to express more precisely what those who identity transcendence with all reality have in mind.

If one accepts this terminology, the question remains: How can monism be regarded as a variety of belief in transcendence? If universal spirit, or God-stuff, is in fact identical with the whole of reality, what is left to transcend? The answer is that the idea of reality permeated by transcendent unity expresses a luminous quality of metaphysical completeness for the believer, distinguishing it from the merely mechanical bumping of atoms across space and time contemplated by much of modern natural science. A good example of the monist perspective is the pronouncement by Krishna, earthly embodiment of the god Vishnu, to the hero Arjuna in the "Bhagavad

Gita": "The entire universe is pervaded by me, in that eternal form of mine which is not manifest to the senses. . . . My Being sustains all creatures and brings them to birth."

Monism in its purest form seems to require belief in the literal nonexistence of particular material things (humans, trees, automobiles, microbes, galaxies) as separate and distinguishable entities. As such, it has rarely received full acceptance among any large number of human beings, most of whom have always felt obliged to keep on making practical distinctions among pieces of reality. Its general thrust, however, has provided the basis for major religions, recurring themes in the arts, and solace for some thoughtful minds who find it impossible to believe in anything else.

MONISM IN THE WEST

The Western mind, with its antecedents in Hebraic and Hellenic cultures, has seemed particularly resistant to monism. The tangible material world has perhaps been too much with us to permit full absorption into universal spirit. From the very beginning, however, essentially monistic ideas have been entertained by some important thinkers and artists in the line from which the West descends.

Even in the Hebrew Bible there are occasional passages expressing broadly monistic attitudes, particularly (once more, atypically) in Ecclesiastes:

> One generation passes away, and another generation comes: but the earth abides forever.
> The sun also rises, and the sun goes down, and hastens to his place where he arose. . . .
> The thing which has been is that which shall be; and that which is done is that which shall be done; and there is no new thing under the sun. . . .
> That which has been is now; and that which is to be has already been.[14]

While monism's role in the origins of Judaism was relatively small and tangential, it played a significant part in the development of the other great source of Western culture, Greek philosophy and art. At the very start, Greek stargazers residing during the sixth century BC on the Ionian shore of Asia Minor, already the contact zone between two radically different cultures, asked the questions: May all of reality, truly conceived, be One? And, if One, what is its nature? Thales of Miletus, the first Greek philosopher we know by name, concluded that the "soul is diffused through the whole universe." Thales also speculated that the fundamental element in nature must be water.[15]

Heraclitus, born a bit up the coast in Ephesus toward the end of the sixth century, thought that the fundamental element more likely was fire. Heraclitus was impressed by the transient nature of existence: "You could not step twice in the same river; for other and yet other waters are ever flowing on." But he agreed with Thales that all aspects of nature reflect a fundamental unity: "God is day and night, winter and summer, war and peace, plenty and want." Heraclitus concluded that human ethical categories seen from the perspective of eternity are ultimately irrelevant—a supposition that has been common to monism: "Good and evil are the same. . . . To God all things are beautiful and good and right, though men suppose that some are right and others wrong."[16]

Among all the philosophers of antiquity, Parmenides, living during the fifth century BC at the other end of the Greek world in the colony of Elea in the Italian peninsula, struck the most consistently monistic note. Parmenides decided that the fundamental nature of the universe is composed of neither water nor fire nor any other tangible element, but rather of an abstract quality that he called simply "Being."[17]

The Sophists, as we observed in chapter two, turned away in fifth century Athens from speculation on the fundamental nature of reality and concentrated on practical questions of ethics and statecraft. Socrates agreed on the priority of ethical concerns, but argued that these can be dealt with only through reference to a transcendent level of being, essentially theistic rather than monistic. Plato at times wrote in a monist vein, as in the *Phaedo*: "Surely the soul can best reflect when it is free of all distractions such as hearing or sight or pain or pleasure of any kind—that is, when it ignores the body and becomes as far as possible independent, avoiding all physical contacts and associations as much as it can, in its search for reality." Like Socrates, however, Plato usually found the fallen world of politics all too real to be consigned serenely to a plane of nonexistence. Practical politics, rather, operates on the unformed level of matter, where the true philosopher may shape it to approach the timeless standard of the ideal.[18]

Among the post-Socratic schools of philosophy that flourished in Athens and later extended their influence throughout the Mediterranean world, the most monistic in tendency was Stoicism. "Monism and immanence," Robert Todd writes, "are the central ideas in Stoic physical theory." This tendency toward identification of transcendence with all existence was particularly developed by Stoic philosophers in imperial Rome. Marcus Aurelius, pausing from his duties as emperor, advised: "Constantly regard the universe as one living being, having one substance and one soul; and observe how all things have reference to one perception, the perception of this one living being; and how all things act with one movement; and how all things are the cooperating causes of all things that exist."[19]

Belief in determinism fostered a certain indifference to human suffering, to others' as well as one's own. Marcus Aurelius wrote, "Death certainly, and life, honour and dishonour, pain and pleasure, all these things equally happen to good men and bad, being things which make us neither better nor worse. Therefore they are neither good nor evil." Zeno, one of the founders of Greek Stoicism, told of beating a slave for stealing. The slave pleaded that it was his fate to steal, to which Zeno replied: "Yes, and to be beaten, also."[20]

Stoicism was much admired by some of the early Christian fathers and deeply influenced the development of Christian ethics. Christianity, however, rejected Stoicism's monist metaphysical outlook in favor of rigorous theism.

SPINOZA: THE SPIRITUALITY OF MATTER

In the sixteenth century, the availability in the West of printed editions of some of the Roman Stoics, particularly Cicero and Seneca, produced a revival of interest in vaguely monistic ideas. "The infinite is everywhere," wrote the seventeenth-century neo-Stoic, Lord Herbert of Cherbury, "and every part refers to some element of the whole."

Benedict (Baruch) de Spinoza, one of the founders of modern Western philosophy, born in 1632, went further toward conceiving a generally monistic metaphysic. A Jew whose family had fled from Portugal to the Netherlands several generations before to escape the Inquisition, Spinoza was a largely self-taught scholar who made his living grinding lenses for recently invented microscopes and telescopes. In his earliest writings he expressed a religious sensibility that was neither traditionally Jewish nor Christian. Though he built on the subjective rationalism developed by Descartes, he rejected the distinction between matter and spirit, and the idea of a theistic God, both of which Descartes had retained. In *God, Man, and His Well-Being,* composed in his late twenties, he wrote: "There is no finite substance. If we can prove that there can be no limited substance, then every substance belonging to the divine being must be unlimited."[21]

In the *Ethics,* his major work, modeled in presentation on Euclid's geometry, Spinoza argued a series of propositions that he maintained follow logically from each other. "God," he deduced, "is the immanent, and not the transitive, cause of all things." But even the immanent God is controlled by a deeper determinism: "Things could have been produced by God in no other manner and in no other order than that in which they have been produced."[22]

As with the Stoics, Spinoza's monism liberated him from the sectarian prejudices and narrow dogmas that characterized many of the traditional religious persuasions of his time. He composed a generously humanistic ethic: "The man who has properly understood that everything follows from the necessity of the divine nature, and comes to pass according to the eternal laws and rules of nature, will in truth discover nothing which is worthy of hatred, laughter, or contempt . . . but, so far as human virtue is able, he will endeavor to *do well*, as we say, and to *rejoice*." To reach this conclusion, however, he appears to attribute qualities of meditated love and caring to "divine nature" that are more truly theistic than consistently monistic.[23]

Not surprisingly, Spinoza's pantheistic ideas got him in trouble with both fellow Jews and the Netherlands's dominant Calvinist clergy. Despite his family's prominent role in Amsterdam's Sephardic community, the elders of his synagogue excommunicated him in 1656. Civil authorities followed up by temporarily banishing him from the city. He eventually moved to the somewhat more tolerant environment of The Hague, where he remained until his death in 1677.

Fearing religious repression, Spinoza did not attempt publication of the *Ethics* during his lifetime. But the manuscript was privately circulated, winning him a good deal of intellectual attention, including a visit from the famous German rationalist, Gottfried Wilhelm Leibniz (who first heard of him through their common interest in optics). Following Spinoza's instructions, the *Ethics* was publicly issued a few months after his death.

In the Europe of his time, Spinoza's attraction to monism was unusual but not unique. The painter Jan Vermeer, Spinoza's near neighbor in Delft, rendered townscapes and domestic interiors in a manner that conveys keen respect for the integrity of material objects, recalling the philosopher's belief in the inherent spirituality of all kinds of matter. Interestingly, Vermeer—like Spinoza—was fascinated by the new science of optics.

In the eighteenth century, Spinoza's philosophy was harshly attacked both by religious writers and by tough-minded empiricists like David Hume. With the coming of the nineteenth century, however, participants in the romantic movement found his pantheistic tendencies sympathetic to their own attraction to a form of monism. Goethe and Coleridge acknowledged his influence, and the German romantic poet Novalis called him "the God-intoxicated man."

After its role in romanticism, monism during the nineteenth and twentieth centuries played a significant, though still distinctly limited, role in Western art, religion, and philosophy. The principal source of its influence in the West, however, has been neither the Stoics nor Spinoza but contact with the religions of the East, where in modified forms it has always been culturally dominant.

HINDUISM: "THOU ART THAT"

Around the middle of the second millennium BC, swarms of fierce Aryan tribesmen—part of the same overflow from the Eurasian steppe that sent the

Greeks into Europe and other invaders into the Middle East—began pouring through the Khyber Pass into the fertile valleys and plains of northern and central India. The invaders found there the remains of a high civilization that had flourished in the Indus River region from about 2500 to 1700 BC. This civilization, based on the great cities of Mohenjo-daro and Harappa, worshipped a form of the Mother Goddess, carried on a brisk trade with the Middle East, and achieved levels of organization and comfort "unequaled before the advent of the Roman Empire." Reasons for its decline remain obscure—possibly involving changes of climate or deforestation caused by the expanding agricultural economy. In any case, the ancient cities of the Indus region proved easy prey for the advancing Aryans, who pillaged and burned them so thoroughly that memory of their very existence was lost to history for thousands of years.

Many survivors from the old Indus civilization fled south into the cone of the Indian peninsula, contributing to an ethnic distinction between light-skinned northern Aryans and dark-skinned southern Dravidians that continues to the present day. Some scholars trace division of the population into rigid social castes to the conquerors' determination to preserve sharp political and economic distinctions between themselves and the conquered.

The Aryans, like the early Greeks, brought with them a pantheon of warrior gods and their consorts. These were celebrated in the Vedas, collections of hymns written in Sanskrit, which, according to Klaus Klostermaier, "are probably the oldest religious text still used by a living religion." The Rig Veda, the oldest (probably composed about three thousand years ago) and most important, includes many frank appeals to the gods for worldly success: "Like fire kindled by friction, do inflame me! Illumine us! Make us rich!" Already, however, there are notes of the monism, or pantheism, that was to become characteristic of Indian religion; for example: "I breathe a strong breath like the wind and the tempest, the while I hold together all existence. / Beyond this wide earth and beyond the heavens I have become so mighty in my grandeur."[24]

The invading Aryans were apparently horrified by the "phallus worship" practiced by fertility cults in the older civilization, and attempted to impose their own sterner religion. As in Greece and the Middle East, the major deities in the developing pantheon—Brahma, "the Creator"; Vishnu, "the Preserver"; and Shiva, "the Destroyer"—were usually given male identities, but the Mother Goddess was never so fully supplanted in India as usually occurred farther west. "The Mother is the consciousness of the Divine," writes a modern Indian scholar, Sri Aurobindo, "or it may be said, she is the Divine in its consciousness force."[25] The older religion of the Indus civilization, expressing cosmic unity and taking themes of erotic sensuality from nature, became integrated into the ruder faith of the conquerors. The resulting combination of Aryan and Dravidian strains produced the rich, multifaceted, and diverse body of traditional Indian religions that we know collectively as Hinduism.

The term Hindu was applied by Moslem invaders in the thirteenth century to peoples they found living in the Indus region. It was not, however, used as a religious designation until the nineteenth century when it was employed by the British to identify, for administrative purposes, the assortment of traditional Indian religions left after separate classifications of Islam, Buddhism, Jainism, Sikhism, and a few others. The term was accepted only gradually among Hindus themselves, and fully only after the split between India and Pakistan at the end of British rule in 1947.

Hinduism has no single founder or prophet like Abraham, the Buddha, Jesus, or Mohammed. It is composed of a wide variety of sects, cults, and local traditions, many of which direct primary worship to one or another of its deities, particularly Vishnu (in the north) and Shiva (in the south.) The deities themselves take many different names and sometimes adopt an alternate sex or become hermaphroditic. "Nothing can be asserted about Hinduism that cannot also be denied," writes Nancy Wilson Ross.[26]

Yet the underlying view of reality held among most practicing Hindus, of whom there are about 700 million in India today and about 290 million elsewhere, seems surprisingly uniform, perhaps more so than within Christianity or Islam. The basic Hindu worldview was set forth as early as the eighth century BC by the Indian sage Aruni, counseling his son: *tat tvam asi*—"Thou art that." This credo, rooted in the Vedas, asserts the identity of the individual soul with the whole of objective reality.

Aruni's teachings form part of the Upanishads, commentaries on the Vedas composed by various sages from the fifteenth to the sixth centuries BC. Other Upanishads impart knowledge of Brahman, "the Soul of the Universe, the invisible, the uncreated Infinite which is manifest in all visible and created things" (not to be confused with Brahma, the creator god; or the Brahmins, members of Hinduism's priestly caste).[27]

Even more central to Hindu tradition than the Vedas and the Upanishads is the "Bhagavad Gita" (the "song of God"), the long poem that forms part of the great Indian epic, the *Mahabharata*, composed between the sixth and third centuries BC. In the Gita, which some devout Hindus recite in its entirety every day, the god-figure Krishna seeks to overcome qualms that the hero Arjuna has developed on the eve of the great battle between his clan, the Pandavas, and its rival, the Kurus. Krishna describes the presence of God-stuff in every particle of matter:

> I am the fresh taste of the water; I
> The silver of the moon, the gold of the sun,
> The word of worship in the Vedas, the thrill
> That passes in the ether, and the strength

> Of man's shed seed. I am the good sweet smell
> Of the moistened earth, I am the fire's red light,
> The vital air moving in all which moves,
> The holiness of hallowed souls, the root
> Undying, whence hath sprung whatever is.

Toward the end Krishna sums up: "But what need have you, Arjuna, to know this huge variety? Know only that I exist, and that one atom of myself sustains the universe."[28]

Westerners surveying the vast and complex pantheon of Hindu gods, goddesses, and sacred beasts are likely to seek parallels in familiar Greek, Roman, and German mythologies. In fact, their natures are quite different. The huge relief carved into stone at Mamallapuram, along the eastern seacoast near the tip of the Indian peninsula, depicts the images of gods, goddesses, elephants, monkeys, deer, sorcerers, and demons, all centered on the meditating hero, Arjuna. These, however, are not intended to depict distinct entities, as in Western mythologies, but rather are *all aspects of a unified whole*, inhabiting the mind of Arjuna (like characters in a James Joyce novel) and at the same time identical with "the soul of the Universe."

Hinduism is often thought of as an otherworldly religion. It does indeed draw some individuals to lives of otherworldly mysticism and asceticism. But viewing events in the material world as in some sense illusory and beyond human control may also be interpreted to release the individual to distinctly this-worldly pursuits. It should be remembered that the immediate purpose of the "Bhagavad Gita" in the context of the *Mahabharata* is to overcome Arjuna's *moral* inhibitions against participating in the slaughter of his clan's rivals, the Kurus, who are also his kinsmen. Krishna reassures Arjuna:

> Life cannot slay! Life is not slain!
> Never the spirit was born; the spirit shall cease to be never;
> Never was time it was not; End and beginning are dreams![29]

Elsewhere in the *Mahabharata,* Bhisma, hero of the Kurus, declares: "It is the warrior's eternal duty to die in battle, not to meet his end at home." As William James observed, the underlying teaching of the "Bhagavad Gita" is that "only those need renounce worldly actions who are still inwardly attached thereto."[30]

Besides accommodating warrior values, Hinduism also finds a place for erotic love. During the first millennium AD, the sensuous aspect of Indian religion, perhaps inherited from the old Dravidian fertility cults, played a growing part in worship and art. "The accent on the female," Joseph Campbell writes, "and specifically as an erotic object, steadily increases, until by the twelfth and thirteenth centuries there would almost appear to be in Indian mysticism little else."[31]

Hinduism's approach to this-worldly responsibilities is shaped by the concept of *dharma*, which P. V. Kane writes is "one of those Sanskrit words that defy all attempts at an exact rendering in English or any other tongue," but can be roughly defined as "the privileges, duties, and obligations of a man, his standard of conduct as a member of the Aryan community, as a member of one of the castes, as a person in a particular stage of life." Dharma in some ways resembles the Western idea of natural law, but is more derived from inherited wisdom and less from exercise of reason. Klaus Klostermaier explains: "Dharma has its roots in the structure of the cosmos, and the socio-ethical law of humankind is but one facet of an all-embracing law encompassing all beings."[32]

Like some formulations of natural law, dharma is often interpreted to reinforce a hierarchical view of society. Kostermaier maintains that "Dharma presupposes a social order in which all functions and duties are assigned to separate classes whose smooth inter-action guarantees the well-being of society as a whole."[33]

In many ancient civilizations, rivalry developed between the warrior and priest classes. In India, this competition was decisively won by the priests, the Brahmins. The warrior class, the *Ksatriyas*, fitted in below the priests; followed by the farmers and merchants, the *Vaisyas*; and the unpropertied laborers, the *Sudras*. These four classes became the bases for the four original castes. As time went on, these further subdivided into more than 3,000 hierarchically arranged castes identified with particular occupations or trades. Beneath all of these were the untouchables, perhaps descendants of the Indus region's original inhabitants.

Perhaps the dominant role of the Brahmins helped tie the Indian class system even more tightly to religion than in most other cultures. According to the Rig Veda, the Brahmin caste issued from the head of the original world spirit, the *Ksatriyas* from its chest, the *Vaisyas* from its belly, and the *Sudras* from its feet. With religious backing, the inflexible structure of castes not only legitimized exploitation of class by class, but also hindered development of economic and social initiative.

Since the composition of the Upanishads, traditional Indian religion has taught the doctrine of transmigration, according to which the individual spirit passes through a series of rebirths into human or animal bodies, reflecting the extent to which the spirit has clung to material desire in a particular life. The objective of the spirit is to break free of this cycle and be absorbed into the true reality of cosmic unity. "From the unreal lead me to the real," implores ones of the Upanishads. "From death lead me to immortality."[34]

The balance between good and bad deeds in each life is determined by *karma*—a concept something like the Western idea of destiny. "Karma," Kostermaier writes, "keeps in motion the vicious circle of action, desire, reward, and new action. The karma of future births is worked out in the present birth; and karma acquired in this birth, good or bad, works toward a future birth." The individual spirit is to some extent responsible for the karma that it bears, but karma also is the product of cosmic fate. "Karma," Nancy Wilson Ross interprets, "is the Master Law of the Universe, but there is no Law Giver."[35]

Hinduism cannot be said to be consistently, in the purest sense, monistic, either now or in the past. The gods and goddesses of the *Mahabharata* are too distinct and real to be absorbed totally into cosmic unity. The individual spirit, the *atman*, appears to have some kind of separate existence before it escapes from the round of rebirth into Brahman. As the Buddha pointed out, the very concept of a struggle between spirit and matter appears to grant some differentiated reality to matter.

The idea of cosmic Oneness, "the Brahman without passions and without parts," is, however, more defining for Hinduism than for any of the theistic religions that rise from the Hebraic root. Concentration on Oneness has enabled Hinduism to carry its believers, common people as well as sages, to a level of detachment at which ordinary lusts, ambitions, sufferings, or regrets may lose much of their sting or attraction. It has helped keep religion a more pervasive force in India than in any Western country, including the United States. Mahatma Gandhi, the religious sage and political prophet who helped lead the struggle to end British rule during the first half of the twentieth century, claimed that traditional Indian religion gave the nation "a path of national God-realization, attained through simple duty, self purification, and self rule."[36]

Despite these strengths, Hinduism, considered from a social and moral point of view, has lacked important conceptual resources that rise from more theistic traditions. First, absence of a concept of the individual as a person created in the image of God has left a gap in support for human rights, particularly the rights of women, lower caste Hindus, and non-Hindu. Indian women are still beaten and even murdered by their husbands with disturbing frequency, and sectarian violence against non-Hindus has contributed to repeated civil disorders. Gandhi himself was assassinated in 1948 by a Hindu fanatic who believed he had gone too far in defending the rights of the Moslem minority. Second, identification of sin with bad karma rather than with personal wrongdoing fosters political corruption and tolerance of authoritarian government. And third, concentration on the timeless One, in contrast to the loving God of the biblical tradition who acts through and judges human experience, creates little spiritual motivation for practical acts aimed at making an imperfect world a somewhat better place.

Robert Bellah writes that the dominant attitude of traditional Indian religion has been that "the world is a burning house and that man's most urgent need is to escape from it." This view, whatever its spiritual or psychological appeal in a troubled time, does not seem to provide a reliable moral foundation for stability, justice, and growth in a free society.[37]

BUDDHISM: BEYOND ILLUSION

During the final decades of the sixth century BC and the early years of the fifth, the same period in which Western philosophy and drama were being hatched in Greece, the Hebrew prophets were active in Israel, and Confucius and Lao-tzu were current in China, two charismatic reformers separately proposed major revisions of India's traditional religion. Both reform movements attacked the theological bases of the caste system, sought to purge mythological and erotic elements from inherited religion, and went further than the Vedas and the Upanishads in the direction of pure and consistent monism. Each eventually gave birth to a new religion.

Varhamana, a monk who took the name Mahavira after his enlightenment toward the end of the sixth century, recommended strict asceticism, if necessary to the point of starvation, as a means for breaking free of the illusory separateness of the human self. He preached reverence toward nature as the bearer of world spirit (*jiva*), and counseled his followers to avoid destruction of any living thing, including insects. Finding all hierarchical class structures, including the caste system, reflections of materialist non-spirit (*ajiva*), he advocated complete human equality and admitted converts to his ascetic order without regard for their class background. Mahavira's followers called themselves Jainas ("conquerors"), and his beliefs evolved into the Jain religion, which continues to this day in India with about two million believers.

With far greater consequences for the shared pool of human values and fundamental belief systems, the other sixth-century reform movement grew from the teachings of Siddhartha Gautama, born in 563 BC to a royal family of the warrior caste, the *Ksatriyas*, in the kingdom of Sakia, part of present-day Nepal near the slopes of the Himalayas. Young Gautama, though married to a beautiful princess and trained by his father for a princely career, began to brood over the inevitability of human suffering and death. Though his wife had borne him a son, he left home and wandered across India, seeking instruction from the wisest and most famous Brahmins of his time. He delved deeply into the Vedic classics, but found them wanting in pure spirituality. Like Mahavira, he pursued extreme ascetic exercises, believing that these might lead him to enlightenment. The effects of these were so debilitating, he later recalled, that "my limbs became like some withered creepers with knotted joints; my buttocks like a buffalo's hoof; my ribs like rafters of a dilapidated shed." But he achieved no awakening.

Finally, seated one night beneath the bodhi tree in northern India, the truth came to him in a flash of spiritual insight: *"All existence whatever is unsubstantial."* The fragmented appearance of the material world is simply illusion, as the classics hinted but never consistently maintained. If this is so, the illusion of material existence is not so much to be conquered as seen through. Extreme asceticism is pointless and may itself be a distraction from truth: "Neither abstinence, nor going naked, nor shaving the head, nor a rough garment, neither offerings to priests, nor sacrifices to gods will cleanse a man who is not free from delusions." Oneness—Nirvana—is indeed absolute, and is attainable to the human spirit through "right contemplation." With this realization, Gautama, at the age of 35, became the Buddha, "the enlightened one."[38]

The Buddha at first questioned whether his discovery could be imparted to others, but his new sense of spiritual exhilaration led him to at least try. Preaching his first sermon a few weeks later near the holy city of Varanasi (Benares), he set forth the "noble eightfold path" through which Nirvana can be reached: right views; right aspirations; right speech; right conduct; right livelihood; right effort; right mindfulness; and, finally, right contemplation. "This," he concluded, "is my last existence. There will now be no more rebirth for me!" Five of his listeners, ascetic monks, were converted on the spot.[39]

For the remainder of his long life the Buddha traveled through India, preaching the way to enlightenment, making further converts, above all opening minds through his serene example. Among his converts were his deserted wife and son, and even his father, the old king. It should be noted, however, that his father won from him the promise that he would recruit no monks without the consent of their parents—a rule still observed in some forms of Buddhism.

The Buddha's message was by no means an affirmation of the warmth of human companionship. He taught (or later followers attributed to him) that "if one lives in the midst of company, love of amusement and desire arises; strong attachment for children arises; let therefore one who dislikes separation, which must happen sooner or later from those beloved, walk alone like a rhinoceros."[40]

When he died at the age of 80, his last words to his disciples were characteristically enigmatic: "Decay is inherent in all compound things. Work out your own salvation with diligence."[41]

After the Buddha's death, his teaching continued to spread rapidly across India, particularly among the growing merchant caste, the *Vaisyas*—who perhaps were glad to find a religion that did not validate the power of the Brahmins. After a particularly bloody war in the third century BC, the warrior king Asoka, who had gained control over much of India, turned to Buddhism as a pacifying force. For a time it seemed that Buddhism was becoming India's prevailing faith. By the third century AD, however, the traditional Vedic religions were making a comeback. Some Brahmins identified the Buddha as one more incarnation of the often-incarnated god, Vishnu. Ultimately, Buddhism almost vanished from the land of its birth.

Unlike Jainism, Buddhism won large followings in other parts of Asia. Theravada Buddhism, which became dominant in Ceylon and most of Southeast Asia other than Vietnam, reverently maintained the strict monism taught by the Buddha. Mahayana Buddhism, which prevailed in the mountain kingdom of Tibet, and made large inroads in China, Korea, Vietnam, and Japan, in contrast, developed the concept of the *bodhisattva*—the enlightened person who temporarily foregoes Nirvana in order to return to help others toward enlightenment.

The Mahayana variant, while losing some of classical Buddhism's rigor, provided a vehicle for more humanistic responses to practical problems of injustice and poverty. Mahayana Buddhism attracted converts in China for the very reason that it offered qualities of compassion and charity not found in the pragmatic Confucianism favored by the scholarly elite. Incorporation of compassion, however, seems to require a value resource beyond consistent monism.

Zen Buddhism, a variant developed in Japan during the thirteenth century AD, emphasized "two supreme ideals—fidelity and indifference to suffering." This self-denying ethic, Richard Storry points out, provided moral support for the military code of Japan's warrior aristocracy.[42]

During Buddhism's first few centuries, believers made no physical images of the religion's founder, following the Buddha's rejection of the importance or even reality of individual personality. Toward the end of the first century AD, however, in the northeast Indian province of Gandhara, where the influence of Hellenistic humanism descended from conquest by Alexander the Great was strong, Buddhist craftsmen began sculpting images of the Buddha seated in the classic lotus position. These became models for the most popular icon of Buddhist art—a paradoxically personal symbol of a scrupulously impersonal religion.[43]

Classical Buddhism of the Theravada school carries monism about as far as it can go. Even the Mahayana and other schools that have adopted some humanistic modifications retain a basically monist orientation. "Buddhism," Max Weber wrote, "is the most radical solution of the problem of theodicy, . . . contrasting the world's transitory events and behavior with the serene and perduring being of eternal order—immobile divinity, resting in dreamless sleep." Buddhist doctrine, Louis Dupre observes, proposes "no other ideal than the attainment of pure emptiness."[44]

Theoretical lack of interest in the temporal world of apparent reality has allowed Buddhism to remain remarkably free of dogma. John B. Cobb maintains that "Buddhism has only one commitment, namely, to enlightenment." In the Buddhist view, enlightenment requires no particular faith—only a willingness to think things through without prejudice, as the Buddha recommended. Other religions, therefore, are readily accommodated. In Japan a Buddhist monk and a Shinto shamaness have sometimes married, forming a team to offer services from either religion, depending on the occasion. (Most Japanese, it has been said, live Shinto and die Buddhist. Many subscribe with an easy conscience to both religions.) The only thing forbidden, in Buddhist belief, is for a religion to claim for itself absolute truth—though this rule itself is of course a kind of absolute.

Buddhism has obviously brought great spiritual satisfaction and release from anxiety to millions during the more than two-and-a-half thousand years of its existence. Its various branches now count about 300 million members, ranking it fourth in membership among the world's religions, behind Christianity, Islam, and Hinduism. In recent times it has regained a relatively small but significant foothold in the land of its origin. The 2,500th anniversary of the Buddha's enlightenment was celebrated in India with considerable fanfare in 1956. Though the overwhelming majority (more than ninety-five percent) of Buddhists are Asians, Buddhism has played an important part in the growing influence of monism in the West.

Belief in the essential nonreality of the differentiated material world, with its numerous apparent problems and attractions, has naturally led Buddhism to take a rather disinterested view of secular politics. Though Buddhist sages have produced a sizable literature on government and social ethics, these works mainly offer advice to rulers and subjects in countries where Buddhism is the established religion. In modern Asia, Buddhism has at times been identified with nationalist movements resisting Western colonialism. In Tibet, Buddhists during the twentieth century have done what they could to fend off domination by secular Chinese governments, first nationalist and then communist. In South Vietnam, religious persecution by the Roman Catholic leadership of the pro-Western regime in the 1960s drove Buddhist monks to acts of protest, including self-immolation by fire.

In the main, however, Buddhism, following the logic of a belief system that values "total emptiness," has given a wide berth to political and economic concerns. According to the great historian of religion Ernst Troeltsch, Buddhism "presents the opposition to politics in its most acute form."[45]

MONISM AND MODERNITY

As mentioned above, monism played an important, though always subordinate, role in the European romantic movement of the early nineteenth century. Its spirit is reflected, for example, in Goethe's dictum: "Everything transient is but a symbol," and in William Blake's claim "to see a world in a grain of sand / and a Heaven in a wild flower."

After the waning of romanticism, monism continued to influence succeeding waves of Western intellectual and artistic expression. Henry David Thoreau's meditations during his stay at Walden Pond in the 1840s as self-appointed "inspector of snow-storms and rain-storms" in part reflect monist attitudes. Like other New England transcendentalists, Thoreau had been deeply impressed by contact with artifacts and bits of philosophy floating back from the Orient with Yankee traders.

In the closing decades of the nineteenth century, some impressionist painters, particularly Monet and Seurat, reached beyond self-consciousness to convey direct perception of spiritualized matter. Going beyond impressionism, Paul Cezanne painted human figures, still lifes, and mountain landscapes in geometric arrangements that express an even more consistent and profound monist vision. Cezanne, John Goulding writes, elevated "things to some region where art becomes religion." Cezanne's work after 1879, when he was forty, is flooded by a powerful sense of transcendence. It is humanity, conveyed by individual personalities, that is absent. In modern art, the tradition of Cezanne has been carried on most directly by Matisse—cool, detached, and focused on metaphysical order.

In literature, James Joyce sought the universal through total immersion in the particular. During the period between the two world wars, allusive poets like Ezra Pound, T. S. Eliot, and Wallace Stevens experimented with monist detachment as a possible means for transcending gathering social catastrophe and spiritual exhaustion. After his conversion to Christianity, Eliot still used monism as his point of departure for *Four Quartets*, written during the Second World War.

> Time present and time past
> Are both perhaps present in time future,
> And time future contained in time past.
> If all time is eternally present
> All time is unredeemable
> What might have been is an abstraction
> Remaining a perpetual possibility
> Only in a world of speculation.[46]

Some modern scientists, uncomfortable with Western traditions of theism but reluctant to lose hold altogether on transcendence, have been drawn to monist ideas. Alfred North Whitehead wrote: "The misconception which has haunted [Western] philosophic literature through the centuries is the notion of independent existence. There is no such mode of existence. Every entity is only to be understood in terms of the way in which it is interwoven with the rest of the universe." Whitehead found in this interweaving a kind of mystical unity. The explosion of the first atomic bomb in the New Mexico desert in 1945 reminded Robert Oppenheimer of lines from the "Bhagavad Gita": "Suppose a thousand suns should rise together in the sky; such is the shape of Infinite God." Some aspects of contemporary physics, such as Julian Barbour's theory that time is an illusion resulting from false perception of multidimensional but entirely spatial reality, seem vaguely monistic.[47]

Some sectors of contemporary feminism, regarding traditional Western theistic religions as irredeemably patriarchal, have given currency to monistic sentiments, often associated with revived celebration of the Neolithic Mother Goddess. At a highly publicized feminist conference in Minneapolis in the fall of 1993, sponsored by the women's divisions of several mainline Protestant denominations, enthusiastic participants chanted allegiance to the goddess Sophia. Some got themselves quoted making disparaging remarks about Jesus Christ. Rosemary Reuther, an influential feminist theologian, describes herself as a Christian, but recommends worship of "the great matrix of being, the Primal Matrix, the great womb within which all things, Gods and humans, sky and earth, humans and non-humans, are generated," in place of Christianity's triune God.[48]

Monism plays a part in the New Age religions, some also linked to the Mother Goddess, that attempt to fill spiritual gaps left by disenchantment with traditional faiths. Vulgarized monism hovers behind much contemporary pop-science, science fiction, and popular music.

THE MONIST SOLUTION

Monism, once its claims are understood, is intellectually fairly simple. Unlike its theistic rivals, it makes no distinction between the creator and the created. It is therefore more easily kept consistent than other belief systems founded on transcendence.

All belief systems that acknowledge—or celebrate—the authority of a transcendent (supernatural) will, power, or idea over the natural world must regard this authority as being in some sense absolute. Theistic scriptures, discourses, sermons, and hymns are filled with affirmations of the dependence of the human individual and group on transcendent will. But if transcendence is accorded omnipotence and omniscience—and it is hard to see how it cannot be and still be absolute—how can there be any real freedom for the finite and created? Theistic thinkers such as St. Paul, Augustine, Calvin, and Kant have shown that answers can be given to this question, even within the context of some kind of predestination, that do not end in monism. But the answers of monism are so much more simple, so austerely self-sufficient, so breathtakingly direct: freedom for the created and finite does not in any real sense exist; therefore truly differentiated matter does not exist; therefore the only thing that does exist is the undifferentiated universal. All perceptions, all sufferings, all appetites to the contrary are simply products of illusion.

The arguments for and against monism obviously do not rest on its political or economic effects. If monism does not provide a firm moral foundation for democracy or a free society or a rising standard of living, what difference does that make if the values that attract us to these things are themselves parts of the illusion—distractions from the only thing that really matters, absorption into the transcendent One?

Monism engages the human imagination and the human spirit in the profoundest possible terms. For multitudes of people, going back at least to the time of the Mother Goddess, it has in one form or another provided the key to spiritual release, enlightenment, or exaltation.

But for other multitudes—more multitudes—it has not. There lurks within human nature the stubborn response: *It is not so.* One source of the human negation of monism is expressed by Dr. Johnson's common sense proof of the existence of matter by "striking his foot with mighty force against a large stone." And by Carlyle's comment when told of Margaret Fuller's announcement that she had accepted the universe: "Gad! She had better!" At a more philosophic level, there is the question, given monism's assumptions, of where the illusion of differentiated existence comes from. Is not the experience of illusion, at least, real? And if real, is it not then in some sense differentiated? The Buddha himself acknowledged at least the appearance of "the fact of suffering."

Perhaps these responses for most incorrigibly time-and-space-bound mortals are enough, but intuitive rejection of monism may go deeper. Perhaps the only thing worse than all the sufferings, disappointments, partings, and impairments of human life would be to believe that these things have never really existed. For one thing, to believe seriously in the fundamental nonexistence of life's troubles would require giving up belief in the good things as well—the sweetness of life and all that goes with it. Even more important, belief that all suffering is the result of illusion must turn sufferers into dupes. All the endurance against hardship through all the ages, all the bearing of loss and pain, all the courage in situations that seem hopeless, all the struggle—all have been for nothing, because all have been nothing. The price for disappearance into "total emptiness" is sacrifice of the reality, and with it the dignity, of everything human. It is a price that most people, even in cultures where the insights of monism have exerted a strong appeal, have finally been unwilling to pay.

Monism has much to say to the modern world. When other systems appear to fail, philosophically and practically, it may offer a last resort for some, even for many. But it is not a promising source for moral renewal of democracy or nonauthoritarian civil society.

5

◁═══▷

Absolutism:
Nothing but the Truth

The commonwealth must be made to agree with the church, and the
government thereof with her government.

      —Thomas Cartwright, sixteenth-century Puritan divine

As for the multitude, it has no right other than to be led and, as a faithful flock, to follow its pastor.

      —Pope Pius X

The entire system of government and administration, together with the
necessary laws, lies ready for you. If the administration of the country
calls for taxes, Islam has made the necessary provision; and if the laws
are needed, Islam has established them all.

      —Ayatollah Khomeini

Monism in its pure form must find the moral and spiritual needs of a free society ultimately irrelevant—perhaps useful in dealing with the practical concerns of the imperfectly enlightened, but distracting from the realization of true being at a higher plane. Such cannot be said of theism, the alternative current of faith and belief through which humans have conceived and experienced transcendence.

Under theism, the natural world known by the ordinary senses is in fact real, but has in some way become estranged from "the Primal Origin of all things [in which] we live and move and have our being." Human society, and human life itself, thus may play a key role in the divine cosmic drama through which the created universe is finally reconciled to transcendent purpose and love.[1]

Theistic value systems are analytically divisible into three major strains,

79

often intertwined in actual history and experience. This chapter will deal with the oldest—and for a long time the most socially powerful—of these, the value system family of absolutism, which establishes both transcendent will and the social institutions through which God conveys His purpose to humanity as authoritative sources of value.

All persons and groups who believe in the existence of transcendent and objective standards of truth, goodness, and beauty are in a sense absolutists. In this book, however, the term is limited to those who hold that a particular human group or institution is uniquely and infallibly endowed with knowledge of such standards.

Absolutism embodies many of the qualities associated with religion that are feared and resisted by advocates of social freedom. It is important to our subject, not only because of its major role in Western history, but also because it is closely involved with the origins of other value systems from which ideas of freedom spring.

TEMPLE AND STATE

From the earliest time in human experience, the appearance of contact with transcendent authority has been a source of political power within the social group. In primitive societies, such contact was usually monopolized by the tribal 'big man,' who used it to reinforce his control and to maintain the group's working cohesion. When the big man or chief conveyed the directives of the supernatural, he invoked the tribe's idealized image of itself. "Ancient peoples," Robert Wilken reports, "took for granted that religion was indissolubly linked to a particular city, nation, or people."[2]

With the emergence of states in Mesopotamia and Egypt at the end of the fourth millennium BC, this identification became more intense. In early Mesopotamian states, "the temple was the most imposing structure (or set of structures), and was not only a 'house of worship' but a sanctuary, a palace, and a storage place and redistributive center."[3]

In the state, religion—like certain economic and professional functions—became the province of specialists. Responsibility for keeping society on the right side of the gods was turned over to a new class of officially designated priests. In agricultural societies, Peter Brown relates, urban settlements and even prosperous rural villages "had enough agrarian surplus to support small numbers of people thrown clear by their religious vocation from their family and their fields."[4]

According to Peter Farb, priests were "people selected by society to become experts in the performance of sacred ritual." They learned their role "through long and arduous training." Unlike their religious rivals, the shamans, who sought to ignite some spiritual spark within the individual person, priests largely addressed themselves to the needs, desires, and apprehensions, both spiritual and mundane, of the group as a social whole. Though their interests might at times diverge from those of the political ruling class, they, like the rulers, were concerned with the group as an organic unit enduring through time rather than with individual moments of inspiration or deliverance.[5]

Priests led ceremonies aimed at maintaining balance between too much and too little rainfall, assuring the return of the life-giving sun, and securing the regularity of the seasons. They kept the calendar by which seeds were planted and crops harvested, based on the movements of heavenly bodies. In wartime, they invoked the gods' wrath against enemies of the state. Partnerships between warrior kings and priests, Patricia Crone reports, produced "a division of power and privilege between temple and state to the exclusion of the rest of the community."[6]

AKHENATON'S BIG IDEA

As states became more complex, the deity associated with social authority was almost always male, corresponding to the father in the patriarchal family and the king in the military state. Northrop Frye writes that: "The supreme god was thought of increasingly as a sky-father."[7]

Particularly in Egypt, where the dominance of the sun and the dependence of the agricultural economy on the annual flooding of the Nile suggested centralized authority, cosmic as well as political, the state—personified by the ruling pharaoh—became the controlling object of worship. Sir Leonard Woolley observed that: "The two central features of the Egyptian scene were the triumphant daily rebirth of the sun and the triumphant annual rebirth of the river. Out of these miracles the Egyptians drew their assurance that Egypt was the center of the universe and their assurance that renewed life may always be victorious over death." The great pyramids, built during the middle of the third millennium, were constructed as tombs for particular pharaohs. They also provided perfect metaphors for the hierarchically organized Egyptian state, with the god-pharaoh at the top and the lesser orders stretched out beneath. For the Egyptians, Frye points out, "pharaoh was not only the shepherd of his people, high priest as well as king, but also an incarnate god, identified with Horus in his life and with Osiris after death."[8]

Egypt's state-sponsored religion was directed by its numerous and tightly structured priestly class. "The priesthood became a profession. The priests and officials attached to the local temples were united in a single sacerdotal organization embracing the whole land with the high priest of Amon of Thebes as its supreme head; and the political power of that organization grew until it could in the end control and even supplant the divine pharaoh himself."[9]

Into this situation in the fourteenth century BC burst a new young pharaoh, Amenhotep IV, who took the name Akhenaton, after his god Aton, the sun. Akhenaton has been called "the first individual in history." For whatever reason—some suggest hostility toward his father, the formidable Amenhotep III/Akhenaton was moved to challenge the entire structure of traditional Egyptian religion. All things, gods and goddesses as well as the material universe, he concluded, are the product of one generating force: Aton. A master of language as well as a thinker and statesman, he composed (or at least inspired) hymns addressed to his creator God.

> O sole God, beside whom there is no other,
> Thou didst create the earth according to thy heart
> While thou wast alone . . .
> Thou hast made the distant sky to rise therein,
> In order to behold all that thou hast made,
> Thou alone.

Aton was no mere tribal god, solely concerned with the welfare of Egypt. "How excellent are thy designs, O lord of eternity! / There is a Nile in the sky for the strangers / And for the cattle of every country that go upon their feet.[10]

Akhenaton at first tolerated the practice of traditional religion, but diverted the public funds formerly controlled by the priests to the worship of Aton. The temple hierarchy had gained possession of about one-fifth of Egypt's cultivatable land. Concern over the priests' growing power may have been part of what caused Akhenaton to start thinking about religion in the first place. When the priests fought back, Akhenaton cracked down hard. Aton worship was imposed as Egypt's official religion. "By a royal order all the old gods of Egypt were proscribed; the priesthoods were dispossessed, the temple services were forbidden, and the names of the gods were erased from reliefs and sacred monuments." Since Akhenaton's father's name was associated with the former state-sponsored religion, his was among the titles that were obliterated from public buildings.[11]

Akhenaton's religion was not quite monotheism. It was never fully distinguished from simple worship of the sun, which is almost as old as humanity. Some lesser deities, including Akhenaton himself, retained their places in a pantheon under Aton's supervision. The new religion had little ethical content. But Akhenaton went further than anyone before in recorded history in developing the idea of a single God who is creator and master of all being.

Akhenaton failed. Egypt's common people were not attracted by his new religion. "The idea of a 'sole god' did not appeal to them," Woolley concludes, "for they were accustomed to, and liked, gods in plenty: they were therefore driven back more than ever to the minor cults and superstitions which had always meant more to the humbler classes of Egyptian society than did the formalized worship of the state." Akhenaton was deposed; polytheism was restored by his son-in-law and successor, Tutankhamen ("King Tut"); and the traditional priesthood regained its privileges and power. Akhenaton's conceptual breakthrough seemed to leave little trace on Egyptian culture.[12]

Some memory may have lingered. Two centuries later a young Hebrew, raised at the court of another pharaoh, cast his lot with his oppressed people and their single, omnipotent God, Yahweh.

PEOPLE OF THE COVENANT

Moses' belief in monotheism had deeper roots than Akhenaton's abstract formulation of Aton. According to biblical history, around 1900 BC a herder of livestock named Abram entered the future land of Israel. After Abram had encountered many adventures and endured much hardship, God ordered him to take a new name, Abraham, and endowed him with a solemn covenant: "I will establish my covenant between me and you, and your off-spring after you throughout their generations, for an everlasting covenant, to be God to you and to your offspring after you, the land where you are now an alien, all of the land of Canaan, for a perpetual holding; and I will be their God."[13]

God's covenant with Abraham, while not superseding the one He had made much earlier for all humanity with Noah, was a pledge to a particular people who were to be God's special instrument, known by the name of Israel, given by God to Abraham's grandson, Jacob. God's covenant with Israel was not, at least as initially interpreted, to be to the detriment of other peoples: "All the families of the earth shall be blessed in you and your off-spring." But Israel was chosen to be God's designated envoy.[14]

The biblical idea of a covenant between God and his people, it should be made clear, is not a contract. It is not a bargain. God sets all the conditions, and Israel's role is to respond. Occasionally, as in Abraham's pleading with God to spare Sodom if only fifty, finally reduced to ten, righteous men can be found within its walls, God enters into a kind of dialogue with one of the patriarchs. But this is not to be confused with negotiation between equal parties. God listens to pleas, but He does not make deals.

God's people were to discover His will as a gradual dawning. Returning from captivity in Egypt seven centuries after Abraham, the children of Israel received, through Moses on Mount Sinai, written directives to acknowledge Yahweh's sole transcendent authority. To these theological commands were joined the moral imperative to "honor thy father and thy mother," in effect establishing the two-parent family as the basic social unit, and moral prohibitions against murder, adultery, stealing, bearing false witness, and even coveting one's neighbor's wife, servants, livestock, or "any thing that is thy neighbor's."[15]

God's covenants with Abraham, Moses, and the other patriarchs were made not for the salvation of individual souls but for the destiny of an entire people. "Judaism," Rabbi Joseph Klausner writes, "is not only religion and it is not only ethics: it is the sum total of all the needs of the nation, placed on a religious basis." By associating the law of the tribe with the will of God, the omnipotent creator, the Hebrew Bible vastly magnified the authority of the social group—and of those designated to speak in the group's name. "Sin in Israel," the religious historian Wayne Meeks points out, "is rebellion against the one God who made all and to whom all are responsible. It is the violation of a relationship, . . . [the] betrayal of a solemn treaty."[16]

Besides blessing a particular people, God in the Hebrew Bible acts through time. Unlike either the animistic spirit-gods or the impersonal timeless unity of monist religions, Israel's God is deeply concerned with the concreteness of history—with what happens on a given day, in a given battle, in the course of a particular migration, and with how these things contribute to His long-term plans for humanity. The Hebrew prophets, Mircea Eliade writes, seem to have been the first thinkers who "succeeded in transcending the traditional vision of the cycle (the conception that ensures all things will be repeated forever), and discovered a one-way time."[17]

In its early years, Israel was governed by a body of elders who essentially acted as a theocracy, combining political and religious functions. But the people, the first book of Samuel reports, eventually longed for a king to lead them in competition with other nations of the Middle East. God reluctantly complied and anointed first Saul, who proved to be a disappointment, and then David, who united the tribes of Israel and established a mighty kingdom. David and his son and successor, Solomon, presented themselves as instruments of God's absolute authority. Under the "Israelite conception of the Davidic kingdom as God's vice regent, the law of the king, his commandments, his will, . . . brook no contradiction."[18]

The Davidic kingdom prospered for a short time at the beginning of the first millennium BC. In Jerusalem on Mount Moriah, the site where Abraham had been prepared to sacrifice his son Isaac before God sent a new sign, Solomon built a splendid Temple to house the ark of the covenant.

But then Israel, a relatively small nation among the warring empires that surged back and forth across the Middle East, began to encounter trouble. In 931 BC the nation split into a northern kingdom, based on Samaria, and a southern kingdom, based on Jerusalem, reflecting an earlier division between the houses of Saul and David. In 722 Samaria fell to the army of Assyria, obliterating the northern kingdom, and Jerusalem narrowly escaped. At the beginning of the sixth century, the southern kingdom again found itself threatened by the advance of a powerful empire, this time Nebuchadnezzar's Babylon.

Why had God deserted His people? The prophets—products of a tradition in Israel that authorized religious and political criticism by inspired individuals who stood outside official channels—provided the answer: God's people had deserted Him rather than the other way around, falling into sin and violating the covenant.

The prophets were heard but not heeded. Perhaps the odds were simply too great. In 586 Jerusalem fell to the Babylonians, Solomon's Temple was destroyed, and many of the Hebrews were carted off to captivity in Babylon, where they first called themselves Jews.

Adversity, far from erasing Israel's faith, ultimately strengthened her sense of heroic, God-ordained nationalism, backed up by transcendent will. "If I forget thee, O Jerusalem," the Psalmist promises, "let my right hand forget her cunning. If I do not remember thee, let my tongue cleave to the roof of my mouth; if I prefer not Jerusalem above my chief joy."[19]

THE LORD OF LIGHT AND THE DEMON OF THE LIE

In 539 BC Babylon itself fell to an even more ferocious conqueror. The Persians, an Indo-European people (in contrast to the Semitic Assyrians and Babylonians), led by Cyrus the Great, had earlier in the sixth century swept down from the high plateau of Iran on their way to establishing the world's most extensive international empire up to that time. The Persians' religious beliefs were attributed to their prophet, Zoroaster (or Zarathustra), who probably lived a little before the time of Cyrus.[20]

Like Judaism, the Zoroastrian religion broke with the old cyclical nature religions and portrayed history as a drama through time, with a beginning, a middle, and an end. According to Zoroaster, the world was created jointly by Ahura Mazda, the Lord of Life, Wisdom, and Light, and his evil twin, Angra Mainyu, the Demon of the Lie. Ahura Mazda made the world to embody his plan for perfectly harmonious existence but Angra Mainyu, at the very moment of creation, corrupted every fragment of being. Human life has been torn between these two conflicting designs ever since. The struggle, however, is not truly equal. The Lord of Life is destined at the end of history to conquer the Demon of the Lie, thereby restoring the state of perfect harmony that was his original intention.

Human beings serve Ahura Mazda's goals, not simply through performance of prescribed rituals, but also by pursuing worldly goods. "The man who has a wife," instructs the Vendidad, the Zoroastrian Book of Law, "is far above him who lives in continence; he who keeps a house is far above him who has none; he who has children is far above the childless man; he who has riches is far above him who has none." Outside the Law, following the evil ways of Angra Mainyu, are those "that cannot make their living save through violence to cattle and herdsmen."[21]

Belief that human existence provides the arena for a tug-of-war between absolute good and absolute evil no doubt made life spiritually exciting and promoted rigorous obedience to the tribe's moral code. It also instilled hatred and contempt for those conceived to be subjects of the Demon of the Lie. "Fight with all your weapons . . . the followers of the Evil One," Ahura Mazda exhorts his adherents, "for these seek to wreck houses, raze villages, despoil clans and provinces; they can cause only disaster and death." At "the End of Days, [these] wicked ones" will be condemned to "destruction and eternal darkness, . . . foul food and the worst curses." The righteous, in contrast, will enjoy "the bliss of divine fellowship, and fullness of Health, Immortality, Justice and Power, and the Good Disposition."[22]

ISRAEL UNDER SIEGE

Scholars suggest that contact between the Jews and the followers of Zoroaster during the Babylonian captivity probably reinforced the tendency, already present in Judaism, to view human life as a cosmic battleground between moral absolutes. The figure of Satan, Prince of Darkness, became more clearly defined as the embodiment of pure evil.

Besides influencing Jewish culture, the advent of the Persians made life physically and socially less oppressive for the Jews. Cyrus, perhaps recognizing some similarity between Judaism and Zoroastrianism in contrast to surrounding pagan religions, permitted many of the exiles to return to Jerusalem. The Temple on Mount Moriah was rebuilt.

During the next four centuries the Jews endured as subjects of exploitative foreign regimes. In 333 BC Alexander the Great, in the course of conquering the Persian Empire and the eastern Mediterranean world, established Greek rule in Palestine. Upon Alexander's death ten years later, his empire was divided among his generals into three separate kingdoms, based on Egypt, Syria, and Macedonia. Ptolemy, the general who ruled Egypt, acquired Palestine as one of his provinces. In 198 BC the province was shifted to Syria, ruled by the Seleucids, descendants of another of Alexander's generals.

The Ptolemies and the early Seleucid rulers were relatively tolerant of the Jewish religion, but the third Seleucid monarch, Antiochus IV, set out—for reasons that remain unclear—to eradicate Judaism from the face of the earth. Torah scrolls were seized and burned. Jews who persisted in their faith were summarily executed. In the Temple, an altar was installed for the worship of the Greek god, Zeus Olympius, and in 167 BC a pig was sacrificed on the altar, deliberately insulting Judaic tradition.

Pushed beyond endurance, a small group of Jews led by Judas Maccabeus in 166 rose in revolt. Overcoming apparently overwhelming odds, the Maccabean revolt succeeded. Israel once more became an independent Jewish nation. Jewish worship was restored in the Temple—an event commemorated by the holiday of Hanukkah.

In the next generation, members of Judas Maccabeus's family, the Hasmoneans, made themselves hereditary rulers of Palestine. The Hasmoneans and other upper-class Jews soon began taking on Greek airs.

In 63 BC a Roman army arrived under the command of Pompey the Great. After a short siege, Jerusalem fell to the Romans. Pompey and his staff entered the Temple's Holy of Holies, where the ark of the covenant was supposed to be kept. Reportedly, they found it empty. The Romans took control of the kingdom, sometimes ruling through puppet Israelite monarchs, sometimes through direct military government. Independent Jewish nationhood ended for almost two thousand years.

By the time of Jesus in the early decades of the first century AD, Judaism was threatened by two unwelcome realities: political domination by Rome and increasing Hellenization of upper-class Jewish society. Not counting Christianity, at least five reactions to these challenges can be distinguished. Each tried in its own way to preserve and convey the seed of Judaism.

The Herodians

The Herodians, clustered around the family of Herod the Great, whom the Romans had installed as "procurator of Judea" (southern Palestine) in 37 BC, went furthest in accommodating Roman rule and adopting Hellenic culture. Herod, though married to a descendant of Judas Maccabeus, was only partly Jewish and was little trusted by either the Jewish religious authorities or the common people. His anxiety when the magi informed him of the birth of a King of the Jews, as recorded in the Gospel of Matthew, was well founded. A shrewd politician and prodigious builder of public works, Herod was convinced that Israel's future lay with Rome. He constructed public baths, amphitheaters, and a base for the Roman fleet at Caesarea.

At the same time, Herod tried to present himself as a legitimate Jewish monarch. He faithfully obeyed the ritual laws, remodeled the Temple, and maintained a private synagogue at Masada.

One of Herod's sons, Herod Antipas, whom the Romans made tetrarch (governor) of Galilee (part of northern Palestine), was less solicitous of Jewish opinion. He married Herodias, widow of his half-brother, in direct violation of Jewish law, thereby provoking (according to the Christian Gospels) vociferous condemnation by the prophet and visionary, John the Baptist. Though Antipas wished only to imprison John, Herodias was not content with halfway measures. She won her husband's assent to John's beheading as reward for the famous dance of her daughter, Salome. Herod Antipas makes a brief appearance in the crucifixion drama when he questions Jesus, apparently out of intellectual curiosity, as a Roman humanist might do.

The Zealots

The Zealots, a general term covering a number of revolutionary groups, were polar opposites of the Herodians in their reaction to the Romans. The Zealots promoted armed uprisings and acts of terrorism to restore Israel's independence. One of Jesus' twelve disciples, Simon, had been a Zealot.

The climax to the Zealots' resistance to Rome came with a revolt that began in 66 AD, leading to the slaughter of the Roman garrison in Jerusalem. Rome responded with customary ferocity. In 70 an army led by Titus, a future emperor, overwhelmed Jerusalem, massacred Jewish survivors, destroyed the Temple, and leveled much of the city, including the city walls. A band of surviving Zealots escaped to Masada, Herod's old stronghold, where they made their last stand. After a prolonged siege, on the night before the Romans planned their final assault, the remaining defenders killed first the women and children and then themselves—a mass suicide memorialized by the modern state of Israel as a symbol of unyielding resistance.[23]

The Essenes

The Essenes joined the Zealots in abhorring Roman domination and Hellenistic culture, but they saw no escape in a military or political solution. Instead they withdrew to monastic communities in the desert beside the Dead Sea, like the one at Qumran, of which we know from the Dead Sea Scrolls, found in 1947 by a Bedouin shepherd boy. No less than the Zealots, the Essenes looked forward to a coming victory of the "sons of light," as they called themselves, over the "sons of darkness," which included unfaithful Jews as well as foreigners. But they expected that this triumph would be miraculously achieved by a "Prince of Light," sent by God. In the meantime they devoted themselves to prayer, contemplation, and transcription of sacred manuscripts.

The Sadducees

The Sadducees, conservative members of the official Jewish religious community, neither plotted rebellion nor withdrew from the world. They concentrated on maintaining the written Law, set forth in the five books of the Torah, as the foundation of the integrity of the Jewish nation. Their chief constituency lay among rural landowners outside Jerusalem. Intense traditionalists, they criticized the Pharisees, their archrivals within the Sanhedrin (Judaism's supreme council), for approving oral interpretations of the Law. They may be thought of as loosely corresponding to the "high and dry" party within the nineteenth-century Church of England.

Some leading Sadducees joined the plot to kill Jesus, apparently in part because they feared that the enthusiasm he aroused among the Jewish populace might provoke the Romans to violent repression. The high priest Caiaphas, a Sadducee, argued: "It was expedient that one man should die for the people."[24]

The Pharisees

The Pharisees agreed with the Sadducees that strict adherence to the Law was the key to the survival of Judaism, but the Pharisees regarded interpretation of tradition as a continuing process. The Law, they maintained, could be enriched and clarified through scholarly dialogue. Unlike the Sadducees, they were open to new ideas. For instance, they believed in the immortality of the individual soul, an idea the Jews may have picked up from the Persians or the Egyptians.

The Pharisees' hostility toward Jesus should be placed in the context of their theology and their view of the embattled situation of Judaism at that time. Jesus' claim to be the Son of God seemed to strike at the very heart of their understanding of monotheism. If it caught on, they must have feared, the Jews might become just another polytheistic people. Israel, the Pharisees believed, could be preserved during the Roman occupation through strict internal discipline. But if deviation from what they regarded as fundamentals of the Law was countenanced, Judaism was likely to slip away into the cosmopolitan mish-mash of Mediterranean cultures.

Destruction of the Second Temple by the Romans in 70 AD created just the crisis the Pharisees had feared. Without the Temple, traditional Judaism could hardly continue. The Pharisees were ready with the institutions of the synagogue (a Greek word meaning "house of assembly") and the rabbinate, which will be discussed in chapter nine on the origins of transcendent idealism.

FIRST CHRISTIANS

The early Christian church, even more than Judaism, was threatened by external attack and internal dissension. The first Christians not only were persecuted by the Romans and condemned by the parent body of Judaism, but also soon had to deal with conflicting interpretations of the exact nature of Jesus' role and mission. Many of the apostle Paul's letters, which became a principal foundation of church doctrine and theology, were written to combat deviations from the main line of Christian faith.

Jesus' own teachings combined radical assertion of the unique value and dignity of each human soul with his call for formation of a resolute and disciplined body of believers to carry the faith to the earth's farthest reaches. "No city or house divided against itself," Jesus warned, "will stand." And: "Whoever is not with me is against me, and whoever does not gather with me scatters." His Father's house, he said, has "many mansions;" but God's ultimate aim for humanity is "one fold and one shepherd."[25]

The apostles set about forming a society of believers who would spread the good news and carry out Jesus' injunctions to feed the hungry, house the homeless, minister to the sick, and comfort the afflicted. Though almost all the original Christians were Jews, the apostles understood from the start that the faith must be open to people of all nations.[26]

The early Christians at first assumed that Jesus' promised return must be imminent and that the material world of ordinary experience would soon come to an end. But as the years passed and those who had personally known Jesus began to die off—often through martyrdom—his caution that "the day and the hour no man knows, nor the angels of heaven, but my Father only," was read in a new light. Christians accepted the need to build an institutional church prepared to last through the ages.[27]

CHURCH AND EMPIRE

Despite assurances by church leaders that Christianity posed no threat to imperial government, the Romans soon found the Christians' insistence that the one true God had entered human history in the person of their crucified leader, Jesus, intolerable, and persecution began. When the city of Rome was devastated by fire in 64 AD, the Emperor Nero, fearing public anger, blamed Christian subversives. On Nero's order, Christians were hung in the public gardens and burned alive as human torches. During the next three centuries vast numbers of Christians went to their deaths in Roman amphitheaters and arenas.

The historian Robert Lane Fox writes that "In the early church, martyrdoms were exceptionally public events, because Christians coincided with a particular phase in the history of public entertainment: they were pitched into the cities' arenas for unarmed combat with gladiators or bulls, leopards and the dreaded bears." The martyrs, one Christian recorded, "included a good proportion of women, not merely slave girls but well-born women and virgins." Persecution was not constant but might be renewed at any time. It was sometimes at its worst under emperors like Marcus Aurelius who prided themselves on their moral enlightenment. Even when not actively persecuted, Christians were subject to social discrimination and blackmail by petty government officials and informers.[28]

The early church at the same time had to deal with religious cults claiming to follow Jesus that deviated from mainline Christianity. One group, the Gnostics, offered a completely spiritualized version of Jesus, and concentrated almost wholly on direct mystical contact between the individual believer and God. Others extended the apostle James's emphasis on humanitarian good works, while rejecting James's cultural conservatism, thereby launching a tendency that later produced such humanist departures from orthodox trinitarian Christianity as Arianism, Nestorianism, Socinianism, and Unitarianism.[29]

In the second century, the tough-minded North African moralist and polemicist Tertullian waged relentless combat against what he saw as deviation from the true faith. The church has no place for questioning spirits, he maintained, because "questions make people heretics." Despite Jesus' invitation to "seek, and you shall find," Tertullian saw no need for further seeking now that the church had become repository of all truth: "Away with the one who is always seeking, for he never finds anything; for he is seeking where nothing can be found." Controversy over church doctrine, he claimed, "has the effect of upsetting the stomach or the brain."[30]

Tertullian had no fear of official persecution. "The blood of martyrs is the seed of the church," he declared. Nor was he troubled by secular philosophers who questioned the credibility of the miracles recorded in the Bible. The faith, he wrote, "is certain because it is impossible"—provoking outrage among rationalists in his own time and ever since.[31]

The church fathers yielded nothing to their oppressors on issues of principle, but sought practical accommodation with the Roman government. Origen, the church's first systematic theologian, argued that Christians through their prayers helped maintain the security of the empire: "Although we do not believe in being fellow soldiers with him, we do fight on behalf of the emperor." Tertullian went further and claimed that many Christians served as loyal soldiers in the emperor's army. "We pray for [the emperor]," he wrote, "a long life, a secure rule, a safe home, brave armies, a faithful senate, an honest people, a quiet world, and everything for which a man and a Caesar may pray."[32]

In 313 official persecution of Christianity at last came to an end. The Emperor Constantine—whether to gain the support of Christians for his swelling political ambitions; or to please his mother, the ardent Christian St. Helena; or because God had opened his heart—ordered "complete toleration" for anyone who "has given up his mind either to the cult of the Christians" or any other cult "which he personally feels best for himself."

In 383 the Emperor Theodosius took the further fateful step of making Christianity the empire's officially established religion. The civil servants whose forebears had delighted in tormenting Christians rushed to get themselves baptized. Toleration of other religions or of dissent within Christianity ceased. Heretics and dissenters, the emperor decreed, were condemned as "authors of sedition and as disturbers of the peace of the church."

Only recently an outcast, the church almost at once became a powerful force within the state. In 390, Ambrose, bishop of Milan, excommunicated Theodosius himself for having ordered mass punishment of the people of Thessalonica, where an army commander had been murdered, and required the emperor to pay public penance before being received back into the church. "Which is the more important," Ambrose wrote the emperor on another occasion when the interests of church and state conflicted, "the parade of discipline or the cause of religion? The maintenance of civil law is secondary to religious interest." Ambrose's assertion of church authority had a darker side. When Theodosius ordered a bishop in Mesopotamia to pay for rebuilding a Jewish synagogue that had been burned by Christians, Ambrose insisted that the church was exempt from such charges and the emperor backed down.[33]

Ambrose, descended from the old Roman upper class, was the first in a long line of Roman Catholic churchmen who used religious authority to shape the moral tone and structure of society. As bishop of Milan, where the imperial court had taken up residence, Ambrose "saw it as his duty to make plain . . . the uncompromising antithesis between the true, Catholic Church and its enemies." To assure the church's triumph, he proposed an alliance between church and state through which the empire would be "held together by undivided loyalty to a single mighty cause, that of Christ and His True, Catholic Church."[34]

Ambrose's greatest single contribution to the development of Christianity probably came through his role in the conversion of a restless young North African intellectual teaching in Milan: Augustine of Hippo. Augustine's work taken as a whole provides one of the essential foundations in the West for transcendent idealism. Some of its elements also had absolutist implications and effects. Both his overall worldview and its absolutist elements will be discussed in chapter ten on the development of transcendent idealism.

While Rome declined in the West during the centuries after Ambrose and Augustine, a new burst of religious vision and enthusiasm, also sprung from the Judaic root, erupted in the East. This new wave soon challenged all the works of the church fathers, and for a time seemed to imperil the survival of Christianity itself.

ISLAM: NO GOD BUT GOD

Islam, writes modern Islamic scholar Khalid Bin Sayeed, professes to be a "political religion." It is of course much more than that: among other things, a comprehensive account of life and the universe; a dynamic faith that currently claims the allegiance of more than one billion souls, second only to Christianity among the world's religions; and creator of a high culture which has produced such serene architectural masterpieces as the Dome of the Rock in Jerusalem, the Blue Mosque in Constantinople, the Alhambra palace in Spain, and the Taj Mahal in India. Sayeed, however, is right when he states that the exceptionally close interaction between religion and government has been an important and distinguishing characteristic of Islamic society. As Ayatollah Khomeini, the inspiration and leader of the Islamic revolution that took control of Iran in 1979, put it: Islam "is a religion where worship is joined to politics and political activity is a form of worship."[35]

Social absolutism, under which established religion and authoritarian government are closely linked, has seemed to flow naturally from a belief system rooted in Islamic faith. "Oh, you who believe," orders the Qur'an, "obey God and obey the Apostle and those charged with authority among you. If you disagree among yourselves about anything, refer it to God and the Apostle." The literal meaning of *Islam* is "submission," and of *Moslems*, "those who submit." The submission required is to Allah, the one God, ruler of all that is. But Allah's authority in most Moslem countries, with a few modern exceptions, has traditionally been extended to the state, which performs Allah's will.

Islam, as is well known, is theologically based on the Qur'an, presented to the prophet Mohammed by the angel Gabriel in the early seventh century AD—the first Moslem century, dating from the *hejira* (flight) of Mohammed from Mecca to Medina. A successful merchant in the Arab trading city of Mecca, Mohammed was forty when he answered the call of Allah to proclaim a monotheistic faith that would continue and purify the Jewish and Christian religions which he had discovered in the Bible. Rejected by the polytheistic business elite of Mecca, Mohammed and a few followers escaped across the desert to the distant city of Yathrib—later called Medina, "the city of the prophet." Yathrib had a sizable Jewish community that Mohammed hoped would accept him as their promised Messiah. When the Jews proved unreceptive, he concentrated on the city's Arabs and the Bedouins in the surrounding countryside, whom he soon persuaded to follow him in formation of an Allah-inspired society. After a campaign of raids on camel caravans and desert battles aimed at strangling Mecca's commerce, Mohammed in 630 AD triumphantly returned to his home city where he established himself as religious and political ruler.

In both Mecca and Medina, Mohammed received a series of revelations from Allah, which were transcribed in one hundred fourteen chapters, or *surrahs*. These make up the Qur'an, a prophetic book about the same length as the New Testament. The Qur'an identifies Mohammed as the last and greatest of a line of prophets that began with Adam and includes, among others, Noah, Hud (Noah's brother), Abraham, Moses, and Jesus. Mohammed did not claim divinity for himself, and denied the divinity attributed by Christians to Jesus, which he regarded as a violation of pure monotheism.

Mohammed asserted that the Qur'an conveys a religion that belongs to the same theistic family as those presented in the Bible. It also expresses themes that, though present in the biblical tradition, are generally downplayed or even condemned by the older religions. It may be said to reflect a suppressed subcurrent within the biblical narrative—a way not taken, a rejected variant. It is the way of Ishmael and Esau, the way of hunters and wanderers and Bedouin tribesmen who maintained their ancient habits in the harsh country beyond the settled communities of the Middle East. It is the way of the desert—more passion than intellect (though Islam produced a distinguished tradition of scholarship), more poetry than program, more focused on God's power than on His regard for each human soul (though Islam, like Christianity, teaches that each individual will be held personally responsible to God on the Last Day).

Augustine had provided Christianity with a "just war" doctrine, under which military action may be justified, even obligatory, under certain circumstances (such as defense of the innocent). But for Christianity and post-exilic Judaism, war was regarded as inherently evil, to be undertaken only under exceptional circumstances. Mohammed deplored the conduct of war as organized slaughter, as introduced by the Greeks and later practiced by the Romans, but his angel did not require him to disguise his satisfaction in the kind of chivalric combat that delighted his Bedouin followers, so long as its object was extension of Islam. The prophet was himself a warrior, wounded in battle at Medina against an army sent by Mecca in 625. "God," says the Qur'an, "has preferred those who fight for the faith before those who sit still, by adding unto them a great reward."[36]

The Qur'an values success and has no place for a concept of God as a savior who suffers with humankind. Mohammed found it inconceivable that Jesus, an admired prophet though not divine, would have permitted himself to be crucified. "They [the Jews] did not kill him nor did they crucify him, but he was made to resemble one crucified. . . . Nay! God exalted him in his presence," the Qur'an relates.[37]

After Mohammed's unexpected death in 632, his relatives and lieutenants agreed among themselves to preserve centralized religious and political control under a single ruler, titled the caliph. Abu Bakr, father of the prophet's favorite wife, was chosen first caliph. For a time the agreement held. Moslem armies burst out of the Arabian peninsula into a Middle East where centuries of inconclusive struggle between the Byzantine and reconstituted Persian empires had left a political wasteland. Damascus, Antioch, and Jerusalem fell in quick succession. All of Syria and Iraq were soon under Moslem control. "The strategy of the Arabs in their wars of conquest," the Middle Eastern historian Bernard Lewis writes, "was based very largely on the skilled use of desert power. . . . The Arabs were at home in the desert; their enemies were not." Turning west, Arab forces conquered Egypt and launched naval expeditions that captured Cyprus, Crete, and Rhodes.[38]

With the 656 AD assassination of Uthman, the third caliph, unity within the Islamic high command broke down. Rival factions among Mohammed's family and in-laws engaged in virtual civil war for the leadership, based on disputed claims over what had been the prophet's intention for the line of succession. After several more assassinations and battles, Uthman's family, the Umayyads (members of the old Mecca elite who had once led the opposition to Mohammed) achieved dominance. Dissidents, however, remained loyal to the memory of Ali, Mohammed's cousin and husband of the prophet's daughter, the legendary Fatima. After a brief tenure as fourth caliph, Ali, too, had been murdered. His supporters believed that Mohammed had selected Ali and his biological descendants to lead Islam. This division became the initial basis for the enduring split within Islam between orthodox Sunnis and Shi'ites—followers of Ali.

The objective of the Moslems' policy of holy war, *jihad*, was not conversion of individuals. The Qur'an includes no counterpart of the Great Commission at the end of the Gospel of Matthew. The aim of *jihad*, rather, was expansion of territories that would be governed by Islamic principles. Inhabitants of the conquered lands were permitted to convert, at first in somewhat subordinate status to the Arabs, but by the end of the eighth century with full rights as members of the Islamic community, the *umma*. Jews and Christians, as fellow "people of the Book," were allowed to maintain autonomous religious communities, but were required to pay a special tax, the *jizyah*. To escape the *jizyah*, many Jews and Christians converted to Islam. Zoroastrians and Hindus were later accepted as honorary "people of the Book." Pagans—persons belonging to none of the tolerated religions—were given a choice between acceptance of Islam or death.

No division within the *umma* was recognized between the religious and political functions. In Islamic theory, all social authority flows from religion. Islamic law, the *Shari'ah*, is based on principles derived from the Qur'an and a compilation of anecdotes about the life of Mohammed, the *hadith*. In practice, since religion so permeates the life of the community, political rulers have found it necessary to manipulate religion for secular purposes. "By a tragic paradox," Bernard Lewis writes, "only the reinforcement of the state could preserve the cohesion of community, and the Islamic state, as it grew stronger, was obliged to make many compromises on the social and ethical ideas of Islam."[39]

In the eighth century, close entanglement of Islam with worldly politics contributed to development of a countertrend of personal mysticism known as Sufism. Richly varied and individualistic, Sufism introduced strands of monism, ecstasism, and transcendent idealism that are in tension with Islam's absolutist tendencies. Though apparently influenced by both Christianity and Buddhism, Sufism presents a distinctively Islamic form of mysticism, perhaps traceable to Islam's original inspiration in the nocturnal wildness of the Arabian Desert. Ignited by Sufi mystics, Islam began a final surge of expansion during the twelfth century, largely peaceful, that carried it across India and Southeast Asia to Indonesia, which now contains the world's largest population of Moslems. (India is second; Pakistan, third.)[40]

During its first thousand years, Islam in most times and in most places, with a few notable exceptions, had the upper hand in political, military, and cultural encounters with the West. For the last three hundred years, the tides of history have flowed much the other way. By the middle of the twentieth century, most Moslem countries had fallen far behind the West, economically, politically, and militarily. Discovery of oil riches in some Moslem nations seemed at first chiefly to confirm their roles as economic and political appendages of the West. Heavily armed Arab nations after 1947 suffered repeated humiliating defeats by the vastly outnumbered state of Israel. Understandably, the spiritual morale of most Moslem peoples was severely shaken. "The fundamental crisis in Islam in the twentieth century," wrote the Harvard scholar William Cantwell Smith, "stems from an awareness that something is awry between the religion which God has appointed and the historical development of the world which He controls."[41]

There no doubt have been a number of reasons for the relative decline of Islamic societies during the last three hundred years. Among the most important appears to be the absolutist belief system that many commentators, both Moslem and non-Moslem, associate with Islam itself. When most of the world was governed by more or less authoritarian regimes, the discipline imposed by absolutist religion normally advantaged Islamic states. But after several Western societies in the seventeenth and eighteenth centuries began increasingly to open themselves to political, economic, intellectual, and religious freedom, restrictions imposed by Islamic absolutism seemed to impede social progress. In the twentieth century, Moslem societies such as Turkey, Iran, and Egypt have at times sought to incorporate elements of Western culture, even at the cost of violating traditional Islamic ways.

The final third of the twentieth century has witnessed significant Islamic resurgence. Observing the current moral and social troubles of Western societies, and mindful of the horrors unleashed by various Western ideologies, many Islamic peoples have been moved to reaffirm or rediscover the strengths of the old faith. Samuel Huntington writes that "Moslems in massive numbers [have turned] toward Islam as a source of identity, meaning, stability, legitimacy, development, power, and hope, hope epitomized in the slogan, 'Islam is the solution.' "[42]

Some Moslem intellectuals and politicians continue to seek an "Islamized" middle way through which aspects of modernity are made compatible with traditional spiritual and moral values. Others, most spectacularly Iran, but also with growing influence in states as varied as Pakistan, Turkey, Egypt, and Algeria, aim for root-and-branch expulsion of Western influences and restoration of a "revived" Islam. "The heart of the revivalist worldview," writes American Islamic scholar John Esposito, is the conviction that the decline of the Moslem world has been caused by "departure from the straight path of Islam"; and that this decline will be reversed by "return to Islam in personal and public life [which will] ensure the restoration of Islamic identity, values, and power."[43]

Moral values rising from Islam may indeed offer at least partial remedies for some of the rapacious egoism and dehumanizing secular collectivism that now plague much of the West. The question remains whether the traditional Islamic belief system is inherently hostile to other values, such as individual human rights and intellectual freedom, on which democracy and economic progress also depend. For devout Moslems this will not be the most important question. They will ask, rather, whether at least some aspects of economic rationalization and social liberalization violate the commands of Allah. But for Islam's well-wishers in the West, and for millions within Moslem societies who continue to yearn for the better life that Western ideals and techniques have seemed to offer, the question of compatibility has burning urgency.

Part of the problem seems to be the historic tendency to interpret Islam as dictating what Khalid Bin Sayeed calls a "total ideology." All religions generate values that, among other things, become normative components in social and political ideologies. But the West has learned—partly and imperfectly learned—that ideologies also involve economic and political theories, assumptions, and empirical observations and measurements that are not themselves inherent to religion. Total identification of ideology with religion fosters absolutization of factors that are properly treated as contingent and relative—one of the besetting perils of all absolutist belief systems.[44]

The Catholic moral theorist George Weigel persuasively suggests that Islam "may well need a Reformation, [and is] waiting for Augustine, [who taught that] the 'secular world' has a legitimate autonomy and integrity of its own, despite its corrupt condition." Augustine and the Reformers drew on the teachings of Jesus and Paul, and on the earlier sermons of the Hebrew prophets. These, too, form part of the common heritage of Islam.[45]

CATHOLIC EUROPE

"We almost didn't make it," the art historian Kenneth Clark said at the start of his celebrated series of lectures on Western civilization in 1969. He meant that for several centuries after the fall of Rome a thoughtful observer might reasonably doubt that civilized human society would ever return to Western Europe. While Islam grew and flourished, and while the eastern Roman Empire maintained a wealthy and cosmopolitan society, civilization in the West virtually collapsed.

Political life regressed from the state to the levels of the chiefdom and even the tribe. Ordinary people were at the mercy of wandering bands of pillagers. To protect themselves they accepted rule by barbarian chiefs who carved unstable principalities from the empire's carcass. Commerce broke down and technological skills were lost. In some places even the memory of Rome disappeared. Legends developed that·a race of giants had built the ruined aqueducts and causeways the Romans had left behind. Some vestiges of learning and cultural elegance were kept alive by Christian monks in Ireland.[46]

During the so-called Dark Ages and the Middle Ages that followed, recurring epidemics of plague and other contagious diseases, climaxed by the Black Death—which reduced Europe's population by about one-third in the fourteenth century—assured that life for many would be miserable and short. Even in the fifteenth century, when the Middle Ages were coming to an end, material existence for most human beings remained stark and threatening. "Calamities and indigence were more afflicting than at present," the Dutch cultural historian Johan Huizinga wrote. "Illness and health presented a more striking contrast, the cold and darkness of winter were more real evils. . . . All things in life were of a proud and cruel publicity. Lepers sounded their rattles and went about in processions, beggars exhibited their deformity and their misery in churches."[47]

Through all these travails, Christianity kept alive the hope for personal salvation and the sense of human solidarity that Jesus had proclaimed. Building on the theological framework created by Augustine, as well as on the Bible and the teachings of the other church fathers, the Catholic Church preserved the essentials of the faith. The Abbey at Mont Saint-Michel, raised on a massive rock off the northwestern coast of France in the tenth century and later reconstructed in Romanesque and Gothic styles, is symbolic of the church in its perhaps most heroic age, withstanding the storms of time, maintaining the light of faith. Henry Adams wrote that the great Gothic cathedrals, whose construction began in the reviving Europe of the twelfth century, expressed "an emotion, the deepest man ever felt—the struggle of his own littleness to grasp the infinite."

The medieval papacy, Ernst Troeltsch writes with some hyperbole, "realized the ideal of Plato's republic and the ideal of the Stoic universal commonwealth." The church taught that in the ideal world (the City of God), society would be "organic," with all units operating smoothly together on the basis of shared love. But in the fallen world of human reality, disrupted by sin, the need for "patriarchal" authority, imposing order through force, was recognized.[48]

In the thirteenth century Thomas Aquinas, in his *Summa Theologiae*, presented a definitive statement of the worldview underlying medieval understanding of human responsibility and social morality. Utilizing texts of Aristotle, brought back to the West by crusaders returning from contact with Moslem scholars in the Middle East, Aquinas sought, as Augustine had with Plato, to create a systematic structure for biblical revelations and moral directives through application of Greek metaphysics and social theories. Discussion of Aquinas's synthesis and its effects, including its absolutist aspect, will be covered in chapter ten on the development of transcendent idealism.

Schism

Partly because of the increased assertiveness of the papacy, the division between Rome and the Eastern Orthodox Church in the eleventh century became irreconcilable. The immediate cause of this split was a somewhat esoteric dispute over the exact nature of the trinity, but the cultural and functional differences were deep and long-standing. The Eastern Church had never developed a doctrine like that formulated for the West by Augustine on the distinction between church and secular authority. In what remained of the eastern Roman Empire, over which the Byzantine emperor maintained unified political control until the fall of Constantinople to the Turks in 1453, the church came to function as a virtual appendage to the state in secular matters.[49]

After the Orthodox Church achieved the conversion of Slavic peoples in the eighth century, its relationships with Russian and other Slavic rulers were maintained, much as in Byzantium. In lands controlled by Islam, Orthodoxy, representing a tolerated religion, occupied a similar role with Moslem sultans.

Perhaps in part because it was excluded from effective participation in politics, the Orthodox Church turned inward, defining itself in more purely spiritual and liturgical terms. Something no doubt was lost through neglect of the social aspect of the Christian message but the spiritual penetration and insights gained are seen not only in the great iconographic art of the Orthodox Church in the Middle Ages, but also in the works of such modern writers in the Orthodox tradition as Tolstoy, Dostoyevski, Solzhenitsyn, and even Chekhov.

In the West, the growing political involvement of the papacy inevitably attracted secular rulers to try to bring it under their direction. The papacy became first a player, then a pawn, in the European power game. In the fourteenth century, French monarchs acquired working control of the papacy and for sixty-eight years even moved the papal court away from the tumultuous urban environment of Rome to the tranquil setting of Avignon in Provence. For a time in the late fourteenth and early fifteenth centuries, the church had first two and then three competing popes, each backed by rival national and ecclesiastical groups—the so-called Great Schism.

The church's internal corruption brought cries for reform within and challenges from without. Near the beginning of the thirteenth century, St. Francis of Assisi experienced a vision in which Christ on the cross commanded him: "Go and repair my house, which is in total disrepair." In the fourteenth century, the Franciscan philosopher William of Ockham warned the church to curtail its political pretensions. St. Catherine of Siena wrote of the need for *riforma*.

The papacy responded in part by giving intermittent support to internal reform groups, such as the Franciscan and Dominican orders, and by commissioning its agents, including the Dominicans, to root out heresy wherever it could be found by almost any available means.

The medieval church's acceptance of absolutist doctrines and methods must have seemed justified in a world torn by disorder and threatened by conquest, as a means for preserving Christian orthodoxy. Without some such strategy, the vessel conveying the faith might not have survived. But in moving so far toward absolutism, the church involved itself with practices infected by bigotry, corruption, and repression, similar to those that Jesus had condemned.

THE BURDEN OF ESTABLISHMENT

The Protestant Reformation of the sixteenth century was the culmination of ferments and processes long underway within the Catholic Church itself. Besides its spiritual and cultural manifestations, the Reformation unleashed personal and social values that became major sources for movements toward democracy and individual freedom in the modern world. The new Protestant churches did not, however, wholly purge themselves of absolutist tendencies in medieval Christianity, and in some instances introduced theological and political innovations that gave rise to hardy new absolutist growths.

Both Martin Luther and John Calvin, the principal initiators of the Reformation, held that civil government should not only enforce moral regulations but also require "that a public manifestation of religion may exist among Christians." In 1533 Calvin approved Geneva's execution for heresy, by burning at the stake, of the Unitarian Michael Servetus. Thomas Cartwright, a sixteenth-century English Puritan divine, wrote: "Civil magistrates must rule according to the rules of God prescribed in his word . . . so they must remember to subject themselves unto the church, to lick the dust of the feet of the church." Puritans in the English colony of Massachusetts in the early 1660s hanged four Quakers (who had returned after repeated beatings) on Boston Common; and in 1692 Salem executed twenty alleged witches—seventeen of them women—not unusual in Europe at that time, but a troubling legacy from America's origins.[50]

The Catholic Church responded to the Reformation by three related strategies that came to be known as the Counter-Reformation. First, the church acted to clean up corruption within its own ranks and structure. Second, it instituted practices aimed at revitalizing faith among the laity, such as daily mass, private one-on-one confessions by individuals to priests, and increased celebration of saints and the Virgin (which in Protestantism had been largely annulled). And, third, through devices like the Inquisition and the Index, it ruthlessly repressed any expression of dissent against papal authority.

The Counter-Reformation was aesthetically embodied in the new baroque style in art and architecture—flamboyant, decorative, and dynamic. Works by creative masters such as Bernini, Caravaggio, Rubens, and Van Dyck conveyed both its spiritual majesty and its accompanying social arrogance.

Europe was plunged into a series of bloody wars, lasting off and on for more than a century, between contending forces of the Reformation and the Counter-Reformation. Pragmatic peace was finally established by the Peace of Augsburg in 1555 and confirmed by the Peace of Westphalia in 1648, achieved through the principle that subjects of every nation must accept the religion favored by their sovereign.

In states with Catholic rulers, Catholicism remained obligatory; while in states ruled by Protestants, mostly Lutheran or Anglican, some form of Protestantism was legally established. Where Protestant churches were established, monarchs usually took a good deal of former church property for themselves and their cronies, whose loyalty was thereby sealed. Calvinist establishments were relatively rare, in part because Calvinists were not politically dominant in many states, but where Calvinists did manage to get the political upper hand, as in Scotland and Massachusetts, they sometimes justified John Milton's complaint: "New Presbyter is but old Priest writ large."

Official establishment brought favored churches, both Catholic and Protestant, riches, social authority, and the power of moral censorship. But it also linked them in the public mind with oppressive feudal regimes. When these regimes came under challenge by liberal reformers and popular revolutions in the eighteenth and nineteenth centuries, established churches were inevitably targeted.

After the outbreak of the French Revolution in the 1780s, the Catholic hierarchy for the most part dug in loyally behind the feudal regimes the church regarded as its protector. Pope Pius VI in 1790 categorically condemned the French Declaration of the Rights of Man: "This equality, this liberty, so exalted by the National Assembly, thus reach their goal only in upturning the Catholic religion, and that is why it has refused to declare her 'dominant' in the kingdom, although this title always was accorded to her." The pope previously had taken no notice of the American Declaration of Independence but now extended his scorn to that charter of liberty as well.[51]

In predominantly Protestant countries, established churches generally aligned themselves with old-fashioned paternalist conservatism. In Britain, the established Anglican Church was popularly identified as "the Tory party at prayer." In Germany, Lutheran clergy in the 1870s enthusiastically supported Chancellor Bismarck's *Kulturkampf* against Catholic influence and opposition to liberalism—designed, Bismarck said, to make the new German empire a "Christian state."

During the twentieth century, church establishment proved a heavy burden on religious faith, as James Madison had wisely foreseen in the debates over religious liberty that followed the American Revolution. As old-line feudal regimes fell before the rising tide of democracy and the upheavals caused by the First and Second World Wars, officially established churches in most countries were eliminated or severely modified. Church observance and attendance sharply declined in all European countries except Ireland and Poland, where the Catholic Church was closely identified with national aspirations.

Until the 1960s, however, the Catholic Church continued to hold that, wherever it was politically feasible, Catholicism "ought to be, by constitutional law, the one religion of the state." Pope Pius XII, an austere descendant of old Roman aristocracy, led the church during the tumultuous years from 1939 to 1956 and declared: "That which does not correspond to truth and the norm of morality has, objectively, no right either to existence or to propaganda or to action."

At the Second Vatican Council in Rome in the early 1960s, under the leadership of the American delegation, and with the blessing of the reformist Pope John XXIII, all of this changed. Despite stout resistance from traditionalists, the council in its last days approved a Declaration on Religious Liberty, largely written by the American Jesuit scholar, John Courtney Murray, holding that "the right to religious freedom has its foundation in the very dignity of the human person." The council's action, Murray said, affirmed "the validity of religious freedom, . . . as a legal institution, a juridical norm, a civil and human right." With passage of the declaration, wrote

Robert Cushman, an American delegate-observer, "a very ancient order of things—at least in principle—passed away. In principle, the era of Constantine—sixteen hundred years of it—passed away."[52]

Some Catholic clerics and intellectuals, and some ordinary lay traditionalists, no doubt continue to yearn for the old days of close linkage between church and state. But in the United States at least, the chief legacy of Catholicism's historic absolutist tendencies is its somewhat greater emphasis on the aspect of Christianity that promotes social solidarity and collective responsibility—a worthwhile balance to the focus on personal experience and commitment more closely associated with Protestantism.

FUNDAMENTALISM

Early in the twentieth century, a group of evangelists in the United States took the title "fundamentalists" to express their devotion to literal interpretation of the Bible as God's revealed word and what they regarded as other basic truths of Christianity. The historian of American evangelicalism, George Marsden, defines a contemporary fundamentalist as "an evangelical who is angry about something."[53]

The sociologist James Davidson Hunter and others have argued that the fundamentalist phenomenon is virtually worldwide. "All fundamentalist sects," Hunter writes, "share the deep and worrisome sense that history has gone awry. What 'went wrong' with history is modernity in its various guises. The calling of the fundamentalist, therefore, is to make history right again."[54]

Use of "fundamentalism" as an umbrella term for almost all conservative religious groups can be seriously misleading, Hunter concedes. Still, there do seem to be common elements in the contemporaneous emergence of "back to basics" religious movements in many parts of the world. Evangelical and fundamentalist Protestants, conservative Catholics, and Orthodox Jews share a belief that powerful forces in their respective faiths have conceded too much to modernizing secularism. Moslem Islamists reassert the distinct identity of Islamic culture. Orthodox Christians raise ancient cultural battle flags in Eastern Europe. Even Hindus, formerly not much concerned with questions of orthodoxy, rally in large numbers to an Indian political party that defines a Hindu way of life. By no means all of these groups are absolutist in culture, theology, or politics, but many seem drawn, in a world they find deprived of sense or meaning and drowning in materialist passions, to the reassuring conviction that they are after all "God's people"—the chosen elect divinely equipped with political, social, and economic answers, as well as religious solutions, to all the world's problems.

THE CLOSED SOCIETY

Absolutism, besides the religious revelations and insights it has conveyed, played a major role in inspiring, protecting, and transmitting the cultural breakthroughs that have carried humankind from brute survival to a safer, more comfortable, more varied, and more stimulating existence. It is the rock on which social order has often been based. As was noted in the examination of the medieval period, it was probably essential to the survival of civilization in much of Europe after the fall of Rome. In contrast to secular collectivism, it offers a view of reality that connects human life with a richer, higher, eternal level of being.

These achievements, however, have not come without cost. Unleavened by other value systems, absolutism demands submergence of the individual human life into a divinely authorized social group. While it has sometimes broadened minds and hearts to consider possibilities beyond the conventional wisdom of the accepted social status quo, it has often blocked further development or discussion of these thoughts by insisting on conformance to its own inflexible dogmas. While repressing random indulgence of individual human cruelty and lust for domination, it sublimates these drives into social structures that can crush or disfigure human life: holy wars, sacrificial torture and murder, inquisitions, witch burnings, sacramental mutilations of body and spirit, and approved exploitation and humiliation of supposed inferiors.

Absolutism defines a personality type as well as a kind of society. The personality type may in fact continue for a time after the religious foundation on which it is based has vanished. Variations on the type abound in literature, embodied by such characters as Henry Fielding's pompous Reverend Thwackum, Dickens' sanctimonious Pecksniff, Jane Austen's domineering Lady Catherine de Bourgh, Victor Hugo's relentless Inspector Javert, and Shakespeare's priggish Malvolio in Twelfth Night (to whom Sir Toby Belch memorably responds: "Dost thou think, because thou art virtuous, there shall be no more cakes and ale?"). Probably most of us in the modern West have some strains of absolutism in our characters. These traits can get us through difficult encounters and steer us away from destructive behavior but, as Sigmund Freud pointed out, the price paid in neurotic symptoms and strained relationships for such security is often exorbitant.

Many contemporary writers claim that absolutism is dying a natural death in the modern world. Francis Fukuyama, for example, argues that societies that repress free exchange of ideas will inevitably lose out economically and militarily to free societies. Social freedom will therefore become universal, and "the end of history" will soon be upon us.[55]

I doubt it. While it is true that a free society is likely to be more economically productive, and therefore wealthier and better able to support a formidable military machine, neither history nor current experience indicates that these qualities alone create a stable society or satisfied citizens. As Khalid Bin Sayeed has pointed out, the current rise of Islam in the most developed and democratic Islamic societies suggests that "rapid economic change and urbanization" do not quench spiritual longings.[56] The growth of fundamentalism in the United States, and similar movements in other developed countries, may have some economic and social causes, but it expresses a sense of moral and spiritual dislocation. Human beings, all experience shows, "do not live by bread alone"—nor by shopping malls, nor space flights, nor military arsenals, nor even by participation in democratic politics. A free society that does not serve moral and spiritual goals beyond egoistic desire will probably give way to a system that does. Capacity and commitment to offer such goals will for the foreseeable future give attraction to absolutism.

Even in moral and spiritual terms, however, absolutism has always had serious shortcomings. Since early in human history, it has been challenged—even among theistic belief systems—by other routes to transcendence.

6

◆━━━━◆

Ecstasism: "Chariot of Fire"

A soul which has love . . . is herself Love, and can to the Virtues say, "I bid farewell to you."

—Marguerite Porete

With *ecstasism* we at last reach a value system family that combines access to transcendence with celebration of freedom in terms close to those set forth in the definition in chapter 1. Where absolutism preaches obedience to divinely established authority, ecstasism offers liberation and may at times call for revolution.

From earliest times there were probably individuals whose interest in theistic religion was mainly personal. Their aim—on cold winter nights in the caverns of the Dordogne, or long before through spiritual experiments on the central African veld—was not so much winning the favor of the gods for the tribe's welfare, as finding entrance through their own deeper consciousnesses to the splendid and supernatural reality at the root of experience.

Ecstasism is not an entirely satisfactory term for the value system family that glorifies participation by the individual soul in transcendence. It may seem too vague and indefinite, but it has been used by some philosophers and social theorists to approximately identify the constellation of ideas and experience covered by this category. Max Weber, for example, wrote of *ecstasy* as "an instrument of salvation or self-deification . . . tending either toward greater intensity of life or toward alienation from life." Karl Mannheim used *ecstatics* to designate a category of intellectuals who "renounce participation in history [or] existence as such." Martin Heidegger employed *ecstase* to name a process through which subjective experience penetrates universal being.[1]

The literal meaning of ecstasy, from the Greek *ekstasis,* is "being put outside oneself." But in religious discourse, art criticism, and ordinary language it has come to convey, among other things, liberation from an old self formed by social convention and parental authority to a new self, enjoying raptures of transcendent bliss. Ecstasism's goal is summed up by Nietzsche's credo: "To impose upon becoming the character of being—that is the supreme will to power."[2]

THE SHAMAN'S TALE

Ecstasism attaches its highest value to direct experience of transcendence. But many ecstasists are prepared to use the knowledge or power so gained for practical purposes in everyday life. Unlike monism in its purest form, ecstasism does not require renunciation of mundane interests. Among primitive peoples—and among many in more technologically advanced societies even today—ecstatic devices, such as charms, incantations, and magic potions, are utilized for distinctly this-worldly purposes: to punish an enemy, to attract a desired lover, to cure physical ailments, or to secure economic good fortune.

In the primitive band or tribe, as we have seen, the big man usually monopolized contact with the supernatural higher powers, particularly on matters concerning the broad welfare of the tribe, such as war and maintaining abundance of game. Even at this early level of social development, however, certain persons were regarded as religious specialists. These were often individuals subject to fits or spells, troubled by emotional afflictions, or living on the outskirts of the tribe. Probably in part because of their very strangeness, they were reputed to have access to ethereal spirits whose help was sought in moments of exceptional desire or fear. These specialists in supernatural services we know by the generic title *shaman*.

"The word shaman," Peter Farb writes, "comes from the Tungus language of Siberia, but the shaman is important among all the Eskimo bands and among many American Indians." Shamans were "born, not made." They supplied love potions, and talismans against "dog bite, gout, headache, or fever." Sometimes, Wayne Meeks reports, they cast "spells to wreak vengeance by inducing coma or death or illness."[3]

In the chiefdom and the state, the new class of professional priests took over many of the group's religious functions formerly managed by the tribal leader. Priests also performed more personal religious services, such as inducing fertility in the womb, providing charms against illness and misfortune, and seeing the dead into the hereafter. The trained priesthood substituted standardized ritual for the shaman's "divine madness."

The shaman did not disappear under the new order, however. He continued at the edge of society, where he had always been, offering access to the deeper secrets of transcendence. Many of his former domestic services were now routinely dispensed by the state's established religion, but when erotic or vengeful impulses became strong, the shaman was likely to receive a call.

The priest and the shaman inevitably became rivals. Though their ministrations were in some sense complementary, they presented competing routes to the same powers. As the religion of the priest gave rise to absolutism, so the religion of the shaman provided a model for ecstasism.

DIONYSUS UNLIMITED

Ecstasism found some of its roots in the old fertility religions that flourished in the Mediterranean world before warrior peoples began pouring down from the Eurasian steppe early in the second millennium BC. It thus rose from the same religious stock that in the East helped produce monism.

The religions the steppe tribes brought with them were stern, masculine, and self-denying. As we have seen, their pantheons eventually made way for some of the older deities associated with carnival spirit and erotic pleasure, but the resulting mix was heavily weighted toward mastery, moderation, and order. Nietzsche called the cultures produced by such religions Apollonian, after the Greek god of the sun.

The official religion of classical Greece, Giovanni Filoramo writes, "established solid barriers between humans and the gods; to violate them even in thought, was to commit the infamous sin of hubris. [Such religion] was like an item of clothing, received at birth and worn on certain ritual occasions, but able to be discarded in everyday life without any special trauma. [It produced] an atmosphere, a particular aura, which one learned to breathe early in life, an ambiance in which one was taught to move and behave correctly."[4]

From early in Greek history, even in Homeric times, this kind of religion was not enough for many people. Women in particular, excluded from pursuits of civic or economic power, turned to cults descended from the old fertility religions. Many became devotees of Dionysus, also known as Bacchus, god of wine and revelry, who specifically offered *ecstasy*— "annihilation of the ordinary bounds and limits of existence." Born of a tragic union between Zeus and the mortal princess Semele (who died because she could not stand exposure to Zeus's thunderbolts), Dionysus always stood (or danced) apart from the lofty gods and goddesses of Olympus. He was modeled on the satyr god of a pre-Hellenic orgiastic nature cult. His attraction rose "either through the influence of those narcotic potions of which all ancient religions speak in their hymns, or through the powerful approach of spring, which penetrates with joy the whole frame of nature."[5]

In fifth century BC Athens, female worshipers of Dionysus, forming squads of Bacchants, raced through the hills on spring nights. They wore fawn skins and crowns of ivy, and shouted their ritual cry, "*Euoi!*" Waving wands of fennel, they danced under the moon to rhythms of the flute and *tympanon.*

A favorite Greek myth, dramatized by Euripides, tells of Pentheus, king of Thebes, who was discovered spying on the Dionysian revels, and torn to pieces by feverish Bacchants, including his own mother, Agave. For Euripides, Pentheus seems to have represented self-confident Athenian politicians projecting their egos into civic arrogance. In its broader context, the myth conveys a warning against ignoring the deeper spiritual and erotic needs of human nature.

Nietzsche believed, at least in his youth when he wrote *The Birth of Tragedy,* that synthesis of Apollonian and Dionysian strains in Greek culture produced the classic achievements of Hellenic art and drama. Dionysian passion, he maintained, was expressed with "clarity and precision [by] the dream-interpreter Apollo, who projects before the chorus its Dionysian condition." Excessive reliance on reason in Greek philosophy after Socrates, Nietzsche argued, suppressed the Dionysian side of Greek culture, exposing it to the cruder materialisms of Macedonia and Rome, and ultimately to Christian bigotry.[6]

These fifth-century mystery religions, formed around worship of Demeter and Orpheus as well as Dionysus, certainly provided release for drives and emotions that the established state religion did not satisfy. They carried forward the exploration of the subjective self that earlier had been launched by poets like Archilochus and Sappho. Their secret initiations and rituals gave average Athenians escape from the pressures of political and commercial life. As social corruption became pervasive, and Athens's economic and political power declined, their popularity grew, eventually coming to embrace almost all Athenians.

The spiritual raptures offered by the Greek mystery religions in some ways resembled the experience of enlightenment exalted by monistic religions about the same time in India, but the mystery religions aimed at psychic exhilaration of the individual soul rather than at obliteration of the self into cosmic nothingness. Dionysus was a far more personal savior than Brahman in his various incarnations. "The religion of the mysteries," Edith Hamilton observed, "was individual, the search for personal purity and salvation. It pointed men toward union with God."

This emphasis on the individual person, combined with a theistic conception of transcendence, made the mystery religions a fertile resource for a new faith entering the Mediterranean world from very different origins in the Middle East.

"THE LIGHT OF MEN"

The Hebrew Bible introduced the concept that each human being is a unique person directly responsible to God, but the person so conceived is almost always placed within a context of social relationships. There are exceptions. The prophetic book of Ezekiel presents a surrealistic vision of humanity stripped to existential nakedness: "O ye dry bones, hear the word of the Lord." And the Song of Solomon, the book most often read in medieval monasteries, interpreted allegorically, conveys images of romantic love that in their subjective intensity recall Sappho.

> Behold thou art fair, my love; behold thou art fair; thou hast doves' eyes beneath thy veil . . .
> Thy two breasts are like young roes that are twins, which feed among the lilies.
> Until the day breaks, and the shadows flee away, I will get me to the mountains of myrrh, and to the hills of frankincense.[7]

In the Christian Gospels of the New Testament, the dignity and worth of the individual personality transcends tribal identity. Jesus cut through convention to the core of human nature that precedes extensive social conditioning: "Except you be converted and become as little children you shall not enter into the kingdom of heaven." The person who seeks salvation must be prepared to leave "house or wife or brothers or parents or children for the sake of the kingdom of God."[8] The key to salvation is faith in God's will and love: "Take no thought for your life, what you shall eat, or what you shall drink; nor yet for your body, what you shall put on. . . . Consider the lilies of the field, how they grow; they toil not, neither do they spin. And yet I say unto you, that even Solomon in all his glory was not arrayed like one of these."[9]

The personal note in Jesus' teaching is so strong that some commentators have argued that it consists of little else—that he was a wandering preacher, something like the Buddha though with a different eschatological message, asking only that his followers believe in his divinity in order to be saved. His teaching, in this view, belongs almost entirely within the category of ecstasism. This interpretation, as has often been pointed out, ignores the social responsibilities that flow from the second of Jesus' great commandments: "You shall love your neighbor as yourself." It also overlooks his assurance that he came "not to abolish the law or the prophets," but to "fulfill" them. Jesus' teaching in its fullness goes far beyond ecstasism, but he did share with the ecstasists a belief in the unique importance of each individual soul.

After Jesus' death and resurrection, his disciples had no doubt that their primary mission was to spread the good news that God in Jesus' person had directly entered mortal existence, thereby fundamentally altering the human condition. In the familiar story in the book of Acts, Peter and John, going one afternoon into the temple, encounter "a man lame from birth" asking alms. Peter responds: "Look on us." The man gives "heed unto them, expecting to receive something of them." Then Peter says: "Silver and gold have I none; but such as I have give I you: In the name of Jesus Christ rise up and walk." Taking the alms-seeker by the right hand, Peter "lifted him up; and immediately his feet and ankle bones received strength." The man, the story concludes, "walked, and entered with them into the temple, walking, and leaping, and praising God."[10]

The personal and spiritual side of Christianity is particularly emphasized in the writings attributed to the disciple John, who was perhaps influenced by Neoplatonic mysticism bubbling in the cultural atmosphere. John opens his Gospel: "In the beginning was the word, and the word was with God, and the Word was God." From God's being came "life; and the life was the light of men. . . . The Word was made flesh, and dwelt among us." Jesus, in John's account, distinguishes sharply between flesh and spirit: "That which is born of the flesh is flesh; and that which is born of the Spirit is spirit." To unleash the spirit, which was humanity's original gift, the individual must "be born again."[11]

John's first epistle reaffirms that "God is light, and in him is not darkness at all." He recommends avoidance of entanglement with this-worldly concerns: "Love not the world, neither the things that are in the world. If any man loves the world, the love of the Father is not in him." John's emphasis on personal spirituality does not contradict the more socially oriented accounts of the other three Gospel writers, or the messages of Paul or James, but he expresses a spiritual, sometimes mystical, strain stressing personal salvation that has remained an important current within Christianity ever since.[12]

The early church, as we have seen, included a variety of tendencies, not necessarily conflicting, but differing in emphasis, and sometimes at their extremes drifting toward heresy. Some formulators of Christian doctrine concentrated on building an institutional church. Others, like the Alexandrian priest Arius, founder of Arianism, developed the humanist side of Jesus' teaching. A considerable number of the most devout pursued the quest for inner purity and light as the essential route to salvation, following the line of John.

During the second century in eastern Syria and Egypt, Wayne Meeks relates, "the adoption of asceticism as the central definition of the Christian ethos reached its most radical expression." In Syria ascetic monks lived as *solitaries* on the edges of villages and towns, practicing spiritual exercises and providing services for town folk who visited their huts, something like those offered by the ancient shamans. In Egypt some monks formed communities on the edge of the desert, giving rise to the institution of the monastery.[13]

Toward the end of the third century, a young Egyptian landowner named Anthony gave all his money to the local poor and set out for the desert to struggle against the "demon of fornication" and other instincts distracting him from his spiritual quest. After twenty years of ascetic discipline in a cell at the bottom of an abandoned fort, he emerged, satisfied that his physical body had "received a portion of that *spiritual body* which it is to assume in the resurrection of the just." Friends marveled "that his body had maintained its former condition, neither fat for lack of exercise, nor emaciated from fasting and combat with demons. . . . The state of his soul was one of purity." Surrounded by disciples, Anthony lived for the next forty-six years in a monastic community he founded at a remote site on the eastern desert, which he felt "mirrored the huge serenity that had descended on his heart."[14]

Anthony was by no means the most extreme of the ascetics. In Syria, Peter Brown writes, crowds "flocked out to catch a glimpse [of Symeon Stylites] perched on his sixty-foot column on the mountain ridge of Telnesin. [Standing] with arms outstretched in prayer, [Symeon's] broken body was a living image of the power of the Crucified."[15]

Ascetics like St. Anthony and St. Symeon were valued by the larger church as examples of exceptional devotion. However, there were others who, while claiming inspiration from Jesus, broke entirely with the main body of Christian tradition. These were criticized and condemned by the church with resolute fury.

GNOSTICISM: THE WAY NOT TAKEN

Attacks by the church fathers on alternative interpretations of Jesus' mission were so successful that until recently surviving information about the dissenters came mostly from their critics. Archaeological discoveries have produced a fuller picture of moral and theological debates within the broad Christian community in its early centuries, but our knowledge of what those who lost the argument actually believed and taught remains fragmentary.

The most formidable dissident group called themselves "Gnostics," after the Greek word *gnosis*, which means approximately "inside knowledge." Circulating widely through the Mediterranean world during the second century, Gnostics claimed they had access to teachings that Jesus had communicated exclusively to his innermost circle of disciples. Taking over some of the teaching of the second century heterodox mystic Marcion, the Gnostics taught that the material world was created by a contentious spirit whom they identified as the Old Testament's Yahweh. Jesus' mission was to restore knowledge of underlying spiritual reality to a chosen elite. "What the Gnostic Christian finally came to 'know,' " Elaine Pagels writes, "is that the gospel of Christ can be perceived on a level deeper than the one shared by all Christians. . . . It becomes a path of spiritual awakening, through which one discovers the divine within."[16]

The Gnostics seem to have drawn on the so-called Gospel of Thomas, a collection of sayings attributed to Jesus, probably composed in Syria during the second century (though a few scholars date its origin much earlier.) Although widely read at the time, Thomas's work had been lost and forgotten until 1945 when a copy was found in a jar containing Coptic manuscripts by two Egyptian farmers. It goes much further toward ecstasism than the four canonical Gospels, and is less concerned with social relationships than even the Gospel of John. Thomas's Jesus says: "Blessed are those who are solitary and superior for you will find the kingdom." In Thomas's version Jesus expresses love for the poor, but he sees little point in trying to make this world a better place: "Whoever has become acquainted with the world has found a corpse, and the world is not worthy of the one who has found the corpse." His advice is not to get involved with the toils and tribulations of ordinary people: "There are many standing at the door, but it is the solitaries who will enter the bridal chamber"; and, "Be passersby." (No good Samaritans wanted!) Self-knowledge is the key to salvation: "When you come to know yourselves, then you will become known, and you will realize that it is you who are the sons of the living Father."[17]

The most influential of the Gnostics seems to have been an Egyptian intellectual named Valentinus who, after education in Alexandria, moved to Rome around 140 AD to set up his own school. Like the Jesus presented by the Gospel of Thomas, Valentinus taught that "fully to know one's inner self is to know the ineffable God." Pursuit of self-knowledge, he maintained, requires withdrawal from the physical world experienced through the senses.[18]

Valentinus and other Gnostic teachers appealed particularly to upperclass Roman women who were gaining increased social freedom during the second century. Female liberation, the Gnostics held, depends on elimination of all differences between male and female, going right back to the separation of Eve from Adam's body. "Separation is the problem," Valentinus insisted, "reunification the solution." But such reunification requires total absorption of female nature back into the male: "Enter through the rib from which you came, and hide yourself from the beasts."[19]

Some Gnostics interwove elements of Christianity with the ancient mythology of the Mother Goddess. In one account, Sophia (a feminine spirit of Wisdom) rather than Yahweh is presented as creator of the physical universe. The Gnostic Sophia, Giovanni Filoramo writes, "performs the function of mediator between God and matter, between the divine economy and its fulfillment." Her role is ambiguous: "I am the honoured one and the scorned one. I am the whore and the holy one." Encountering Christ, she "first covered her face with shame, but, having seen him with all his fructifying power, she ran to him and received strength through his appearing."[20]

Recognizing the appeal of Gnosticism to bored or frightened spirits in the deteriorating social world of the second century, the early church fathers set about discrediting its arguments and practices. Clement of Alexandria deplored its incoherent alternation between "radical asceticism" and "unbridled libertinism." Tertullian blasted the chaotic anarchy of what he claimed was a typical Gnostic community: "They enter on equal terms, they listen on equal terms, they pray on equal terms . . . they do not care if they profess different doctrines, provided that they all help to destroy the truth."[21]

Gnosticism took a variety of forms and sometimes offered conflicting teachings during the century or so that it prospered. However, as Filoramo points out, all versions of Gnosticism differ essentially from the main body of Christianity in that they offer Christ, not as a redeeming moral savior, but as "the Man of Light, [who] does no more than recover that part of himself, his spiritual substance, that had fallen prisoner to the darkness. [The Gnostic Savior] does not come to reconcile humankind with God, but to reunite the Gnostic with Himself."[22]

Though ultimately crushed as a living institution by the church fathers and the hostile Roman government, Gnosticism survived as a religious tendency among the submerged currents of Europe's cultural underground. Its legacy maintained a presence in folk mysteries and superstitions, and through the Hermetic philosophy circulated by various medieval and Renaissance spiritualists. It penetrated Christian mysticism, surfaced in some manifestations of the Protestant Reformation, and has supplied a rich vein in the artistic and cultural outpourings that descend from nineteenth-century romanticism. Recently, since discovery and translation of some of its original texts, it has been taken up by some religious intellectuals, particularly among feminists, who are attracted by its equalitarian spirit, de-emphasis on sin, and attention, however ambiguous, to women.

MEDIEVAL MYSTICISM

Advocacy and practice of ecstasism have by no means been limited to Christianity and the West. From the eighth century, Islam has included a major strain of Sufi mysticism, which has emphasized the personal and other-worldly aspects of theistic religion. Some forms of Hinduism, particularly those centered on worship of Shiva, have developed the concept of a personal savior who liberates something like a born-again spirit. Primitive tribes in Africa, the Americas, and the Pacific Islands have carried on explorations through art, music, and dance, sometimes abetted by narcotics, of the subjective unconscious. Even the common-sense culture of China has provided space for village soothsayers who offer routes to spiritual ecstasy. This chapter, however, will deal mainly with manifestations of ecstasism within the Western tradition, identifying ecstatic outgrowths of other cultures as they have influenced the West.

From the beginning, mainstream Christianity, as we have seen, had an important dimension of mysticism, modeled on the teachings of Jesus as conveyed by John, and the imagery of Paul: "By one spirit are we all baptized into one body, . . . and have all been made to drink into one Spirit." This strain sometimes shaded toward ecstasism, as in the exercises of pillar saints like Symeon Stylites.

Christian mysticism has always included both monistic and ecstatic tendencies. The monistic element has been stronger in the Eastern church, and the ecstatic in the West. It is a mistake to try to distinguish too sharply between these strains—some individual mystics display aspects of both.

Meister Eckhart, whose fourteenth century writings were declared heretical by the Catholic Church, leaned toward monism, though he was a Westerner: "All creatures are mere nothing; I do not say that they are little or aught: they are nothing. That which has no entity, is not. All creatures have no being, for their being depends on the presence of God." On the other hand, Heinrich Susso, Eckhart's successor in the Rhineland, inclined toward ecstasism, writing of his beloved Eternal Wisdom: "She soars high above in a sky with clouds, she is bright like the morning star and shines like the radiant sun; her crown is eternity, her robe beatitude, her speech sweetness, her kiss absolute delight; she is remote and near, high aloft and below; she is present and yet hidden; she lets herself be approached and yet no one can grasp her."[23]

The medieval church welcomed spiritually oriented monastic orders and individual mystics as sources of inspiration and religious renewal, but it feared the challenges to authority they often represented. "The Church in the Middle Ages," Johan Huizinga wrote, "tolerated many religious extravagances, provided they did not lead up to novelties of a revolutionary sort, in morals or in doctrine. So long as it spent itself in hyperbolic fantasies or ecstasies, superabundant emotion was not a source of danger. . . . [But] the same sentiment became dangerous, as soon as the fanatics of chastity, not content with shutting themselves up in their own spheres of purity, wanted to apply their principles to ecclesiastical and social life."[24]

St. Francis of Assisi and St. Catherine of Siena both preached highly personal and spiritual forms of Christianity, but both were tolerated by the church and canonized soon after their deaths. Spiritual individualists who went further, however, were ruthlessly persecuted by church authorities.

Some ecstasists moved outside the bounds of the church altogether. Early in the thirteenth century, the Free Spirit movement, centered in Cologne from where it quickly spread through much of Europe, taught that the individual spirit moved by love can—through subjective ardor—gain direct access to God. Some participants in the movement interpreted it to encourage unrestrained sex. "They committed rapes and adulteries and other acts which gave bodily pleasure, and to the women with whom they sinned, and the simple people they deceived, they promised that such sins would not be punished," wrote the abbot of St. Victor, himself a mystic within the Christian mainstream. Others concentrated on service to the poor. Women played leading roles in some parts of the movement, claiming equality with men. According to the intellectual historian Orlando Patterson, "What all versions had in common was the belief that perfect freedom was possible by finding the God within oneself and identifying with it, and that the church with its masses, sermons, and prayers were unnecessary to achieve this."[25]

Marguerite Porete, a leader among the Free Spirits, declared: "A soul which has . . . love is herself Love, and can to the Virtues say, 'I bid farewell to you.' " The church declared her work heretical, but she refused to recant. In June 1310, Marguerite "was burned alive by a huddle of priests, solemnly praying for the freedom of her soul."[26]

RADICAL PIETISM

The Protestant Reformation of the sixteenth century emphasized the aspect of Christianity that focuses on salvation of the individual soul. Martin Luther, John Calvin, and other mainstream Protestants kept this spiritual individualism channeled within institutional structures that maintain civil and church authority, and support social services.

On the outer edge of the Reformation, however, some religious visionaries pressed for unconditional removal of all mediating structures between the individual spirit and God. The term *pietism* was first used in the seventeenth century to designate a movement among German Protestants to promote intense personal purity. The origins of this tendency within Protestantism, however, go back to the early days of the Reformation, and beyond that to such medieval phenomena as the Free Spirits and the twelfth-century Waldensians, and even, in the view of some scholars, to second-century Gnosticism.

In the first phase of the Reformation, the pietist tendency gave birth to Anabaptism, named for the belief among its advocates that the sacrament of baptism should take place after a mature decision to accept Christ rather than in infancy. Ulrich Zwingli, the mainstream Reformer who had brought Protestantism to Zurich, proposed that a liturgical dispute within the local church be settled by appeal to the city council. Simon Stumpf, speaking for a faction that emphasized direct experience of the Holy Spirit by the individual, replied: "Master Ulrich, you do not have the right to place the decision on this matter in the hands of my lords, for the decision has already been made, the Spirit of God decides." Those sharing Stumpf's view seceded and formed their own Anabaptist congregation.[27]

Some pietist sects, like the Quakers and the Mennonites, practiced strict asceticism and sought to draw converts to the "inner light" by exhortation and example. "I was sent to turn people from darkness to the light that they might receive Christ Jesus," wrote George Fox, founder of the Society of Friends. Others, however, felt authorized to take whatever actions were necessary, including violence, to achieve a new order in which sin and corruption at last would be conquered.

In Germany in 1524, a Protestant clergyman named Thomas Muntzer, defying both Luther and the civil authorities, called for an armed uprising to establish a just society. "The living God," Muntzer proclaimed, "is sharpening his scythe in me, so that later I can cut down the red poppies and the blue cornflowers." Muntzer was speedily captured and executed by the German nobility. But ten years later Protestant ecstatics following his inspiration gained control of the town of Munster, where for more than a year they operated a "New Zion," featuring common ownership of property and free love. All single women were required to have sex with any man who asked. A reign of terror was instituted to crush dissent. When the town's defenses were finally overrun, the victorious nobility ruthlessly tortured and murdered surviving rebels.

The politically militant interpretation of pietism was applied during the next century in the English civil war by the Levelers and the Fifth Monarchy Men, so named because they believed the final monarchy of Christ forecast in the Bible was at hand. Fighting valiantly for the Puritan cause, until Cromwell found it necessary to suppress them, the Fifth Monarchy Men invoked as their slogan the declaration of the twelfth-century mystic Joachim of Flora: "Justice shall be done though the world perish for it."

The practices of the Munsterites, the Levelers, and the Fifth Monarchy Men exhibit the perhaps surprising but common inclination among ecstasists: if and when they turn from contemplative spiritual experience to some kind of social action or involvement, they tend to adopt many of the behavioral characteristics of their conceptual polar opposites and political antagonists, the absolutists—in fact, to become absolutists. This inclination results paradoxically from ecstasism's downgrading of the authority of social forms. If the individual communicates directly with transcendence, without need for guidance or mediation by any kind of human institution, then his inspiration is by definition uncorrupted by this-worldly distortions. When applied in ordinary time and space, therefore, the ecstasist's orders from divinity, including those dealing with social organization and authority, can brook no dissent. The promised land of eternal peace and justice may be just a step, or a battle, away. Opponents are instruments, even if unwitting, of evil. No resistance, therefore, can be tolerated "though the world perish for it."

Radical pietism was brought to the New World by, among others, the antinomian Puritan Anne Hutchinson, who arrived in the recently established Massachusetts Bay Colony in 1634, seeking the spiritual freedom she could not find in England. The colony's governing elders at first welcomed the purity of her Christian witness. However, they soon began to worry that her rejection of all social authority might undermine church and civil discipline. The true Christian, she said, "must see nothing in himselfe, have nothing, doe nothing, onely he is to stand still and waite for Christ to do all for him." A court presided over by the redoubtable John Winthrop in 1637 ruled that Mrs. Hutchinson's ideas "tend to slothfulness, and quench all indeavor in the creature." Unrepentant antinomians were condemned to banishment. After wandering for several years along the New England frontier, Anne Hutchinson was murdered by Indians in 1643.

Her teaching and example, however, were not forgotten. Almost thirty years after her death, William Coddington, a surviving antinomian who had shared her banishment, wrote to the governor of Massachusetts: "You may as well withhold the flowing of the Tide into Massachusetts Bay, as the Working of the God of Truth in the Hearts of his People in the Massachusetts Jurisdiction, or to limit the Holy One to a Company or Tribe of Priests."[28]

True to Coddington's prediction, antinomianism, though usually not by that name, became a recurring theme in American history, playing a role in the numerous Baptist and Wesleyan revivals of the eighteenth and nineteenth centuries, the proliferation of idiosyncratic sects like the Shakers and the Spiritualists, and the storm of transcendental philosophy that broke over New England in the 1840s. In the 1960s, hippies and student radicals protesting against the Vietnam War were sometimes described as "antinomians."

Whatever their flaws or shortcomings, pietist sects deserve great credit for taking the lead in attacking some of the worst evils in Western society while most of the mainstream churches, both Protestant and Catholic, remained silent. In 1688 Francis Daniel Pastorius, leader of a group of German pietists who settled in Germantown outside Philadelphia, was joined by three Mennonites in issuing a call for the abolition of slavery—the first such in America and among the first in Western history: "Here is liberty of conscience, which is right and reasonable. Here ought to be likewise liberty of ye body." The Quakers soon joined the fight against slavery, and both Quakers and Mennonites championed the cause of American Indians.

ROMANTICISM: "CLOUDS OF GLORY"

With some of its roots in pietism, the romantic movement that exploded through Western culture and politics toward the end of the eighteenth century set off effects that remain intellectually and socially active to the present time. Romanticism has never had a simple meaning or character, but all its varying manifestations have shared devotion to some form of human freedom as a transcendent ideal.

Arthur O. Lovejoy in his seminal book, *The Great Chain of Being*, published in 1936, listed among the characteristics of romanticism: "the naturalization in art of the 'grotesque;' the quest for local color; . . . the distrust of universal forms in politics; the aesthetic antipathy to standardization; the identification of the Absolute with the 'concrete universal' in metaphysics; the feeling of 'the glory of the imperfect;' the cultivation of individual, national, and racial peculiarities. . . ." Charles Taylor in his perhaps equally important 1989 book, *Sources of the Self*, summed up the romantic goal: "perfect fusion of the sensual and the spiritual."[29]

No one did more than Rousseau to uncover the themes that led to romanticism. As we saw in chapter three, Rousseau's doctrine of the "general will" provided the conceptual foundation for several kinds of modern secular collectivism. Before attaching the machinery of collectivism to the engine of personal liberation, however, he created a vision of the socially unencumbered free spirit that thereafter had a life of its own.

Rousseau's fictional sage, the Savoyard vicar, set the standard that was to become romanticism's ideal: to "be myself, at one with myself, no longer torn in two, [so that] I myself shall suffice for my own happiness." Such freedom, Rousseau wrote in a letter published in 1758, is to be achieved, not among jaded sophisticates in big cities, but "in the open air, beneath the sky, where you must gather and surrender to the sweet sentiments of happiness." Spiritual liberation, he maintained, empowers the individual to explore deeper ranges of passion and commitment. The heroine of his novel *Nouvelle Heloise* tells her lover: "My darling, I love you as one must love, with excess, madness, rapture, and despair."[30]

Romanticism also tapped into the independent spirit expressed by folk poets like Robert Burns:

> A fig for those by law protected!
>   Liberty's a glorious feast!
> Courts for cowards were erected,
>   Churches built to please the priest.

Romanticism's defining moment came with the French Revolution of 1789. Here at last was a concrete challenge to the stale conventions associated with feudal monarchies and established churches. Wordsworth, looking back years later, recalled "Bliss was it in that dawn to be alive, / But to be young was very heaven!" The Revolution's decay into terror and dictatorship caused disillusion, but succeeding generations of romantics continued to be stirred by what they took to have been its launching spirit. Shelley wrote "The world is weary of the past / Oh might it die or rest at last."

From the start, however, romanticism's revolt was directed against not only inherited autocracy, but also the cool, rationalistic side of the Enlightenment that had been developed by writers like Helvetius and Voltaire. Even Isaac Newton came in for lumps as a reductionist from the visionary poet and painter William Blake.

> The Atoms of Democritus
> And Newton's Particles of light
> Are sands upon the Red sea shore,
> Where Israel's tents do shine so bright.

Wordsworth joined the attack on scientific demystification: "Our meddling intellect / Mis-shapes the beauteous forms of things:— / We murder to dissect." And Soren Kierkegaard, the nineteenth-century Danish theologian who conveyed many romantic themes, was sure: "Faith begins precisely there where thinking leaves off."[31]

For many romantics the greater enemy was the new industrialized and urbanized world that commerce and science were bringing into being. In this world, Blake warned, "England's pleasant pastures and mountains green" were giving way to "dark Satanic Mills." Wordsworth indicted the new culture of business: "Rapine, avarice, expense, / This is idolatry; and these we adore." Byron, in the third decade of the nineteenth century, already forecast coming environmental catastrophe:

> I had a dream, which was not all a dream.
> The bright sun was extinguished, and the stars
> Did wander darkling in the eternal space,
> Rayless, and pathless, and the icy earth
> Swung blind and blackening in the moonless air.

Dislike for the effects of modernity led some writers to invoke selective elements of the past as both refuge and rebuke. The German philologist Johann Gottfied Herder, a major source of romantic ideas, praised the Middle Ages as a time of imagination, feeling, and rural simplicity, contrasted with current urban luxury, artificiality, and vice. Wordsworth longed for the "plain living and high thinking" of an earlier England. John Keats nostalgically recalled "the gentleness of old Romance, / The simple plaining of a minstrel's song." Walter Scott, above all, thrilled British and American audiences with his tales of medieval heroism and chivalry—so much so that Mark Twain later complained that the whole American South had been infected by "Sir Walter's disease."

Many romantics maintained roots in some form of Christianity. "Trailing clouds of glory do we come," Wordsworth wrote, "From God, who is our home." The German romantic philosopher Friedrich Schelling insisted: "Without the conception of a humanly suffering God—a conception common to all the mysteries and spiritual religions of the past—history remains wholly unintelligible." Coleridge affirmed at least a broadly theistic view of existence:

> He prayeth best, who loveth best
> All things both great and small;
> For the dear God who loveth us,
> He made and loveth all.

The romantics' interpretation of Christianity, however, generally placed little emphasis on human guilt or sin. For Rousseau and (by implication) the romantics, Charles Taylor points out, "The source of the higher love . . . has become the voice of nature. The doctrine of original sin, in its orthodox understanding, has been abandoned." In Rousseau's view: "The first impulses of nature are always right; there is no original sin in the human heart." Wordsworth promised: "Nature never did betray / The heart that loved her."

Rejecting traditional Christianity's teaching on the inherent limitations of human nature, romanticism incited the individual to drive straight for personal perfection. "The essence of self," wrote the German poet Novalis, "is at one with the essence of essences—God, Universe, Being—and . . . the quest for the true or inward self holds out the promise of proximity or even union with the divine in the realization of selfhood." Coleridge similarly attested: "The primary Imagination I hold to be the living Power and prime Agent of all human Perception, and as a repetition in the finite mind of the eternal act of creation in the finite I AM."[32] In America, the patron saint of New England transcendentalism, Ralph Waldo Emerson, solemnly concurred: "Trust thyself. Nothing is at last sacred but the integrity of your own mind." Or as Walt Whitman more exuberantly put it: "I sound my barbaric yawp over the roofs of the world."

W. H. Auden pointed out that for the romantics "the divine element in man is . . . held to be neither power nor free will nor reason, but self-consciousness. Like God and unlike the rest of nature, man can say 'I.'" Exaltation of the self led many romantics to become obsessed with experience for its own sake. "This craving to raise as high as possible the pyramid of my life," Goethe wrote, "the base of which has been given and established for me, outweighs all else, and scarcely permits a moment's relapse." Goethe's Faust, Auden observed, "does not seduce Marguerite because he desires her or become a swampdrainer because he wants to do good to mankind, but because he wants to know what it feels like to be a seducer and a benefactor."[33]

In this perspective, the artist becomes the exemplar for humankind. Herder went so far as to declare the artist "a creator God." The poet and dramatist Friedrich Schiller, another prime source of romantic ideas, slightly less boldly found the poet "the only authentic human being." According to Shelley, the poet "strips the veil of familiarity from the world, and lays bare the naked and sleeping beauty which is the spirit of its forms."

A favored way of achieving spiritual perfection among the romantics was through union with a person of the opposite sex—as we say, romantic love. The identification of romanticism with sexual union became so close that in general parlance the word romance has come to mean little else. Some declarations of love by the romantics are straightforward expressions of desire. Shelley proposes:

> Nothing in the world is single,
> All things by a law divine
> In one another's being mingle—
> Why not I with thine?

But many include an element of melancholy. Keats, perhaps foreseeing his own early death, broods: "Ay, in the very temple of Delight / Veil'd melancholy has her sovran shrine. . . ." Byron, more robustly, recalls a former lover's embrace: "When it sparkled over aught that was bright in my story, / I knew it was love, and I felt it was glory."

The effects of the romantic revolution on music were even larger than on literature—a subject that can be no more than touched on here. Scott Burnham observes that, where the works of eighteenth century masters like Haydn and Mozart are "artful play with convention and representation," the music of Beethoven, perhaps the greatest of romantic composers, produces "the sense of an earnest and fundamental presence burdened with some great weight yet coursing forth ineluctably, moving the listener along as does the earth itself." The same could be said of Schubert or Wagner.[34]

Some romantics, resembling the detached pietists, rejected involvement in civil politics, which they regarded as hopelessly degrading and corrupt. But others, like the militant pietists, entered enthusiastically into political combat, or at least offered political visions that others might follow. Blake, in the voice of Milton, declared:

> I will not cease from Mental Flight,
> Nor shall my Sword sleep in my hand,
> Till we have built Jerusalem
> In England's green and pleasant Land.

Shelley urged his readers to "defy power, which seems omnipotent." Byron died of a fever contracted while fighting for Greek independence. Wordsworth, living on into the Victorian age as a revered member of the cultural establishment, became conservative, but never renounced the political enthusiasms of his youth. Goethe and Schiller fed currents of political liberalism in Germany. Schiller's and Beethoven's *Ode to Joy* is in part a political anthem.

The two great iconic symbols of political romanticism are neither British nor German but French: Delacroix's dramatic painting of *Liberty Leading the People*, portraying a heroic, tri-color–waving, bare-breasted Marianne leading aroused citizens to battle against the restored Bourbon monarchy in the Revolution of 1830; and Victor Hugo's Jean Valjean on the Paris barricades (though it should be remembered that Valjean went to the barricades primarily to rescue his ward's lover, Marius, a true militant romantic, rather than for any political reason).

Political romanticism has always carried a torch for the French Revolution's announced ideals: *Liberte, Egalite, Fraternite.* Its passions have sometimes been channeled into support for emotional causes that undermine or even contradict its professed values, but it has maintained fires of enthusiasm—Blake's "Chariot of fire"—that have warmed human souls and "kept hope alive" in some of history's darkest hours.

NIETZSCHE: SEEKING THE OVERMAN

Friedrich Nietzsche, the troubled genius whose powerful negations loomed over twentieth-century culture and philosophy, has been called a "confirmed anti-Romantic." It is true that he tried to distance himself from what he regarded as the romantics' sentimentality and softness. "I deny morality," he wrote, "in the same way as I deny alchemy. . . . I also deny immorality: not that innumerable people *feel* themselves to be immoral, but I do deny that there is any *justifying reason* for them to feel so."[35]

Yet Nietzsche shared the romantics' devotion to the potentialities of the unencumbered human spirit—in fact went further in that direction than most of the early romantics. "Beyond your thoughts and feelings, there stands a mighty ruler, an unknown sage—whose name is self. In your body he dwells; he is your body," he wrote in *Thus Spoke Zarathustra*, the first installment of which appeared in 1883 when he was thirty-nine years old.

"Do not throw away the hero in your soul! Hold holy your highest hope!" Nietzsche's thought went through a complex process of development from his origin in the household of his father, a conservative German Lutheran pastor who died when he was five, and his early classical education. But by the publication in 1872 of his first important work, *The Birth of Tragedy*, that process, according to the Nietzsche scholar Peter Levine, "had already arrived at the last stage."[36]

But did Nietzsche, like the romantics, relate the self to a transcendent source of value? Or was he a secular egoist—one who bases all value on the individual self? Or even a nihilist—one who denies the existence of any objective value in life whatever? Both modern egoists and nihilists have claimed him as one of their own, and some passages in Nietzsche's writings seem to support their contentions. He strongly repudiated any form of traditional theistic religion, particularly Christianity, which he believed had emasculated the Western spirit. "God is dead!" he announced, embracing a conclusion from which most earlier skeptics had shrunk. He rejected moral restraints, whether traditional or developed by reason: "Everything is false! Everything is permitted!" Humanist standards like Kant's categorical imperative, he argued, are just one more blight on human confidence: "Who is the great dragon whom the spirit will no longer call lord and god? 'Thou shalt' is the name of the great dragon. But the spirit of the lion says, 'I will.' " Strength provides its own justification: "To expect that strength will not manifest itself as strength, as the desire to overcome, to appropriate, to have enemies, obstacles, and triumphs, is every bit as absurd as to expect that weakness will manifest itself as strength." Action is normative: "The doing is everything."[37]

Nietzsche, however, felt no affinity for the kind of egoism celebrated by some of the laissez-faire capitalists and their apologists. "Far from the market-place and from fame," he wrote, "happens all that is great: far from the market-place and from fame the inventors of new values have always dwelt." He also deplored racism and tribal nationalism. He specifically disowned the anti-Semitism entertained by his sometime friend and admirer, Richard Wagner.[38]

What then of nihilism? Did Nietzsche agree with Theodore Dreiser, another writer whom his work influenced, that: "Life is nothing but a God damned stinking game"? He went a long way toward that view. As Levine observes, he rejected "the very structure of rationality which allows us to recognize truth and falsehood, opinion and fact." His dislike for Socrates and almost all subsequent Western philosophers, at least up to his predecessor in German *Sturm und Drang* speculation, Arthur Schopenhauer, was based on his conviction that they attempted to impose objective meaning on existence through reason.[39]

At the last resort, however, Nietzsche does not give up on transcendence.

Longing for transcendence, in fact, seems to be the underlying force that animates his philosophy. "We have only," he wrote in *The Birth of Tragedy*, "to place Faust, who storms unsatisfied through all the provinces of knowledge and is driven to make a bargain with the powers of darkness, beside Socrates in order to realize that modern man has begun to be aware of the limits of Socratic curiosity, and to long, in the wide, waste ocean of knowledge, for a shore." The creative individual is not, after all, spiritually self-sufficient: "Only as the genius in the act of creation merges with the primal architect of the cosmos can he know something of the eternal essence of art."[40]

Acknowledgment of a "primal architect" did not guide Nietzsche to a compassionate ethic or a democratic politics. Quite the contrary. His protagonist Zarathustra concludes that: "Pity is the final sin." He aims for "the height where no more rabble sits by the well." Preachers of "equality" are "tarantulas, and secretly vengeful." Women, in particular, must be kept in their place: "You are going to women? Do not forget the whip!"[41]

Nietzsche maintained that experience and knowledge of genuine transcendence have been blocked in the West by millennia of Christianity and rationalism. In pre-Socratic Greece, such qualities were won through a golden synthesis of Apollo and Dionysus. Regaining them now would require a superior being, whom Nietzsche calls the Overman. Nietzsche's mission is to "teach the Overman." The Overman will be "beyond culture, but . . . able to exploit this as an advantage." He will have the strength, Levine summarizes, "to act creatively despite . . . knowledge that nothing is true or false, good or evil." His emergence will mark the embodiment of transcendence in human form—but in a far different character than that taken by Jesus. Nothing must be permitted to stand in his way: "When the ends are great, [any strategy is permitted] even if it resorts to the most frightful means." The Overman, in short, is the last word in ecstatic individualism.[42]

Perhaps it is unfair to hold Nietzsche responsible for selective use of the Overman doctrine by Nazi torturers and murderers to justify their crimes. He no doubt would have detested them, as he despised rabid nationalists in his own day. On the other hand, the twentieth century has shown that totalitarian fascism is at least one of the destinations to which a doctrine glorifying amoral self-fulfillment may lead.

In person, Nietzsche was anything but the human "beast of prey" extolled by his writings. Stefan Zweig, an intellectual admirer, described him while he was working on *Zarathustra* as a "myopic man [relying on] innumerable bottles and jars and potions: against the migraines, which render him all but senseless for hours, against his stomach cramps, against spasmodic vomiting, against the slothful intestines, and above all the dreadful sedatives against his insomnia."[43]

In 1889 Nietzsche went mad, apparently in part as a result of syphilis.

Until his death in 1900 he was confined, at first in an asylum and later under the care of his mother and sister. Whatever else may be said of him, he seems to have been, even in his creative years, as his biographer Walter Kaufmann writes, "an utterly lonely man."[44]

WOODSTOCK NATION

The West was probably more receptive to ecstasism during the twentieth century than at any time since the Bacchants romped over the hills around Athens during the fifth century BC. While science, corporate business, and government bureaucracy combined to rationalize public life to an unprecedented degree, individuals were persistently drawn to the irrational, the instinctual, and the occult.

In the late 1960s and the early 1970s a social uprising associated with ecstatic practices and goals shook established cultures to their foundations and for a time seemed even to threaten governments. The 'rebellion' of the sixties achieved few lasting institutional changes, but left a cultural underground that has continued to affect popular attitudes and recreational tastes. Drug-induced ecstasism is practiced in most Western societies by a substantial minority, including some highly visible performers in the arts, professional sports, and entertainment. On another track, religious cults promising ecstatic deliverance attract significant followings. These range from moderately eccentric charismatic sects to hysterical communes that at the monstrous extreme produced the mass suicide of the Jim Jones cult in Guyana in 1979, and the confrontation ending in tragedy between law enforcement authorities and the followers of David Koresh outside Waco, Texas, in 1993.

The popularity of ecstasism in part expresses reactions by individuals against the spiritual barrenness and imposed regimentation of the highly rationalized public world, and attempts at subjective escape from the twentieth century's public horrors (wars, genocide, danger of nuclear annihilation). But it also has been fed and shaped by influential cultural forces.

Romanticism, though now disparaged by many academic critics, continues to provide serviceable outlets for rebellious spirits. The novels of Herman Hesse, written early in the century and cherished throughout by disaffected youth, for example, are described by a French scholar as proclamations of "the Romantic sentiment *par excellence*: the sentiment of the limits imposed by destiny and the desire to break through these limits, to destroy the human condition, to break out of everything." The protagonist of Hesse's most widely read book, *Steppenwolf*, declares: "The likeness of man, once a high ideal, is in the process of becoming a machine-made article. It is for madmen like us, perhaps, to ennoble it again."[45]

Many romantic writers assert benign attitudes toward the mass of humanity, but some display the arrogance and ruthlessness that romanticism's glorification of the self can induce. D. H. Lawrence, characteristically ahead of his time, wrote thirty years before the Holocaust: "If I had my way, I would build a lethal chamber as big as the Crystal Palace, with a military band playing softly and a cinematograph working brightly; then I'd go out in the back streets and main streets and bring them in, all the sick, the halt, the maimed: I would lead them gently, and they would smile a weary thanks; and the band would softly bubble out the Hallelujah Chorus."

The psychoanalytic studies of Sigmund Freud, begun in Vienna during the 1890s, profoundly affected twentieth-century art, academic discourse, and intellectual babble. With the advent of TV talk shows, Freud's doctrines have come to permeate popular culture, eliciting revelations of intimate personal secrets, real or imagined, from compliant guests. Freud himself, while aiming to reduce the psychic cost of repression of instincts during infancy, was a staunch defender of civilizing discipline. His techniques, however, inherently exalt the autonomous individual, and his ideas have become weapons for artists and intellectuals who regard inherited morality and conventions as jailers of spiritual freedom.

Modern art includes strains of egoism, monism, and even transcendent idealism. Its dominant thrust, however, through a tradition that goes back at least to Gauguin and Van Gogh, has been toward ecstasism. Qualities of personal expression in late nineteenth-century art came together in Picasso's *Les Demoiselles d'Avignon*, conveying the artist's reaction to forms suggested by "five confrontational whores posed theatrically on a little stage." The subject of this and much of Picasso's later work is not the scene before his eyes, but his internal struggle to convert its images into shapes and values expressing his personal temperament. "In working," Picasso wrote, "one must always be against." Unlike his great rival, Matisse, Picasso does not sublimate self-consciousness through containment in classic forms, but rather searches deep within his individual psyche for universal significance.

Following Picasso, contemporary art has to a great extent abandoned representation of three-dimensional objects painted from the perspective of the individual observer, which had characterized Western art since the Renaissance. Pure abstraction, claimed the painter Wassily Kandinsky, is "absolutely necessary and can in no way be avoided."[46] But this change has not reduced emphasis on the self. Quite the contrary: the artist's inner emotional or spiritual experience has become in most cases the sole subject of his or her art. All artists interpret the world through personal insights and forms, but representational art portrays a shared world of objective reality with which viewers are in a general way familiar, not because we know Renaissance Italy, or seventeenth-century Holland, or nineteenth-century

France, but because we recognize aspects of commonly experienced natural existence.

Art's move away from representation early in the twentieth century was in part reactive to competition from the recent invention of photography. But the deeper cause of this transformation was a loss of belief in the significance of the world of objective things in which most people more or less participate. What matters for much of modern art is not the common world of human experience, but how the individual artist feels. Among lesser artists this often leads to simple egoism—sometimes perverse egoism. But all the great moderns, including Picasso, Miro, Magritte, Pollock, and de Kooning—and in a different way, Matisse and Mondrian—have used their subjective experience to explore personal spiritual visions. What has usually been lost has been, not in all cases transcendence, but its relation to nonabstract human community. The "clarion note of modern art," John Updike writes, is that "the creator owes his public nothing but himself (or herself, needless to say)."[47] As art becomes more self-centered, it reinforces drives toward self-centeredness in the larger society.

Another source of modern engagement with ecstasism is popular music. Rising originally from traditional African-American themes of joy and sorrow, which interacted with elements from rural Appalachia and from other ethnic cultures, American blues, jazz, and rock have expressed personal longings and visions of splendor that have touched millions, not only in the United States, but all over the world. In the 1960s, working-class Britons added to this mix qualities of proletarian defiance and ambition, more personal than political: it's time to get ours. The result has been raucous, loud, compelling entertainment, merchandised through a vast, complex, and often crime-ridden industry. First introduced as the rhythmic beat for public dancing, jazz and its descendants have gone through numerous cycles from danceable music to music mainly for the ear and back again. Much popular music performs the ancient folk-art function of providing outlets for high spirits and releases for confined emotions. Less benignly, the popular music industry, Martha Bayles writes, has attracted "people . . . less interested in music than in using such a powerful medium for culturally radical purposes."[48]

In the late 1960s, all these forces and trends, catalyzed by the seemingly purposeless tragedy of the Vietnam War, came together to produce an explosion of rebellious attitudes and behavior, mainly among the young, particularly the privileged and well-educated young, at first in the United States and then throughout the West. Revolution seemed in the air. Actual revolution for a few days in the spring of 1968 appeared to have toppled the government of President Charles de Gaulle in France, spreading briefly to other parts of Western Europe—until de Gaulle made a dramatic comeback and governments steadied.

Protesters in the United States, though always a small minority even among the young, bombed government buildings, closed down universities, and helped drive Lyndon Johnson from the presidency. Simone de Beauvoir, a heroine among the disaffected, declared that society could "change only as a result of sudden cataclysmic upheaval on a global scale." But it was a revolution peculiarly without program or direction. "The revolution would make itself," rebellious students insisted. According to a manifesto issued by student radicals at the Free University of West Berlin in 1967, "The existing society can not change itself in any fundamental or qualitative way from within, only from outside in the name of totally different objectives and probably only by necessary defensive use of extralegal violence. . . . The present task is to insist on the revolutionary negation, for what is urgent is not the detailed outline of the free house of the future but the destruction of the oppressive prisons of the present."[49]

As mentioned in chapter two, Herbert Marcuse and other gurus of the 1960s seemed to license egoistic self-indulgence, but the more philosophic among them enclosed this message within a rationale of ecstatic universalism. "Imagination," Marcuse wrote, "envisions the reconciliation of the individual with the whole, of desire with realization, of happiness with reason. While this harmony has been removed into utopia by the established reality principle, phantasy insists that it must and can become real, that behind the illusion lies knowledge." The psychiatrist Wilhelm Reich, another favorite oracle of the period, claimed that removal of social hang-ups would end human conflict because "man who attains genital satisfaction is honorable, responsible, grave, and controlled, without making much of a fuss about it." But change would require, and justify, drastic action. "When repression has become so effective that for the repressed, it assumes the (illusory) form of freedom," Marcuse conceded, "the abolition of such freedom readily appears as a totalitarian act."[50]

In the United States, the rebellious mood of the 1960s reached a kind of climax at a rain-drenched rock music festival near the community of Woodstock in upstate New York during the summer of 1969, where more than 300,000 people gathered, after causing a traffic jam that closed the New York Thruway, and drank, smoked pot, listened to rock bands, and joined in orgies of emotion and sex. The celebrants gave themselves the name, partly ironic, "Woodstock Nation." It was not, they made clear, a conventional kind of nation, with boundaries, institutions, interests, or laws. Rather, it was the free nation of the future, composed of autonomous individuals come together to share, sing, take dope, and make love.

After Woodstock, the rebellion of the sixties seemed to recede. The following spring, when President Nixon sent American troops into Cambodia chasing Vietcong, hordes of protesters descended on Washington with the announced intention of shutting down the federal government and forcing a reversal of policy. The administration appeared to waver but in the end held firm. In 1972, Nixon was reelected by a huge majority. After Nixon was driven from office by the Watergate scandals, the United States accepted defeat in Vietnam in 1975 and things settled down. Succeeding generations of students, unimpressed by the effects of rebellion and attracted once more by the fruits of capitalism, appeared socially passive, if not conservative. "The sixties were like a bomb blast," a suburban high school principal said in 1979, "that left rings that each year we see less signs of." The 1980s all over the West became an era of political conservatism.

Ecstasism, however, has continued to fill spiritual gaps left by the decline of traditional transcendent belief systems. For a sizable minority, it defines a chosen lifestyle. For many others following conventional careers, it provides weekend or after-hours release from workday stresses: Saturday night fever! Jonathan Larson's 1996 hit Broadway musical, *Rent*, based loosely on the Puccini opera, *La Boheme*, substitutes AIDS for tuberculosis as the scourge hanging over the party. At a recent Saturday matinee, the audience seemed to represent a cross between a political rally and a revival meeting. The play's concluding coda is: "There is no future / There is no past . . . / No day but today." The situation of the story's characters, who are HIV positive, is truly tragic and worthy of pity, but living for the ecstatic moment on the assumption that there is "no day but today" is itself an invitation to tragedy. A society converted to the play's point of view would surely be headed for ruin.

THE BATTLECRY OF FREEDOM

Ecstasism by its nature offers at most no more than short-term relief from the West's pressing moral and spiritual problems. Experience shows that it tends either to disintegrate into simple egoism, as happened with many children of the sixties, or to provide a lure for totalitarian movements, as occurred in Europe between the two world wars. Its inherent flaws and perils have been imaginatively embodied by creative writers in the West during the past two hundred years through characters as varied as Faust, Ahab, Raskolnikov, Kurtz, and Scarlett O'Hara.

Yet ecstasism's ability to touch deep qualities within the human spirit, from the time of the shamans onward, can hardly be doubted. All of the above fictional characters, except perhaps Kurtz, represent qualities of strength and courage as well as evil. Since the Renaissance, many of the West's most creative artists, including Michelangelo, Shakespeare, Beethoven, Goethe, Goya, Dostoyevski, Wagner, Melville, Picasso, and Joyce, have expressed aspects of ecstasism in their works—though most of these have also conveyed values drawn from other belief systems, including transcendent idealism. Ecstasism has provided a magic route to the sublime—however socially inadequate or even destructive its message often ultimately has been.

Finally, forms of ecstasism have defended human freedom and integrity in times of great crisis. It is therefore appropriate to conclude this chapter with the tribute by William Wordsworth, perhaps the greatest of romantic poets, to Toussaint L'Ouverture, liberator of Haiti, murdered in 1803 by Napoleon's soldiers:

> There's not a breathing of the common wind
> That will forget thee; thou hast great allies;
> Thy friends are exultations, agonies,
> And love, and man's unconquerable mind.

7

Civil Humanism: Virtue in the Mind of the Beholder

Civic humanism denotes a style of thought . . . in which it is contended that the development of the individual towards self-fulfillment is possible only when the individual acts as a citizen, that is as a conscious and autonomous participant in an autonomous decision-making political community, the *polis* or republic.

—J. G. A. Pocock

In their separate ways, monism, absolutism, and ecstasism all provide versions of the experience of transcendence for which humans appear instinctively to hunger. None of these, however, seems to generate values sufficient to sustain a free society. Perhaps, then, we should try to get along without transcendence as a moral and civic foundation—or treat it as an allowable taste, like an interest in travel or a love of music—and concentrate on finding a purely secular value system that combines support for individual rights with incentives for social responsibility. Just such an enterprise has consumed vast amounts of intellectual effort and ingenuity in the West since the Enlightenment of the eighteenth century.

I call attempts to achieve a coherent moral synthesis between individual rights and social responsibility without reference to transcendent purpose *civil humanism*. It also may be labeled "secular humanism," an expression often used in both scholarly and popular discourse.[1]

Civil humanism also has obvious affinities to "civic humanism," a term coined in the 1960s by Hans Baron to designate a mode in literature and philosophy initiated in Florence during the early fifteenth century by writers like Coluccio Salutati and Leonardo Bruni, and since extended by J. G. A. Pocock and others to a "republican" tradition which they claim flourished in the West from the fifteenth to the nineteenth centuries. *Civic* humanism,

133

however, is best reserved for the particular qualities of the Florentine school and its descendants—though certainly a form of *civil* humanism.

"THE SCHOOL OF HELLAS"

Efforts to find a secular foundation for social freedom did not begin with the Enlightenment. Indeed, many Enlightenment writers looked back to the Renaissance, and beyond that to classical Athens and Rome, to find models that would meet their need.

The first major effort to launch a form of democracy—rule by the people—came in Periclean Athens in the fifth century BC, with roots reaching back to democratic reforms introduced by Cleisthenes at the end of the sixth century. Pericles, a member of the old Athenian aristocracy, put himself at the head of the city–state's more democratic party in 461, and for more than thirty years thereafter usually dominated a government that extended its authority over much of the Mediterranean world and broadened democracy at home. Under Pericles' administration, the arts flourished, and a new class of intellectuals pushed out frontiers of speculation and knowledge. Athens, Pericles said, became "the school of Hellas."

Athenian democracy of the fifth century, as has often been pointed out, was a kind of "democracy of the club." Women, the many foreigners who were attracted by the city–state's social climate, and the huge population of slaves had no part in government. In its dealings abroad, Athens proved imperialistic and unprincipled. Internally, general economic prosperity did not prevent, and may have quickened, the growth of rancorous class antagonisms. Although Pericles took away many of the privileges of the old aristocracy, the income gap between rich and poor steadily widened under his administration. Members of the aristocratic party, scornful of rule by democratic politicians, plotted restoration of oligarchic government.

Periclean democracy nevertheless represented a genuine, though limited, attempt to place government, as Pericles said, "in the hands of the many and not of the few." In his 430 BC funeral oration for the Athenian dead at the end of the first year of the war with Sparta, Pericles (as reported by Thucydides) set forth the ideals of Athenian democracy: "There is no exclusiveness in our public life, and in our private intercourse we are not suspicious of one another, nor angry with our neighbor if he does what he likes; we do not put on sour looks at him, which, though harmless, are not pleasant." Democracy, rightly understood, he maintained, nurtures rather than obstructs pursuit of individual excellence: "While the law secures equal justice to all alike in their private disputes, the claim of excellence is also recognized; and when a citizen is in any way distinguished, he is preferred in the public service, not as a matter of privilege, but as the reward of merit." Pericles saw no need to call on traditional sources of moral inspiration: "We shall not need the praise of Homer or of any other panegyrist whose poetry may please for the moment, although his representation will not bear the light of day."[2]

In 429, Pericles died. The war with Sparta and its allies continued on and off for twenty-five more years, with the tide gradually turning in Sparta's favor. Dissension within Athens grew. In 404 Sparta achieved final victory. The oligarchs, with Spartan support, took control in Athens and instituted a reign of terror against their political opponents. Within a few years, after Sparta had lost interest in Athenian politics, surviving democratic leaders regained authority and settled scores—among other things ordering the trial and death of Socrates.

Athens gradually recovered its economic prosperity and even got back some of its empire. Democracy of a kind was restored, but the civic idealism of the Periclean era never returned. Classical humanism declined into selfish egoism, as described in chapter two. Internal struggles between oligarchs and democrats persisted. Many citizens began to long for a tyrant to assure order. The "center," in W. B. Yeats's sense, did not hold. Politicians, to win public favor, spent funds on games and festivals that should have gone for defense. In 338 Philip of Macedon descended on Greece, and the effective independence of Athens, along with other city–states, died soon after.

ARISTOTLE: THE PERFECT GENTLEMAN

The intellectuals and scholars who gathered in Athens during the fifth and fourth centuries created a tradition of rational discourse that was perhaps classical humanism's finest flower. But most of the major intellectuals—with the important exception of Herodotus, the father of history—were not admirers or supporters of Athenian democracy. Socrates, as presented by Plato, seems almost the ideal humanist, declaring before his judges in the *Apology* a standard for intellectual freedom that continues to ring through the ages: "I thought . . . that I ought not to do anything common or mean when in danger; nor do I now repent the style of my defense; I would rather die having spoken after my manner, than speak in your manner and live."[3] But Socrates and Plato concluded that democracy is the enemy of the truly independent mind and spirit. Plato, applying Socrates' principles, went on to construct a model for authoritarian government on which, as we have seen, subsequent collectivist and absolutist systems have drawn.

When Aristotle, born in the colonial town of Stagira in 384, arrived in Athens at the age of eighteen to study in Plato's Academy, Athenian civic life was long past its prime. Profiting from the decline of Sparta, some Athenian politicians and businessmen were again aspiring to dominate Hellas, but the vitality of Athens' democracy continued to ebb. Aristotle remained at the Academy for twenty years, becoming the school's acknowledged star, second only to the master. But when Plato died in 347, he left instructions that Aristotle should be passed over for leadership of the Academy.

Moving on, Aristotle, after some adventures in Asia Minor, took up residence in 342 at the Macedonian court as tutor to Philip's son, Alexander, already at age thirteen a youth of extraordinary promise. Aristotle remained in his tutorial role until Philip's assassination in 336. Alexander, succeeding to his father's throne and quickly achieving mastery over all Greece, ruled through daring and charisma rather than by cultivation of classical virtues. Aristotle seems to have been puzzled and even disappointed by his product. While conquering most of the known world during his short lifetime, Alexander picked up many of the traits and pretensions of a traditional Oriental despot.

After his experience in Macedonia, Aristotle returned to Athens to open his own school, the Lyceum, as rival to the now dispirited Academy. For twelve years he wrote and lectured, making the Lyceum Athens's new intellectual center. Paradoxically, Aristotle's connection with Alexander ultimately undermined his position in Athens. While the young monarch campaigned across Asia and Africa, extending Hellenistic culture, Athenian patriots plotted to reassert their city's independence. Fearing that his Macedonian ties made him a target, and recalling Socrates' fate, Aristotle, aged sixty and ailing, once more moved on, so that, as he said, Athens would not "sin twice against philosophy." He died in Euboea in 322—the year after Alexander's death, and while the Macedonian army was snuffing out the last remnant of Athens's freedom and democracy.

During his long career in scholarship, Aristotle wrote comprehensively on most fields of human knowledge, ranging from metaphysics through natural science to rhetoric, politics, and aesthetics. He combined careful observation with astute analysis. His conclusions were so authoritative that more than a thousand years later most Western scholars and philosophers still assumed that whatever Aristotle had written on a subject must be correct.

At the heart of his work was his study of human behavior in society. Thales and the other early Ionian philosophers who concentrated on questions of being, he wrote, "knew things that are remarkable, admirable, difficult and divine—but useless." Aristotle did not intend to be useless. He had little interest, moreover, in the human individual as a solitary creature.

Aristotle's standard of behavior for "man as man" was based, like the physical ideals of classical sculpture, on deduction of what must be humanity's potential for excellence and perfection. His social philosophy assumes the authority of a controlling purpose, a *telos*, in human life. Humanity's *telos* is inherent in human nature itself, not ordained by a personal deity like the God of the Hebrew Bible. Aristotle, Harvey Mansfield Jr. points out, "supposed that nature indicates to human beings what is good for them."[4] In Raphael's famous painting of the School of Athens, Plato points up toward the heavens (transcendence), while Aristotle extends his right hand parallel with earth (nature).

In the *Eudemian Ethics,* Aristotle provides some place for an abstract deity that may be humanity's ultimate object for "service and contemplation"; but this deity is "not a superior who issues commands." The foundation for human ethics, and therefore politics, lies much closer at hand. "There are three things which make men good and virtuous: nature, habit, and rational principle," he wrote.[5] Like Alexander Pope two thousand years later, he believed that "the proper study of mankind is man."

Aristotle maintains that the *telos* of every living thing may be determined by discovering what it is best at doing. For humankind, the distinguishing quality is exercise of reason: "In men rational principle and mind are the end toward which nature strives." Humanity's *telos* dictates perfection of the body as well as the mind: "The care of the body ought to precede that of the soul, and the training of the appetitive part should follow: nonetheless our care of it must be for the sake of reason, and our care of the body for the soul."[6]

Full development of human rationality requires participation by man in society. "Man is by nature a political animal." By this Aristotle does not mean that humans are biologically programmed for collective behavior, in the manner of the honeybee or "any kind of herd animal." He means rather that humanity's highest calling, reason, depends on social intercourse: "It is evident that the state is a creation of nature. . . . He who by nature and not by mere accident is without a state, is either a bad man or above humanity; he is like the 'tribeless, lawless, heartless one,' whom Homer denounces."[7]

Cultivation of the qualities that make a good society is based on "virtue." Virtuous behavior is usually defined through location of the "mean" in any range of dispositions or categories of action. Courage, for instance, lies midway between rashness and cowardice; temperance between self-indulgence and prudish intolerance. "Virtue must have the quality of aiming at the intermediate, [because] in that condition of life men are most ready to follow rational principle."[8]

Promotion of virtue is necessarily a responsibility of the *polis*: "It is difficult to get from youth up a right training for virtue if one has not been brought up under right laws, for to live temperately and hardily is not pleasant to most people, especially when they are young. For this reason their nurture and occupations should be fixed by law; for they will not be painful when they have become customary." The best instructor in virtue is not rational argument but habit. "We are by nature able to acquire [virtues], and reach for complete perfection through habit."[9]

Aristotle finds merit in democracy as an effective instiller of virtue—thereby distinguishing himself from Socrates, Plato, and most other leading Athenian intellectuals. "If the people are not utterly degraded, although individually they may be worse judges than those who have special knowledge, as a body they are as good or better." To Socrates' contention that government, like the arts and sciences, should be left to experts, he responds that members of the consuming public are best able to judge their own interests: "The guest will judge better of a feast than the cook." By giving ordinary people a say in government, democracy produces a broadly held sense of citizenship. It is therefore "safer and less liable to revolution than oligarchy."[10]

Aristotle does not intend, however, that the general public shall have much control over day-to-day direction of government, or that persons from working-class backgrounds shall rise to high office. He is suspicious of the rich, whose "encroachments . . . are more destructive to the constitution than those of the people." In keeping with his principle of moderation, he believes that "the best political community is formed by citizens of the middle class." But actual government is best left to persons of independent means, who have time and leisure for unpaid public service. In this way, "the poor will keep to their work and grow rich, and the notables will not be governed by the lower class." He believes in "equality for equals," but is by no means a leveler: "Virtue is not the ruin of those who possess her, nor is justice destructive of a state; therefore [a] law of confiscation clearly can not be just."[11]

Aristotle specifically rejects the proposal by Socrates, endorsed by Plato, that ownership of all economic enterprises should be held in common and administered by the state for the public good. Like any modern capitalist, he argues that property "which is common to the greatest number has the least care bestowed upon it." In the good state "property should be private, but the use of it common."[12]

Most Greek intellectuals justified slavery as a necessary evil. Aristotle, however, defends slavery as a positive good because, he claims, it suits the naturally slavish dispositions of servile peoples. Unlike Plato, who favored equal participation by women (though within an authoritarian structure), Aristotle would give almost no rights to women, whom he regarded as "misbegotten men."

Despite these serious limitations, Aristotle's model commonwealth was much more liberal, in the humanist sense, than those proposed by other intellectuals of his time. His civic ideals closely followed those celebrated in Pericles' funeral oration. In the twilight of Athenian democracy, Aristotle constructed a reasoned argument for broadly based democratic rights and freedoms.

Aristotle's moral influence long outlived the classical world for which he wrote. Through adaptations by Moslem scholars like Avicenna and Aver-roes, his philosophy formed the basis for a civil humanist strain within Islam. In the thirteenth century AD, Thomas Aquinas melded Aristotle's eth-ics with biblical transcendent idealism to produce a powerful synthesis, the effects of which will be examined in chapter ten. During the Renaissance, Aristotle, along with Plato, provided the philosophic foundation for a new flowering of civil humanism in the West.

After the eighteenth-century Enlightenment, civil humanism, though in-creasingly influential in many sectors of Western society and thought, moved away from reliance on Aristotle. This divorce came in part because of Aristotle's close identification with medieval scholasticism, and in part because science undermined belief in the idea that nature is guided by moral purpose. Civil humanists sought justification and ethical direction from a variety of other philosophic systems, some of which will be discussed in the next chapter.

More recently, these modern formulations of civil humanism have come to seem faulty. Some civil humanists have turned back to Aristotle—sometimes through the mediation of Aquinas, but often in the secular origi-nal. Since most of these cannot bring themselves to argue seriously for Aris-totle's mechanical but nonetheless teleological physics, they have had to get along without a *telos* for humanity inherent in nature.

In his influential 1981 book *After Virtue*, Alasdair MacIntyre, a modern Aristotelian, developed the ingenious argument that a person's motivation for moral behavior may be something like that which prevents a dedicated chess player from cheating at chess: if the player "cheats, he or she will be defeating not me, but [by the standards of chess] himself or herself." Unfor-tunately, a good many people, if the stakes are high enough, seem prepared to cheat for material rewards in the game of life. (Perhaps life is really not very comparable to a "game," after all.) MacIntyre has since tied his Aristo-telianism to motivation supplied by Christianity.[13]

Aristotle, in both the ancient and modern worlds, usefully clarifies many moral and social issues. But his system, particularly without the authority of inherent moral purpose deducible from nature, which modern science has undermined, gives no strong motive in difficult circumstances for ethical public behavior. In the *Nicomachean Ethics*, Aristotle argues persuasively for the morally binding force of friendship in personal relationships. He concedes, however, that ties between "fellow citizens . . . seem to rest on a sort of compact [which is] full of complaints; for as they use each other for their own interests they always want to get the better of the bargain."[14]

In his own time, Aristotle's teaching did not discernibly affect the decay of Athenian democracy or persuade the Athenians to make the kind of com-munity sacrifice and effort that would have been needed to provide any chance of successfully resisting the Macedonians (on which Aristotle himself may have been at least ambivalent). Standing alone, it is unlikely to rescue us from our present predicament.

ROMAN LEGACY

Alexander's massive empire could not survive his death. His generals divided the lands he had ruled into three contentious kingdoms and an extended period of social and political turmoil followed.

Division in the East opened the way for emergence of a new hegemonic power in the West. By the end of the second century BC, Rome had achieved practical mastery over most of the Mediterranean world. The Romans had begun as a coalition of tribes camped on the hills beside the Tiber River. According to legend, the city was founded by Romulus in 754 BC. Like the Greeks, the Romans, even (or perhaps particularly) in the Augustan age, seem to have retained some memory of a more tranquil, equalitarian civilization in the Mediterranean basin before the arrival of invading conquerors from the north, with their gods of battle. "Before Jove's day," Virgil recalls in the *Georgics*, "no tillers subdued the land. Even to mark the field or divide it with bounds was unlawful. Men made gain from the common store, and Earth yielded of herself more freely when none begged of her gifts. . . . Then came iron's stiffness and the shrill sawblade—for early man cleft the splitting wood with wedges; then came divers arts. Toil conquered the world, unrelenting toil, and want that pinches when life is hard."

Such nostalgia did not deter the Romans from savage practice of the arts of war. What distinguished Rome militarily, according to John Keegan, was the exceptional ferocity of its soldiers. While most Mediterranean peoples, including the Greeks, had developed some distaste for violence, and even some moral scruples about treatment of noncombatants, the Romans kept up the systematic brutality their ancestors had brought long before from the Eurasian steppe. The Roman custom upon entering a conquered city, the military historian Polybius wrote, was to "kill everyone they met and to spare no one, and not to start looting until they received their order." The purpose of this behavior was "to strike terror." An observer, the historian continued, "can see in cities captured by the Romans not only human beings who have been slaughtered, but even dogs sliced in two and the limbs of other animals cut off."[15]

As in Athens, Rome from an early time was divided between economic classes, at first the patricians (upper class) and the plebeians (common people). A third force was introduced during the third century BC as the equestrian order, or knights—originally persons who could afford to own a horse and therefore were eligible for service in the cavalry. The equestrians came to include many of the "new men," often drawn from towns outside Rome, who were acquiring fortunes as bankers, traders, and publicans (public contractors) under the wing of the expanding Roman state.

Despite these class differences, the Roman people for many centuries maintained a high degree of social and political unity. The landed upper classes and the small farmers, who made up most of the common people, were on easy terms with each other. Differences in wealth were not extreme. The patricians and equestrians provided the officers and cavalry, and the common people the foot soldiers, for the legions that were making Rome militarily supreme.

The Roman Republic, which at the end of the sixth century had replaced the monarchy inherited from Romulus, operated under an unusual mixed form of government (a model for the system of checks-and-balances adopted by the American founders). Broad executive authority was vested in two consuls, elected for a term of two years; the aristocracy was represented by the senate, and the general public expressed its will through a popular assembly. At times of national crisis, the entire system was temporarily superseded by a dictator—appointed with unrestricted powers for a term of six months—after which he gave up his office, as in the case of Cincinnatus who in the fifth century BC returned to his farm after leading the republic to victory over a rival tribe. Roman society under the republic, the political historian Lily Ross Taylor reports, was hierarchically structured, but ordinary citizens enjoyed "some measure of personal liberty."[16]

Toward the end of the second century BC, Rome's social solidarity began to waver. Provincial governors and knights "brought back to Rome the fabulous wealth of the provinces, the gold and silver of Spain and Macedonia, the riches gained from the bounteous agricultural products of Sicily, Sardinia, and Africa. They also brought back an abundant supply of slaves." Small farmers found they could not compete with the cheap grain imported from the provinces. Members of the upper classes bought land around Rome to form great estates worked by slave labor. Citizenship was extended to all residents of Italy south of the Po River, reducing the value of each citizen's vote in the assembly. Former farmers who had lost possession of their land, as well as immigrants from the subject territories, flocked into the city of Rome. "The city rabble," Taylor writes, "was not bound to the upper classes by the ties which had once united small farmers and aristocrats."[17]

Rome was torn by fierce struggles between a party of the upper classes claiming to defend constitutional liberty, known as the *optimates*, and a party claiming to represent the interest of the common people, known as the *populares*. In 46 BC Julius Caesar, an aristocrat and victorious general with a following among the *populares*, made himself dictator. When he showed no inclination to relinquish power, members of the old upper class, including some who had prospered through his favor, struck him down in the senate.

In the subsequent civil war, Octavian, Caesar's grandnephew and son by adoption, was the ultimate victor. He had the senate declare him "Augustus"—the name by which he is known to history. Augustus always presented himself as the guardian of the republic. "At the age of nineteen on my own responsibility and at my own expense," he wrote in his autobiography, "I raised an army, with which I successfully championed the liberty of the republic when it was oppressed by the tyranny of a faction."[18] But in practice he kept all power in his own hands and the republic as a political reality was dead. Social solidarity was reestablished, but on a more authoritarian and hierarchical basis, modeled on the military chain of command.

Rome continued to expand its territory under the emperors who came after Augustus. Most of the subject peoples, few of whom had any experience of political freedom, seem to have welcomed the firmness of Roman rule, with resulting peace and opportunity for economic growth. Edward Gibbon wrote, with some hyperbole but essential accuracy: "The obedience of the Roman world was uniform, voluntary, and permanent. The vanquished nations, blended into one great people, resigned the hope, nay even the wish, of resuming their independence, and scarcely considered their own existence as distinct from the existence of Rome."[19]

The Romans borrowed heavily from Greek humanist culture, of which they considered themselves the heirs. "To study the humanities carefully," Ovid wrote, "makes behavior gentle and permits people not to act savagely." The Romans generally did not rise to the originality of thought or purity of expression achieved by the Greeks, but they excelled at practical application of humanist ideas and forms in arts such as oratory and architecture.

As we saw in the chapter on monism, Roman intellectuals and politicians were particularly attracted to the Stoic school of Greek philosophy. The fatalist strain in Stoicism probably appealed to soldiers for whom death and disaster were regular companions. Stoicism also provided a metaphysical framework useful to statesmen and jurists called upon to administer the most extensive empire the world had ever known.

The ruling classes of earlier empires, such as the Assyrian, the Babylonian, and the Persian, had based their authority on force, and had frankly employed state power to serve their class interest. Even the Athenians had assumed that force and national interest were determining factors outside the *polis*. The Romans aspired to more than that. The monist tendency within Stoicism pointed them toward the idea that there is a single body of universal ethical law inherent in nature, superior to the positive laws of particular states. Augustus had been educated by Stoic tutors, and in Orlando Patterson's view, probably "saw in the Stoic conception of providence a spiritual and inner representation of his own providential power in the world."[20]

The Roman Stoics mingled monism with the Aristotelian version of classical humanism to lay the foundations for the concept of natural law. "If our intellectual part is common," Marcus Aurelius argued, "then reason also, in respect to which we are rational beings, is common; if this is so, common also is the reason which commands us what to do, and what not to do; if this is so, there is a common law also; if this is so, we are fellow citizens; if this is so, we are members of some political community; if this is so, the world in a manner is a state." Epictetus, viewing the hubbub of Roman life from the perspective of a slave, put the idea of universality in more common terms: "We may learn the will of nature from the things in which we do not differ from one another. . . . Will you not remember, no matter who you are, or whom you rule, that we are kinsmen, that we are brethren by nature?"[21]

Roman jurists, like Gaius and Ulpian, employed the Stoic insight of universality to develop a code of jurisprudence that they claimed was prescribed by nature for all human beings. Such natural law, they maintained, applied even to relations among states. "Whatever natural reason has established among men is observed by all nations and is called the law of nations," Gaius wrote.

The idea that life proceeds inexorably along a preordained course beyond human control induced the Stoics to find value in faithful performance of one's assigned social role rather than in pursuit of social ideals. "For this is your duty," Epictetus counseled, "to act well the part that is given to you; but to select that part belongs to another." This attitude fit well with the Roman military ethos, and no doubt was useful to the managers of an authoritarian state.

Stoicism reinforced the Roman insistence, even under the republic, on a hierarchical structure for society. Cicero wrote that "Nature has provided not only that those men who are superior in virtue and in spirit should rule the weaker, but also that the weaker should be willing to obey the stronger." Marcus Aurelius agreed: "We were born for each other's sake. . . . I was born to be their [the people's] protector, as the ram is to his flock and the bull to his herd."[22]

In the end, acceptance of Roman rule depended on the force of Roman arms and the vigor of Roman administration. When Rome's political vitality at last began to erode, due to moral corruption in the ruling class and growing alienation among the common people, the empire crumbled. Long before the Western empire ended in the fifth century, many persons were looking to sources outside secular philosophy for moral guidance and spiritual awakening.

Rome left, nevertheless, a memory of the benefits that a universal state, administered at least in part through a humanist formulation of natural law, might bring. The belief system around which Roman life was ordered, particularly under the emperors but also to a great extent under the republic, was always primarily collectivist and authoritarian. But Rome conveyed to the West the ideals of classical humanism, and cast these in a structure of universalism that few among the classical Greeks had ever imagined.

The darker side of Rome's legacy was the model and taste it provided for unrestricted exercise of executive power. Later kaisers and czars adopted both Caesar's name and some of his methods. Their republican opponents railed endlessly against the evils of "Caesarism," but many emulated Caesar's pursuit of earthly domination and glory.

"SPRINGTIDE OF THE MODERN WORLD"

During the Dark and Middle Ages that followed the collapse of Roman authority, further experiments with civil humanism were discouraged by custom, condemned by religion, and prohibited by law. The Christian Church preserved the biblical idea that each human soul is uniquely valuable, and limited the reach of authoritarian governments, but increasingly emphasized the absolutist aspect of the Augustinian synthesis. Kingdoms that competed for control of former Roman territories were founded on force, usually blessed by the church. They treated criticism and dissent as evidences of treason.

Independent thinkers were never wholly absent, however. The ninth century Irish scholar Erigena wrote: "Authority sometimes proceeds from reason, but reason never from authority. For all authority that is not approved by true reason seems weak. But true reason, since it rests on its own strength, needs no reinforcement from any authority." In the twelfth century, the theologian Peter Abelard declared: "The first key to wisdom is assiduous and frequent questioning. . . . For by doubting we come to inquiry, and by inquiry we arrive at truth." The passionate letters of Abelard's lover, Heloise, present a woman candidly exploring and expressing the deepest motivations of a subjective self. In the thirteenth century, the scientist Roger Bacon proclaimed that: "man, by use of nature, can do all things."

In self-governing cities and towns after the eleventh century, elected councils asserted principles of liberty and community, derived from Christian, Roman, and Germanic sources. A twelfth-century French town enacted a charter declaring that it had "elected to be governed by a common oath association, so that each one may sustain his neighbor as brother as need arises."[23]

In general, however, feudal monarchs and nobility collaborated with an absolutist church to keep the common man and woman socially, politically, and culturally repressed. Most people, it seems, willingly gave up any thought of personal liberties in return for some measure of order and security in a dangerous world, and hope for salvation in the life to come.

Early in the fourteenth century, as noted in the chapter on egoism, a new wave of confidence and optimism burst across the West, beginning in Italy. Writers and artists took up humanist themes and interests, often employing classical models that had been brought back from the East by returning crusaders. According to Boccaccio, Dante's Christian epic *The Divine Comedy* "was first to open the way for the return of the Muses, banished from Italy." After Constantinople fell to the Turks in 1453, Byzantine scholars and artists fleeing west quickened the classical revival. Europe, wrote the English historian John Addington Symonds, "was, as it were, a fallow field, beneath which lay buried the civilization of the old world. . . . These men of the Renaissance enjoyed what we may term the first transcendent springtide of the modern world."[24]

More recent scholars have argued that the change was not so abrupt, and that the medieval world was not so "intellectually barren and inert" as Symonds and others claimed. Certainly there were earlier cultural awakenings, particularly in the ninth, tenth, and thirteenth centuries, but there is no doubt that a major turn occurred during the fourteenth and fifteenth centuries. Scientists and adventurous voyagers undertook, in the phrase of Jules Michelet, "the discovery of the world and the discovery of man." Scholars elaborated mathematical concepts, inherited from classical antiquity by way of Islam, with momentous consequences for banking, trade, manufacturing, and warfare. Artists painted from the perspective of the individual observer, and poets wrote in languages actually spoken by contemporary peoples. The printing press, introduced in the West by Johannes Gutenberg in 1456 after transmission from the Orient, made books widely available to the middle class.

Renaissance humanism fed on the moral implications of Christianity. Jesus Christ, the scholar Erasmus maintained, taught that "the crown of wisdom is that you know yourself." Through application of philology to the Greek texts of the Gospels, humanists like Erasmus and Lorenzo Valla sought recovery of the *philosophia Christi*, "the philosophy of Christ." Painters and sculptors like Michelangelo, Leonardo da Vinci, Raphael, Botticelli, and Titian created humanized representations of stories from the Old and New Testaments.

At the same time, artists began portraying the pagan gods and goddesses of antiquity in works like Botticelli's *Birth of Venus*, Bellini's *The Feast of the Gods*, and Titian's *Venus and Cupid*. In *The Feast of the Gods,* based on a tale by Ovid, the Olympians appear far gone in drunkenness and revelry, with Priapus slyly slipping his hand under the skirt of the sleeping nymph, Lotis. Titian's numerous and sensuous studies of Venus depict a goddess who relishes her naked beauty. Renaissance painters also took up, for fat commissions, portraiture of contemporary grandees and their families, sometimes mingling these with biblical subjects, as in Titian's portrayal of the Madonna and Child surrounded by members of the Pesaro family in the Church of the Frari in Venice.

Even in their secular works, however, most artists and poets sought to relate their presentations to transcendent ideals and forms. Michelangelo, Charles Taylor observes, "is deeply imbued [with the idea] that earthly beauty is the mortal veil through which we see the divine world." Leonardo searched for transcendent "reasons" in nature. "Nature is full of an infinity of reasons which has never been in experience." The "vile, wretched" side of human nature, Petrarch declared, can be redeemed only through "nobility of the soul."[25]

Renaissance man—and in a different role, Renaissance woman—resumed and pushed further the classical pursuit of human perfection. Jacob Burckhardt, in his magisterial nineteenth-century book on Renaissance Italy, argued that intellectuals and artists of the period "first gave the highest development to individuality, and then led the individual to the most zealous and thorough study of himself in all forms and under all conditions." In Kenneth Clark's more recent view: "The discovery of the individual was made in early fifteenth-century Florence."[26]

Some Renaissance writers, particularly Machiavelli, may have given license to the release of egoism, but the great Renaissance artists and theorists, including Machiavelli, were not themselves egoists. Machiavelli, despite his cynicism, was an ardent patriot for the Florentine republic. Leonardo Bruni, another Florentine, proclaimed that: "the excellence of one can flourish only when developed in collaboration with the diverse excellence of others." According to Burckhardt, the "moral force" linking the individual to the common good was a modernized version of the old Aristotelian concept of virtue, whether or not rooted in religion: "the sentiment of honour . . . that enigmatic mixture of conscience and egoism which often survives in the modern man after he has lost, whether by his own fault or not, faith, love, and hope."[27]

Excellence and freedom, at least freedom of expression, Renaissance man believed, are inextricably connected. "Such civic excellences as the arts and letters," Leonardo Bruni held, can "flourish only under conditions of liberty." Vasari, the sixteenth-century painter and art historian who coined the term Renaissance, asked himself why the artists of Florence were superior to all others. He concluded: "The spirit of criticism: the air of Florence making minds naturally free, and not content with mediocrity."[28]

Some Renaissance intellectuals, as J. G. A. Pocock and others have shown, translated humanist values into republican politics. Bruni claimed that "Florence was descended from the Roman republic," and idealized "the citizen as warrior and the warrior as citizen." Matteo Palmieri, another

Florentine intellectual, insisted that the good life requires participation in politics: "He who passes his life in solitude and is neither experienced nor skilled in important matters, in public offices, and in the business of the community, will never become just and courageous."[29]

In political practice, Renaissance humanism seems to have abetted the rise of a new breed of centralizing monarchs like the Bourbons in France and the Tudors in England. The trend toward political centralization grew in part from the price explosion of the fifteenth century, which weakened—some scholars say impoverished—the old nobility, and strengthened the bourgeoisie, who generally backed the new autocrats; and in part from military innovations that favored national governments. Tough-minded centralizers like Henry IV in France and Elizabeth I in England were also aided by practice and acceptance of Machiavelli's new science of politics. Civil humanism, moreover, by undermining traditional loyalties and ancient pieties, helped open the way for structural change in government and society. In the short run at least, the new forms of political organization were not likely to be republican. The Florentines, Pocock concedes, "did not fully succeed in solving the problem [of motivating republicanism] and showing how a self-sufficiently virtuous republic could exist in the secular time which was a consequence of its own finitude."[30]

Scholars differ over the relationship between the Renaissance and the Reformation, which broke with full force across Western Europe during the sixteenth century, a few years after Erasmus and the Florentines had composed their major works. Reinhold Niebuhr maintained that the Reformation was a revolt against *both* Catholicism and the Renaissance. The Reformation, he argued, rejected not only "the dogmatic control of religious thought by the church," but also the Renaissance's confidence in "the autonomy of reason" as the key to human perfection. Hugh Trevor-Roper, in contrast, writes that Calvin was "the heir of Erasmus," carrying on "in a more intolerant age [the Erasmian attack on the] external apparatus of official Catholicism." In any case, the two together, whether in concert or at odds, delivered the one-two punch that was to shatter forever the relative unity and security of Catholic Europe.[31]

SHAKESPEARE: BETWEEN TWO WORLDS

No one grasped better than William Shakespeare the intellectual and religious forces that were dividing the West at the end of the sixteenth century. Both the Renaissance and the Reformation had come late to England, but by the reign of Queen Elizabeth both were generating a social dynamism that was moving the island kingdom from the wings to a major role in European politics and culture.

Besides being unmatched master of the English language and a first-rate dramatist, dealing with eternal issues of the human heart and soul, Shakespeare provides—through symbols that go deeper than reason—acute impressions of contending ideas and social passions that battled within the collective consciousness of Elizabethan England.

Shakespeare's declared alignment was with the modernizers. He staunchly championed the Tudor monarchy that was leading England toward a modern state and economy. He demonized Richard III, the last Yorkist king, representing the old feudal nobility, who had been deposed by Henry VII, first of the Tudors. The Tudor accession, he had Henry promise, will bring "smooth-fac'd peace, / With smiling plenty, and fair prosperous days!" He jubilantly celebrated—almost invented—the cause of English nationalism: "This blessed plot, this earth, this realm, this England," he declared, will be guarded by "We few, we happy few, we band of brothers." He gave lines to Faulconbridge, bastard son of Richard the Lionhearted, at the end of *King John*, that ever after would be recalled by Englishmen in periods of national emergency:

> This England never did, nor never shall,
> Lie at the proud foot of a conqueror . . .
> Come the three corners of the world in arms
> And we shall shock them! Nought shall make us rue
> If England to itself do rest but true!

At the same time, he understood, and brooded over, what was being lost. The ghost of Hamlet's father, the murdered king, may be interpreted as representing (among other things) the dying Catholic feudal order, which had given not only political structure but also purpose and meaning to life. (John Shakespeare, the playwright's father, died a Catholic in 1601, the year Shakespeare completed *Hamlet*.)[32] Claudius, Hamlet's uncle and the deposing usurper, may be interpreted as representing (among other things) the ruthless "new men" pushing their way to power at Elizabeth's court—with the implied connivance of the Queen! *Hamlet* at one level is an intensely personal family tragedy; but it is also an extended metaphor for clashing belief systems. T. S. Eliot once wrote that *Hamlet* "is dominated by an emotion which is inexpressible, because it is in *excess* of the facts as they appear."[33] The "objective correlative" that Eliot missed is supplied by Christendom's collective guilt and anxiety over threatened loss of teleological confidence. The time that is "out of joint" is public and metaphysical as well as personal.

Shakespeare's Macbeth and Lady Macbeth, Caesar and Brutus, and the villainous Edmund in *King Lear* ("I grow; I prosper. / Now, gods stand up for bastards!") are all, in varying ways and with varying motives, usurpers.

Their bad ends offer examples that served the regime's political interest in discouraging thoughts of treason, like those fomented by supporters of Mary, Queen of Scots. But they would also have reminded Shakespeare's audience that the Tudors were themselves in a sense usurpers, disestablishers of the Catholic Church as well as of the previous regime.

Through Falstaff, Shakespeare expresses much that was warm and merry—as well as much that was brutal and corrupt—about the displaced order. "Banish plump Jack," the fat knight tells his fellow roisterer, Prince Hal, "and banish all the world." Falstaff speaks for that genial company who recall with pleasure having "heard the chimes at midnight." "What is honour?" he asks, turning the guns of egoism on the humanist ethic. "A word. What is that word honour? Air. A trim reckoning! Who hath it? He that died a Wednesday." When Hal becomes Henry V he does indeed "banish plump Jack." The old rogue dies, the King having "kill'd his heart."

Harold Bloom is right in arguing that Shakespeare was among the first to foresee the potentially nihilistic consequences of the rejection of transcendence, at first no more than covert or implied, that had begun with the Renaissance. But he goes badly wrong in claiming that Shakespeare made himself spokesman for this tendency. The dramatist, rather, looked into the future and weighed the spiritual and moral trade-offs with an ironist's eye.[34]

Shakespeare sometimes conveys the humanists' delight and pride in human aptitudes, as in Hamlet's tribute: "What a piece of work is man! how noble in reason! how infinite in faculties! in form and moving how express and admirable! in action how like an angel! in apprehension how like a god! the beauty of the world, the paragon of animals!" But in lines right after this exuberant passage, he immediately undercuts the entire image: "And yet to me what is this quintessence of dust? Man delights not me—no, nor woman neither." Elsewhere Shakespeare gives full voice to the nihilism that intellectual speculation and social conflict were breeding in Western consciousness: "[Life] is a tale / Told by an idiot, full of sound and fury, / Signifying nothing" (Macbeth); and, "As flies to wanton boys, are we to the Gods. / They kill us for their sport" (King Lear).

Some of Shakespeare's characters rebut nihilism with the Stoic version of humanism: "Men must endure / Their going hence, even as their coming hither, / Ripeness is all" (Lear). And some with Augustinian Christianity: "There's a divinity that shapes our ends / Rough-hew them how we will." (Hamlet).

While siding with the modernizers within the ruling class, Shakespeare was by no means a social revolutionary. In Troilus and Cressida he gives Ulysses a speech that elegantly states the case for social hierarchy:

> O when degree is shak'd,
> Which is the ladder to all high designs,

> Then enterprise is sick! . . . Take but degree away, untune that string,
> And hark what discord follows! and things meet
> In mere oppugnancy.

Shakespeare foresaw that the ultimate chief beneficiaries of a world in which commerce rather than military force is dominant would not be aristocratic courtiers and poets, but ordinary people freed to make their ways as far as work and wit would carry them. He seems to have viewed this prospect with mixed emotions.

He had no use for the self-righteousness of middle-class Puritans who were advancing in the latter part of Elizabeth's reign—satirizing these in the character of the "virtuous" Malvolio in *Twelfth Night*. His comedies abound with characters practicing common occupations: weaver, carpenter, tinker, constable. He often portrays these as buffoons, but he also endows them with practical common sense and a kind of dignity. In *Much Ado about Nothing*, for example, constable Dogberry at first appears a mere clown, but Shakespeare gives him lines in response to taunts from a bellicose soldier that convey both the insecurity and the defiant sense of achievement current among artisans and small merchants rising into the middle class: "I am a wise fellow; and which is more, an officer; and which is more a householder; . . . and a fellow that hath had losses and one that hath two gowns and everything handsome about him." Bottom, the redoubtable weaver in *A Midsummer Night's Dream*, is amorously pursued by the bewitched queen of the fairies after being turned into a donkey by the impish Puck. He has his farcical aspect, but he also has "had a dream, past the wit of man to say what dream it was. . . . I will get Peter Quince to write a ballad of this dream: it shall be called 'Bottom's Dream,' because it hath no bottom."

In *The Tempest*, perhaps the last play written entirely by Shakespeare, Caliban, a "deformed slave" who has been serving the benevolent wizard Prospero on an isolated island, may be interpreted as representing the playwright's fix on the uprooted urban proletariat gathering in London. Such people, Shakespeare apparently feared, would be prey to unscrupulous politicians, threatening the established social order. When a party of travelers is shipwrecked and scattered on Prospero's island, Caliban thinks he sees his chance for freedom. He foolishly identifies a drunken butler, Stephano, as a prospective liberator:

> A plague upon the tyrant that I serve!
> I'll bear him no more sticks, but follow thee,
> Thou wondrous man.

Stephano, thinking to make himself master of the island, encourages Caliban's rebellion. Caliban celebrates:

'Ban, 'Ban, Ca—Caliban
Has a new master get a new man.
Freedom, high-day! high-day, freedom! freedom, high-day, freedom.
Stephano: O brave monster! lead the way.

Shakespeare, like most artists, provides no systematic social or existential philosophy. He creates dramatic symbols that represent the social and intellectual forces that were shaping his world—and in many cases continue to shape our own. For the most part, he does not judge these. But in *The Tempest*, after Caliban and Stephano have been brought to heel, and Prospero (like Shakespeare?) has decided to "break my staff [and] drown my book," he permits himself to survey the future, in the voice of his daughter, Miranda, with humanistic optimism and enthusiasm, perhaps touched by irony:

O wonder!
How many goodly natures are there here!
How beauteous mankind is! O brave new world
That hath such people in it!

8

◆━━━━◇

The Crisis of Modernity

What counts as a decent human being is relative to historical circumstance, a matter of transient consensus about what attributes are normal
and what practices are just or unjust.

—Richard Rorty

I n the eighteenth-century Enlightenment, civil humanism gave birth to
the body of ideas and attitudes that we now call modernity—defined
by Martha Bayles as "credulity toward natural science and skepticism
toward all other truth claims." Modernity transformed human experience
during the last two centuries, and produced technological breakthroughs
and scientific accomplishments that have made life for millions, particularly
in the West, longer, safer, freer, more comfortable, and more interesting. It
has provided capacities, literally, to reach toward the stars and to break into
the atom. It has dispelled some of the irrational terrors that have haunted
human consciousness since the infancy of the race, and it has brought the
world closer together than would have seemed remotely feasible even a few
generations ago.

At the same time, modernity has created the technical means for actual
extinction of civilization and humanity itself. It has contributed to the increased horrors of modern war and political repression. While enlarging opportunities for self-expression and self-fulfillment, it has undermined bonds
of family and community on which past societies have depended for order
and cohesion. Through its skepticism toward "truth claims" not derived
from science, it has challenged many of the beliefs and convictions about
the universe and the human condition that have given meaning and purpose
to existence for most people in ages past, and for most even today.

In the closing decades of the twentieth century, there developed a general
sense that modernity had fallen into a kind of crisis—unable to cope with
many of the moral problems that its material successes have helped create,

153

and itself the cause of some of the discontents and social malfunctions speci-
fied in the opening chapter.

During and since the Enlightenment, civil humanist writers and thinkers
have proposed intellectual frameworks that they claim can take the place of
traditional moral and spiritual belief systems. This chapter will examine
some of the more notable of these, and consider civil humanism's contention that it can, unaided, support values sufficient to sustain a functioning
free society.

THE ENLIGHTENMENT PROJECT

The writers and artists of the Renaissance were either, like Petrarch and
Erasmus, dedicated Christians seeking through reason and classical models
to purify their faith; or, like Machiavelli, closet materialists who carefully
kept expression of their skepticism within socially acceptable bounds. The
philosophers and publicists who launched the eighteenth-century Enlightenment, in contrast, found it necessary, and in many cases exhilarating, to
build foundations for public and private morality outside revealed religion.[1]

William Davenant and Daniel Defoe, English journalists and critics of
the early eighteenth century, helped sow the seeds of the Enlightenment,
J. G. A. Pocock observes, and "were the first intellectuals on record to express an entirely secular awareness of social and economic changes going on
in their society, and to say specifically that these changes affected both their
values and their modes of perceiving social reality." Louis Dupre writes: "In
the eighteenth century, the idea of God ceased to be a vital concern of our
intellectual culture." Men of the Enlightenment, Henry May maintains, believed "that we understand nature and man best through the use of our natural faculties," and denied that "revelation, tradition, or illumination [are]
the surest guide for human beings." According to Ernst Cassirer, the Enlightenment regarded religion as "a barbarous thing, a strange and uncouth
mass of confused ideas and gross superstitions, a mere monstrosity."[2]

Not all Enlightenment thinkers were overtly anti-religious or even anti-
Christian. Many subscribed to deism, a creed first developed in the latter
part of the seventeenth century by Lord Herbert of Cherbury. Deism conceived God as analogous to a watchmaker who made the universe and then
left humans to cope with it through their own devices, particularly reason—
much as in Aristotle's idea of the unmoved mover.[3]

In France, Voltaire (the single most influential source of Enlightenment
ideas, whose long career spanned the middle section of the eighteenth century) was unflagging in his attacks on the established Catholic Church, but
conceded that most human beings cannot get along without some kind of
religion. For the intellectual elite, he declared, some version of deism should

suffice. But for the great mass of human beings, something like the Christian idea of God was still needed to preserve personal morality and social order. "I want my attorney, my tailor, my servants, even my wife to believe in God," he wrote, because "then I shall be robbed and cuckolded less often." He warned his friends not to speak of atheism in front of the servants for fear they would have their throats cut in bed at night.[4]

Voltaire's younger contemporary Helvetius was more thoroughgoing in his condemnation of religion: "In every religion the first objective of the priests is to stifle the curiosity of men, to prevent the examination of every dogma whose absurdity is too palpable to be concealed. . . . Religious intolerance is the daughter of sacerdotal ambition and stupid credulity." Diderot, editor of the great *Encyclopedie*, agreed: "The Christian religion is to my mind the most absurd and atrocious in its dogmas: the most unintelligible, the most entangled and obscure . . . the most intolerant of all."

Dispensing with religion, the Enlightenment was left with the problem of how the moral authority needed to hold society together was to be conceived. Voltaire's solution was a kind of two-tier system of beliefs, with rational pooling of self-interests for the deistic elite, and Christian promises of salvation or hellfire damnation for the masses. Over time, the religion of reason might extend more broadly: "Reason must first be established in the minds of leaders; then gradually it descends and at length rules the people, who are unaware of its existence, but who, perceiving the moderation of their superiors, learn to imitate them." But, with God absent, what was to deter members of the liberated elite from pursuing their individual or class interests at the expense of the common good?

Some Enlightenment thinkers shared Adam Smith's confidence that unrestricted competition among rational selves, perhaps cushioned by a spirit of innate benevolence in human nature, would automatically serve the interest of society as a whole (or the sum of separate individuals who make up society). Others followed Rousseau in counting on a new collectivism defined by the democratically determined "general will" to produce both personal freedom and social order.

But for most of the *philosophes*, let alone most ordinary people, neither egoism nor collectivism alone provided a morally or spiritually adequate substitute for Christianity. Some other bond, then, was needed. For some, nature itself supplied the answer. Diderot for instance wrote: "How short would be the code of nations, if it conformed rigorously to that of nature! How many vices and errors would man be spared!" Liberated from conventional morality, Diderot found in the code of nature a warrant for uninhibited practice and display of sex: "What has genital action, so natural, so necessary, and so just, done to you, that you exclude its sign from your conversations, and that you imagine that your mouth, your eyes, and your ears would be soiled by it?" For Voltaire, who did not care much for nature, progress toward an increasingly civilized society is inherent in history: "We may believe that reason and industry will always progress more and more; that the useful arts will be improved; . . . that philosophy, universally diffused, will give some consolation to the human spirit for the calamities which it will experience in all ages."[5]

These proposed solutions, however, did not do much to fill in the details of precisely how individual freedom was to be related to the common good without recourse to transcendence. By the end of the eighteenth century, Charles Taylor points out, deism "was becoming less and less believable, was going the way of earlier conceptions of cosmic order, and was in any case roundly rejected by [scientific] naturalism."[6] Constructing a plausible bond between freedom and social morality, then, was to become the Enlightenment project—a challenge that confronts civil humanists to the present day.[7]

KANT: "THE MORAL LAW WITHIN ME"

The most ambitious, and in some ways the most profound, attempt at solving the Enlightenment problem was made while the Enlightenment was still young by the German philosopher Immanuel Kant. Partly of Scottish ancestry, Kant brought together the tradition of hardheaded British empiricism launched by Hobbes and Locke, and extended in the eighteenth century by the Scottish school of commonsense realism, with the continental tradition of speculative rationalism begun by Descartes. To this mixture he added a large serving of Rousseau's romantic idealism.

Kant had been raised in a pietist branch of Lutheranism, in which his working-class parents were devout communicants. He owed his education to the interest of the family's Lutheran pastor, and he remained a lifelong professing Christian. He founded his ethics, however, not on revealed religion but on the operation of reason. His solution, therefore, if valid, would meet the moral and epistemological needs of civil humanism, whether or not Kant was himself a civil humanist.

Though he became an international intellectual celebrity after publication of his *Critique of Pure Reason* in 1781, he never ventured more than a few miles from Konigsberg in eastern Prussia, where he was born in 1724, and spent his entire career as professor of philosophy at the local university. He was a skilled geographer, but never saw a mountain or an ocean. Barely five feet tall and afflicted by a deformed chest, he practiced a strict program of physical exercise that helped him live to the age of eighty. Kant seems to have been among the most methodical of men. According to an old story, the people of Konigsberg were able to set their clocks by the timing of his daily constitutional walk. One day he appeared late on his rounds; it was the day on which he had begun reading Rousseau.

With Kant, philosophy moved from the busy worlds of politics, journalism, and commerce, and the sacred world of the church, to the more detached halls of academe. He presented his arguments in ponderous professional jargon. Yet Kant did not lack human sentiment. He learned from Rousseau that life must be based on the heart as well as the head. In another old story, he noticed that his argument that God's existence cannot be proved through logic alone in the *Critique of Pure Reason* brought tears to the eyes of his aged servant. He then wrote the *Critique of Practical Reason* to provide practical reassurance that God after all exists.

Kant joined and reinforced the Scottish empiricist David Hume's demolition of the old scholastic arguments for the existence of God. All such arguments, Hume and Kant claimed, contain as a hidden premise the ontological argument—the contention that the idea of God as the greatest conceivable being by its own inner logic proves God's existence, because a being that does not exist by definition could not be the greatest conceivable. This argument, and everything that follows from it, they maintained, is nothing but a trick with words. "To posit a triangle," Kant wrote, "and cancel its three angles is contradictory, but to cancel the triangle together with its three angles is not a contradiction."[8] Kant did not, however, share Hume's conviction that human beings are alone in an indifferent universe. "Ultimately," Hume had written, "the life of a man is of no greater importance to the universe than the life of an oyster." Kant argued: "In order to set ourselves a common purpose in conformity with the moral law, we must assume a moral cause of the world (an author of the world) . . . in other words, that there is a God."[9]

Kant also did not follow Hume in denying the possibility of establishing what is morally good through unaided reason. What *ought* to be, Hume argued, can never be derived solely from what *is*. Moral judgment always rises, not from "a speculative proposition or affirmation [but from] an active feeling or sentiment." Reason, on questions of value, is "the slave of the passions." Hume, a successful writer and man-of-the-world in prosperous eighteenth-century Edinburgh, did not find this conclusion disturbing. He had less confidence than his friend Adam Smith in the benign effects of economic competition and the normal benevolence of human nature, but he believed that humans have enough natural good will, supplemented by the force of custom and guided by an enlightened monarchy, to produce social stability.[10]

Kant, in contrast, set out to discover through reason an objective basis for morality. He believed he had found this in the "categorical imperative"—the rule that the individual should "act as if the maxim of your action were to become by your will a universal law of nature." The categorical imperative, Kant argued, is conceived by an autonomous human self able to make moral choices, in some sense free of physical causation: "When we think of ourselves as free, we transfer ourselves into the intelligible world as members, and recognize the autonomy of the will." Even if God did not exist, the categorical imperative would command obedience. God's moral role is to fuse the will and the spirit—the "highest good" which "must be possible."[11]

Kant's moral system, J. B. Schneewind points out, is founded on "a purely formal principle." The categorical imperative derives its moral authority from "the need to avoid self-contradiction." Unlike any moral philosopher before him, Kant makes this "the sole principle of morals."[12]

Kant's categorical imperative is obviously similar to the biblical Golden Rule—"Do unto others as you would have them do unto you"—which has counterparts in many religions. His corollary maxim to "act that you use humanity, whether in your own person or that of any other, always at the same time as an end, and never merely as a means,"[13] is a splendid moral directive from which many of the foundational beliefs of democracy and a free society can be derived. But it seems to spring more from a long religious and moral tradition than from abstract calculation. Kant himself at times acknowledged this connection. Christianity, he wrote in the *Critique of Judgment*, "enriched philosophy with far more definite and purer conceptions of morality than morality itself could have previously supplied. But, once these conceptions are found, they are *freely* approved by reason." The Gospel, he told his students, "was the first to present us with a pure morality, and as history shows, nothing else came near it."[14]

Kant's moral system, because it is based on rules conceived by a morally sovereign self, is often said to give priority to the "right" over the "good." This means that it calls for a certain kind of moral behavior regardless of what the ultimate good may be. But for Kant the "right" appears to become the "good." Duty comes to play a role much like that of God in theistic religions: "*Duty*! Sublime and mighty name that embraces nothing charming or insinuating but requires submission."[15]

The categorical imperative has often been criticized because its dictates may vary depending on the context in which it is applied. Believers in laissez-faire economics, for example, would not hesitate to make maintenance of an unrestricted free market a "universal law." But those whose social goal is complete economic equality find reliance on the market inadequate or destructive. The categorical imperative is not much help in settling this dispute, a problem shared by the Golden Rule and similar maxims. The deeper problem with the categorical imperative, from a practical standpoint, is its abstract, mechanical character. It is not likely to win assent from most actual human beings, even philosophy professors, in the way that religious, patriotic, or ideological creeds are able to do.

Kant has remained popular among some liberals and communitarian conservatives, even some who find his reasoning abstruse, because he seems to offer a theoretic basis for personal liberty within a context of community obligation that avoids the emphasis on individualism and self-interest characteristic of ideologies descended from Locke and Adam Smith. The trouble is that his dry maxims do not have the capacity to move humans to action—a lack that collectivist successors like Hegel and Marx filled with loyalties that were all too concrete, and that modern bureaucracies overcome through inflexible legalism.

In the conclusion to his *Critique of Practical Reason*, Kant wrote that his mind was moved by "ever new and increasing awe and admiration [for] the starry heavens above me and the moral law within me"—the words inscribed on his tomb in Konigsberg cathedral. These are words, after all, of a religious seer, whose inspiration does not dim with time. But "the starry heavens above" do not in themselves provide much practical moral guidance, and "the moral law within me" seems to require a source in something beyond reason.

UTILITARIANISM

Kant's genius was to mingle the rigor of British empiricism with various kinds of continental idealism. The English utilitarians of the next generation, coming more in the direct line from Hume and the Scottish realists, tried to keep the rigor while dispensing with the idealism.

Utilitarianism, as formulated in the closing decades of the eighteenth century by Jeremy Bentham and James Mill, dealt with the Enlightenment problem by ignoring it. The utilitarians traced all human value to the pursuit of pleasure and avoidance of pain. Personal freedom was valued, not as an inherent right ("nonsense on stilts," Bentham sneered) but as a device to increase the production of pleasure. By the same token, community was valued solely for its utility in promoting pleasure and minimizing pain. "The community," Bentham wrote, "is a fictitious *body*, composed of the individual persons who are considered as constituting as it were its *members*. The interest of the community then is, what?—the sum of the interests of the several members who compose it."[16]

Utilitarianism is distinguishable from simple egoism, utilitarians claim, by the formula it provides for measuring and determining social policy: "the greatest happiness of the greatest number." In making this calculation, "everybody [is] to count for one, nobody for more than one." Democracy is thus given a philosophic foundation without moving from a totally materialist view of reality.

Utilitarianism was enormously popular among statesmen, reformers, and social theorists in nineteenth-century England. It gave industrial capitalists and their publicists moral justification for sweeping aside traditional attachments and restraints, as well as newly discovered "rights," that might interfere with the efficiency of markets or block economic development. Political reformers employed its cool logic to attack the feudal system of representation that disenfranchised millions of middle-class and working-class citizens and kept power in the hands of the landed aristocracy. Imperial administrators adopted it as a guide for paternalistic government of subject peoples. Early socialists used it to deflate claims that private property is based on inherent moral rights.

Almost from the moment utilitarianism was conceived, however, critics appeared to charge that it carried implications that are potentially dehumanizing to political, economic, and cultural life, and opened the way to tyranny rather than liberation. These criticisms have continued to the present day.

In the first place, critics charge, the whole business of reducing pleasure and pain to precise arithmetic measurements misses the core of human experience. It makes no provision for qualities that intrinsically give some pleasures more value than others. "Other things equal," Bentham wrote, "pushpin [a bar game] is as good as poetry"—thereby provoking lasting outrage among lovers of high culture. Bentham did not shrink from the logic of ethical relativism. Condemnation by modern Europeans of the Greek and Roman practice of exposing unwanted infants to die as "unnatural," he declared, 'means nothing. . . . All it can serve to express is, the disposition of the person who is talking of it.'"[17]

Second, utilitarianism on its own terms gives the individual no real reason to value the good of the group or urgent needs of unrelated others above his own pleasure. "In the absence of strong and lasting benevolent impulses," John Rawls argues, "a rational man would not accept a basic structure merely because it maximized the algebraic sum of advantages irrespective of its personal effects on his own basic rights and interests."[18] Third, basing social policy on abstract calculations of pleasure and pain assigns too much power to those entrusted to do the calculating, licensing technocratic oppression. And fourth, dismissal of the concept that certain human rights are fundamental and inalienable may justify cruelty and intolerance when these serve the mood or interest of the majority. "If enough cheering Romans pack the Coliseum to watch the lion devour the Christian," Michael Sandel points out, "the collective pleasure of the Romans will surely outweigh the pain of the Christian, intense though it be. Or if a big majority abhors a small religion, and wants it banned, the balance of preference will favor suppression, not toleration."[19]

John Stuart Mill, son of James, tried to disarm some of these criticisms by introducing an external moral standard. Influenced by the nineteenth-century English romantics, particularly Coleridge and Carlyle, Mill the younger attempted to synthesize strict utilitarianism with pursuit of nobility in human life. "I regard utility as the ultimate appeal on all ethical questions," he wrote. "But it must be utility in the largest sense, grounded on the permanent interest of man as a progressive being." Mill acknowledged that "man as a progressive being" may sometimes choose a more painful course over one likely to maximize pleasure, not merely as a short-term trade-off of some pain for more ultimate pleasure, but under some circumstances a permanent deficit of pleasure: "It is better to be a human being dissatisfied than a pig satisfied; better to be Socrates dissatisfied than a fool satisfied."[20]

Unfortunately for utilitarianism, as has often been pointed out, Mill's resort to an outside moral standard causes the whole system to crash on the rocks of incoherence. The "ultimate appeal on all ethical questions" may be the pleasure-pain calculus, or it may be "man as a progressive being," whatever that may mean. It cannot be both. If it is the pleasure-pain calculus, Mill should have preferred the pig and the fool.

Mill left no doubt that in a combat between lions and Christians, he would be on the side of the Christians. Philosopher and politician, an important officer in the British East India Company for more than twenty years, champion of the movement for woman's suffrage, he was the very model of a nineteenth-century English liberal. Civil libertarians still invoke the standard for personal freedom Mill set forth in his essay *On Liberty*: "The sole end for which mankind are warranted, individually or collectively, in interfering with liberty of action of any of their number, is self-protection. . . . The only purpose for which power can be rightfully exercised over any member of a civilized community, against his will, is to prevent harm to others. His own good, either physical or moral, is not a sufficient warrant."[21]

Mill hedged his standard with qualifications that made it adaptable to the political realities of his time and his own idea of the requirements of civilization. "Despotism is a legitimate mode of government," he conceded, "in dealing with barbarians, provided the end be their improvement, and the means justified by actually effecting that end." His application of the principles of free speech and freedom of the press would fall considerably short of rights advocated by most current civil libertarians: "An opinion that corn-dealers are starvers of the poor, or that private property is robbery, ought to be unmolested when simply circulated through the press, but may justly incur punishment when delivered orally to an excited mob assembled before the house of a corn-dealer, or when handed about among the same mob in the form of a placard." Eccentric behavior must not be permitted to go too far: an individual "must not make a nuisance of himself to other people." Self-destructive conduct that becomes a burden on others deserves moral and even legal restraint: "Whenever . . . there is a definite damage, or a definite risk of damage, either to an individual or to the public, the case is taken out of the province of liberty, and placed in that of morality and law."[22]

Mill's actual doctrine, taken in its entirety, therefore, would not satisfy many who currently cite his views. But his underlying principle certainly upholds the rights of individuals in a free society: "The only freedom that deserves the name, is that of pursuing our own good in our own way, as long as we do not attempt to deprive others of theirs, or impede their efforts to obtain it."[23]

Unlike Bentham, Mill saw a continuing need for a kind of religion to provide moral support for a free society. He had great respect for Jesus as a prophet who offered "the pattern for perfection for humanity." But he believed that Christianity as it had been understood was no longer intellectually credible, and in any case promotes qualities such as passivity, dogmatism, and irrational faith that undermine his idea of "man as a progressive being." What was needed instead, he argued, was a new "Religion of Humanity."[24] Unlike Rousseau's civil religion, Mill's Religion of Humanity would not primarily serve the interest of the state but rather would inspire adherence to a humanist ideal. How would content for this ideal be determined? Through dialogue among members of the intellectual elite—among people like John Stuart Mill. Symptomatically, Mill's confidence in the intellectual elite was such that he proposed a form of democracy in which voting would be weighted according to intellectual attainment, with unskilled laborers at the bottom, and well-established liberal professionals at the top.[25]

Mill, Isaiah Berlin wrote, "left the true utilitarian spirit" far behind.[26] In the process, he sacrificed the analytic rigor achieved through strict application of the pleasure-pain calculus. As compensation, he gained support for values such as individual rights, personal honor, and human solidarity, which are necessary foundations for a free society, and which Bentham had scorned. But Mill ultimately based these values on the thin ice of elite opinion in a given era.

The mainline of utilitarianism, descended from Bentham, has been carried on in various forms by a strong school of professional philosophers, and has given both public and private bureaucracies useful tools for measuring results and guiding policy. But it has never won wide acceptance as a compelling moral or spiritual foundation for a free society. If pursuit of pleasure and avoidance of pain are the base values from which all else flow—"the ultimate appeal on all ethical questions"—moral judgments come down to personal tastes, voluntarily accepted and subject to discard when interest or humor shifts. Pure utilitarianism, on its own terms, offers no plausible bridge from self-interest to human solidarity.

Recognizing this difficulty, the eminent late nineteenth-century utilitarian philosopher Henry Sidgwick wrote: "If we are not to systematize human activities by taking universal happiness as their common end, on what principles are we to systematize them?" Hitler and Stalin, as well as Larry Flynt and the Reverend Jim Jones, would have answers.

PRAGMATISM

Utilitarianism has always carried some flavor of the environment of commerce, empire, and social reform with which it was associated in Victorian England. The related philosophy of pragmatism, in contrast, has had a distinctly American twang—though it also has exercised considerable influence among European intellectuals.

Pragmatism has operated in American life on two levels. It has been both a broad cultural tendency going back to colonial times, and a particular school of philosophy that originated in the latter part of the nineteenth century. As the former, it has expressed qualities of practicality, energy, and relative informality that have always characterized the American way of doing things. "You must be up and doing," Cotton Mather exhorted his Puritan parishioners in early eighteenth-century New England. "What is practicable," Thomas Jefferson wrote to John Adams a century later, "must often control what is pure theory." "Can do" based on "what works" has been a national axiom. In this sense, pragmatism has contributed greatly to the success of American industry, the stability of American democracy, and the openness of American life. It has also played a role in fostering political and business corruption, and licensing ruthless pursuit of personal success without much regard for who gets hurt.

As a school of philosophy, pragmatism was launched in the 1870s by the Harvard logician Charles Sanders Peirce in order to produce a functional vocabulary useful to science. It first received wide public attention through the books and lectures of Peirce's Harvard colleague, the charismatic psychologist and philosopher, William James. Peirce eventually changed the name of his own system to "pragmaticism," a term so ugly, he said, that nobody would be likely to steal it.

As developed by James, John Dewey, and more recently Richard Rorty, pragmatism responds to the Enlightenment search for a moral bond between the individual and society without reference to transcendence by holding that this problem, like many traditional philosophic conundrums, is essentially meaningless. Pragmatists maintain that both truth and value depend, not on correspondence with objective realities "out there," or on internal coherence, but on what actually works in achieving, as James wrote, more "satisfactory relations with our surroundings." The

Enlightenment problem as conventionally stated implies the existence of "individuals" and "society" as distinct entities when they are in fact aspects of a fluid historic process. "The actual 'laws' of human nature," Dewey declared, "are laws of individuals in association, not beings in a mythical condition apart from society."[27]

Support for democracy, pragmatists argue, may represent a "taste," but it is a taste with the force of history behind it. "We should see allegiances to social institutions," Rorty writes, "as no more matters for justification by reference to familiar, commonly accepted premises—but also as no more arbitrary—than choices of friends or heroes. Such choices are not made by reference to criteria. They cannot be preceded by presuppositionless critical reflection, conducted in no particular language and outside of any particular historical context." The business of life is to create tools that will serve the values history has given us. In the course of developing such tools (like free speech and representative assemblies) we shape and reform our values.[28]

James had grown up in a tradition of Protestant spiritualism and never endorsed the Enlightenment's rejection of personal theism. Though in no way an orthodox Christian, he maintained a wavering belief in some kind of transcendent force at work in the universe. "The total expression of human experience," he wrote, "as I view it objectively, invincibly urges me beyond the narrow 'scientific' bounds. Assuredly, the real world is of a different temperament—more intricately built than science allows. . . . Who knows whether the faithfulness of individuals here below to their own poor over-beliefs may not actually help God in turn to be more effectively faithful to his own greater tasks?" His work, therefore, belongs more to the category of transcendent idealism than to civil humanism.[29]

On the other hand, John Dewey, who succeeded James as principal formulator of pragmatism, confined his philosophy to purely secular values, though conveyed with fervor drawn from the evangelical Protestantism in which he had also been raised. As a young man he lost all faith in "the mystery of a power outside of nature and yet able to intervene within it." While James had steered pragmatism toward support of individualism, Dewey moved it in a much more collectivist direction. He began his philosophic career in the Midwest in the 1890s as an ardent Hegelian. By the time he arrived at Columbia University in New York City in 1904, to begin what turned out to be a tenure of forty-three years as both philosopher and educational theorist, he had given up Hegel. He always retained, however, the German philosopher's enthusiasm for collective dynamism.

Dewey counted himself a warm advocate of democracy. But he rejected the view, which he correctly attributed to the American founders, that democracy is based on "prior non-political rights inherent in the very structure of the individual." Democracy, he argued, "cannot be conceived as a consecration of some form of government which has already attained constitutional sanction. [True democracy] consists in a trend of conduct that causes choices to be more diversified and flexible, more plastic and more cognizant of their own meaning, while it enlarges this range of unimpeded operation."[30]

Dewey's distrust of static forms led him to doubt the need for institutions that most people thought were essential to democracy: "There is no sanctity in universal suffrage, frequent elections, majority rule, congressional and cabinet government. These things are devices evolved in the direction in which the current was moving." In 1929, he expressed admiration for Soviet Russia's "enormous constructive effort . . . in the creation of a new collective mentality; a new morality I should call it, were it not for the aversion of Soviet leaders to all moral terminology." Six years later, he recommended "the substitution of the intelligence that is exemplified in scientific procedure" for the rough-and-tumble of traditional democratic politics. By 1939, after Stalin's purges, he grew disenchanted with the Soviet Union, and regretted that "the theory which has made the most display and the greatest pretense of having a scientific foundation should be the one which has violated most systematically every principle of scientific method."[31]

Dewey remained vague on the standards that were to guide democratic evolution. "Growth itself," he declared, "is the only moral 'end.' " Growth toward what, he indicated, is a question that will be answered through continuing experiment. "The relation of individual freedom to organization is seen to be an experimental affair. It is not capable of being satisfied by abstract theory."[32]

After a period in the intellectual doldrums during the decades following the Second World War, pragmatism was given new life in the 1980s through the work of the social and cultural philosopher Richard Rorty. In Rorty's hands, Dewey's tradition of social liberalism has been infused by strains derived from European postmodern existentialism (which finds some of its own distant sources in the writings of Peirce and James). The resulting mix has produced a philosophic cocktail attractive to many scholars and intellectuals.

Postmodern intellectuals, Rorty prescribes, need to proceed on two tracks, one aimed at achieving personal autonomy through "irony," the other at social solidarity through political liberalism (by which he means the broad tenets of social democracy). "The closest we will come to joining these two quests is to see the aim of a just and free society as letting its citizens be as privatistic, 'irrationalist,' and aestheticist as they please so long as they do it on their own time—causing no harm to others but using no resources needed by those less advantaged."[33]

The goals of Nietzsche and J. S. Mill, Rorty claims, can be realized "in alternate moments" through application of values that are entirely secular. "In its ideal form, the culture of liberalism would be one which was enlightened, secular, through and through. It would be one in which no trace of divinity remained, either in the form of a divinized world or a divinized self. . . . It would drop, or drastically reinterpret, not only the idea of holiness but those of 'devotion to truth' and of 'fulfillment of the deepest needs of the spirit.' "[34]

Neither irony nor liberalism, in Rorty's system, relates to any standard of truth or value outside physical experience. "Ironist theory is . . . a ladder which is to be thrown away as soon as one has figured out what it was that drove one's predecessors to theorize," a metaphor also employed by the existentialist philosopher, Ludwig Wittgenstein. All social morality is relative: "What counts as a decent human being is relative to historical circumstances, a matter of transient consensus about what attitudes are normal and what practices are just or unjust." (In a footnote in his 1989 book, *Contingency, Irony, and Solidarity*, Rorty admits that he does not really believe that moral and aesthetic judgments are entirely subjective: "The distinction between true and false . . . is as applicable to statements like 'Yeats was a great poet,' and 'Democracy is better than tyranny,' as to statements like 'The earth goes around the sun.' [But] there is no practicable way to silence doubts on such matters.")[35]

Yet Rorty rejects "Nietzsche's insinuation that the end of religion and metaphysics should mean the end of our attempts not to be cruel." Secular liberals, he maintains, are guided by a sense of obligation "to keep trying to expand our sense of 'us' as far as we can." He does not say why.[36]

At the operational level, pragmatism is a trait and habit of mind that has done good service in breaking through crusts of restrictive formality and inherited prejudice, and puncturing intellectual fantasies. "What works?" is surely a question that always needs to be asked when dealing with real-world problems. In this form, it is not really new. "Two principles have to be kept in mind," Aristotle wrote, "what is possible, what is becoming: at these every man ought to aim." And Marcus Aurelius: "That which is useful is the better." But as an ultimate source for freedom or social responsibility—or for that matter as a standard for truth or beauty—it has never been adequate. As Rorty concedes: "There is no *neutral*, noncircular way to defend the liberal's claim that cruelty is the worst thing that we do."[37] As an effective foundation for public or private morality, pragmatism, almost comically, fails its own test: It does not work.

RAWLS: THE VEIL OF IGNORANCE

Political liberalism in the United States, and to a great extent in Western Europe, got along for about two decades after the Second World War with an ideological framework supplied by some combination of utilitarianism and pragmatism. Liberalism, allied in Europe with social democracy, was the reigning public philosophy, with little need for theoretic justification. Religion was tolerated, even praised, but kept socially in check.

By the end of the 1960s, however, liberalism was in trouble. The Vietnam War had turned many intellectuals and students who formerly had been among liberalism's warmest advocates against the liberal establishment in the federal government. Opposition to the war was approaching the level of civil insurrection. Explosive riots by blacks in major cities led many to question the reality of civil rights progress. Establishment liberalism ("Consciousness Two," in the parlance of the time) seemed implicated in a corporate culture that demanded conformity and regimentation. Traditional values of work, family, and community appeared undercut by liberal assumptions. A new breed of conservatives and just ordinary people were asking questions for which liberalism had no easy answers.

Fortuitously, the Harvard philosopher John Rawls in 1971 published *A Theory of Justice,* a book that claimed to provide a comprehensive theoretic basis for equalitarian liberalism. Initial reactions in the liberal press were rhapsodic. Many scholars, though usually more guarded than the press, expressed admiration. Some hailed Rawls's work as the long-sought solution to the Enlightenment problem of balancing freedom with community in a secular context.

The analytic foundation to Rawls's argument is an ingenious intellectual device that he calls "the original position." In the original position, "a group of [hypothetical] persons" have agreed, in order to "decide once and for all what is to count among them as just and unjust, [to be placed behind a] veil of ignorance," which prevents any individual from knowing "his place in society, his class position or social status; . . . his fortune in the distribution of natural assets or liabilities, his intelligence and strength"; and even, most crucially, "his conception of the good, the particulars of his rational plan of life, or . . . the special features of his psychology such as his aversion to risk or liability to optimism or pessimism."[38]

Persons so situated, guided only by reason and self-interest, Rawls contends, will, after exhaustive deliberation, come to agree on two principles as essential standards for justice: first, that "each person is to have an equal right to the most extensive total system of basic liberty compatible with a similar liberty for all" (what might be called the J. S. Mill principle); and, second, that no social or economic inequalities will be permitted unless they benefit "the least advantaged" members of society, and are produced through "conditions of fair equality of opportunity."[39]

The novelty among these standards is the requirement, which Rawls calls the "difference principle," that any social or economic inequality must benefit "the least advantaged." Under the difference principle, unequal incomes or wealth will be permitted only if their elimination would actually make the least advantaged worse off. Where no such effect can be demonstrated, government, through the "principle of redress," must act to remove all inequalities.[40]

It turns out that by "the least advantaged" Rawls does not mean the absolute bottom of society, or the physically incapacitated or insane, but "the representative unskilled worker [or] persons with less than half the median income and wealth." Nevertheless, the redress he calls for, to iron out inequalities that violate his standard, would require massive and continuing government intervention.[41]

Along with much praise, Rawls's book eventually received severe criticism from writers on both the political right, who did not like his justification for large and intrusive government, and the left, who objected that his system still leaves too much leeway for market capitalism. Professional philosophers faulted parts of his reasoning. Despite these rebukes, the book's influence has been huge, affecting politicians, government planners, journalists, and liberal religious activists, as well as secular intellectuals. In a second book, *Political Liberalism*, published in 1993, Rawls responded to his critics, and clarified and modified some of his earlier positions. But his basic argument has remained little changed.

One of the qualities that makes Rawls's thesis persuasive for many readers is the image that he offers of persons assembled in the original position as a kind of discussion group in which we can imagine ourselves participating. As members of such a hypothetical group, readers can conceive giving up knowledge of what would be their wealth and rank in society, and even not knowing their "intelligence, strength, and the like." If under these conditions we would choose the principles of justice that Rawls proposes, we can further conceive, if there is no strong countervailing reason, feeling bound by our agreement when we come out from behind the veil of ignorance and learn our actual situations. Rawls stipulates that he assumes his rulemakers will be motivated to apply the standards they choose by a "sense of justice"—the source of which is not at first clear.[42]

Ultimately, however, as a number of scholars have pointed out, Rawls goes too far. By requiring, *as is essential to his argument,* that we not know our "conception of the good, [or our] aversion to risk or liability to optimism or pessimism," Rawls has stripped us of qualities that are intrinsic to our very existence as persons. As Daniel Bell observes, for Rawls's hypothetical individual, "the person has disappeared." The subjects participating in the exercise are not really people like us. They are not really people at all. "Not persons," Michael Sandel concludes, "but only a single subject is to be found behind the veil of ignorance." Rawls's "persons" is a figure of speech, disguising a single decision-maker, a kind of impersonal computer, that Rawls has programmed with assumptions about value.[43]

Do Rawls's assumptions amount to a plausible surrogate for inherent human values? It is crucial to Rawls's argument that a rational human being, acting out of self-interest, would, if he did not know his actual situation, choose a society in which economic and social risks are held to a minimum, even if this means sacrificing a chance for exceptional gain. But is preference for low-risk security inherently more rational than willingness to "shoot the moon?" It would seem that this is an existential decision that each actual person will make for himself or herself.

Historically, most Americans, forced to the choice, have preferred a society in which there are opportunities for great success, even at the cost of accepting considerable risks. When George McGovern ran for president in 1972, he proposed that all inheritances be effectively limited to $500,000. When his pollster discovered that this proposal was enormously unpopular among low-income blue-collar workers, McGovern was amazed. "These people," he said, "must think they are going to win on a lottery ticket." Maybe so. But more likely they were expressing preference for a society in which they, or more likely their children, might through hard work and good fortune acquire riches that could be passed on, over one in which equality was guaranteed. This choice will offend some conceptions of a good society, but it is not inherently irrational. Reason can help weigh such decisions, but it does not finally make them. They are based on a hunch, on a passion—on "liability to optimism or pessimism."

What about Rawls's requirement that standards of justice be determined without knowledge of our "conception of the good?" Perhaps we can imagine agreeing to rules for society behind a veil of ignorance that prevents us from knowing what we regard as ultimate good—what we value most in life. But when we come out from behind the veil and learn our actual idea of the good, is it really conceivable that we will agree to these rules if they fundamentally violate what we now know we regard as life's most important values? This scenario is like a group of campers who are lost in the woods without a compass on a starless night, and agree to vote which direction is the most likely route out. If the stars appear, and they are able objectively to determine direction, will they then feel bound to take the route they voted for if it turns out to be wrong?

Rawls's answer to this is that his is a *deontological* system, in which the "right" takes precedence over the "good." In teleological systems, such as Christianity, Aristotelianism, or utilitarianism, the right is defined as that which contributes best to "maximizing the good." But in a deontological system, such as Kant's, the authority of the right—our sense of duty—is superior even to what we regard as the ultimate good.[44]

Where does this authority come from? Rawls *does not* mean the circumstance under which people with competing ideas of the good may be willing to compromise on the dictates of these ideas for the sake of social peace. His standard of justice represents objective principles that "once and for all [will determine] the kinds of social cooperation that can be entered into and the forms of government that can be established." This standard derives moral force from "an overlapping consensus of reasonable religious, philosophic, and moral doctrines in a society regulated by it."[45]

In his later book, *Political Liberalism,* Rawls insists that his standard of justice is "political not metaphysical"—it makes no claim to offering a "comprehensive philosophical doctrine" identifying ultimate good. But the many "reasonable" ideas of ultimate good competing within a democratic pluralist society, he claims, generate sufficient shared moral authority, a "sense of justice," to motivate acceptance and enforcement of the standards he proposes. Good citizens will regard the right (social justice) as politically superior to their separate metaphysical goods.[46]

Rawls's distinction between the good and the right expresses a fallacy. His idea of a liberal equalitarian society is simply one more idea of the good. A society in which his idea of justice reigns is, in his mind, the best society. For Rawls, as for Kant, the right *becomes* the good. It may have powerful moral claims, but there is no reason why persons holding other ideas of the good should accept it as superior. This does not mean that people holding competing ideas of the good—such as those prescribed by different religions or ideologies—will not for the sake of peace agree to political compromise of their differences, or that social peace is not itself a value that competing ideas of the good may support in common. But this is not Rawls's argument.

Even if his assumptions were accepted, it is at least doubtful that Rawls's system would provide a firm philosophic basis for liberalism in any traditional sense of that term. As Robert Nozick points out, Rawls's assertion of collective ownership of all character and talent undercuts the sanctity of human personhood that the whole enterprise was meant to affirm.[47]

Rawls's work is richly reasoned and gives useful insights into many contemporary moral and social problems, but in the end it does not provide an argument for his kind of equalitarian liberalism that will convince many who do not share his particular values to begin with, let alone solve the Enlightenment problem of balancing freedom with community without appeal to transcendence.

COMMUNITARIANISM

During the 1980s, the growing moral and social crises in the United States, and elsewhere in the West, helped give rise to a new breed of "third way" intellectuals and social activists who call themselves "communitarians." Some communitarians trace their lineage to Aristotle, some to Kant, some to Rousseau, and some even to the Bible. In the 1990s, "civil society," a favorite communitarian buzzword, became a widely heralded moral solvent, attracting the attention of politicians like Bill and Hillary Rodham Clinton in the United States, and Tony Blair in Britain.

Some communitarians, such as Daniel Patrick Moynihan, Richard John Neuhaus, Jean Bethke Elshtain, and Michael Lerner, are declared theists. Their work is firmly in the tradition of transcendent idealism, which will be discussed in the next chapter. Others, such as Michael Sandel, William Galston, and Amitai Etzioni are religion-friendly, though usually cautious about identifying themselves with a particular religious faith.

Many communitarians, however, including Michael Walzer, Alan Wolfe, and Benjamin Barber, are resolutely secular. Their work may properly be described as an effort to carry on the Enlightenment project by other means.[48]

Communitarians, Nicholas Onuf writes, "dream of shelter from a hostile world of imperious bureaucrats, numbing materialism, and mindless nationalism." But secular communitarianism generally comes down to a variant of pragmatism, seeking to provide justification for having the moral cake of social solidarity, while, through individual rights, eating it too, without reference to transcendence. As such, it relies on vague ethical intuitions or unrooted social consensus—neither of which has ever done much to stem moral decline in a society undergoing rapid change.

Some secular communitarians, while not themselves in any serious sense religious, make a place for a Rousseauian "civil religion." As the record of the twentieth century shows, however, civil religion manufactured to serve the objectives of the state at best confuses patriotism with religion, and all too readily serves to provide spiritual cover for an authoritarian regime.[49]

AN UNSOLVED PROBLEM

Philosophical concepts and operational strategies—including some not discussed here, such as Edward O. Wilson's "scientific materialism," Lawrence Kohlberg's theory of stages of psychological maturity, and Eric Posner's attempt at synthesizing self-interest with social norms[50]—have aroused interest among intellectuals. Some have attracted followings among segments of the general public. But, as answers to pollsters and current behavioral problems show, none has truly filled the gap left in Western moral consciousness by the declining influence of religion. The general moral crisis in the West continues; the Enlightenment problem remains unsolved. As James Q. Wilson writes: "We have come face to face with a fatally flawed assumption of many Enlightenment thinkers, namely, that autonomous individuals can freely choose, or will, their moral life."[51]

Most efforts to harmonize individual rights and social responsibility without recourse to transcendence rest on some version of the contention that human reason alone from its own resources can produce authoritative moral norms, as in Kant's formulation of the categorical imperative. This claim, however, was decisively challenged early in the Enlightenment, as we have seen, by David Hume, using the same weapons of logic and empirical analysis with which he and Kant had upset the traditional scholastic proofs for the existence of God. "Reason," Hume wrote, "is, and ought to be, the slave of the passions, and can never pretend to any other office than to serve them." An *ought* proposition, he maintained, can never be derived solely from an *is* proposition—by which he seems to have meant that moral authority can never be generated solely through rational analysis without recourse to sentiment or faith. Hume's arguments have often been disputed, but the case for the independent moral authority of reason has never truly recovered from his refutation. "It has become evident," writes the contemporary linguistic philosopher Karlis Racevskis, "that Reason cannot both be ethical and instrumental: it cannot be, at the same time, a human nature or ethical essence *and* a capacity for shaping nature and the world."[52]

Some contemporary philosophers, including Rorty and other pragmatists, argue that an aesthetic preference for a free society is itself sufficient basis for any other values that such a society may require. It is true that polls show large majorities in the United States and other Western countries supporting basic democratic institutions. But statistical evidence and common observation make clear that such abstract support does not deter many individuals from indulging in all kinds of lying, cheating, abusive behavior, even outright crimes, which undermine the moral foundations on which a free society depends. Declining participation in elections in the United States and many other Western nations indicates disinclination among many to undertake even the minimum tasks of citizenship. A mere taste for democracy does not by itself seem to motivate the behavior needed to assure a free society's survival.

Theoretically, some as-yet-undiscovered formulation of civil humanist beliefs and strategies might fill the moral, social, and personal needs that civil humanism has so far failed to meet. But two centuries of unsuccessful trying, often by brilliant and ingenious thinkers, offer an unpromising prognosis for the future.

Secular egoism and secular collectivism are internally consistent belief systems, whatever their baneful effects for human life. They can be acted on. But civil humanism, the attempt to wed self-interest to a sense of the common good without reference to a transcendent source of value, seems not to cohere. It breaks down into its component parts, either releasing unbridled egoism or fostering submission to collective rule by the state. As Alfred North Whitehead put it, secular humanism "gives no foothold for any forecast of the future around which purpose can weave itself."[53]

This failure has practical real-world consequences. Most people do not, of course, worry about whether arguments conceived by Richard Rorty or John Rawls or the secular communitarians make cognitive sense. But a secular culture that is intellectually and spiritually hollow at its core provides a fertile breeding ground for destructive long-term behavioral trends now afflicting much of the West, including the United States.

Civil humanists respond that there really is no choice—either ethics and morality and standards of justice must come from purely human sources or they will come from nowhere. "The hard truth," B. A. Ackerman writes, "is this: There is no moral meaning hidden in the bowels of the universe." Bernard Williams concurs: "We know the world was not made for us, or we for the world, that our history tells no purposive story, and that there is no position outside the world or outside history from which we might hope to authenticate our activities."[54]

If they are right, the modern world seems destined to drift indefinitely—or until catastrophe intervenes—without a moral compass fixed on objective reality. Humanism divorced from religion, Ernst Troeltsch predicted, will proceed to a "tragic or comic end," and "lead to dissolution, decomposition, and spiritual anarchy." The hard dogmatists of absolutism and the excited fanatics of ecstasism, as well as the gentle fatalists of monism, are prepared to fill this vacuum.[55]

There remains, however, another alternative: the seventh and last of our categories of value systems, which will be discussed next as a possible source for moral regeneration and guidance in the twenty-first century.

9

Transcendent Idealism: Roots

> Only someone who submits to the authority of the universal order can genuinely value himself and his neighbors, and thus honor their rights as well.
>
> —Vaclav Havel

We come, finally, to the last of the value system families, which founds individual human rights and social responsibility on mandates derived from transcendent purpose at work in the universe—in other words, from God's love and concern for each human life. I call this value system category *transcendent idealism*.

Transcendent idealism generates ideas and arguments similar to some associated with formulations we have encountered in earlier chapters. Like Immanuel Kant, for example, transcendent idealism holds that effective morality must be founded on an objective moral imperative; but unlike Kant, it relates this imperative to the will of personal deity. Like the nineteenth-century American transcendentalists, such as Emerson, it celebrates the spiritual side of human nature; but unlike Emerson, it is attentive to humanity's seemingly incorrigible attraction to sin and moral corruption. Like various social idealisms descended from the French Revolution, it champions the pursuit of social justice, but it insists that justice pursued without regard for genuine liberty (not the Rousseauian or Hegelian kinds) leads inevitably to tyranny. In all of these cases, and others like them, transcendent idealism differs from seemingly parallel belief systems in that it finds no route to either freedom or justice that does not pass ultimately through reverence for God's grace and love.

Transcendent idealism is not inconsistent with or opposed to moral *realism*. It could reasonably be labeled transcendent humanism, were it not for humanism's current common identification, in both general and scholarly discourse, with secularism and relativism. In contrast to some other systems

175

founded ultimately on religious faith, transcendent idealism affirms the reality and significance of material existence. Unlike some forms of ecstasism, it looks outward to the created world of things and events, as in the paintings of Durer and Rembrandt, and the novels of Jane Austen and Tolstoy, rather than exclusively inward to the subjective self. Unlike absolutism, it accepts the fallibility of all human institutions, including those that claim to receive their authority directly from God.

Transcendent idealist ideas and themes have played a part in many cultural traditions. The Babylonian *Epic of Gilgamesh*, derived from a narrative first composed around 2000 BC, tells in part of a young ruler instructed in civic responsibility through divine inspiration. The Indian epic, the *Mahabharata*, gives at least vaguely theistic sanction to the idea that "absence of cruelty" is the highest human ideal. The Mahayana Buddhist concept of the *bodhisattva*, a kind of savior who returns after achieving enlightenment to assist others, has transcendent idealist overtones. The Chinese sage Mencius, who lived in the fourth century BC, grafted concepts of theistic oversight and popular wisdom onto Confucian tradition, producing the formulation: "Heaven sees as the people see; Heaven hears as the people hear."[1]

The principal sources of fully developed transcendent idealism, however, are unquestionably cultural traditions based on the great religions descended from the Hebraic root. Among these, Islam, while including a doctrine of human free will, has generally lacked a concept of constitutional separation between organized religion and the state, and has tended in practice toward absolutism. Judaism and Christianity, too, as we have seen, have hosted a number of sometimes conflicting value systems. Nevertheless, the chief conveyor of transcendent idealist values and ideas in the modern world has been the Judeo-Christian cultural tradition—not the same thing as the separate religious faiths on which it is based, but fed by them.

PROPHETIC JUDAISM

As is well known, much of the Hebrew Bible deals with the travails and triumphs of a particular people, Israel, singled out by God's covenant. But that, of course, is not where the story begins. The first ten chapters of the book of Genesis start with God's creation of "the heaven and the earth" and all living things, and then relate the origins and early experience of the human race.

Humanity was created by God, according to the first account in Genesis, "male and female," in His image, with the charge to "be fruitful, and multiply, and replenish the earth, and subdue it." For this purpose, humanity is given "dominion" over all other species. In the second account, God forms man "of the dust of the ground," and then woman of the same flesh, from man's rib. In contrast to the pagan Mother Goddess, Northrop Frye points out, the creator God of the Bible "is a deity who does not bear or nurse his children and hence a god who makes the world rather than one who brings life into existence by giving it birth." His creation "suggests planning and intelligence." The "divine presence" reported in the Bible "may be experienced in or through nature, but should not be ascribed to nature."[2]

God places the first man and woman in "a garden eastward of Eden" amid "every tree that is pleasant to the sight, and good for food." He gives them free use of the garden and its bounty, with one exception: they must not eat "of the tree of knowledge." The first woman, Eve, is tempted by "the serpent" to eat the fruit of the tree of knowledge, so that she and her husband, Adam, will "be like gods, knowing good and evil." Eve succumbs to this temptation, and shares the fruit with Adam, "who was with her, and he ate." This fall from grace, according to the Bible, tainted all succeeding generations of humanity with original sin.[3]

The exact meaning and significance of the fall have been endlessly debated by theologians and scholars. At least part of its content may be the discovery of self—the quality that made humanity distinctively human and endowed humans with extraordinary capacities and powers, but also the source of many of our troubles.

Genesis goes on to relate the consequences of sin, including the murder by Cain, the first offspring, of his brother Abel. "Cursed from the earth," Cain departs to "the land of Nod, east of Eden," where he takes a wife (whose origin is not explained), raises a family, and founds the first city. By chapter six, human behavior has become so bad that God decides to send a flood that will destroy most living things "from the face of the earth." God spares only one good man, Noah, along with his family, and two of every living thing, which He orders Noah to take into the ark that will ride out the flood. When the waters recede, God "said in his heart, I will not again curse the ground any more for man's sake," and grants Noah a covenant "between me and you and every living thing of all flesh, [that] the waters shall no more become a flood to destroy all flesh"—a covenant embracing all humanity, in fact all living things, that long precedes His later covenants with the Hebrew patriarchs.[4]

In chapter eleven, Genesis takes up the story of God's particularly chosen nation, Israel, and its special role in fulfilling God's purpose. Much of the rest of the Hebrew Bible narrates the unfolding of God's special relationship with the Jewish people. Though Israel's ultimate role is to be a blessing for "all families of the earth" and "a light to the Gentiles," Abraham and his descendants are sure that God intends them to triumph decisively over their tribal enemies, if necessary through ruthless application of military force.

As Israel's history progressed, however, and the Jews encountered many setbacks and much internal strife, some of the Bible's authors began to find

a deeper meaning in God's purpose. From the beginning, God is more concerned with justice and righteousness than with material prosperity. "The
way of the Lord," God tells Abraham, is "to do justice and judgment." In
Leviticus 19:18, God commands Israel through Moses to "love thy neighbor
as thyself." The Psalmist, confronting the hard realities of human existence,
finds reassurance in God's love: "Surely goodness and mercy shall follow
me all the days of my life: and I will dwell in the house of the Lord for
ever."[5]

The belief system set forth in the Hebrew Bible goes beyond tribal solidarity to messages that are both more universal and more individualistic. The
biblical idea that a single creator, God, acts through time and history,
Wayne Meeks points out, necessarily denotes a universal moral authority
that applies to all peoples: "Individuals, communities, and empires will be
weighed at last by God's standard of perfect righteousness." At the same
time, the idea that each human being is made in God's image is inherently
individualistic. Even the concept of the fall as the result of human choice
indicates a capacity for personal will. Outside the biblical tradition, Germain Grisez writes, "no one developed any very clear conception of human
free choice. The notion of freedom of choice for human persons is related
closely to the conception of God as a free creator, man made in God's
image, and of God confronting man with the Covenant or the Gospel, and
demanding that man freely respond by a commitment of faith or by a rejection."[6]

This body of ideas had major moral and political implications, though
not always at once realized. The Hebrews, for example, from an early time
condemned infanticide, which had, William Langer found, "existed everywhere since time immemorial as a means for disposing of deformed infants
and limiting the size of population during periods of extreme privation."[7]
In this as in other areas, biblical teachings became the source for a widely
held human normative tradition.

The Hebrew Bible celebrates the establishment by David, just before 1000
BC, of successful kingship based on Jerusalem. But it also honors the inde-
pendent holy man Nathan, who calls David to repentance for having sent
Uriah the Hittite to death in battle out of lust for Uriah's wife, Bathsheba.

Particularly after the emergence of the prophets in both the northern
kingdom (Israel) and the southern kingdom (Judah) around 800 BC, the
moral and social values rising from the Bible were made explicit. Amos, a
southerner active in the northern kingdom before its fall to the Assyrians in
722, rails against parasitic overlords who exploit the rural poor: "Because
you trample on the poor and take from them levies of grain, you have built
houses of hewn stone, but you shall not live in them; you have planted pleasant vineyards, but you shall not drink their wine." His theme is taken up by
the first Isaiah: "Woe unto them that turn aside the needy from judgment,

and take away the right from the poor of my people." Micah condemns rich men who "are full of violence" and whose tongues are "deceitful in their mouths." More than a century later, Jeremiah is even more vehement in identifying internal rot as a greater threat to Jerusalem than the approaching Babylonian army: "How long shall the land mourn, and the herbs of every field wither, for the wickedness of them that dwell therein?"[8]

The prophets were not, for the most part, social revolutionaries. Jeremiah assumes the permanence of a hierarchically structured society. Isaiah's God urges: "Come now, and let us reason together. . . . If you be willing and obedient, you shall eat the good of the land."[9] Most of the prophets agree, however, that true righteousness requires an active social conscience, as in Isaiah 1:17: "Seek judgment, rescue the oppressed, defend the orphan, plead for the widow."

After Jerusalem fell to the Babylonians in 586, as Jeremiah had predicted, and many of the Jews were forcibly transported to Babylon, the later prophets tended to concentrate on personal spiritual liberation or salvation, as in second Isaiah's redemptive promise: "They that wait upon the Lord shall renew their strength; they shall mount up with wings as eagles; they shall run and not be weary; they shall walk and not faint." The later prophets, however, continued to seek moral and social as well as spiritual reform. Third Isaiah, in a passage cited later by Jesus, declares that the Lord has anointed him "to bring good news to the oppressed, to bind up the broken-hearted, to proclaim liberty to the captives, and release to the prisoners." The prophets, Robert Benne writes, "progressed from a nationalistic messianism in which God delivers the nation from its enemies to an ethical messianism in which God saves the good who unjustly suffer at the hands of evildoers."[10]

As their troubles persisted, the Jews pondered the problem of why God permits bad things to happen to good people. The book of Job, apparently composed sometime after the return of most of the Jews from the Babylonian captivity toward the end of the sixth century, tells of the trials and tribulations of a "blameless and upright" landowner and farmer named Job. God allows Satan to test Job's faith by taking away his wealth, killing his children, and afflicting him with boils "from the sole of his foot to his crown." Surveying these disasters, Job's wife advises him to "curse God and die." Job "cursed his day" but refuses to renounce his faith: "Shall we receive good at the hands of God, and shall we not receive evil?"[11]

The rest of the book largely recounts a series of exchanges between Job and three "comforters," later joined by a fourth, who urge him to recognize that his misfortunes are merited punishments for personal, though previously unrecognized, misconduct or unrighteousness. Job denies his guilt: "I will say to God, Do not condemn me; let me know why you contend against me. Does it seem good to you to oppress, to despise the work of your hands and favor the schemes of the wicked?" Job accepts God's authority, but will not stop claiming his innocence: "Though he kill me yet I will trust in him; but I will defend my ways to his face."[12]

Finally God Himself confronts Job and rebukes him for questioning the ways of the Almighty:

> Then the Lord answered Job out of the whirlwind:
> "Who is this that darkens counsel by words without knowledge?
> Gird up your loins like a man, I will question you, and you shall declare to me.
> Where were you when I laid the foundation of the earth?
>   Tell me, if you have understanding . . .
> Have you commanded the morning since your days began, and caused the
>   dawn to know its place,
> so that it might take hold of the skirts of the earth,
>   and the wicked be shaken out of it? . . .
> Can you bind the chains of the Pleiades,
>   or loose the cords of Orion? . . .
> Do you know the ordinances of the heavens?
>   Can you establish their rule on the earth?[13]

After verse upon verse of some of the most powerful poetry on transcendence ever written, Job at last submits:

> "I know that you can do all things,
>   and that no purpose of yours can be thwarted . . .
> Therefore I have uttered what I have not understood,
>   things too wonderful for me, which I did not know.[14]

Some modern commentators complain that Job had the better of the argument, and should have stuck to his guns. This, however, was not the view of those who composed the story. The meaning intended by the original authors may to some extent be debated, but clearly they aimed to convey that the God who made the universe has purposes that are beyond human comprehension, and that man, if he is to gain the strength and confidence that come from knowing God's presence, must finally simply accept God's will.

Note, however, that Job in his submission does not promise to stop asking questions: "I will question you, and you declare to me." And God, in a final rebuke to the comforters, who seem to be oracles of conventional wisdom, indicates that He prefers Job's searching to their platitudes: "My wrath is kindled against you . . . for you have not spoken of me what is right, as my servant Job has." To the annoyance of some modern readers, the story ends with God restoring "the fortunes of Job when he had prayed for his friends; and the Lord gave Job twice as much as he had before."[15]

As we saw in chapter five, for a brief time under the independent state founded by Judas Maccabeus in the second century BC, Israel's troubles, like Job's, seemed to be lifting. But with the arrival of the Romans in 63 BC, oppression returned. After a period of rule by puppet governments, Jewish patriots in 66 AD rose in revolt aimed at expelling Roman domination. Despite heroic struggle, the rebels proved no match for the Roman legions. In 70, Jerusalem fell and the Second Temple was destroyed.

As long as the Temple existed, most Jews felt little need for local places of worship. There are few recorded references to synagogues before the time of Herod the Great. But with the Temple gone, the local community synagogue, instituted by the Pharisees, moved to a central place in Jewish life. "Separate not thyself from the congregation," commanded the great first-century rabbi, Hillel.[16]

In 32 AD, Jews in southern Judea, led by Simon bar Kosba (Bar Kokhba), whom some believed to be the promised Messiah, staged a new uprising. After some initial successes, bar Kosba's revolt was bloodily suppressed. The Roman emperor Hadrian changed the very name of Jerusalem to Aelia Capitolina, and Jews were barred from the city. Substantial Jewish communities, nevertheless, continued to exist in Palestine, particularly in the rural interior.

In both Palestine and the far-flung Jewish Diaspora, the synagogue and the rabbinate developed along parallel, though for several centuries largely independent, lines. The rabbi, a teacher rather than a priest in the conventional sense, at first had no authority over the synagogue, a place for communal worship and organization of charity. Rabbis functioned in scholarly academies and the rabbinic courts. The earliest rabbinic writing, the Mishnah, a collection of laws based more on oral tradition than on the written Torah, was completed around 200 AD. During the fourth and fifth centuries, rabbis compiled the two Talmuds, one in Israel, and the other, which became known as the Babylonian Talmud and proved the more influential, in the revived Persian Empire. These provided learned commentaries on the Mishnah. To these were added during the final centuries of the Roman Empire the teachings of the Midrashim, a series of scholarly discourses on the Hebrew Bible.[17]

Loss of the Second Temple encouraged concentration by the rabbis and other Jews on the core moral and cultural values of Judaism. "Deeds of loving-kindness," taught Rabbi Yohanah ben Zakkai, Hillel's successor, "are religious acts equal to the rituals of atonement formerly performed in the Temple." With political action blocked, scholarship was particularly esteemed. The Babylonian Talmud declares: "A religious scholar is superior to a prophet."[18]

Judaism survived. The seed of faith, planted by Abraham and cultivated by Moses and the prophets, continued to flourish. In the Middle Ages, Talmudic scholars such as Saadiah Gaon, Judah Halevi, and Maimonides, carrying on the tradition of oral debate begun by the Pharisees, explored the relationship between duties owed directly to God (ritual) and duties owed to other humans although ultimately to God (justice). God's covenant with His people was preserved into medieval and modern times. "The other nations vanish," Maimonides wrote in the twelfth century, "but the Jews last forever." Even the horrific events of the first half of the twentieth century were not to prove him wrong.[19]

It would be absurd to claim that the ancient Hebrews held fully developed concepts of democracy or a free society. They first experimented with a kind of theocracy under which the individual had few rights, and then adopted monarchy as a means for remaining militarily competitive. Hebrew scripture speaks positively of freedom, but this usually does not go beyond release from actual slavery.

Nevertheless, the Hebrew Bible and the rabbinic writings through which Judaism was interpreted and applied are originating sources for many of the moral ideas from which constitutional democracy and republican government were to spring: the unique and equal value of each human life; the root of community in God's covenant with His people; maintenance of social order through rule of law (also held by other Middle Eastern peoples going back at least to Hammurabi, but strengthened among the Hebrews by foundation in God's commandments conveyed through Noah and Moses); the injunction to improve the earth through work; the imperative of social justice; and the community's obligation to care for "the stranger, the fatherless, and the widow." With good reason, the founders of a new republic millennia later in a distant land took as one of their mottoes a passage from Leviticus (though somewhat out of context): "Proclaim liberty throughout all the land unto all the inhabitants thereof."[20]

THE BIRTH OF TRAGEDY

Some among the Greeks of the classical period, as we have noted in earlier chapters, groped toward monotheistic solutions to the moral tensions between individual and group interests in complex societies, as well as to the deeper puzzles that rise from humanity's capacity to conceive levels of happiness and beatitude that seem beyond human reach for any very extended period. "God is one," Xenophanes wrote as early as the sixth century BC, "supreme among gods and men, and not like mortals in body or mind."[21]

Plato, above all other Greek philosophers, even Socrates, who fired his imagination, conceptualized a unifying transcendence that shapes and gives meaning to human life. Man's goal, he has Socrates conclude in *Theaetetus*, is "to become like God, as far as this is possible; and to become like him, is to become holy, just, and wise." The process of formulating this goal, Werner Jaeger surmised in *Paideia*, generates "the incessant secret excitement that marks the efforts of Socrates and his friends in Plato's dialogues, as they endeavor to acquire knowledge of virtue in itself and of good in itself." It is the end they have "been striving to reach—even although it can never really enter a state of permanent possession and unmoved satisfaction."[22]

In *Phaedo*, Plato identifies "the divine" as "that which naturally orders and rules," in contrast to "the mortal" which "is subject and servant." In *Timaeus*, he hypothesizes an "artificer," who is "father and maker of all the universe." When he wrote the *Laws* near the end of his life, he had reverted to a more standard polytheistic concept of "the gods"; but these are revered as "the chiefest of all guardians, [who] guard our highest interests."[23]

Plato's god, though sometimes presented with an aura of mysticism, is never more than an intellectual abstraction. He does not walk and talk with human interlocutors, like the God of Abraham, Isaac, and Jacob. He follows a pattern of the ideal and eternal, which in a sense preceded him and limits his action. Plato would probably have regarded it as blasphemous to imagine that this god would have created humanity "in his image." Lacking the concept of a personal god, Plato's version of theism, however sublime, has no place for the idea that each human life is uniquely sacred. As a result, it justifies absolutist religion and authoritarian collectivist politics, and has been an antagonist rather than a friend to democracy.

The closest approach to transcendent idealism among the classical Greeks came not in philosophy but in drama. Tragedy had originated in Athens during the sixth century in choral presentations that formed part of the annual festival of Dionysus. Around 535 BC an actor named Thespis—thus, "thespian"—introduced the innovation of separating himself from the singing and dancing group to carry on spoken dialogue with the chorus leader. According to Aristotle, Aeschylus early in the fifth century added a second actor, and Sophocles a few years later a third. Sophocles introduced rudimentary scene painting.

The young Nietzsche, as we saw in chapter six, argued that the tragedies of Aeschylus and Sophocles derived their power from a synthesis between Dionysian frenzy and Apollonian form. There is probably much truth to this insight, in the sense that beauty of language and dramatic structure make repressed drives and anxieties in human nature acceptable to consciousness. But this in itself does not explain the deep pessimism and gloom expressed by the tragedians of the Periclean age, while Athens' power and prosperity were still at their height. Aeschylus causes Cassandra to lament in *Agamemnon*, first presented in 458 BC, soon after Pericles achieved political ascendancy:

> Alas, poor men, their destiny. When all goes well
> a shadow will overthrow it. If it be unkind
> one stroke of a wet sponge wipes all the picture out;
> and that is far the most unhappy thing of all.[24]

Sophocles, in the concluding lines to *Oedipus the King*, produced in 429 soon after the Peloponnesian War began, repeats the traditional Greek warning: "Look upon the last day always. Count no mortal happy till / he has served the final limit of his life secure from pain."[25] And Euripides (whom Nietzsche regarded as the betrayer of Dionysian inspiration) gloomily forecasts in *Medea*, produced in 431:

> Greatness brings no profit to people.
> God indeed, when in anger, brings
> Greater ruin to great men's houses.[26]

Perhaps some inherited guilt from the warrior Hellenes' ancient conquest of a more pacific culture worshipping the Mother Goddess may have lain buried within the Greek mind. It may be no coincidence that many of the tragedies are set in motion by wronged women of Asian origin. (The Athenians were reputed to have interbred more with the earlier population than the Spartans or other Greeks had done.) Or the portents of coming civil discord may already have affected sensitive spirits. (Both Sophocles and Euripides wrote their final works after things had begun to go badly for Athens, though before Athens' final defeat by Sparta.) Or the dramatists may simply have exposed the fundamentally tragic situation of humankind, however pleasant temporary circumstances may be.

It also seems fair to argue, however, that the great tragedians sensed that, even when Athenian success was at its zenith, the civil humanist solution embraced by the Periclean age was not working—that the civic life of the *polis* had come to rest on unstable moral and spiritual foundations. Aeschylus and Sophocles, in different ways, sought to mend the defects of civil humanism through appeals to forms of theistic religion. Euripides, who accepted the Sophists' fundamental materialism while deploring its effects, attempted no such solution—which was perhaps why Aristotle declared him "the most tragic of the poets."

Aeschylus, the earliest of the three, had fought at Marathon and remained his whole life a patriotic Athenian. It should be remembered that the *Oresteia*, his great trilogy recounting events flowing from the murder of Agamemnon, returned victorious from Troy, by his adulterous wife, Clytemnestra, is in its conclusion a success story. Orestes, their son, pursued by the Furies for his revengeful slaying of Clytemnestra, is acquitted by the goddess Athene in a trial on the Acropolis in Athens, laying the foundation for civil justice. The city grown from these roots, the Chorus predicts, will be:

> civilized as the years go by,
> sheltered under Athene's wings,
> grand even in her father's sights.[27]

This happy ending, however, hardly erases the horrors rising from the crimes and executions that have gone before. Aeschylus provides no endorsement of the belief in the moral sufficiency of human reason that lay at the heart of Periclean humanism. Athene preserves a place for the Furies, supernatural enforcers of primordial taboos, as guardians of morality:

> I advise my citizens to govern and to grace,
> and not to cast fear utterly from your city. What
> man who fears nothing at all is ever righteous?

The Furies, somewhat incongruously, promise to resist both "the life of anarchy" and "the life devoted to one master" in defense of the presumably democratic "in-between" which "has the power / by God's grace always, though / his ordinances vary."[28]

Humanity's troubles, Aeschylus maintains, rise from its tendency to defy the will of a vaguely monotheistic god, identified with the Olympian Zeus. "The philosophy of Aeschylus," Jaeger observed, "could not exist without that faith." In *The Persians*, produced in 472, only eight years after the Greeks' great victory in the naval battle at Salamis, Aeschylus has the ghost of King Darius warn:

> Insolence, once blossoming, bears
> its fruit, a tasseled field of doom, from which
> a weeping harvest's reaped, all tears . . .
> Zeus is the chastener of overboastful
> minds, a grievous corrector.[29]

In *Prometheus Bound*—the first play in a trilogy, the other two segments of which have not survived—Aeschylus seems to question the moral authority of the traditional Zeus. Prometheus, who in earlier Greek mythology had been treated as a mischievous spirit who angered Zeus by stealing fire from heaven, is transformed by Aeschylus into a heroic, though doomed, benefactor of humankind. "In a single word," cries the defiant Prometheus, chained to his rock by orders of the vengeful Zeus (who does not appear in the play), "I am the enemy of all the Gods that gave me ill for good." We cannot know if in the trilogy's two lost plays the rebellious Prometheus is somehow reconciled with the omnipotent father god ("only Zeus is free"), but the play is evidence that Aeschylus, while distrustful of humanist optimism, was searching for a formulation that would close the gap between omnipotent deity and human ideas of justice. In the final lines of the play, Prometheus appeals to a feminine aspect of divinity:

> O Holy mother mine,
> O Sky that circling brings the light to all,
> you see me, how I suffer, how unjustly.[30]

Even more than Aeschylus, Sophocles was an active participant in governance of the Athenian state during its days of glory. A successful general and politician, he was a friend and ally of Pericles. Like Aeschylus, he could write with pride of Athens, as in *Oedipus at Colonus*, composed at the very end of his life, when he was ninety and his beloved city was in clear decline:

> Last and grandest praise I sing
> to Athens, nurse of men,
> for her great pride and for the splendor
> Destiny has conferred on her.
> Land from which fine horses spring!
> Land where foals are beautiful!
> Land of the seas and the sea-farer![31]

Yet from the time he first entered a winning play in the Dionysian festival at the age of only twenty-eight (defeating Aeschylus), he seems to have questioned the civil humanist premises of Periclean culture. Sophocles, Alasdair MacIntyre writes, attacked "Athenian hubris for an impious confidence in the effectiveness of the skillful use of power, a confidence which has displaced a proper care and respect for the relationship of the city to divine law."[32] The Athenian democracy in which he was a leader, Sophocles seems to have felt, was doomed by its own arrogance and greed.

Unlike Aeschylus (though like Shakespeare), Sophocles was capable of writing simple horror plays, like his version of *Electra*, that are little more than potboilers. But when at the top of his form, notably in *Ajax, Philoctetes*, and the three Theban plays, he plunged further into the most profound puzzles of the human heart and soul than any other writer in classical antiquity.

The Theban plays, though all deal with events in the lives of Oedipus and his family, were written as single plays, at widely different points in Sophocles' career, rather than as parts of a trilogy. This enabled him to go deeper into a particular character, though at the expense of Aeschylus's broader scope.

Antigone, produced first though it comes last in the story's chronology, tells of the aftermath of a civil war for control of Thebes between Oedipus's sons, Eteocles and Polynices, in which both have perished. Creon, uncle of the two dead princes, has assumed control of the state, and decides for political reasons that Eteocles shall be buried with full honors but that Polynices' body must be left to rot on the field of battle. Antigone, daughter of Oedipus and fiancee of Creon's son, Haemon, feels compelled by family honor to bury Polynices.

Creon is presented by Sophocles as the very embodiment of the authoritarian state:

> The man the state has put in place must have
> obedient hearing to his least command
> when it is right, and even when it's not.[33]

Antigone, though she is impelled by "the laws of old tradition," is also representative of a kind of personal willfulness that Sophocles does not wholly admire. From the beginning, she seems in love with her coming martyrdom:

> For me, the doer, death is best.
> Friends shall I lie with, yes friend with friend,
> when I have dared the crime of piety.[34]

When Creon orders her execution for defying the state, the Chorus, while granting her "respect," admonishes: "Your self-sufficiency has brought you down." But the fall of Creon, whose son has joined Antigone in death, is more terrible:

> O crimes of my wicked heart,
> harshness bringing death.
> You see the killer, you see the kin he killed.
> My planning was all unblest.[35]

In *Oedipus the King*, produced twelve years later in the year of Pericles' death, Sophocles probed more deeply into the underlying contradictions of Athenian humanism. Pericles, whatever his shortcomings, had been no Creon; Creon's authoritarianism was the very kind of polity Pericles claimed to have displaced. But in Oedipus, Sophocles presents a prize model of Periclean man, enterprising and civic-minded. "The resemblances between Oedipus and Pericles," the classicist Bernard Knox wrote, "though it is true they have often been exaggerated and overinterpreted, are still striking and not to be lightly dismissed."[36]

The play, as is well known, tells of Oedipus, king of Thebes, who unwittingly on his way to the throne has killed his father and married his mother. When the city is stricken by "a deadly pestilence," Oedipus seeks to discover the moral pollution that everyone assumes must be the cause. Jocasta, his wife—and mother—though she does not know the truth, advises against prying too far beneath the surface: "Best to live lightly, as one can, unthinkingly." But Oedipus is confident of his powers: "I account myself a child of Fortune, / beneficent Fortune, and I shall not be / dishonored." When told by the blind prophet Teiresias that his persistence will be his ruin, he replies: "I do not care, if it has saved the city."

The play's philosophic framework is set by the Chorus, declaring the transcendent source of moral law:

> May destiny ever find me
> pious in word and deed
> prescribed by the laws that live on high:
> laws begotten in the clear air of heaven,
> whose only father is Olympus;
> no mortal nature brought them to birth,
> no forgetfulness shall lull them to sleep;
> for God is great in them and grows not old.[37]

When the full awfulness of the truth is revealed, and Jocasta commits suicide, Oedipus, whose sin has been hubris, accepts responsibility. He blinds himself and is led from the city by his daughters, Antigone and Ismene:

> Take me away, my friends, the greatly miserable,
> the most accursed, whom God too hates
> above all men on earth![38]

Thirty-five years later, in the last year of his own life, Sophocles again took up the story. *Oedipus at Colonus* relates the old wanderer's arrival at Athens, where Apollo's oracle has foretold he will meet death in a sacred grove outside the city. The counterpart of Pericles is now Theseus, king of Athens, while the aged Oedipus seems to speak with the voice of Sophocles himself. Antigone, whom we saw die in the first play, reappears as her father's faithful guide, and we learn how her moral will was forged. An earlier Creon also appears, scheming as usual.

Oedipus has come to doubt his personal guilt in the tragic events at Thebes years before:

> How was I evil in myself?
> I had been wronged, I retaliated; even had I
> known what I was doing, was that evil?

He nevertheless finds some purpose in his suffering: "One soul, I think, often can make atonement / For many others if it be sincere." Theseus, a tough-minded realist, offers help in protecting Oedipus's children, but he has no interest in religious speculation: "I know I am only a man: I have no more / To hope for in the end than you have." For Oedipus, that is not enough. At the end of his long journey, he invokes a mysterious power that is both human and transcendent:

> I know it was hard, my children.—And yet one word
> makes all these difficulties disappear:
> That word is love.[39]

Euripides, the last of the great tragedians, detected no trace of transcendent meaning in the growing social and military troubles of post-Periclean Athens. As we saw in chapter two, he criticized the city's political and moral corruption, but the standard he invoked was entirely secular. Like Sophocles' Theseus, Euripides insists on recognizing that he is "only a man," and expects his audience to do the same. Sophocles is supposed to have said that the difference between himself and Euripides was that he showed men as they ought to be, while Euripides showed them as they actually are.

Euripides employs the clumsy device of the *deus ex machina* to tidy up the endings to some of his plays. But this only underlines his essential contempt for any idea of supernatural being. His view is neatly expressed by Hecuba's bitter aside in *The Trojan Women*:

> O gods! What wretched things to call on—gods!—for help
> although the decorous action is to invoke their aid
> when all our hands lay hold on is unhappiness.[40]

All three tragedians shared belief that the culture based on civil humanism in Athens was breaking down, more from internal corruption than from outside challenge. Aeschylus and Sophocles searched in this decay for evidences of transcendent significance, but, like Plato, lacked the conceptual foundation for fully developed transcendent idealism. Euripides finally found no hope at all, human or divine.

THE NEW COVENANT

More than three hundred years after Plato, in the tumultuous first century AD, came Jesus of Nazareth, preaching a message of hope, redemption, and love. As Jaroslav Pelikan has shown, interpretations of Jesus' exact role and meaning have varied greatly during the ages that have followed. But as Pelikan also writes: "Within the church, but also far beyond its walls, his person and message are in the phrase of Augustine, a 'beauty ever ancient, ever new.' " In a very real sense, as the author of the epistle to the Hebrews wrote in the first century, "Jesus Christ is the same yesterday and today and for ever."[41]

Jesus in some ways resembles the prophets of the Hebrew Bible, particularly Isaiah, whom he often cites. Like them, he calls for obedience to a loving God and caring service to the stranger, the poor, the sick, and the oppressed. But from early in his ministry Jesus makes clear that he regards his role and meaning as crucially different from those of the prophets. The prophets, even Moses, had claimed to be no more than chosen human agents of God. Jesus reveals, at first to his inner circle of disciples, and then more openly, that he is the promised Messiah, conveying God's direct participation in human experience, through a body and mind fully human. After completion of his earthly mission, moreover, God's presence will continue through the Holy Spirit (in Hebrew, *Ruah*, a feminine noun.)

This doctrine of the Holy Trinity, the single God who is three-in-one, was not put into definitive theological language until the Council of Chalcedon in 451, but its basis is fully set forth in the New Testament. For monotheists outside Christianity, it has ever been a scandal, constituting departure from strict belief in a single transcendent deity. For Christians, it is the central mystery of faith, embodying the "new covenant" which God, through Jesus, has conferred on all humanity.

Except for the accounts in Matthew and Luke of Jesus' birth in Bethlehem, and Luke's report of his visit with his parents to the temple in Jerusalem when he was twelve years old, we know almost nothing about his early life. In the three synoptic Gospels (Matthew, Mark, and Luke), Jesus as a young adult was baptized in the Jordan River by John the Baptist, an apocalyptic prophet whom Luke identifies as his cousin. He then fasted for forty days and forty nights in the wilderness—traditionally the rocky desert just west of the Jordan—after which he was visited by Satan, who sought to tempt him.

Lesser devils, ancient animistic spirits something like the Furies that pursued Orestes in the *Oresteia*, appear at various points in the Gospels, for example as the demons that Jesus drove from a human sufferer into the Gadarene swine. Their access to supernatural knowledge was shown by their instant recognition, while it is still hidden to most humans, that Jesus is the Christ. The Satan who visits Jesus in the wilderness is far more powerful than any of these. He is the personification of absolute evil in the universe, the same who tormented Job and, as the serpent, tempted Eve.

Satan, according to Matthew, tries three strategies to attract Jesus away from God and into his service. All three rely on his awareness that Jesus is subject to the mortal aspirations of humankind, both high and low. First he proposes: "If you are the Son of God, command that these stones be made bread"—appealing to the humanist dream of boundless material plenty without need for labor. Jesus replies, citing Deuteronomy: "Man shall not live by bread alone, but by every word that comes from the mouth of God." Satan then carries him to the pinnacle of the temple in Jerusalem and urges him to use his powers to leap into space—in effect defying the laws of physics in a burst of ecstasist hubris. Jesus, considerably less tempted by this vain suggestion, responds simply, again citing Deuteronomy: "You shall not tempt the Lord your God." Satan, at last falling back on the primordial human sin of inflated egoism, offers Jesus rule over "all the kingdoms of the world and their splendor." Jesus now easily dismisses him: "Get you behind me, Satan! For it is written, 'Worship the Lord your God, and serve only Him.'"[42]

Some of the moral and ethical directives presented by Jesus in the course of his ministry seem in tension with each other. He orders his disciples to place their duty to him and his teachings above loyalty to their families: "Forsake houses, or brothers, or sisters, or father, or mother, or wife, or children, or lands, for my name's sake"; but specifically sanctifies the family, alone among human institutions: "What God has joined together, let no man put asunder." He approves departure from the strict Jewish law when this serves human welfare: "The sabbath was made for man, and not man for the sabbath"; but insists that he has come to fulfill, not supplant, the law. He is highly critical of the rich: "It is easier for a camel to go through the eye of a needle than for a rich man to enter into the kingdom of God," and advises a rich young man seeking salvation to "sell your possessions, and give the money to the poor, and you will have treasure in heaven; then come, follow me"; but in the parable of the talents draws a moral lesson from a primitive capitalist's tough-minded rebuke of a cautious servant: "You ought to have invested my money with the bankers, and on my return I would have received what was my own with interest." He preaches what sounds like extreme pacifism: "Do not resist an evildoer. But if anyone strikes you on the right cheek, turn the other also"; but he uses at least metaphors of armed struggle: "Do not think that I have come to bring peace to the earth: I have not come to bring peace but a sword." As we have seen in earlier chapters, some of Jesus' teachings, taken in isolation, can be interpreted to express absolutism, ecstasism, monism, or even civil humanism.[43]

Some modern biblical scholars, on the basis of what seems very flimsy evidence regarding texts that are almost two thousand years old, have concluded that Jesus did not really say many of the things the Gospels report him saying. The notorious Jesus Seminar of academicians goes so far as to vote on particular sayings, ruling those not approved as inauthentic. Liberals using this form of analysis can produce a Jesus who is primarily a social activist. Thomas Jefferson was an early lay pioneer at this tactic. But of course evangelicals can play the same game, creating a messiah whose concerns are almost entirely spiritual. If both sides cut all the passages that give them trouble, the result would be accounts greatly reduced in moral and spiritual substance. It seems far more reasonable, from standpoints of both credible scholarship and practical faith, to accept the Gospels we have as authentic accounts by writers who had known Jesus or were reporting things they had been told he had said. The tensions in the canonical Gospels relate much more closely to the rough realities of actual human existence than the superficially more consistent contents of purged versions.[44]

In any case, Jesus provides a series of general principles on which his operational directives are based. He first, as reported by Matthew, cites the familiar Golden Rule: "In everything do to others as you would have them do to you." The problem with the Golden Rule, as we have seen, is that it provides no deterrent for persons indulging in condemnable, or at least questionable, practices who would be happy, or think they would be happy, to have these practices made general laws.

Later in Matthew, Jesus, when asked what is the greatest commandment, replies: "You shall love the Lord your God with all your heart, and with all your soul, and with all your mind. This is the greatest and first commandment. And a second is like it: You shall love your neighbor as yourself." Jesus thus sets human social responsibility within the broader context defined by love of God. He makes the critical norm, not strict law observance or social fairness, but actual love—goodness of will, as Augustine would interpret it—which he regards as the only reliable basis for just and harmonious human relationships. He does not, in this connection, require denial of self. He seems to regard positive self-love, understood as part of God's gift, as a healthy human quality, in fact as the measure by which humans are to determine their responsibility to each other.[45]

Jesus does not stop there. As reported by John, he takes the step the Old Testament prophets could not take. After telling his followers to "keep my commandments," he delivers a final commandment: "Love one another as I have loved you." He thereby ties ethics and morality to his *personal* love, expressing God's love for humanity. Transcendence is brought to earth. God's love is made directly normative in human affairs. "Inasmuch as you have done to the least of these," Jesus said, "you have done also to me."[46]

Jesus' new commandment raises both the sanctity of each human life and the authority of universal moral law to unprecedented heights. The "first outstanding characteristic" of the "Gospel ethic," Ernst Troeltsch observed, "is an unlimited, unqualified individualism." This may be overstatement, but it is true that Jesus offers salvation to individuals, whose souls "enter heaven one by one," not to groups. For God, there is no averaging out; though ninety and nine are saved, the Heavenly Father cannot be content if even one is lost. The class, the group, the nation are not what count. What counts is the individual human soul. Jesus calls for abandonment of the old self, motivated by avarice and pride. But the goal he sets, rather than obliteration of the self, as with the Buddha, is realization of a higher self.[47]

At the same time, Jesus, as his ministry proceeds, casts his moral directives in universal terms. His mission is for the inhabitants of "all nations," rather than for a particular group or race. Though many people may not know it, all have been potentially redeemed by his sacrifice and love. In the body of Christ, wrote the apostle Paul, following the logic of Jesus' teaching, "there is neither Jew nor Greek, there is neither bond nor free, there is neither male nor female."[48]

In other passages, Jesus seems to concede the need, in a fallen world, for more pragmatic sanctions. Seeking to trap him, some of his opponents among the Pharisees ask, "Is it lawful to pay taxes to Caesar or not?" Jesus gets them to produce a Roman coin. "Whose head is this," he asks, "and whose title?" They answer, "Caesar's." He concludes: "Render therefore to Caesar the things that are Caesar's, and to God the things that are God's." Some modern scholars have made rather too much of the claim that Jesus, by showing that the Pharisees possess the Roman coin, was branding them as collaborators with the occupying power. Jesus' point seems clear: there is a place in society for civil authority that is not tied directly to religion. But note also that Jesus sets a *limit* to the reach of civil authority—there are things that are Caesar's, but there are also things that Caesar is forbidden to touch. He thereby lays the foundation for doctrines of religious freedom and an independent church that are to be recurring themes in Christianity.[49]

Jesus' mission won wide support in his home region of Galilee. His entrance into Jerusalem on Palm Sunday was greeted by the Jewish populace with great enthusiasm. But he outraged or frightened Palestine's civil and religious establishments. Six days later, these forces crucified him on Calvary.

The story of Jesus' death on the cross, Charles Taylor points out, is lifeaffirming, in contrast to the resignation recommended by many classical philosophers. Jesus values life, this life, as well as the life to come. His sacrifice is therefore agonizing and real. "The Christian martyr," Taylor writes, "in giving up health, freedom, or life, doesn't declare them to be of no value. On the contrary, the act would lose its sense if they were not of great worth. To say that greater love hath no man than this, that a man give up his life for his friends, implies that life is a great good." Jesus taught that the ultimate meaning of human life is found in transcendence. But transcendence shines through to this life, to the here and now. What happens in this world is important, not just to individual humans or to human society, but to God: "Thy will be done on earth as it is in heaven." Contrary to the views of Western Stoics and Eastern monists, the pain suffered by humans in this life is real, but the reward for suffering endured is everlasting.[50]

The story of the Gospels does not, of course, end with the crucifixion. Jesus returns. The disciples, who had been demoralized and scattered, are transformed and united. "The hinge on which that faith turned," writes the English theologian and religious historian C. H. Dodd, "was the belief that Jesus, having been put to death by crucifixion, 'rose from the dead.' This is not a belief that grew up within the church, or a doctrine whose development might be traced. It is the central belief about which the church itself grew, without which there would be no church and no Gospels, at least of the kind we have."[51]

Jaroslav Pelikan declares: "Regardless of what anyone may personally think or believe about this, Jesus of Nazareth has been the dominant figure in the history of Western culture for almost twenty centuries."[52] From that dominance grew a church that has been associated with many evils and much foolishness. But it is also the source of the central moral and ethical tradition of the West, and increasingly, during the nineteenth and twentieth centuries, of much of the rest of the world as well.

10

⟵⟶

The Great Tradition

The natural law is the same for all, both as a standard of right action
and as to the possibility that it can be known.

—St. Thomas Aquinas

I live and love in God's peculiar light.

—Michelangelo

While we are aspiring toward our true country, we be pilgrims on earth.

—John Calvin

I n 1955 the literary historian and critic F. R. Leavis published a book
called *The Great Tradition*—his title for the tradition of high moral realism in the English novel from Henry Fielding and Jane Austen to Henry
James and Jospeh Conrad. Leavis held that the major writers in this tradition are characterized by "a vital capacity for experience, a kind of reverent
openness before life, and a marked moral intensity."[1]

The term Great Tradition can be used more extensively to designate the
long line of thinkers, prophets, and artists, including most of Leavis's stars,
who have participated in the development of transcendent idealism in the
West. This chapter will examine the works of some of the principal shapers
of this broader Great Tradition from the first through the seventeenth centuries, with particular reference to their roles in forming the values and ideas
on which a free society is based.

YEARS OF STRUGGLE

Christianity, the religion that grew up around the good news brought by
Jesus, did not have an easy time in its founding years, as we saw in chapter

195

five. Observing Paul's injunction to obey the "governing authorities" in all except matters of faith, leaders of the early church sought accommodation with the Roman state. The authorities were not receptive. They regarded the Christians' refusal to worship the emperor as both impious and dangerously subversive. Besides, the Christians made easy scapegoats for troubles within the empire. Brutal persecution followed.

Hardened by adversity, Christians began developing novel ideas about relations between religion and the state. Taking their cues from Jesus' distinction between "things that are Caesar's" and "things that are God's," and Paul's admonition to "be not conformed to this world," they gradually evolved truly revolutionary concepts of religious freedom. Early in the third century, tough old Tertullian, though he had no qualms about enforcing absolutist authoritarianism within the church, complained that the Roman state was "taking away religious liberty so that I may no longer worship according to my inclination, but am compelled to worship against it." Origen, the church's first systematic theologian, went further. Christians, he declared, "when tyrannized . . . by the devil, may form associations contrary to the devil's laws, against his power, to protect those whom they succeed in persuading to revolt against a government which is barbaric and despotic."[2]

Internally, the church was governed by bishops, "normally elected by presbyters [priests] and congregations, and, from the early second century, with the consensus of neighboring bishops." Presiding bishops arrived at decisions after wide consultation with other bishops, and discussion with presbyters and laity. The early church, the political scientist Antony Black writes, "generated the entirely new idea of a general consensus achievable by representatives of all peoples in an ecumenical council of bishops. . . . It was without precedent and turned out to be of central importance for the history of political thought and institutions."[3]

After Constantine declared tolerance for Christianity and other independent faiths in 313, followed by Thedosius's establishment of Christianity as the empire's official religion in 383, the church's political problems for a time seemed over. Ambrose, bishop of Milan, as earlier noted, projected a kind of partnership between church and state, under which the church would assure "undivided loyalty" to the state, and the state would impose religious orthodoxy on its subjects. Christianity seemed headed toward becoming a typical state-sponsored religion, with the church holding substantial temporal powers, but the state for that very reason finding it necessary to exercise political control over the church.

Events intervened. In 410, only thirteen years after the death of Ambrose, the city of Rome was sacked by Visigoths led by their warrior chief, Alaric. Barbarian hordes swept across Western Europe and toward the empire's outposts in North Africa. Newly founded Germanic kingdoms soon began springing up in what would become France, Spain, England, and even Italy.

In the East, the empire, based in Constantinople, would remain a vigorous political actor for many centuries. Even in the West, the forms of empire would be kept up for a while longer, but the authoritative reign of Roman administration and culture, it soon became evident, was gone forever. The church, recently allied with the empire, seemed to have cast its lot with a loser.

Not surprisingly, many who had benefited from the old Roman hegemony began blaming the empire's decline on its desertion of the pagan gods and official support for the previously persecuted faith. Dealing with this challenge, and designing a new role for the church under changed circumstances, fell to Ambrose's great successor, Augustine of Hippo—brought to Christianity in part by Ambrose's sermons, though the two were not personally close.

AUGUSTINE: DEFENDER OF THE FAITH

Augustine's life work went far beyond responding to the church's immediate social situation, and even beyond dealing with persistent doctrinal divisions within the church. Taking up themes set forth in the Gospels and Paul's epistles, he constructed a system of beliefs and ideas that became, at least in the West, a primary source for practically all subsequent formulations of transcendent idealism. He also, somewhat inconsistently, reinforced absolutist tendencies that became another part of the Christian and Western legacies.

Growing up in North Africa near the ancient city of Carthage, Augustine was instructed, though not baptized, in the faith of his devoutly Christian mother, Monica. From his middle-class father, Patricius, who remained a pagan until late in life, he acquired appreciation for the values of civic order and discipline. As a young student in Carthage, he was attracted by the Manichaean cult, based on the teachings of Mani, a Mesopotamian visionary executed by the Persians in 276 AD. Mani had portrayed human life as a struggle between absolute good and absolute evil, similar to the old Zoroastrian conflict between the Lord of Life and the Demon of the Lie. To promote the triumph of absolute good, Manichaeans believed, a chosen elite is justified in applying authoritarian methods. After a few years Augustine reacted against the moral bleakness and philosophic implausibility of the Manichaean vision, but he may have retained something of the Manichaeans's habit of absolutizing political issues.

An ambitious academic, Augustine moved at the age of about twenty-eight to Rome, and then on to Milan, which had become the seat of the imperial court. He continued to feel the tug of the religion of his mother, who joined him in Italy. Against this was balanced the delights of an ardent sex life. He kept a beautiful young mistress and fathered an illegitimate son. "Lord," he later recalled praying, "grant me chastity and continence, but not yet."[4]

In Milan, Augustine was impressed by the arguments and example of Ambrose. Final conversion, as related years later in his *Confessions*, came one afternoon in a Milanese garden where he heard a child's voice calling: "*Tolle, lege; tolle, lege.*" ("Take up and read.") He opened the New Testament epistles and read in Paul's letter to the Romans: "Put on the Lord Jesus Christ, and make no provision for the flesh, to gratify its desires."

Baptized by Ambrose, and blessed by the dying Monica, Augustine returned to his home in North Africa intending to take up a life of religious contemplation. Much to his dismay, he was soon inducted into the priesthood as assistant to the aged bishop of Hippo, near Carthage. When the bishop died in 404, Augustine, once more unwillingly, took his place. "He understood the contribution of desert monasticism to the church," Judith Herrin writes, "but abandoned the idea of going on a pilgrimage to Egypt for the more demanding task of administration in the strong but divided church of Africa."[5] For the next twenty-five years, usually in poor health, he not only carried out the pastoral and administrative duties of bishop, but also acted as civil judge, a job that went with his church office at that time, all the while turning out a huge volume of sermons and meditations, an autobiography, and his theological studies.

From his church in Hippo, Augustine witnessed the sack of Rome and the approach of barbarian raiding parties in North Africa. He shared the sentiments of doom and foreboding that engulfed his parishioners, who had relied on the security provided by Roman order. He may also have sensed that it would be a very long time before any comparable political structure would restore relative peace and stability to what had been the Roman world.

Augustine responded to this political catastrophe, and the social chaos that grew from it, with two conceptual formulations. First, he taught that the Kingdom of God proclaimed by Jesus far transcends any earthly government, including the Roman Empire or any of its successors. Though the church may utilize the services of civil government, its moral authority is in no way derived from association with the state. Second, he cast the church as the enduring and authoritative vessel of God's moral law on earth.

In claiming an authoritative role for the church, Augustine drew on the resources of Greek philosophy, particularly Plato, of which he had learned through reading the Neoplatonic works of the third-century Egyptian philosopher and mystic, Plotinus. As noted earlier, Plato strictly speaking was an absolutist, but the transcendence he hypothesized was so abstract and distant that his philosophy often became in practice a rationalization for the operation of secular authoritarian institutions. Augustine wedded Plato's metaphysic and some of his political ideas to Abraham's theistic God and the opportunity for personal salvation offered by Jesus.

While using the Platonic concept of a transcendent ideal world that sets standards for the material world of becoming, Augustine differed fundamentally with Plato's understanding of human nature. For Plato, bad behavior among humans was the result of ignorance or error rather than of temptation to commit evil within the human psyche. He would not have understood Paul's confession: "The good that I would do I do not; but the evil which I would not, that I do." Through collective social action guided by reason, Plato believed, humans can achieve a morally ideal community that he called the Republic. Augustine, in contrast, guided by the biblical concept of original sin, taught that all human communities, which he called the City of Man, are inherently corrupt, and inevitably must fall short of the transcendent ideal, which he called the City of God. For Augustine, the intellectual historian William Bouwsma writes, "the will is not, after all, an obedient servant of reason; it has energies and impulses of its own, and man is a far more mysterious animal than the philosophers are inclined to admit."[6]

Following Ambrose, Augustine accepted reliance by the church on the state to secure order and impose Christian orthodoxy in the City of Man. He supported suppression by the imperial government in North Africa of the Donatist sect, a locally popular Christian group that went beyond Catholic doctrine in preaching the attainability of social justice through human action. But he had no illusions about the motives or behavior of states left to their own devices. "Without justice," he wrote, "what are kingdoms but great robberies? For what are robberies themselves but little kingdoms?"[7]

The key to maintaining tolerable justice and order in the City of Man, Augustine argued, is moral tutelage of the state by the church. Without guidance from religion, "there is not any justice in any commonwealth whatsoever." Among its other offices, the church is charged with giving moral direction to both secular rulers and their subjects. "You [the church] teach kings to rule for the benefit of their peoples; and you it is who warn the people to be subservient to their kings." One institution, and one institution only, is equipped to carry out this tutelage: the Catholic Church governed from Rome, which Augustine called "the true mother of all Christians."[8]

Augustine, Reinhold Niebuhr observed, surrounded his identification of "the historic church" as God's earthly instrument "with all kinds of qualifications, which later Catholic ages did not have the prudence to maintain." Nevertheless, Niebuhr continued, Augustine viewed the church as being, "despite these qualifications, in some sense the Kingdom of God on earth."[9]

While contributing to the support of absolutism within Christianity, and through it in Western society and culture, Augustine at the same time formed a concept of the human person that became a principal foundation for later ideas of democracy and a free society—"a charter for human freedom and a release for the diverse possibilities of human creativity," as Bouwsma puts it. "Augustine," Charles Taylor writes, "was the first to make the first-person standpoint fundamental to our search for the truth." By writing the *Confessions* as a subjective religious memoir, the first of its kind, he elevated the significance of the individual self. He more or less discovered the idea of human will, which he identified as the instrument for carrying out Jesus' command to "love one another as I have loved you." Christian love, he made clear, was not classical *eros*. It is rather the harnessing of natural desires to the pursuit of transcendent ideals through the agency of personal will (*voluntas*). Justice requires goodness of will.[10]

Human good will, Augustine maintained, following Paul, was entirely dependent on God's grace. "Our wills," he wrote in *The City of God*, "have just so much power as God willed and foreknew that they should have." But this did not negate or diminish the dignity or responsibilities of human freedom: "It is not the case . . . that because God foreknew what would be in the power of our wills, there is for that reason nothing in our wills. For he who foreknew this did not foreknow nothing." The crucial Christian concepts of God's omnipotence and human free will were thus reconciled, as well as has ever been done.[11]

While upholding the sanctity of the individual person, Augustine did not regard salvation as a transaction simply between the individual and God. His vision was a social vision: "the heavenly city." The Stoic philosophers who were prominent in Rome "generally left the impression that social existence was a distraction from the good life, which could be satisfactorily pursued only by withdrawal from the world of men." Augustine, in contrast, "though still yearning for a contemplative life, insisted unequivocally on the obligations of the individual to society, obligations at once of duty, prudence, and love. . . . At the same time the conception of the blessed life opened up by his less intellectual vision of man was not for the few but accessible to all." In Augustine's view, the moral philosopher Jean Bethke Elshtain points out, human social responsibility is based in the first place on "the thread of commonality" that descends from God's special creation of Adam. This act of creation also supported human "individuality and plurality." God, Augustine wrote, created "one individual; but that did not mean that he was to remain alone, bereft of human society. God's intention was that in this way the unity of human society and the bonds of human sympathy should be more emphatically brought home to man, if men were bound together not merely by likeness in nature but also by feeling of kinship."[12]

Christians, who were already in a sense citizens of the heavenly city, Augustine held, had social responsibilities that went beyond those based on clan or civil relationships. Christians made "no scruple to obey the laws of the earthly city, whereby the things necessary for the maintenance of this mortal life are administered." The moral authority of the heavenly city, formed "by the love of God, even to contempt of self," was distinct, however, from the rule of the earthly city, formed "by love of self, even to contempt of God." Augustine's belief in humanity's fallen nature, Elshtain comments, led him to treat human politics as "a politics of limit." The pilgrim ethic, Augustine advised, should be guided by two simple rules: "first, to do no harm to anyone, and, secondly, to help everyone whenever possible."[13]

Deviating from earlier Christian pacifism, Augustine found war under some circumstances, mainly when it was the only way to save human lives, justified, even obligatory. "For the true follower of God even wars are peaceful if they are waged not out of greed or cruelty but for the sake of peace, to restrain the evildoers and assist the good." He was scornful, however, of the Romans' claim that their wars of conquest served the cause of peace. "Consider the scale of those wars, with all their slaughter of human beings, all the human blood that was shed." Even just wars, he warned, risk becoming "self-destroying." No nation can "abidingly rule over those whom it has subjugated by conquest."[14]

For Augustine, the heavenly city can never be fully, or even approximately, achieved through human means. But its attraction gives meaning and direction to human history. He rejected "the eternal round of the ancients," who viewed individuals and societies as bound by endless repetition of purposeless cycles.[15]

Facing the moral wasteland of late antiquity, Peter Brown writes, "Augustine never abandoned the hope against which he judged, ever more sadly, the present misery of the human race." Near the end of his long ministry, he asked: "When will full peace come to even one single person?" For Augustine, the answer was clear: "The time full peace comes to each is the time when peace in its fullness will have come to all the citizens of our Jerusalem."[16]

AQUINAS: THE TEMPLE OF REASON

The medieval church drew heavily on the absolutist aspects of Augustine's teaching. But it never gave up belief in the sanctity of each human person that it also inherited from Augustine, as well as from the Bible and other early church fathers.

By the thirteenth century, thriving commerce, coordinated political control over large territories, and cosmopolitan social and cultural life had begun to return to Western Europe. There had indeed been several earlier revivals, in comparison with which the burst of economic activity and social creativity that followed the Crusades was only the most buoyant and prolonged. The church, under aggressive papal leadership begun by Leo IX and Gregory VII, had broken out of subjugation to secular feudal overlords, and was asserting claims, not simply to independence, but to political dominance. Scholars associated with new religious orders were simultaneously questioning and reinvigorating Christian intellectual and cultural traditions.

Thomas Aquinas, born early in the thirteenth century to a family of southern Italian lesser nobility, achieved a powerful synthesis of traditional church teaching with formerly lost (to the West) Aristotelian doctrines and theories that had long been preserved and cultivated by Moslem scholars in the Middle East, and were being brought back by returning crusaders. As a young man Aquinas joined the recently founded Dominican order, a hotbed of new learning, and spent most of his formative years in the intellectually exciting atmosphere of the University of Paris. Though he retained and elaborated many of Augustine's arguments, he was regarded with suspicion by Augustinian traditionalists, who charged that, copying Aristotle, he placed too much trust in the human faculty of reason. Raised by academic mentors and succeeding popes to high places in the church's scholastic network, he fended off these criticisms, and devoted his career to constructing a comprehensive account of man and the universe, presided over by God, in which everything seems to fit.

While adhering to the biblical concept of original sin, Aquinas developed an intellectual outlook that is considerably more optimistic about human nature than that presented by Augustine. His gaze was fixed on the original perfection and harmony of God's creation before the fall, and he celebrated God's ultimate goodness more than His judgment. These qualities in his hugely influential writings, particularly his *Summa Theologiae*, contributed to the West's growing confidence in human capabilities, on which they no doubt also fed.

From Aristotle and also from the Roman Stoics, particularly Cicero, Aquinas derived the idea that humans are naturally subject to universal objective moral and ethical laws, which are anterior to the particular laws and customs of separate tribes or nations. Combined with the Christian idea of the human person, this classical doctrine of objective universal law produced the Western theory of natural law which has ever since played a major, though far from unchallenged, role in moral, legal, and constitutional doctrine.

Natural law, though it may be grasped without recourse to revelation, Aquinas maintained, was rooted in eternal law, "the rational governance of everything on the part of God." Whether the rules of "rational governance" are themselves determined by God, or whether these in some sense precede God's action, Aquinas does not make clear. Human laws, the actual laws of nations, if they are valid, are applications by human lawmakers to particular situations of the principles set forth by natural law. "Every human law has just so much of the nature of law as it is derived from the law of nature."[17]

Aquinas's association of human laws with God's own law strengthened the hand of the state in dealing with its subjects. Lawbreaking, under the natural law scheme, was not only criminal but also sinful, meriting eternal damnation. But it also had the effect, at least in theory, of subjecting the state itself to judgment by the church and its doctors, experts at interpreting God's law. "Kings," Aquinas wrote, "should be subject to priests."[18]

Belief in natural law opened the way to criticism of the state by its citizens and even to rejection of laws that are inherently unjust—contrary to nature's law. Aquinas declared that man was not bound to obey "a law that inflicts unjust hurt on its subjects . . . provided he avoid giving scandal or inflicting a more grievous hurt." He quoted Augustine: "A law that is unjust is considered to be no law at all." Movement toward a mighty defense for human rights was thereby launched, to be invoked much later by, among many others, Thomas Jefferson in his appeal at the start of the American Declaration of Independence to "the Laws of Nature and of Nature's God."[19]

Aquinas, by instinct and conviction, was a political conservative, in the Burkean sense. "Human law," he wrote, "should never be changed unless, in some way or other, the common weal be compensated according to the harm done in this respect." For Aquinas, Dino Bigongiari observes, "the worst of all laws is preferable to anarchy." He subscribed to many of the popular prejudices of his time, as in his definition of woman as a "deficient and misbegotten" man, whose shortcomings may result from being conceived under "a moist south wind."[20]

He loyally supported the prevailing political institution of kingship: "Government by one person is better than by many," because "provinces and cities that are not ruled by one person are torn by dissension and disputes without peace," while those ruled by "a single king enjoy peace, justice flourishes, and they delight in the abundance of wealth." A people oppressed by their ruler may under extreme circumstances depose their king; but "if the tyranny is not extreme it is better to tolerate a mild tyranny for a time rather than to take action against it that may bring on many dangers that are worse than the tyranny itself."[21]

All social authority, Aquinas maintained, comes ultimately from the pope, acting as God's surrogate on earth. "The authority exercised by rulers" was received "from the Pope and with it conditions and limitations on its use." Political forms are open to rational analysis and debate, but in the end the pope's authority is final: "In the Pope the secular power is joined to the spiritual. He holds the apex of both powers, spiritual and secular, by the will of Him who is Priest and King unto eternity, King of Kings, and Dominus Dominatum."[22]

Despite these endorsements of absolutist attitudes, Aquinas found in natural law principles on which institutions incorporating elements of democracy and espousing social justice would later be built. While upholding the moral authority of the church in politics, he opposed the theocratic impulses of the papacy in his time. In Aquinas's system, the pope "does not wield the two swords." The basis of his argument for democratic participation in social governance is communitarian, not individualistic: "The good of one man is not a final end but is directed toward the common good, and the good of a single household is ordered to the good of the state that is a perfect community." But he viewed the community as an assembly of human souls rather than as the property of the ruler: "The prince holds the power of legislating only so far as he represents the will of the people." Operationally, "all should have a share in the government. In this way peace is preserved among the people, and everyone loves the constitution." The "best form of polity" is a constitutional mixture, including, along with kingship and aristocracy, an element of "democracy—popular rule, in that the ruler can be chosen from the people and the people have the right to choose their rulers."[23]

Representative assemblies introduced for the first time in some local governments during the late thirteenth century were inspired in part by the teachings of Aquinas and other scholastics. Elected city councils often set forth their goals in explicit church language, as in a typical charter preamble: "All belonging to the friendship of the town have agreed by faith and sacrament that each will help the other as his brother in what is useful and honest."[24]

Aquinas felt at home in the growing urban enclaves within the thirteenth century West. Man, he asserted, is "naturally a towndweller," and rural life is "the result of misfortune." Such lifestyle preferences, however, did not lead him to give up the church's traditional suspicion of commerce. Like Aristotle, John Courtney Murray pointed out, Aquinas regarded "commercial dealings" as dangerous sources of "corruption." He restated Aristotle's justification for private property: "Every man is more careful to procure what is for himself alone than that which is common to many or to all; since each one would shirk the labor and leave to another that which concerns the community." An individual may legitimately seek "moderate profit" if he pursues "profit not as his goal but as a recompense for his labor." But Aquinas had little understanding of the functions of the market or of lending money at interest in promoting economic efficiency and growth. The price of a commodity was to be set, not by the impersonal operation of the marketplace, but by calculation of the "fair price" based on the labor that went into its production. "To receive usury for lending money," he wrote, "is unjust in itself, for something is sold that does not exist, and this results in an inequality which is contrary to justice." On the other hand, it was permissible for Christians in need of funds to obtain a loan through payment of "usury," which he did not distinguish from interest, to a man who "is a usurer by profession"—by which he meant Jews. The "standard commercial and financial practices of capitalism," Alasdair MacIntyre concludes, are "incompatible with Aquinas's conception of justice."[25]

Shortly before Christmas day in 1273, when he was forty-eight years old and working at the University of Naples near his birthplace, Aquinas suddenly announced that he could go no further with his still uncompleted *Summa* because, "All that I have written seems like straw to me." From accounts of troubles that he had speaking and walking, some modern scholars have guessed that he may have suffered a stroke. Earlier writers "attributed the change to a mystical experience of the inadequacy of the human mind to express the divine." Two months later, on his way to attend a church council in Lyons, he struck his head on a tree branch across the road, and died soon after.[26]

Some critics of the natural law approach formulated by Aquinas and his intellectual descendants argue that it is based on a teleological view of nature that is unsupported by physical evidence, and has served mainly to protect the privileges of historically dominant groups, such as males, whites, and heterosexuals. The purposeful universe of Aristotle and Aquinas is indeed hard to find in the vast array of seemingly chance relationships presented by modern physics and biology—though Albert Einstein continued to believe that "God does not play dice with the universe." And natural law theorists have often been prone to identify entrenched power structures and prejudices with the laws of nature. Nevertheless, human institutions that have endured for a very long time, such as the family, the community, private property, and organized religion, may reasonably be inferred to serve some permanent, or at least deeply imbedded, qualities in what may just as well be called "human nature." And some widely held human sentiments, such as love among parents and children, abhorrence of crime (to some extent culturally defined), and pity for persons in need, may fairly be said to embody, even if they do not create, authoritative moral standards.

The more serious danger in enthronement of natural law is, as the thirteenth-century Augustinians warned, that it tends to encourage reliance on reason alone as a means for determining ethical and legal norms. Aquinas himself, insisting on the dependence of natural law on divine law, did not take this step, nor have some other natural law theorists in various religious traditions. But since the seventeenth century in the West, the idea that ethics and jurisprudence form a kind of science, parallel to the natural sciences, has helped give rise to numerous attempts at deducing moral values purely through exercise of reason, as we saw in chapter eight. If such attempts are bound to fail, as Hume and his philosophic successors have argued and experience seems to show, the only effective standard for social behavior, lacking transcendent direction, becomes individual self-interest or collective force.

THE REFORMERS

Aquinas was canonized in 1323, less than fifty years after his death. His work, particularly the *Summa*, was soon recognized as the definitive statement of the medieval church's official worldview, comparable in its realm to the sublime cathedrals then rising all over Europe. Succeeding generations of scholastic philosophers, building on Aquinas's foundation, constructed a body of doctrine providing carefully reasoned answers to practically all conceivable questions on faith or morals.

Yet something was lost, as Aquinas himself perhaps recognized near the end of his life. The stones in the temple of discourse erected by the scholastics were so finely chiseled that they seemed at times to shut out the towering heavens above—wild, glorious, and ultimately beyond the grasp of human reason, as related by the Bible. This tension between the spiritual inspiration of the Bible and the intricate doctrinal system derived from it probably contributed more than indignation over corruption in the church hierarchy, or surrounding economic and social changes, to the forces of dissent that finally produced the Protestant Reformation. From the thirteenth century on, spiritually aroused individuals strained against the church's institutional and doctrinal rigidities. Their words and deeds sometimes generated movements for internal reform and renewal, but often set off clashes that shook both the civil and ecclesiastical worlds.

Luther

Martin Luther, the Augustinian monk whose defiance of the papacy at Wittenberg in 1517 triggered the breach from which there proved to be no return, regarded the apostle Paul's insistence that believers are saved "by the faith of Christ, and not by the works of the law" as the crucial lost key to Christian theology. On the basis of this revelation, he denounced the whole system of penances and indulgences through which the papacy was, among other things, financing construction of a new St. Peter's in Rome. The effect of Luther's teaching was elevation of the individual's personal relationship with God above obedience to the church as the foundation of Christian faith. Though he favored retention of much of the church's traditional structure and ritual, Luther justified these as instruments for personal salvation.

Luther did not intend that concentration on faith should cause indifference to works. Faith, he maintained, moves the individual to live a better life. "From faith flow forth love and joy in the Lord, and from love a cheerful, willing free spirit, disposed to serve our neighbor voluntarily, without taking into account any gratitude or ingratitude, praise or blame, gain or loss." Active faith can be expressed through a secular calling as well as through church observance. "You have Christ," he preached, "as your neighbor."[27]

The idea of a secular calling led Luther to approve trade and commerce in a framework of Christian ethics. "Buying and selling are necessary," he declared. "They cannot be dispensed with and can be practiced in a Christian manner." Luther, H. Richard Niebuhr observed, released Christians "from monasteries and the conventicles of the pious for service of their actual neighbors in the world through all the ordinary vocations of men."[28]

Spiritual individualism did not lead Luther to political radicalism. He seems by nature to have been a social conservative, and held, also following Paul, that "the powers that be are ordained by God." Beyond temperament and theology, he realized that to escape John Huss's fate in the previous century he needed the support of at least part of the German nobility, who for their own reasons were smarting under the exactions of the papacy. He strove to make clear that his religious innovations would strengthen rather than threaten existing local political power structures. For Aquinas's endorsement of "passive acceptance" of political "patriarchalism," Troeltsch commented, Luther substituted "positive obedience." When the German peasantry responded to what they took to be Luther's message, and rose in revolt in 1525, he urged the nobility to put down the rebellion with utmost severity. "If [an official] can punish and does not," he wrote in a widely circulated pamphlet, "even though the punishment consists of the taking of life and shedding of blood—then he is guilty of all the murder and evil which those fellows commit."[29]

Luther prescribed the "two swords" solution to the relationship between church and state: the state must be supreme, with church support, in the secular sphere; while the church reigns, with state backing, in the spiritual. Christians, he maintained, have a moral responsibility to perform civil duties. "If the activity of the state benefits Christianity, then true Christians not only may but must participate in it—whether as officials, judges, soldiers, or even hangmen."[30] Luther's doctrine planted the seeds for later ideas of broad-based citizen participation in public life, but it also undermined the church as a practical check on the state's coercive power. For many Lutherans, the state became the worldly embodiment of the organic ideal, opening the way to Hegel and beyond. Luther's crude anti-Semitism reinforced an animosity already all too common in Christian European cultures.

Before his death in 1546, Luther set the ideological direction of the Reformation and established one of its major denominations. He also produced a substantial body of hymns, including the electrifying "A Mighty Fortress Is Our God"—the first in a long series by writers such as Isaac Watts,

Charles Wesley, Julia Ward Howe, and James Russell Lowell that have become major conveyors of the Protestant spirit. "Music," Luther wrote, "is
a noble gift of God, next to theology"; and, more famously: "The devil has
no right to all the good tunes."[31]

Calvin

Luther's fellow reformer in Geneva, John Calvin, went much further in promoting comprehensive reconstitution of church and social life. Calvin
preached that religion should pervade the whole of secular as well as spiritual existence. "The God of Calvinism," Max Weber remarked, "demanded
of his believers not single good works, but a life of good works combined
into a unified system. There was no place for the very human Catholic cycle
of sin, repentance, atonement, followed by renewed sin."[32]

Born in 1509 and reared by middle-class parents within the Catholic
Church in France, Calvin in his early twenties was converted to Protestantism. Passing through Geneva in 1534, he was persuaded to stay on to help
lead the local chapter of the burgeoning Reformation. After brief expulsion
by the town council in 1538, he returned triumphantly to Geneva in 1541.
Though his only official position was moderator of the Geneva company of
pastors, he thereafter led and finally dominated the city's civil as well as
religious life until his death in 1564. His monumental *Institutes of the
Christian Religion*, first published in 1536 when he was only twenty-seven,
became the theological fountainhead of the Reformed branch of Protestantism. Besides promulgating doctrine, Calvin inspired and actively directed a
kind of Protestant International, supporting missions throughout Europe,
particularly in France, Germany, England, Scotland, and the Netherlands,
as well as Switzerland.

Calvin's view of the human lot in its natural state was predominantly
bleak: "unquiet, turbulent, miserable in numberless instances, and in no respect altogether happy." Rescue of humanity from this predicament, he was
certain, required intercession by a God with absolute power and majesty.
Calvin used the idea of natural law, but left no doubt that it was totally
subordinate to God's unconditioned will. For Calvin, the Reformation
scholar David Little points out, "there is no law above or outside God: 'God
is above the order of nature.' " God's presence, Calvin maintained, was
"not the empty, idle, and almost unconscious sort that the Sophists [his tag
for Catholic scholastics] imagine, but a watchful, effective, and active sort,
engaged in ceaseless activity."[33]

In Calvin's interpretation, the Bible teaches that a just God will not indis-
criminately save all human beings, scoundrels and fiends as well as saints.
But a God who is all powerful must have known from the start of creation,
indeed from before creation began, which humans will be saved and which

will be damned. From this conclusion follows Calvin's doctrine of the elect, for which he cites the precedent of Paul in his letter to the Ephesians: those chosen to be saved have been predestinated for their role through all eternity.[34]

The doctrine of predestinated election can generate authoritarian tendencies among the faithful. Calvin, however, like Augustine—and unlike Stoic or Oriental monists—believed in the reality of individual human will: "Ours is the mind, ours the will, ours the striving, which [God] directs toward the good." Though God knows from the start what the outcome of human choice will be, the individual has responsibility to choose between good and evil. Persons so endowed stand on equal footing before God, and require equal treatment under civil law.

Calvin's conception of human existence as a moral battleground, in which actions by individuals play a crucial role, has the effect of concentrating great significance on the events of everyday life. The inspiration of the Bible and the presence of the Holy Spirit, "even now upon earth, commences within us some prelude to the heavenly kingdom, and in this mortal and transitory life affords us some prelibations of immortal and incorruptible blessedness." Calvinism, the church historian Ralph Hancock writes, "represents not at all a repudiation of this world but an intensification of worldly activity, understood as redounding not only to the benefit of God's innocent natural creation but especially to the glory of God."[35]

To better perform their mortal pilgrimage, humans are entitled to make full use of all the resources of this world, including civil government. While Luther regarded temporal life as a secondary, though significant, moral sideshow to the real business of spiritual salvation, Calvin urged his followers to enter civil society to produce a "Holy Community." Civil government "is equally as necessary to mankind as bread and water, light and air, and far more excellent." Calvin, Troeltsch noted, "regards Family, State, Society, and the economy not as concessions to sin but as useful institutions to attack evil."[36]

Some later Protestants, such as the Dutch Arminians, the German Moravians (who traced their lineage to John Huss), and John Wesley, the founder of Methodism in eighteenth-century Britain and North America, rejected the elitist implications of the doctrine of the predestinated elect as inconsistent with God's love. In their interpretation of the Bible, salvation is available to all human beings, without constraints from predestination, though many do not know it. "I felt my heart strangely warmed," Wesley wrote, recalling his born-again experience at Aldergate in 1738. "I felt I did trust in Christ, Christ alone, for salvation; and an assurance was given me that he had taken away my sins, even mine, and saved me from the law of sin and death." Wesley and his followers, and like-minded evangelicals in other denominations, however, retained Calvin's emphasis on this-worldly discipline and enterprise as evidences of faith.

Like Luther, Calvin did not seek fights with established civil power structures. He strongly counseled his disciple John Knox, founder of Presbyterianism in Scotland, against supporting overthrow of the Catholic monarch, Mary, Queen of Scots. Again citing Paul, Calvin declared that: "a man of the worst character with sovereign power possesses divine authority."[37]

Calvin, however, perhaps because his political situation was more secure, went beyond Luther in approving action by elected civil magistrates to resist the power of tyrannical kings. "I affirm, that if they connive [with] kings in their oppression of their people, such forbearance involves the most nefarious perfidy because they fraudulently betray the liberty of the people, of which they know they have been appointed protectors by the ordination of God." He warned that respect for "the authority of governors" should "not seduce us from obedience to Him to whose will the desires of all kings ought to be subject, . . . to whose majesty all their sceptres ought to submit."[38]

Calvin saw merit in democracy: "It is an inestimable gift, when God gives to people the freedom to elect judges and magistrates." But he believed that in practice the most feasible form of government is "aristocracy, or a system compounded of aristocracy and democracy . . . where freedom is regulated with becoming moderation." He called for "equality before the law," but assumed the necessity for a "graduated" social structure, "clearly defined in terms of offices and obligations."[39]

Unlike Luther, Calvin rejected the hierarchical model for internal church governance because "the Holy Spirit willed men to beware of dreaming of a principality or lordship as the government of the church." He found "no comparison of heavenly and earthly hierarchies." He stipulated that ministers should be elected by the people. Ministers, following Calvin's guidance, began discussing the meaning of scripture with the laity. In celebration of the Lord's Supper, Christ's miraculous presence is found, not in the bread and wine as in the Catholic mass, only partly altered by Luther, but in the congregation itself, with all members, women as well as men, fully participating.[40]

Calvin's belief in the limitations of sinful humanity led him to question the competence of the humanly created state. At the same time, his conviction that God wills that most humans should spend their lives improving the material world directed him to approve the spirit of economic enterprise stirring in Europe. The Calvinist system, David Little observes, "ideally at least, sets economic behavior free from the all-encompassing control of the State. Vocational activity becomes by implication a special realm of Christian freedom. There, as in the Church, the Calvinist acts out in an ultimate way his role as the instrument of God's coming Kingdom."[41]

Human responsibility to "replenish the earth and subdue it," Calvin concluded, obliged humans to respect the laws of economics as well as other physical laws. He therefore substantially modified the medieval church's condemnation of usury. Christians, he held, should be free to lend and borrow money at interest so long as such transactions benefit the debtor as well as the creditor.[42]

The question of the exact relationship of Calvinism to the rise of capitalism has consumed the attention of historians in several generations.[43] Certainly there were other forces at work. But it can hardly be doubted that Calvin's authoritative endorsement played a major part in shaping the characters of bankers, merchants, and manufacturers who were transforming the economic life of Europe. Cancellation of the required observance of numerous saints' holidays freed up much time for productive labor in Protestant countries. Calvin himself urged the introduction of cloth and watch manufacturing in Geneva. Theodore Beza, his successor as head of the Geneva church, approved the establishment of the city's first investment bank.

At the same time, Calvin called on the economically successful to share their profits with those less fortunate. He cited Paul's counsel to the Romans: "We that are strong ought to bear the infirmities of the weak, and not to please ourselves."[44] John Wesley's injunction to "make all you can, save all you can, give all you can" is very much in the Calvinist spirit.

Calvin believed that the elect may know of their election through a sure spiritual intuition, linked to Luther's doctrine of salvation through faith. Some Calvinists, not so certain, were considerably tormented on this subject. But many were uplifted by conviction of God's favor, however undeserved. The effect on believers' personal and social morale was immense. Dedicated Calvinists felt "free to mold society to God's will." Such confidence could liberate human minds from the shackles of feudal society. It could also motivate ruthless social behavior, as represented by one of the banners flown by Oliver Cromwell's Puritan army in the English civil war of the 1640s: "Jesus Christ and No Quarter."[45]

Protestantism and Democracy

Partly because they usually were not favored by established monarchies, Calvin's successors generally moved more aggressively than he had to resist authoritarian governments and defend civil liberties. John Knox for a time followed Calvin's advice to steer clear of sedition, but finally told Queen Mary to her face: "If princes exceed their bounds, Madam, and go against that wherefore they should be obeyed, it is no doubt that they may be resisted, even by power"; and sanctioned the insurrection that brought her down.[46] After the St. Bartholomew's Day Massacre in France in 1572, during which mobs incited by the Catholic queen-mother and approved by the government slaughtered thousands of Huguenot Protestants, Beza lifted

Calvin's rule that even oppressive governments should normally be obeyed. Calvinist pastors began speaking of themselves as "tribunes of the people." Cromwell's Puritans defeated and beheaded Charles I in 1649, and for a short time instituted a republican Commonwealth in England.

The Dutch merchant class who dominated the Netherlands followed the more liberal strain of Calvinism, and implemented policies of religious toleration. The English Puritans, in contrast, while they held the upper hand, imposed their version of Calvinism with enthusiastic rigor. Cromwell declared freedom of conscience "a natural right of humanity" and supported some rights for dissenting sects, but the Commonwealth under his leadership maintained a Calvinist state church.

The relatively democratic internal governance of Reformed churches provided models for movement toward democracy in civil government. French Huguenots, making explicit what in Calvin was implicit, argued that: "government was instituted not merely as an element in God's sovereignty, but to guarantee the fundamental rights of the populace." The Pilgrims, a dissident Calvinist sect who preceded the Puritans to Massachusetts, agreed before landing to a democratic system of government that would "frame such just and equal laws, ordinances, acts, constitutions, and offices as shall be thought most meet and convenient for the general good of the Colony."[47]

As we saw in chapter six, Anabaptists on the left wing of the Reformation went far beyond Lutherans or Calvinists in promoting individualism in both religious and civil life, sometimes to the point of anarchy. But as they formed communities, Anabaptists too were driven by their religious beliefs to introduce elements of constitutional democracy. Since they were minorities almost everywhere, except in a few religious enclaves, Anabaptists were motivated to become particularly staunch defenders of religious liberty. The Anabaptist practice of adult baptism expressed the principle that membership in the religious community is through voluntary consent, with implications for civil society.

Whatever their limitations and shortcomings, and whatever their mutual animosities toward each other, Calvinists and Anabaptists jointly during the seventeenth and eighteenth centuries brought to England and its North American colonies political and social innovations that were genuinely revolutionary. Democracy found models in the ancient world, received philosophic inspiration from some Catholic scholastics and Renaissance humanists, and was fed by traditional institutions that went far back into the Middle Ages. But it was the Protestant reformers, particularly in England, who took the first substantive steps toward a new kind of political and social order. The English historian Christopher Dawson, himself a Catholic, has written: "In England the pure Calvinist tradition was united with that of the Anabaptists and independent sects to produce a new movement which was political as well as religious and which marks the first appearance of genuine democracy in the modern world. And in this revolutionary attempt . . . the Calvinist conception of the democratic aristocracy of saints provided the inspiration and the driving force."[48]

REMBRANDT: "FROM DARKNESS INTO LIGHT"

As we saw in chapter five, great artists of the late sixteenth and seventeenth centuries, such as Caravaggio, Bernini, Rubens, and Van Dyke, used some of their works to serve the Catholic Church's dynamic Counter-Reformation aimed at snuffing out Protestantism. Several of these, notably Rubens and Van Dyke, also lent their talents to glorification of the emerging breed of centralizing monarchies such as those of the Bourbons in France and the Stuarts in England. But the greatest of all baroque artists—and surely one of the five or six greatest artists of all time—was a Protestant and a republican: Rembrandt van Rijn.

Almost from the time he began painting in Amsterdam in the late 1620s, Rembrandt was seen by the Calvinist reformers of Holland as the bearer of their response to Rubens, based in nearby Antwerp, and other Catholic masters. As a young artist, Rembrandt was strongly influenced by Rubens—thirty years his senior. In the 1630s he executed several monumental portrayals of the crucifixion of Christ, approaching in power Rubens's dramatic *Elevation of the Cross* and *Descent from the Cross* painted for Antwerp cathedral. In his mature religious masterpieces, however, Rembrandt, like Durer an earlier conveyor of the Protestant spirit, turned to more intimate and inward-looking portrayals, set in scenes from everyday life. In his *Supper at Emmaus*, painted in 1648, Christ's taking of a meal after the resurrection with at first unknowing disciples is rendered all the more profound and mysterious by the realistic ordinariness of its setting.

Rembrandt returned in spirit—though certainly not in style—to aspects of the baroque prefigured in the previous century by Michelangelo, who, while creating heroic masterpieces of Christian art sponsored by the Catholic Church, had been deeply affected by a Protestant circle active in Rome. Like Michelangelo, Rembrandt sought to present the convergence between transcendence and material reality within the human soul. Also, like Michelangelo, he was particularly attracted by the characters and stories of the Old Testament.

Rembrandt's *Bathsheba*, painted in 1654, presents King David's paramour naked, preparing for her rendezvous with the king, while holding in her hand the letter in which David explains that he has secured their union by sending her husband Uriah to certain death in battle. Bathsheba's appearance of introspective contemplation conveys her awareness of her partnership in sin, her acceptance of God's judgment, and yet at the same time her faith in God's reconciling mercy.

In Rembrandt's time, the young Dutch republic was struggling desperately for its survival against the rapacious armies of the mighty Hapsburg Empire. In perhaps his greatest masterpiece, *The Night Watch*, painted in 1642, Rembrandt portrays the assembling republican militia, prepared to do battle in defense of freedom. *The Night Watch*, Simon Schama points out, is the perfect icon of "disciplined liberty."[49] It goes as far as any two-dimensional painting ever has in achieving three-dimensionality—indeed four-dimensionality, since it also moves in time. Hanging now in the Rijksmuseum in Amsterdam, it presents the stalwart republicans coming at us still—from the past into the future, "from darkness into light." It may usefully be compared to another great portrait of aroused revolutionaries, Delacroix's *Liberty Leading the People*, depicting Marianne ushering patriots to battle against the restored Bourbon monarchy in 1830. Delacroix's impassioned rebels are rising to destroy an ancient oppressor. Rembrandt's sober citizen-soldiers are making a new world. In the next century they will reassemble in Philadelphia for John Trumbull's painting of the signing of the American Declaration of Independence.

Rembrandt was never a very regular member of Amsterdam's Calvinist church. When he took to his bed, and impregnated, his housemaid, Hendrickje Stoffels, whom he had hired to take care of his young son after the death of his wife, the church council disowned him. (Hendrickje was probably in an early stage of pregnancy when she posed for Bathsheba.) In his final years, after his paintings had fallen out of fashion, and Hendrickje and their daughter had died, he seems not to have participated in formal religion. Yet his work, from beginning to end, is suffused with the spirit of Protestantism—matched in music in the next generation by the devoutly Lutheran Johann Sebastian Bach, who believed that his music was "an argument for the existence of God."[50]

For more than two centuries after Rembrandt and Bach, transcendent idealist values, often mixed with influences from other value systems, were transmitted by painters, composers, sculptors, poets, playwrights, novelists, and other creative artists of extraordinary genius—Catholics and Jews and Orthodox Christians and some of no particular religion as well as Protestants—whose honor roll includes, among others, Handel, Mozart, Goya, Jane Austen, Balzac, Melville, Tolstoy, Dostoyevski, Thomas Eakins, Mahler, T. S. Eliot, Matisse, Chagall, William Faulkner, Walker Percy, Andrew Wyeth, and Muriel Spark. More recently the running in the creative arts has gone much the other way, with most works expressing some variant or mixture of ecstasism, civil humanism, collectivism, or unbridled egoism. Whether, and when, the Great Tradition will again be fertile with outpourings of creative genius only the future will tell.

11

◇━━━◇

The American Founders, Locke, and the First Amendment

A patriot must be a religious man.

—John Adams

Can the liberties of a nation be thought secure when we have removed their only firm basis, a conviction in the minds of the people that these liberties are the gift of God?

—Thomas Jefferson

The values and ideas on which free societies are based were produced through long and complex development, fed by both religious and secular sources. This process did not reach political fruition in the West until the second half of the eighteenth century. There were important earlier trials in Venice, Florence, Switzerland, the Netherlands, England, and a few other places, but the first enduring experiment with republican government and constitutional democracy in the modern world was launched, though not fully realized, with the signing of the American Declaration of Independence in Philadelphia on July 4, 1776.

This chapter will examine the religious and other values on which the American experiment was founded, the influence on these of the philosophy of John Locke, and the intent of the American founders in placing religious liberty first among the Bill of Rights approved by the First Congress in 1789.

"THE LATTER-DAY GLORY"

Religion was a major motivating force in the migration of settlers to the English colonies in North America during the seventeenth and eighteenth centuries—a fact now carefully concealed from students in some American

215

public schools. This was particularly true of the founders of the Puritan colonies in New England (Massachusetts, Connecticut, and New Hampshire) but also to a great extent of the early settlers of Rhode Island, Pennsylvania, Maryland, and some of the southern colonies.

For the Puritans, America was the promised land of Protestantism. "We go," declared Francis Higginson, leading one of the first bands to the New World, "to practice the positive part of Church reformation, and propagate the gospel in America." The Puritans believed that their arrival in North America might be the prelude to Jesus' promised second coming. " 'Tis not unlikely," preached Jonathan Edwards, the great Puritan theologian and revivalist who helped launch the Great Awakening of the 1730s, "that this work of God's spirit, that is so extraordinary and wonderful, is the dawning, or at least a prelude, of that glorious work of God often foretold in scripture, when the progress and issue of it shall renew the world of mankind." Edwards believed he knew where the great work would commence: "The latter-day glory is probably to begin in America."[1]

The Puritans introduced institutions of democracy in the governance of their colonies, but with participation limited to church members. Even among church members, authority was expected to flow from the top down. John Winthrop, governor of the Massachusetts Bay colony, held that "the people should be seen and not heard, [because] the Community are not men of understanding." John Cotton, the colony's leading divine, agreed that a well-ordered commonwealth requires "obedience of the sons of men."

Neither Massachusetts nor the other Puritan colonies, however, approached the image of theocracy now sometimes attached to them. Church elders, indeed, were not eligible to serve as civil magistrates. As good Calvinists, John Coolidge points out, the Puritans insisted "the civil order is created by human will, and therefore has no claim to worship." According to George Armstrong Kelly, "Though the vested power of a harsh creed was pervasive, state and church were distinct, and the clergy had less control over politics than anywhere in Europe."[2]

Outside the Puritan colonies, government and custom were more tolerant of religious diversity and dissent. In adjacent Rhode Island, Roger Williams, a restless "Seeker" who had found the strictures of Massachusetts too confining, established a colony permitting complete freedom of religious worship. It welcomed many Baptists and Quakers, as well as antinomian Calvinists. Williams's primary goal, as Mark DeWolfe Howe has shown, was to create a social atmosphere favorable to the flowering of Christianity, which he believed was inconsistent with a state-imposed church. "The civil sword," Williams wrote, "may make a nation of hypocrites and anti-Christians, but not one true Christian."[3]

In the middle colonies, tolerance grew from varied origins. New York, taken from the Dutch by the English in 1664, was already pluralist in practice if not in law. The established Anglican Church had to share social space with Presbyterians, Dutch Calvinists, Lutherans, Catholics, and a small community of Jews exiled from Brazil. New Jersey, then sparsely populated, was predominantly Puritan and Quaker, but had no established church.

In Pennsylvania, William Penn launched his "Holy Experiment" in 1682, based on Quaker principles of religious liberty, under which no person acknowledging "one Almighty God . . . shall in any case be molested or prejudiced for his, or her conscientious persuasion or practice." Penn had no doubt of the need for a theistic basis for society: "If we are not governed by God, then we will be ruled by tyrants." But, like Williams, he was convinced that religion flourishes best in an environment of social freedom. Pennsylvania attracted religious refugees from all over Europe, including Baptists, Lutherans, Mennonites, Moravians, Catholics, and Jews, as well as Quakers. Delaware, also controlled by Penn and his family, maintained similar policies of inclusion.[4]

Cecilius Calvert, Lord Baltimore, a Catholic, founded Maryland in 1632 as a haven for fellow English Catholics threatened by religious persecution at home. In pursuit of this plan, Calvert pressured the Maryland assembly in 1649 into passing an Act of Toleration, granting religious freedom to all Christians. In the short term, Calvert's effort failed. In 1655 a Puritan colonial administration, backed by the Commonwealth in England, revoked the Act of Toleration and expelled all Catholic priests from the colony. After 1702, the Anglican Church was officially established, but Catholics remained more numerous and prominent than in any other colony. Charles Carroll of Carrollton, said to be the richest man in North America at that time, became the only Catholic to sign the Declaration of Independence, and his cousin, John Carroll, was consecrated in 1790 as the first Catholic bishop in the United States.

The four southern colonies, Virginia, North and South Carolina, and Georgia, all had established Anglican Churches, which included among their communicants many of the country squires who eventually gave leadership to the American Revolution. Tightly knit communities of Presbyterians, Baptists, Huguenots, and German pietists were given little trouble, though all were required to pay taxes supporting Anglican churches and schools.

Religion, specifically Protestant Christianity, whether or not established, shaped the entire social atmosphere of all the colonies right up until the Revolution. Full church membership, which entailed responsibilities we would now associate with elders, vestry, trustees, or deacons, was relatively small—about twenty percent of the total population. But the great majority of colonists regarded Christianity, indeed Puritanism, as the primary, perhaps only, source of their most important social and personal values. "Puritanism," writes the religious historian Sydney Ahlstrom, "provided the moral and religious background of fully 75 percent of the people who declared their independence in 1776 . . . 85 or 90 percent would not be an extravagant estimate."

The two most widely owned and read books among the colonists, Benjamin Franklin reported, were the Bible and John Bunyan's *Pilgrim's Progress*. According to T. J. Curry: "After a century and a half of colonial settlement in which the overwhelming majority of citizens were Protestants, a contemporary would in many instances have been hard put to define where Protestantism ended and secular life began." Henry May writes: "For most inhabitants of the American colonies in the eighteenth century, Calvinism was . . . in the position of laissez-faire in the mid-nineteenth century England or democracy in twentieth-century America." The intellectual historian Barry Alan Shain agrees: "America was a land shaped by the tenets of reformed-Protestant theology and spiritual or Christian liberty had an important role to play in this formation."[5]

"A MORAL AND RELIGIOUS PEOPLE"

The patriots of 1776 by no means regarded themselves as rebelling against their religious roots. Rather, they viewed their political actions as concrete expressions of their religious faith. America, the Boston firebrand Samuel Adams proclaimed, should become a "Christian Sparta." His equally impassioned colleague James Otis declared that acts passed by the English Parliament unsanctioned by God's law were "contrary to eternal truth, equity, and justice, and consequently void." Members of the Continental Congress who signed the Declaration of Independence in 1776 appealed to "the Laws of Nature and of Nature's God" to justify their cause. The "proclamations and other state papers of the Continental Congress," Edward Humphrey relates, "are so filled with Biblical phrases as to resemble Old Testament ecclesiastical documents." The first official flag of the new republic, authorized by George Washington in 1776, bore the motto: "An Appeal to Heaven." Looking back years later, John Adams wrote to Thomas Jefferson in 1813: "The *general Principles*, on which the Fathers achieved Independence, were . . . the Principles of Christianity, in which all" were united.[6]

All the principal founders, even those like Franklin and Jefferson who were personally skeptical, or even, in the case of Jefferson, at times hostile, toward religion, were convinced of the need for a religious basis for the moral values without which republican government could not succeed. Washington, as commander of the Revolutionary army and later as first president of the new United States, frequently called for public prayers and issued proclamations of thanksgiving addressed to "Almighty God." When he took the oath of office as President in 1789, he added the phrase, "so help me God"—a practice continued by all his successors. In his farewell address, delivered at the end of his second presidential term in 1796, Washington warned that, "whatever may be conceded to the influence of refined education on minds of peculiar structure" (probably a sarcastic reference to Jefferson, with whom his relationship had by then cooled), "reason and experience both forbid us to expect that national morality can prevail in exclusion of religion."[7]

John Adams declared: "Our constitution was made only for a moral and religious people. It is wholly inadequate to the government of any other." Franklin, at a tense moment at the Constitutional Convention, urged that daily sessions be started with prayer, following the practice of the Congress that wrote the Declaration of Independence. In 1802, Alexander Hamilton, probably largely for practical political reasons, proposed formation of a "Christian Constitutional Society," which he hoped would unite religious and economic conservatives.[8]

James Madison, the principal author of the Bill of Rights, had considered becoming a minister during his undergraduate years at Princeton in the early 1770s. He was probably the most personally religious of the major founders; from an early age he had defended religious liberty on religious grounds. In his celebrated *Memorial and Remonstrance* of 1784, through which he successfully opposed Patrick Henry's attempt to restore state financial support for church schools in Virginia after the Revolution, Madison made clear that his aim in advocating separation of church and state was not to protect the public or the state against religion, but to produce a social climate favorable to uncoerced faith. Imposition of Christianity by the state, he argued, "is a contradiction of the Christian religion itself." The example of established churches in Europe showed that state support for religion "is adverse to diffusion of the light of Christianity." Henry's proposed legislation, "instead of leveling as far as possible every obstacle to the victorious progress of truth, with an ignoble and unchristian timidity would circumscribe it, with a wall of defense, against the encroachment of error." Madison coupled the Calvinist view that "there is a degree of depravity in mankind which requires a certain degree of circumspection and distrust" with a cautiously hopeful belief that "there are other qualities in human nature which justify a certain portion of esteem and confidence"—the conception of human nature underlying the system of checks and balances that he, among others, incorporated into the federal Constitution.[9]

Even Jefferson, who became a unitarian and heartily disliked all forms of militant religion, Presbyterian as well as Catholic, acknowledged that a free society requires a public motivated by religious faith. Religion, he maintained, is "the alpha and omega of the moral law." During the Revolution, he became a founding member of the Calvinist Reformed Church in Charlottesville. As president, he appealed in his second inaugural for "the favor

of that Being in whose hands we are, who led our fathers, as Israel of old."
When, after leaving the White House, he laid out the University of Virginia
in Charlottesville, he proposed that the "religious sects of the state" should
be invited to "establish within, or adjacent to, the precincts of the University, schools for instruction in the religion of their own sect."[10]

Some of the founders, particularly Jefferson and Franklin, were attracted
by the watchmaker god of deism. For the most part, however, as Perry
Miller pointed out: "European deism was an exotic plant in America, which
never struck roots in the soil. 'Rationalism' was never so widespread as liberal historians, or those fascinated by Jefferson, have imagined. The basic
fact is that the Revolution had been preached to the masses as a religious
revival, and had the astounding fortune to succeed."

Only when we reach Thomas Paine, publicist for the American Revolution and later a member of the revolutionary assembly in France (from
which he narrowly escaped with his life), do we find a significant figure
openly hostile toward traditional Christianity. The Bible, Paine wrote in *The
Age of Reason*, "is a book of lies, wickedness, and blasphemy, for what can
be more blasphemous than to ascribe the wickedness of man to the orders
of the Almighty?" But even Paine called for belief in a deistic God who en-
forces social justice, and in a hereafter where the good are rewarded and the
evil punished.[11]

CLASSICAL MODELS

Some historians have identified classical humanism, whether received directly from the Greeks and Romans, or through the medium of a "republican" tradition hatched in Renaissance Florence, as an influence on the
founders' social beliefs at least equal to that of biblical Christianity. It is true
that many of the leading founders were well read in the classics and scoured
ancient writers for models for republican government. They studied Roman
history in particular for clues on how to avoid the failure of republican institutions. Their architecture, art, and rhetoric reflect their veneration for the
classical past. Jonathan Mayhew, the Boston pastor who helped organize
resistance to the British in the 1770s, listed Plato, Demosthenes, and Cicero
as authors who had instructed him in "the doctrines of civil liberty." John
Adams and Madison attributed their ideas on mixed government to Aristotle. Among other classical writers often cited were Plutarch, Cicero, Sal-
lust, Tacitus, and Seneca. "It was an obscure pamphleteer indeed," observes
Charles Mullett, "who could not muster at least one classical analogy or
one ancient precept." Jefferson, above all, traced much of his political thinking to the classical ideas and attitudes that he enshrined in Monticello.[12]

Most of the founders, however, looked to classical precedents more for structural form than for moral substance. Sam Adams's ideal of a *Christian Sparta* is representative of this distinction. "The classics of the ancient world are everywhere in the literature of the Revolution," the historian Bernard Bailyn writes, "but they are everywhere illustrative, not determinative of thought. They contributed a vivid vocabulary but not the logic or grammar of thought, a universally respected personification but not the source of political and social beliefs." Many rank-and-file patriots would probably have agreed with Benjamin Franklin that it was "better to bring from Italy a receipt for Parmesan cheese than copies of ancient historical inscriptions." Even among the intellectual elite, classical models often were viewed with candid skepticism. Madison criticized the leveling tendencies he associated with "the turbulent democracies of Greece." Hamilton pointed out that the supposedly democratic Pericles had brought on the Peloponnesian War, leading to Athens's ruin. John Adams was so exasperated by Plato that he decided that the *Republic* must have been intended as "a bitter satyre upon all republican government." Even Jefferson, while embracing the hedonistic individualism of Epicurean philosophy, found in "the teachings of Jesus . . . the necessary social complement to Epicurus."

Barry Shain reports that, after an extensive study of primary documents written by Americans during the Revolutionary era, he found that "the intellectual foundations I uncovered proved to be less classical or Renaissance republican and more Calvinist (or reformed Protestant) than I had anticipated." Americans of the founding generation, Shain writes, had "little interest in forming dialogic communities. . . . Most were more interested in possessing everlasting life through Christ's freely given grace by serving their religious and geographic communities and their families, and by attending to agricultural matters."[13]

LOCKE: PHILOSOPHER OF FREEDOM

The other great intellectual source of the Revolution was of course the eighteenth-century European Enlightenment. The American founders, however, for the most part got their version of the Enlightenment straight from its origins in the writings of John Locke and other English and Scottish political theorists of the late seventeenth and early eighteenth centuries, rather than from its later manifestations among the anti-clerical French *philosophes*.

Some readers will find it odd to think of Locke, a founder of British empiricism, as a transcendent idealist. It is true that Locke was not an idealist in the sense of believing in abstract universals, as conceived by Plato or Hegel. But, like Calvin—and like Rembrandt—he viewed the world of material reality as morally responsible to a transcendent creator. He was thus, in this sense, both an idealist and a realist.

Locke's father had been a captain in the Parliamentary army that over-threw Charles I in the 1640s. He was himself a warm supporter, mostly through his pen, of the Glorious Revolution of 1688 that deposed James I and made William and Mary constitutional monarchs. He firmly rejected the claim by the Stuarts and other defenders of the "divine right of kings" that monarchs inherit their authority directly from God's "positive dona-tion" to Adam.[14]

Like the slightly earlier English empiricist Thomas Hobbes, Locke rooted his epistemology in common-sense self-awareness and all that flows from it. "If anyone be so skeptical as to deny his own existence," he wrote, "let him, for me, enjoy his beloved happiness of being nothing, until hunger or some other pain convince him to the contrary." Unlike Hobbes, however, he placed the self within a larger moral context, established by God: "The eter-nal source of all being must also be the source and original of all power; and so this Eternal Being must also be the most powerful." The "materials of reason and knowledge," he maintained, must come from "experience," con-veyed through "sensation." He made two exceptions: knowledge of self comes through "intuition"; and knowledge of God through "demonstra-tion," by which he meant faith flowing from reflection on the very nature of being.[15]

Like his friend Sir Isaac Newton, Locke was attracted by the Arian ver-sion of Christianity, emphasizing the human side of Christ's nature. But he acknowledged Jesus Christ as "our Savior," who "dissipated this darkness; [and] made the one invisible true God known to the world." The American founders, therefore, experienced no cognitive disconnect between their adoption of Locke and their adherence to Christianity.[16]

God, in Locke's view, set forth in the second of his *Two Treatises on Gov-ernment,* published in 1690, "hath given the world to men in common." But God does not intend that men should simply enjoy the world as they have found it. Rather, following injunctions that go back to Adam, they are to *improve* the world: "He hath also given them reason to make use of it to the best advantage of life and convenience." Improvement, given human na-ture and the human condition, requires the institution of private property: "God, by commanding to subdue, gave authority to appropriate. And the condition of human life, which requires labor and materials to work on, necessarily introduces private possessions."[17]

From this kernel, Locke's entire theory of private property, which is the foundation of his belief in representative government, unfolds. "Though the earth and all inferior creatures be common to all men, yet every man has a property in his own person; this nobody has any right to but himself." When a man, through "the labor of the body and the work of his hands" improves what he finds in nature, "he hath mixed his labor with, and joined it to something that is his own, and thereby makes it his property."[18]

The right to private property is not unlimited. The individual can justly acquire property only up to the point "where there is enough, and as good left in common for others." And he has a moral right only to "as much as he can make use of to any advantage of life before it spoils." The first of these conditions probably seemed to pose no great problem in an age when the riches of the New World offered almost boundless opportunities for enterprise and expansion. The second might at first seem more restrictive, but the developing institutions of the marketplace provided the solution, inherited from the ancient Lydians: money. By exchanging the fruit of his labor for a "piece of metal, pleased with its color," Locke wrote, a man "might heap . . . up as much as he pleased." The rest, one might say, was capitalism. Not surprisingly, Locke was one of the first stockholders in the Bank of England, founded in 1694.[19]

Men form governments, Locke argues, "for the preservation of the property of all members of that society, as far as is possible." The type of government best equipped to achieve this end is not absolute monarchy of the kind proposed by Hobbes. The Hobbesian solution is "indeed inconsistent with civil society" because the unrestrained monarch, "corrupted with flattery, and armed with power," threatens every man's property. Locke (like Aquinas and Calvin) favored a mixed form of government, which he called a commonwealth, including a limited monarchy, an inherited nobility, and a democratically elected assembly.[20]

All men, Locke held, as common heirs to God's original covenant, are endowed with "equal rights [to] natural freedom, without being subjected to the will and authority of any other men." Equality before the law, however, is not inconsistent with substantial differences in social status or wealth: "Age or virtue may give men a just precedence; excellency of parts and merit may place others above the common level; birth may subject some, and alliance or benefit others, to pay an observance to those whom Nature, gratitude, or other respects may have made it due."[21]

Despite his concessions to the actual social and political conditions of seventeenth-century Britain, Locke believed that legitimate government must in the end be founded on the will of the majority of citizens, going back to the original compact among consenting individuals: "It is necessary the body should move the way the greatest force carries it, which is the consent of the majority; which the consent of every individual that united into it agreed that it should; and so every one is bound by that consent to be concluded by the majority."[22]

The founders took from Locke, along with his advocacy of personal freedom and private property, support for religious liberty—a principle in which they were also steeped by the teachings of Roger Williams and William Penn. Locke's *Letter Concerning Toleration*, published in 1689, is one of the great landmarks in the development of the Anglo-American doctrine of religious liberty. Possession of governmental authority, he argued, confers no control over religion, because "it appears not that God has ever given any such authority to one man over another as to compel anyone to his religion." Religion imposed through state coercion is not only oppressive but also ineffective because "though the rigor of laws and the force of penalties were capable to convince and change men's minds, yet would that not help at all to the salvation of their souls."[23]

Locke makes certain exceptions. Public practice of Islam is not to be tolerated because a devout Mohammedan "acknowledges himself bound to yield blind obedience to the Mufti of Constantinople." Atheism, too, cannot be permitted, because "promises, covenants and oaths, which are the bonds of human society, can have no hold upon an atheist." Atheists have no moral right to object, because, "seeking to undermine and destroy all religion, [they] can have no pretense of religion whereupon to challenge the privilege of toleration."

The basis for religious freedom, in other words, in Locke's view, as later in Madison's, rests ultimately on religion. Even those holding proscribed religious beliefs, however, should not be denied the rest of their civil liberties: "Neither Pagan nor Mahometan, nor Jew, ought to be excluded from the civil rights of the commonwealth because of his religion."[24]

Locke's foundation of human freedom on God's covenant with humanity establishes an inherent moral bond for community. His emphasis on the moral right of the individual to own property may obscure other essential sources of cooperative behavior, such as compassion and the right of all persons to share in benefits flowing from socially produced goods, and it may in practice open the door to egoism. But in Anglo-American cultures shaped by Lockean influence, it has also motivated enterprise and provided an effective check against intrusion into personal rights by the socially powerful or overweening government.

Some recent writers, uncomfortable with Locke's individualism and emphasis on private property, have tried to play down his influence on the American founders and build up that of the eighteenth-century Scottish philosopher, Francis Hutcheson.[25] A leading light in the Scottish Enlightenment that included Hume and Adam Smith, Hutcheson traced development of civilization more to an innate human "moral sense" than to the defense of private property.

Whatever attraction Hutcheson may have for liberal communitarians put off by Locke's focus on property, he provides no help for secularists eager to deny the religious sources of the American Revolution. Hutcheson, a Presbyterian minister, was if anything even more convinced than Locke of the need for a theistic basis for morals. "As to direct atheism," he wrote, "or denial of a moral providence, or of the obligations of the moral and social virtues, these indeed directly tend to hurt the state in its most important interests: and the persons who directly publish such tenets cannot well pretend any obligation in conscience to do so."[26]

In any case, Locke's preeminent influence can hardly be doubted. Jefferson, for instance, identified Locke as one of the three greatest men in human history (Newton and Francis Bacon being the other two).

RELIGIOUS LIBERTY

Having won independence and established a new nation, the American founders set about forming a government to implement their interests and ideals. After several years of experiment with the loosely structured system provided by the Articles of Confederation, they devised in 1787 the federal Constitution, under which, with a small body of amendments, the United States has been governed ever since.

As has often been pointed out, the Constitution, unlike the Declaration of Independence, makes no mention of God. (The story is told that Alexander Hamilton was berated by a Princeton professor on a sidewalk in Philadelphia a few days after the constitutional convention completed its work because the Princeton faculty were "greatly grieved that the Constitution has no recognition of God or the Christian religion." Hamilton replied: "I declare, we forgot it!") The only reference to religion in the original document is the Lockean prohibition that "no religious test shall ever be required as a qualification to any office or public trust under the United States." The delegates apparently concluded, after some discussion, that the exact relationship of government to religion was too thorny a subject to deal with during the time available.

Yet the conception of human nature and history underlying the Constitution is, as many historians have observed, profoundly Calvinist. The British historian and diplomat James Bryce wrote: "There is a hearty Puritanism in the view of human nature that pervades the instrument of 1787. It is the work of men who believed in original sin, and were resolved to leave open for transgressors no door which they could possibly shut." The framers of the Constitution, the intellectual historian Glenn Tinder points out, "were heirs of a Calvinist worldview in which both foundations and original sin were emphatically affirmed." The cultural Calvinism of the founders was neatly expressed by Madison in *Federalist 5*, written to promote ratification of the Constitution: "But what is government itself, but the greatest of all reflections on human nature? If men were angels, no government would be necessary."[27]

The first session of Congress in 1789, filling a gap left by the original framers, enacted the Bill of Rights, beginning with the religion clauses of the First Amendment: "Congress shall make no law respecting an establishment of religion, or prohibiting the free exercise thereof." (Congress sent to the states two procedural amendments prior to what we now have as the First Amendment, but these were never ratified.)

Contrary to the assumption underlying some recent Supreme Court decisions, the First Amendment is *not* "neutral" on the public value of religion, though it requires functional neutrality in administration. The First Amendment includes, along with the right to free exercise of religion, rights to free speech and a free press, and "the right of the people peaceably to assemble, and to petition the government for a redress of grievances." The framers clearly considered these latter rights not only as things good in themselves, or even as things precious, like such unspecified rights as the right to travel or the right of privacy. The framers regarded freedom of speech, freedom of the press, and freedom to assemble and petition as *necessary* to the conduct of republican government—as integral to the life of a free society. Without the exercise of free speech and a free press, without free assembly, there could be no republic.

It is reasonable to conclude that they placed the right to free exercise of religion, set forth in the very same sentence, in the same category. Free exercise of religion is not simply a good in itself—though for the great majority of them it surely was that—but also *one of the few essential goods on which all the other goods of a free society depend.*

Other actions by the First Congress that passed the Bill of Rights bear out this interpretation. With the approval of Madison and other framers, Congress appointed chaplains for the House and Senate, and authorized chaplains for the armed forces. It readopted the Northwest Ordinance of 1787, providing a charter of government for the Northwest Territories, which holds that "religion, morality, and knowledge, being necessary to good government and the happiness of mankind, schools and the means of learning shall forever be encouraged."[28]

The First Amendment, however, distinguishes between the good of religion and the other necessary goods that it protects. In the areas of speech and the press, government is left free to advocate its own opinions. But in the area of religion, government is not permitted to disseminate or promote views of its own. In part this distinction reflects realistic acceptance of pluralism. Although the people of the United States were still largely Protestant, there was an increasing variety of Protestant denominations, along with growing communities of Catholics and Jews. A national establishment was not politically feasible.

Beyond pragmatic adjustment, however, most of the framers were convinced, as Madison had argued in the *Memorial and Remonstrance*, and as Williams, Penn, and Locke also had taught, that establishment is bad for religion itself. The condition of established churches under the feudal polities of Europe showed, not only that forced religion violates human rights, but also that state-supported religion is likely to become too closely identified with and manipulated by a particular regime in the City of Man. The framers therefore accompanied the free exercise clause with the establishment clause, prohibiting, at the national level, a state-authorized church.

Just what the framers intended by the establishment clause has in recent years been exhaustively and heatedly debated. By limiting their prohibition to Congress, they left untouched the established churches still maintained by some of the states. But these turned out to be contrary to the spirit of the American ethos, and the last of them was disestablished by Massachusetts in 1833. Since the 1940s, the Supreme Court has held that the Fourteenth Amendment enacted at the end of the Civil War forbids state as well as national establishments.

On the more important question of what establishment entails, at whatever level, opinions have varied widely. Some of those who take what is called the accommodationist position argue that the framers meant no more than that such aid as government may give to religion must be distributed without discrimination among all religious bodies. But the framers were familiar with this kind of arrangement in the multiple establishments maintained by states like New York, Maryland, and South Carolina. It therefore was probably covered by what they meant by the term *establishment*. When they prohibited a national establishment, they must have meant to include it in their prohibition.

The extreme version of what is called the separationist position, though it has found its way into some Supreme Court decisions, seems to me no more plausible. In this view, the framers intended that government and public functions should be insulated against any contact with or acknowledgment of religion. This hardly squares with their adoption of the Northwest Ordinance, their appointment of chaplains, their approval of resolutions of prayer or thanksgiving to God, or the repeated assertions by most of them that a free society requires moral support and guidance from religion.

Strict separationists, on and off the Court, like to invoke Jefferson's "wall of separation" metaphor which comes from a letter written more than ten years after the First Amendment was passed.[29] It has appeared so often in Supreme Court opinions that many Americans probably think it is part of the Constitution. But Jefferson, as secretary of state, had little or no role in framing or enacting the First Amendment. His views on church-state issues were regarded by his contemporaries, even by his friend Madison, as extreme. His attitudes therefore are not very helpful in interpreting the establishment clause.

An influential modern school of constitutional experts, known in the law schools as "noninterpretivists" (because they regard interpreting the original meaning of the Constitution as irrelevant), seeks to avoid the whole question of what the framers intended by claiming that Supreme Court decisions should now be based mainly on the findings of current social science and advanced ethical theory. "The measuring rods," writes the judicial scholar Lawrence Friedman, "are very vague, very broad principles. These are attached loosely to phrases in the Constitution." This approach has been used to justify some of the Court's most controversial decisions, such as the 1973 ruling creating a constitutional right to abortion. In establishment clause cases, however, the Court, even when rendering extreme separationist decisions, has tended to concede the continuing relevance of what the framers had in mind.[30]

The explanation of what became the establishment clause given by Madison, the principal framer, when it was being debated in the House, was simply that "Congress should not establish a religion, and enforce the legal observation of it by law, nor compel men to worship God in any manner contrary to their conscience."[31] This makes clear that there shall be no state church (or churches), paid for at taxpayers' expense or requiring attendance at services (the hallmarks of European establishments); but suggests no exclusion of a good deal of interaction and mutual recognition between religion and government.

Linked with the public value of religion expressed by the free exercise clause, this interpretation of the establishment clause produces a standard that may be called *benevolent neutrality*: acknowledgment that the state, like all creation, is "under God," and therefore has a responsibility to foster a civic life hospitable to religion, but prohibits intervention by the state, direct or indirect, in the conduct of religious bodies, which means no financial support.[32]

This understanding of the religion clauses of the First Amendment is not mine alone. Give or take a few nuances, it was the understanding held by practically all Americans, including Supreme Court justices, during the first three-quarters of our national life—until the Court in the late 1940s began its wavering course toward exclusionism.[33] According to public opinion surveys, it is the understanding still held by most Americans today.

Alexis de Tocqueville, a visitor to the United States during the early nineteenth century, observed: "Religion in America takes no direct part in government, but it must be regarded as the first of their political institutions; for if it does not impart a taste for freedom, it facilitates the use of it. . . . I do not know whether all Americans have a sincere faith in their religion—for who can search the human heart?—but I am certain that they hold it to be indispensable to the maintenance of republican institutions."[34]

The United States has changed greatly since Tocqueville wrote; its boundaries and power have vastly expanded, its wealth enormously increased, its population changed from a still relatively homogeneous nation to one of the most heterogeneous on earth, its culture transformed by the mixed blessings of seemingly boundless technological innovation and invention. The question remains: Can its free institutions endure without support from the kind of religious roots Tocqueville described?

12

⟷

The Values Connection

Each individual has certain basic rights that are neither conferred nor derived from the state. To discover where they come from, it is necessary to move back behind the dim mist of eternity, for they are God-given.

—Martin Luther King Jr.

The American founders believed that republican government and a free society require moral foundations that must be based on religion. If they were right, civil society, entirely within the context of its social and political objectives—though, for believers, not only for those ends—has good reason to maintain a hospitable environment for religion. If they were wrong, religion may sensibly be treated as a purely private matter, and accorded no more attention or recognition than any other allowable taste. Were the founders right?

In the introductory chapter of this book, I suggested ten values as crucial moral foundations for a functioning free society. While many readers may argue over exactly which values should be included, most readers will probably accept most items on my proposed list, give or take a few additions or subtractions, as necessary motivators and guides for a healthy free society.

Here again is the list:

- Belief in the unique value and significance of each human life
- Maintenance of social order through the rule of law
- A sense of continuity, relating each individual life to human community and larger patterns in time and nature
- Belief in moral equality among all humans
- Pursuit of social justice
- Support for majority rule within a constitutional framework of government
- Tolerance of differences in behavior and belief

- A sense of personal and social honor
- Compassion for persons in trouble or need
- Moral realism respecting the human condition

Readers will note that these values are deemed necessary not only to make a free society "free," but also to maintain it as a "society," in the sense of a body able to operate and endure through time. None of these values, of course, are likely to be fully realized or dominant in any actual society— certainly including our own. But a society that does not recognize them as at least moral ideals is not likely to remain free over an extended period, and may not even survive.

Let us now test each of the value system families, reviewing some of the material examined in earlier chapters, as possible sources for these critical values.

SINGLE SOURCE VALUE SYSTEMS

Egoism, the first and perhaps most instinctual of the value system categories, provides the basis for a kind of existential freedom, but it is freedom only of each individual for himself or herself. All value is reduced to a standard of personal "tastes." Not even slavery is prohibited, from the point of view of the enslaver. Egoism's underlying conception of justice remains that set forth long ago by Thrasymachus: "Nothing else but the interest of the strong."

Egoism may motivate prudential arrangements among individuals as a means of escape from the "war of every man against every man," but it gives no support for such arrangements beyond what self-interest requires. Perhaps for the sake of a quiet life many individuals will be prepared under most circumstances to abide by generally approved laws, but for the more robust of spirit, lawbreaking will often seem natural. Even for the normally pacific, when personal interests are seriously at stake, abstract rules will not be constraining. Adoption of social rules by majority vote is simply an indicator of predominant force in numbers, useful to keep in mind but without moral authority. For thoroughgoing egoists, the real law is the law of the jungle: do to others as they would do to you, only do it first.

By the standard of egoism, values such as tolerance, honor, and compassion are no more than sentimental preferences. Those attracted by such qualities may feel free to pursue them, but persons otherwise inclined have no reason to defer to somebody else's personal tastes. Equality for egoists is simply a lowest common denominator among self-interested individuals. Ideas of spiritual continuity with a larger human community or nature as a whole are romantic myths.

Egoists are supreme social realists, if reality is judged solely in the light of self-interest. But it is a reality, as Hobbes remarked, that is likely to be nasty and brutish, if not always poor or short. The trick to successful egoism, as Voltaire pointed out, is to keep most people under the sway of traditional moral authority while oneself pursues selfish pleasures. In the contemporary world, under the scrutiny of mass communications media, this trick, at least for politicians, has become increasingly difficult.

Some egoists, as discussed in chapter two, argue that total reliance on self-interest can be reconciled with civilization in one of two ways: either through the assumption that human nature is so inherently benevolent that once the corrupting effects of such misguided social arrangements as capitalism and nationalism are eliminated, social harmony will automatically prevail; or, conversely, through the opposed conviction that unhampered competition among individuals guided solely by self-interest will just as automatically produce results beneficial to all. Evidence for either of these propositions is extremely weak.

Both civil humanism and the Judeo-Christian tradition, the two principal sources of public morality in the modern West, hold that self-interest is an inescapable and potentially creative part of the human condition. But self-interest liberated from the context of other values is likely to turn society into a joyless cockpit for ruthless struggle among anxious hedonists.

Collectivism, egoism's secular opposite, fills some of the social value needs that egoism scorns or regards as irrelevant. It cherishes community and motivates work for shared social goals. In its Rousseauian model, it may accept a form of democratic participation to determine, at least initially, the public will. It bases a kind of compassion on biological instinct. In the name of "socialist realism," it subjects personal tastes to the test of the actual, and cuts through artificial adornments that decorate traditional class-oriented societies.

Collectivism, however, provides no basis for any idea of freedom that includes individual self-determination. Its standard of justice is Plato's: "Remember, you are created for the sake of the whole, and not the whole for the sake of you." It may at times march under a banner of "equality," but, lacking a concept of individual rights, the equality it offers is only the equality of the hive. For the rule of law it substitutes the unbridled authority of the state. It derides traditional ideas of honor as cloaks for class privilege. For the sake of the collective, as Lenin said, all manners of "stratagem, ruse, illegal method" are justified. It may indulge differences in lifestyle, but holds no tolerance for political dissent.

Whatever its social achievements, therefore, collectivism in practice is the virtual antithesis of a free society. Attempts to identify collectivism with "freedom" through interpretation by "higher consciousness" are semantic tricks, perpetrated by ideological publicists who aim to overcome the attraction of freedom by defining it out of existence.

Monism, the third of the value system categories basing all value on a single source, generates deep spiritual senses of continuity with the human family and with nature itself. It supports belief in equality, not only among humans but among all living things. It is often tolerant of—because essentially indifferent to—competing belief systems.

At least in its purest form, however, monism regards many of the ideas and institutions on which a free society is based—individual rights, standards of justice, law courts, popular elections—and indeed the idea of a free society itself, as ephemeral illusions. Its goals are elsewhere, and it considers pursuit of a free society through human endeavor as one more distraction from achievement of spiritual tranquility.

Some predominantly monistic religions do support democratic values. India, where monistic ideas remain strong, is currently the world's most populous functioning democracy, with lively public debate and participation in politics. Democratic values and institutions in societies with powerful monistic traditions, however, are usually imports from other value systems, mainly civil humanist or transcendent idealist. It is probably not coincidental that such societies, even under formally democratic polities, are slow to achieve economic progress, and often continue to appear largely passive toward social injustices, such as abuse of women and ethnic violence, that are now generally regarded with moral abhorrence, though admittedly not completely overcome, in much of the West.

ABSOLUTISM AND ECSTASISM

Egoism, collectivism, and monism share a common recognition, at least in theory, of only a single source of legitimate value. The other four value system families recognize two, or, in the case of transcendent idealism, three, value sources as inherent realities of human existence.

Absolutism, tracing all value ultimately to transcendence but legitimizing rule in a fallen world by divinely chosen institutions, both sacred and temporal, goes even further than collectivism in promoting community and motivating collaborative effort for designated social goals. Through its supernatural perspective, absolutism creates bonds of continuity that may infuse social traditions with the grandeur of transcendent purpose. It provides divine sanction for the rule of law, as determined by chosen oracles. Its sense of social realism may be breathtakingly pragmatic. Compassion is generally treated as secondary to revealed moral law, but may be viewed as commendable when kept in its assigned place.

Like collectivism, however, absolutism provides little support for ideas justifying individual human rights. Its view of justice is whatever serves the goals and commands of divinely established authority. It shuns democratic participation and notions of equality except as propagandistic tools to strengthen public morality. It is particularly prone to the kind of triumphalism that relentlessly persecutes personal and public dissent.

Though both Western and Islamic forms of absolutism have sometimes evolved toward support for democratic institutions, through association with transcendent idealism, and though absolutist values may at times serve as useful checks against anarchistic tendencies in the modern world, unleavened absolutism remains a formidable adversary of social freedom.

Ecstasism, based on direct experience by the individual of transcendence, in contrast, is often identified in song and story, and sometimes in actual practice, with defense and extension of freedom. Even more than egoism, ecstasism exalts personal self-fulfillment, and may, in its ascetic form, motivate prodigious industry. Through art and literature, it has often conveyed continuity with idealized nature and human community. At crucial points in history, it has inspired valiant resistance against social oppression.

Ecstasism, however, fails the test of moral realism. Its vision of community is devoutly utopian. It creates no adequate structures for enduring political or economic collaboration among imperfect individuals under real-world conditions. Its reliance on the directives of irrational spiritual "happenings" breeds contempt for defined standards of law or justice and institutionalized systems of popular suffrage. In recent art, its concentration on purely personal expression has fostered isolation and division rather than spiritual enrichment. Its version of equality is flawed by its obsession with romantic self-fulfillment.

Ecstasism at times has been an invaluable friend to freedom. But its failures to respect the realities of human nature and the strictures of common human decency have all too often, as the experiences of the French Revolution and many successors have shown, opened the way for oppressions even worse than those it has valiantly struggled to overthrow.

THE SECULAR REPUBLIC

The essential moral resource needed to form and maintain a free society is a value system that legitimizes both individual rights and social responsibility, and establishes a coherent bond between the two. The value system categories so far covered by this chapter's review (except for monism, which claims to transcend the problem) provide powerful foundations for either rights or responsibility, but none creates an effective balance or a basis for prioritizing between the two. This is just the task that, as we saw in chapters seven and eight, civil humanism set out to accomplish.

During the last fourth of the twentieth century, civil humanism made considerable headway toward replacing religion as the principal foundation for moral values in much of the West, and even in many non-Western societies. Mass communications media, particularly television and movies, recently joined by the Internet, have everywhere become prime shapers of public values. Americans now watch an average of twenty-eight hours of television each week—much more contact than even most observant persons have with organized religion. These industries, while aiming much of their entertainment and advertising messages at egoist tastes among their audiences, generally employ civil humanism as their assumed moral backdrop. In most American public schools, civil humanism has become the semiofficial foundation for ethical and moral standards. In higher education, it shares influence with unadorned egoism. Much of psychological therapy and behavioral counseling is guided by values derived from some form of civil humanism. The so-called ethicists who thrive as consultants in both public and private sectors usually base their judgments on citations from civil humanist authorities.

The rise of civil humanism has been accompanied by a decline of many forms of traditional religion. In most European democracies, including Great Britain, Germany, and France, reported regular adult participation in organized religion has fallen below twenty percent. In Sweden, probably the most secularized country, only four percent of adults regularly attend religious services. Only in Ireland and Poland, in both of which the Catholic Church has been closely identified with the national spirit, has religion remained relatively strong; and in both of these, as national independence has become more secure, religious participation and influence have fallen.[1]

The United States is often presented as the great exception to the twentieth-century decline of religion in most of the West. It is true that by many statistical measures Americans remain a predominantly religious people. More than ninety percent tell pollsters they believe in God or "a Higher Power"; more than eighty percent regard themselves as Christians; and about sixty percent say that religion is "very important in their lives." Active participation in organized religion does not match these figures but still is higher than in most other Western democracies. A survey by the National Research Center in 1996 found twenty-five percent of adults reporting weekly attendance at religious services, and an additional twenty-two percent saying they attended at least once a month (both figures probably inflated by the tendency of many people to exaggerate their religious participation).[2]

Beneath these surface signs of relative strength, however, are many indications of decline. The share of Americans reporting weekly attendance at religious services fell by almost one-third from 1972 to 1996, and those reporting at least monthly attendance dropped by one-fifth.[3] Most mainline

Protestant denominations have suffered deep losses in both membership and contributions. Membership in the Roman Catholic Church, the nation's largest denomination, has grown only because of the large influx of immigrants from Latin America. Among groups descended from earlier immigrants from Europe, the Catholic Church, too, has been losing members, as well as priests and nuns.

Evangelical Protestant denominations and independent churches grew rapidly, in some cases spectacularly, during the 1970s and 1980s. Recent survey evidence, however, indicates that growth for most evangelical churches during the 1990s leveled off or even reversed, except among Asian-Americans. The sociologist Christian Smith writes that evangelicals, despite internal vitality, remain an "embattled" minority, whose "strategies of engagement . . . seem to undermine their best efforts at exerting an effective influence in the world."[4]

Jewish social action and fraternal groups are effective participants in American life, but most Jews have little formal contact with religion. Many people who continue to regard themselves as to some degree religious seem to have constructed personal belief systems only remotely related to traditional Christianity or Judaism (as in Robert Bellah's famous discovery of a California career woman named Sheila who had invented a vague religion of her own that she called "Sheilaism"). Religious observance among opinion-forming academic and media elites has dwindled to small fractions.[5]

Most Americans, surveying the world around them, conclude that the role of religion is declining. A Gallup poll in 1997 reported sixty percent believing "religion is losing influence" in the United States.[6]

The rising influence of civil humanism as a source of moral values in the West and the accompanying decline of traditional religion have taken place during a time of general peace and prosperity. Through advances by science and technology, life has grown longer, more comfortable, and more interesting for most Westerners.

For many in the West, however, these material improvements seem to a great extent hollow. Moral decay, reflected in historically high crime rates, broken families, births out of wedlock, illicit drug use, and public and private corruption, undermine senses of well-being and security. Declining participation in elections indicates at least complacency, and more likely, polls show, disillusion, with the operations of democracy.

Perhaps most important, life for many seems to have lost moral direction and meaning. A 1995 study by the Center for Survey Research at the University of Virginia found seventy percent of a national sample believing that American "moral and ethical standards" are in "strong or moderate decline." A 1998 survey by Market Research reports seventy-seven percent viewing "the country's morals and values pretty seriously off on the wrong track." Similar findings are posted by studies in most other Western democracies. The Harvard political theorist Peter Berkowitz concludes: "A growing discrepancy between liberal democracy's need for virtue and its supply of it is no idle hypothetical scenario, but rather an increasingly common description of the actual condition."[7]

Civil humanism gives rhetorical support to many of the key values, such as tolerance, freedom, equality, and community, on which a free society is based. Upon examination, however, these supports often turn out to be founded on moral and intellectual quicksand. Civil humanists cherish the unique value and dignity of each human person in the abstract, but often are quick to reach the threshold where the rights of individuals are subordinated to the interests of social groups. Traditions of law, justice, community, and honor come down, with Rorty and like-minded pragmatists, to personal tastes; or, with Rawls, in their ultimate foundations to assumed axioms. Civil humanists preach tolerance as an essential virtue, but in practice often allow it to be limited by strictures of "political correctness." While supporting both compassion and moral realism, civil humanism provides no deeper moral consciousness for resolving inevitable tensions between the two.

Even the sources of equality, a favorite value with many civil humanists, are surprisingly thin. Rawls, for instance, holds that humans are equal in the same sense that all points within a circle are equally within the circle—not a very persuasive argument against individuals asserting claims to preferred treatment on the basis of alleged personal or class superiority.[8]

Lacking objective standards for balancing individual rights with social need, civil humanism is chronically vulnerable to challenges by ideological forces based on value systems from the other two secular categories, egoism and collectivism. During the first half of the twentieth century, various forms of collectivism captured the loyalties of many in the West who had lost faith in both religion and secular liberalism. During the second half, as the disastrous effects of unchecked collectivism became clear, egoism seemed to hold stronger attraction for most of those to whom the moral claims of either religion or civil humanism had become unconvincing.

As the twenty-first century advances, and the likely tensions between entitlements promised by liberal welfare states and the willingness of individuals to be taxed become pressing, perhaps accompanied by growing social disorders, environmental crises, and threats of international terrorism, the hour of collectivism may come round again. None of these problems seems unsolvable, but their solutions will require more moral direction than can probably be provided by any known forms of civil humanism.

Civil humanists like to point out that some of the social problems now afflicting Western democracies appear more severe in the United States, where by statistical measures religion remains relatively strong, than in Western Europe where religion seems weak. All of the European democracies, however, even after recent immigration, are more culturally homogeneous than the United States. Moral traditions rooted in religion in these countries for a time retain considerable authority, though their spiritual source has weakened. "Swedes are probably the most unreligious people in Europe," a Swedish intellectual observes, "but you cannot understand this country at all unless you realize that our institutions, social practices, politics, and way of life are fundamentally shaped by our Lutheran heritage."[9]

There is considerable evidence that the moral capital so supplied is running thin. Most European countries are now catching up with, or even passing, the United States in problems such as crime, drug use, births out of wedlock, and social disaffection. Sweden, where rejection of religion has gone furthest, has the highest rate of births out of wedlock and one of the highest crime rates in Western Europe—both higher than the United States.[10]

Civil humanism clearly provides some individuals with a basis for personal morality and public ethics that gets them through many of life's difficult choices and strains, and helps make them good citizens. Civil humanist theorists and publicists have made—and no doubt will continue to make—valuable contributions to the development of democratic institutions and practices, both in the West and some non-Western countries, particularly India, Japan, and South Korea (though Christianity has also been an important factor in the democratization of South Korea).

For the great majority of human beings, however, civil humanism has never created sufficient foundations for either a good life or a decent society. Aristotle's version of civil humanism, John Finnis writes, fails to endow most people with "a good that one could love, personal in a way that one might imitate, a guide that one should follow, or a guarantor of anyone's practical reasonableness." The same can be said even more emphatically of the various models of civil humanism that descend from the secular Enlightenment.[11]

All of the belief system families so far reviewed in this chapter may supply values that keep at least the appearance of a free society working for a time. But no one of them, nor all together, are reliable sources for the values operating in concert that are needed for long-term survival of constitutional democracy or republican government.

THE TRANSCENDENT IMPERATIVE

Apart from civil humanism, the principal moral foundation for the development of free societies in the West has been the transcendent idealist strain within the Judeo-Christian tradition. Based on the stories and teachings of the Hebrew Bible and the New Testament, mixed with some aspects of classical humanism, Judeo-Christian beliefs and ideals provide objective authority and motivating inspiration for the key values needed to sustain a free society.

Transcendent idealism derives belief in the inherent sanctity and dignity of each human life from humanity's creation in God's image and God's love for each human person, as established in the book of Genesis, amplified by the Hebrew prophets, and taught by the New Testament. Maintenance of order through law, common to most civilized societies, is reinforced by God's directives to Moses on Mount Sinai. Continuity with human community is sanctified by God's successive covenants with the Hebrew patriarchs and through Jesus' "love commandment." Moral equality is founded on common origin of humankind in God's creation. Social justice is fired by the teachings of the Hebrew prophets and the New Testament's concern for the poor, joined by natural law theories developed by Aristotle and the Stoics. Democratic participation in government and majority rule are derived from universalization of the Greek concept of popular sovereignty. Tolerance, though threatened by absolutist variants of religion, is mandated by expressions of inclusion by some of the Hebrew prophets, Jesus, and Paul.[12] Honor, the quintessential classical virtue, is supported by the Ten Commandments. Compassion, in part expressing a natural human quality, is given moral force by the Hebrews' concern for "the stranger, the fatherless, and the widow," and Jesus' declaration that "as you have done to the least of these, you have done also to me." Moral realism descends from the biblical idea of original sin, and classical humanism's tough-minded portrayal of human nature.

Transcendent idealism provides no simple formulae for resolving tensions between some of these values, such as tolerance and community, or compassion and moral realism, but it does give a perspective for placing all values within a larger context of God's purpose and love.

Empirical research on the actual effects of religion on social and moral behavior in the United States has unfortunately been relatively scarce until recently. (A good deal is now underway.) Such research as exists, however, generally indicates that a strong presence of religion has a positive effect on social stability, personal morality, and volunteer participation in the institutions of civil society—all vital qualities for a successfully functioning free society. Some of the groups and places in which religion is strong are relatively insulated by affluence or location against some of the social troubles associated with urban modernity. But even in low-income neighborhoods of major metropolitan areas, according to the urbanologist John DiIulio, "it is increasingly clear . . . controlling for all relevant individual characteristics, such as race, gender, education, and family structure . . . that the presence of active religious institutions mediates crime by affecting the behavior of disadvantaged youth." A 1998 survey by the National Center on Addiction and Substance Abuse at Columbia University found that "teens who attend religious services regularly are far less likely to use drugs, know drug dealers, or have friends who smoke, drink, or do drugs than those who attend such services less than once a month." A review by Byron Johnson and David Larson of forty academic juvenile delinquency studies published between 1980 and 1997 produced substantial evidence that religion "had a beneficial impact on delinquency."[13]

Drug treatment and juvenile delinquent reform programs operated by "faith-based organizations" appear to have far higher rates of success than those run by purely secular institutions. Church-sponsored programs in Boston, Philadelphia, and Chicago, among other cities, have reportedly significantly reduced juvenile crime. "Convincing a drug addict or juvenile delinquent that Jesus loves him," Daniel P. Moloney argues, "is likely to be more successful than teaching him Aristotle or Kant." Amy Sherman reports the experience of a former addict who had repeatedly relapsed after treatment by government-sponsored recovery programs: "Those programs generally take addiction from you, but don't place anything within you. I need spiritual lifting."[14]

Teen Challenge, a Pentecostal ministry operating 130 programs for drug addicts and juvenile delinquents in forty-three states and Puerto Rico, has produced drug abstention rates of between 80 and 90 percent among former addicts seven years after exiting the program, according to independent scholarly studies, compared to 10 to 26 percent abstention rates among graduates of publicly funded secular programs six years after exiting. (Teen Challenge seeks no government funding. Nevertheless, the Texas Commission on Alcohol and Drug Abuse in 1995 threatened to revoke its license if it did not employ "certified dependency counselors," without regard for faith commitment. Elected in 1994, Texas Governor George W. Bush publicly supported Teen Challenge and appointed a state task force "to examine the benefits of faith-based self-help programs." Faced with this pressure, the state agency backed down.)[15]

Numerous faith-based Protestant, Catholic, and Jewish welfare agencies operate a vast array of soup kitchens, homeless shelters, hospitals, day care centers, senior citizen centers, hospice programs, income support programs, and residential homes, among other services. Many of these receive public funds, and some, as Charles Glenn has shown, play down the spiritual aspects of their missions to accommodate government regulation and secular opinion. Nevertheless, Stephen Monsma, who has extensively studied the operations of faith-based welfare services, concludes: "Religious associations have a basis on which to build a bond or sense of trust and to motivate persons with whom they are working that governmental and other secularly based agencies lack." The African-American social scholar and activist Glenn Loury writes: "Reports of successful efforts at reconstruction in ghetto communities invariably reveal a religious institution, or set of devout believers, at the center of the effort."[16]

These findings are consistent with the results of numerous studies brought together and analyzed in 1996 by the political scientist Guenter Lewy (himself an agnostic on religion). A 1995 study by a research team led by T. David Evans, cited by Lewy, discovered that "religious activities such as attending church, listening to religious broadcasts, and reading religious materials had a significant negative effect on adult criminality." John Cochran and Ronald Akers found in a 1989 study that "religiousness is inversely related to [juvenile] delinquent behavior." A study by the Rand Corporation tracking a nationally representative sample of high school women over two years concluded that negative responses on self-reported "religiousness" was "a strong predictor of subsequent single parenthood." A national survey on divorce by researchers at the City University of New York "revealed that those with no religious affiliation had the second highest rate of divorce (after Unitarians)." The famous *Connecticut Mutual Life Report on American Values in the 1980s* reported that "38 percent of the most religious Americans did volunteer work for a local organization, while only 6 percent of the least religious showed such involvement in their communities."

Of course all these studies, and others surveyed by Lewy, are subject to the methodological pitfalls and imperfections common to all science. Correlation does not prove causal relationship. But their cumulative effect is impressive. As Lewy sums up: "Without overstating the significance of these empirical findings, it is clear that true religiousness can be a force that moderates the crisis of modernity and wards off some of its deleterious effects."[17]

Probably a Judeo-Christian value system's most important contribution to the maintenance of a free society, as here defined, is its projection of a vision of objective meaning and purpose in human life, and underlying order in the universe, growing not from individual choice or social fiat, but from the very nature of reality revealed by religion. Without such a vision, humans appear inevitably drawn to either self-absorbed egoism or submission to a collective social will—or, in Hobbes's formulation, simultaneously to both! Either of these is profoundly incompatible, as ancient and recent history shows, not only with freedom, but ultimately with any kind of civilized existence as we have come to know it in the West. The maxim of the book of Proverbs is still accurate: "Where there is no vision, the people perish."[18]

Other belief systems, as we have seen, offer alternative visions of universal meaning, purpose, and order. But these either reject individual human rights (absolutism), or subvert necessary social authority (ecstasism), or inspire no commitment to making this world of mortal experience a somewhat better place (monism). "The priest and the prophet," Isaiah warned, may "err in vision and stumble in judgment."[19] Civil humanism, while supporting many of the values needed by a free society, provides no objective foundation on which these values can be based. Transcendent idealism, alone among the value system families, consistently sustains an internally coherent structure of values, including liberty, order, community, moral equality, social justice, public participation, tolerance, honor, compassion, and moral realism, from which a free society grows.

If this is so, civil government in a free society has within the limits of its purely civil objectives an important interest in providing a hospitable, though not coercive, social environment for the religious faiths on which transcendent idealism is based. The American founders, then, were right: democracy requires moral and spiritual values which for most people must come from religion.

FAITH IN ACTION

This conclusion leaves many questions of practical application unanswered. The devil, as the politicians like to say, is in the details.

Some of the arguments made by secularists and separationists against any form of public recognition or accommodation of religion carry considerable weight. Many are directed primarily against absolutist forms of religion. But almost all religions, as we have seen, include some absolutist strains. That was one of the reasons the founders included the establishment clause in the First Amendment.

Recognition of the dangers of absolutism, and of the somewhat more subtle lures of ecstasism, should lead religious bodies, particularly Christian churches in the United States which hold at least nominal allegiance from the overwhelming majority of citizens, to proceed with tact and civility in public life. But churches and other religious bodies cannot escape responsibility for moral or social conduct in the particular City of Man in which they happen to find themselves—no more than in Augustine's day.

Historically, some religious bodies have dealt with the perils and dilemmas that arise from involvement of religion with public life by passive acceptance of the prevailing political order. The grim consequences to which this choice may lead are shown by the shameful avoidance by many Christian churches of active resistance against, and even in some cases collaboration with, the rise of Nazism and fascism in Europe between the First and Second World Wars, and the willingness of some religious bodies to come to terms with communism during the postwar era. As Karl Barth said, the religious community is unavoidably obliged to "remind the state of those things of which it is unlikely to remind itself."[20]

This does not mean that the churches or other religious bodies should endorse or advocate particular ideologies or social blueprints. Champions of the current religious right in the United States who cast themselves as chief cheerleaders for unrestricted market capitalism dilute their moral message. Conservative Christian *Voter Guides* that make opposition to gun control or support for term limits "litmus tests of faith" are hardly biblically based.[21]

On the other side, liberal churchpersons who in the name of their churches uncritically support the social or political designs of secular liberalism are at least equally unwise. Churches that at their national conferences adopt detailed lists of social, economic, and foreign policy proposals, resembling political party platforms, often go outside their areas of moral competence and undermine their legitimacy with their own memberships.[22]

Almost all public issues have some moral component. But many issues involve ideological and technical questions on which persons holding similar moral values may reasonably disagree. Religious bodies have three primary missions in public life:

First, to plant and nurture values that, by shaping their members' social consciences, give moral direction to public policies, while recognizing that many of these policies also depend on technical and political judgments on which churches and other religious institutions are not likely to be expert;

Second, to provide or support direct service programs in education, health care, welfare assistance, and moral rehabilitation that meet spiritual as well as physical needs for persons of all ages;

And, third, after careful research, to take stands on public issues in which the moral component is central, such as abuse or exploitation of children, civil rights, persistent poverty, abortion, defense of families, help for the disabled, social bigotry, and political terrorism.

"The first social task of the church," the Protestant theologian Stanley Hauerwas writes, "is to be the church and thus help the world understand itself as world." Or as Pope John Paul II puts it: "In her social doctrine the Church does not propose a concrete political or economic model, but indicates the way, presents principles."[23]

Beyond these primary responsibilities, religious bodies may play useful and responsible roles on complex economic, social, and foreign policy issues as fact-gatherers, sponsors of public forums, and, when invited by contending parties, mediators. The more religious bodies avoid close identification or alignment with a particular party or faction in electoral politics, the more successful they are likely to be at maintaining the degree of trust in the larger community needed to support performance of these civically constructive roles.

Churches and other religious bodies should not be deterred from carrying out their moral responsibilities in public life by the charge, popular with many secularists and some religious leaders anxious not to offend secular political allies, that attempts to "legislate morality" are by their nature absolutist and in practice unfeasible. Even apart from laws against such crimes as murder and stealing, which obviously rest on moral principles, governments regularly legislate moral values, as in laws upholding civil rights or providing protections for persons with disabilities.

Concentration on shared values and avoidance of the absolutist side of religion should reduce but will never fully eliminate the socially divisive effects of differences over religion. Authentic religion arouses deep emotions in the human heart. These are likely to produce some tensions, whether in domestic politics, international relations, or the local schoolyard. Similarly, recognition of religion in civic ceremonies or public schools will inevitably offend some citizens. The question is whether the moral and social benefits that come from keeping religion a presence in the public square justify the expenditures of political will, ingenuity, and civility that are needed to maintain a welcoming arena for religion while minimizing its divisive effects.

Evidence and arguments have been presented in this book that no other value system can play the role traditionally performed by religious faith in forming and nurturing the moral values on which constitutional democracy and a free society depend. Value systems derived from other sources may at least temporarily fill this need for some individuals, but for the community at large, maintenance of a vital religious presence appears indispensable.

Just how this is to be done is best dealt with through pragmatic democratic adjustments at state and local levels. The key changes in direction now needed in the United States are removal of overreaching federal bans against expression of religious values in public schools and civil ceremonies; and impartial government funding of faith-based as well as secular service organizations, such as hospitals and welfare agencies, nondiscriminatingly ministering to public needs.

The Supreme Court in recent years has followed a wavering course with regard to religious expression in publicly supported institutions or activities. In 1990 the Court upheld the constitutionality of the Equal Access Act of 1984, through which Congress required that student-led religious groups should have the same rights to after-hours use of public school facilities as other extracurricular organizations.[24] In 1997 the Court, in the case of *Agostni v. Felton*, moved away from decisions in the 1980s that had barred use of public employees to give remedial instruction to handicapped students in faith-based schools. In 1998 the Court let stand, by an eight-to-one vote, a ruling by the Wisconsin Supreme Court approving a state voucher program for low-income families of students attending religious schools in Milwaukee.[25]

In the spring of 2000, however, the Court, by a six-to-three vote, declared unconstitutional the custom through which a student chosen by classmates at a Texas high school delivered a prayer over the public address system before football games. In the majority opinion, Justice John Paul Stevens held this practice to be "an improper majoritarian election of religion." Chief Justice William Rehnquist, in dissent, charged that Stevens's opinion "bristles with hostility to all things religious in public life."[26]

Predicting the effects of future Supreme Court appointments on religious expression issues is of course hazardous. History has shown that presidents do not always get what they expect when they nominate new justices. In the course of the 2000 national election campaign, the presidential candidates of both major parties emphasized their beliefs that religious faith should play a larger role in public life. How much these commitments will be reflected in future judicial appointments remains to be seen.

Public funding of welfare services provided by faith-based institutions was given an important boost by the—at first—little noticed Charitable Choice provision of the 1996 Welfare Reform Act. At least since the expansion of the welfare state in the 1930s, many faith-based service agencies, such as hospitals, welfare services, child care centers, and homeless shelters, have received substantial financial support from government. A survey by Stephen Monsma in 1996 found that 82 percent of mainline Protestant, 57 percent of evangelical Protestant, 91 percent of Catholic, and 17 percent of Jewish service agencies received more than 20 percent of their funding from government sources.[27]

The new Charitable Choice law, passed with bipartisan backing, requires that states using federal welfare funds not only can but must make financial support available to faith-based institutions on the same basis as offered to other nongovernmental social service providers. Religious organizations receiving such funds are specifically guaranteed "the right to maintain a religious environment by displaying religious art, scripture, religious apparel, and other symbols . . . [and] the right to use religious criteria in hiring, firing, and disciplining employees." Faith-based providers "may not discriminate against a beneficiary on the basis of religion, a religious belief, or the beneficiary's refusal to actively participate in religious practice."[28]

Many religious organizations, fearful that increased public funding will inevitably lead to more government regulation, have been wary in approaching Charitable Choice. Even without burdensome regulation, the sociologist of religion Robert Wuthnow has warned, involvement by faith-based institutions with government may tempt them to accept "subtle reorientation" of their "aims and aspirations."[29] In the fall of 2000, many questions about Charitable Choice, including its constitutionality, remained unsettled.

Monsma cogently argues, however, that experience has shown that "religious associations have a basis on which to build a bond or sense of trust and to motivate persons with whom they are working that government and other secularly based agencies lack."[30] Many of the social ills now afflicting the American people have major spiritual and moral dimensions. Partnership between government and religious institutions is justified in dealing with these problems, *with the essential proviso that the spiritual aspects of services provided by religious agencies are maintained and protected.*

Charitable Choice does nothing for religious elementary and secondary schools looking to publicly financed vouchers for families of their students to help support their operations. Public subsidization has long been available, Charles Glenn points out, for religious groups running day care or higher education institutions, but "this is far from being the case when it comes to K-12 schooling."[31] During the 1990s, as part of the general movement toward choice in education, Wisconsin, Ohio, and Puerto Rico enacted some form of state support for educational vouchers that may be used for religious schools chosen by parents. Despite fierce opposition from public school organizations and civil liberty groups, backing for voucher programs has proceeded on an upward trend. Many parents, concerned over deterioration of public schools in some areas, particularly large cities, as well as reacting against the virtual expulsion from public education of even such recognition of religiously founded teachings as posting of the Ten Commandments (which appear carved in stone above the dais of the United States Supreme Court), have turned or would like to turn to religious schools.

"Schools that have a religious character," Glenn argues, "are likely to be more effective at creating the sort of community that can support learning than are schools whose basis for attendance is the happenstance of geography." The possible loss of the democratizing and community-building roles, beside more purely educational functions, that public schools have traditionally performed in American life, is of major concern. It is good that children should get to know and make friends with fellow students from a variety of faiths within their schools. But if religion and religious expression continue to be treated in many public schools as bacilli potentially harmful to children, many parents will no doubt conclude that transmission of values they cherish, and believe are essential to America's future, can only be achieved through denominational schools, and support for public funding that makes this choice available to low-income as well as wealthy families will continue to grow.

The underlying argument of many secularists, though not of all strict separationists, against public recognition of religion is that religion involving transcendence is simply not credible in the modern world, informed by natural science and shaped by advanced technology. Religion, in this view, is the celebration of an illusion and the sooner we clean it out of our cultural belief systems the better.[32] If this view were held by a majority of citizens, religion—though still protected as a personal right—should be largely confined to private observance. No amount of social benefits could justify maintaining for purely civic purposes a view of life and the universe that most people regarded as fundamentally false. Moreover, in the not-very-long run, it would not work. Richard Niebuhr's warning is worth repeating: "Faith could not defend us if it believed that defense was its meaning."[33]

Fortunately, in the United States at least, this is not the case. A substantial majority of Americans currently retain belief in one of the faiths on which transcendent idealism is based. Under these circumstances, maintaining a hospitable public environment for religion is morally consistent and can be civically transforming. If the argument presented in this book is correct, even moderate secularists, perhaps a majority within the secular minority, should be prepared to approve the presence of religion—real religion, not some watered-down "civil religion" substitute—as a public good.

In some communities beliefs may now be so diverse that no generally acceptable accommodation of varying faiths and nonbeliefs is achievable. But in most, political skills and cooperative spirits can produce balanced recognition of differing religions and parallel secular beliefs represented within the community.

As George Washington said in his farewell address, "reason and experience both forbid us to expect" that for most people "national morality can prevail in exclusion of religious principle." If this is so, the necessary expenditures of will, imagination, and open-mindedness are surely worthwhile.

NOTES

CHAPTER 1

1. Adrian Karatnycky, "The 1999 Freedom House Survey," *Journal of Democracy* (January 2000).

2. *National Vital Statistics Reports* (Hyattsville, Md.: National Center for Health Statistics, 47, no. 18, 29 April 1999), table C, 8. In the late 1990s, the *number* of teen-age births declined, but the *share* of births out of wedlock continued at or near record highs.

3. Almost nine out of ten respondents to a *U.S. News & World Report* survey in 1996 said, "Boorish behavior is rampant." Steve Twomey, "Civil Offense," *Washington Post*, 6 June 1999.

4. Everett C. Ladd, "Everyday Life: How Are We Doing?" *Public Perspective* 10 (Storrs, Conn.: Roper Center, April 1999), 1.

5. The number of persons in prisons rose from an estimated half million in 1980 to more than 1.8 million in 1998. Bureau of the Census, *Statistical Abstract of the United States*, Washington, D.C.: 1997, table 313; "Prison Population Still Rising," *Washington Post*, 15 March 1999.

6. Immanuel Kant, "Toward a Perpetual Peace" in *Practical Philosophy*, trans. Mary V. Gregor (Cambridge: Cambridge Univ. Press, 1996), 334.

7. Francis Fukuyama, *Trust: The Social Virtues and the Creation of Prosperity* (New York: Free Press, 1996).

8. Samuel P. Huntington, *The Clash of Civilizations and the Remaking of World Order* (New York: Simon & Schuster, 1996).

9. H. Richard Niebuhr, *The Kingdom of God in America* (New York: Harper, 1937), 12.

CHAPTER 2

1. Nicholas Humphrey, *The Inner Eye* (London: Faber & Faber, 1986); John Jaynes, *The Origins of Consciousness in the Breakdown of the Bicameral Mind* (Boston: Houghton Mifflin, 1976).

2. Daniel C. Dennett, *Consciousness Explained* (Boston: Little, Brown, 1991), 416; Edward O. Wilson, *On Human Nature* (Cambridge, Mass.: Harvard Univ. Press, 1978), 75.

3. Charles Taylor, *Sources of the Self: The Making of the Modern Identity* (Cambridge, Mass.: Harvard Univ. Press, 1989), 112.

4. "The Epic of Gilgamesh," in *Hastings Encyclopedia of Religion and Ethics*, trans. A. Jeremia (New York: Scribner, 1928), 5:447.

5. Alasdair MacIntyre, *Whose Justice? Whose Rationality?* (Notre Dame, Ind.: Univ. of Notre Dame Press, 1988), 49; Snell quoted in Bernard Williams, *Shame and Necessity* (Berkeley: Univ. of California Press, 1993), 23; Yvon Garlan, *Slavery in Ancient Greece*, trans. Janet Lloyd (Ithaca, N.Y.: Cornell Univ. Press, 1988).

6. Hesiod, *Works and Days*, trans. David W. Tandy and Walter C. Neale (Berkeley: Univ. of California Press, 1996), 53, 73.

7. Archilochus, "Be Still, My Soul," trans. C. M. Bowra; Alcaeus, "Immortalia Ne Speres," trans. C. M. Bowra; Sappho, "To a Bride," trans. Werner Jaeger, in *The Ideals of Greek Culture* (New York: Oxford Univ. Press, 1945), 1:43.

8. Friedrich Nietzsche, *The Birth of Tragedy*, trans. Walter Kaufman (New York: Random House, 1967), 13.

9. MacIntyre, *Whose Justice?* 43.

10. Plato, *The Republic*, trans. Benjamin Jowett (New York: Scribner, 1928), 1:338C1; Plato, "Gorgias," in *Collected Dialogues*, trans. W. D. Woodhead, ed. Edith Hamilton and Huntingdon Cairns (New York: Pantheon, 1961), 483D2.

11. MacIntyre, *Whose Justice?* 65.

12. Euripides, "The Bacchae," in *Complete Greek Tragedies*, trans. William Arrowsmith, ed. David Greene and Richard Lattimore (Chicago: University of Chicago Press, 1958) 4:581.

13. Euripides, "Hecuba," in *Complete Greek Tragedies*, trans. William Arrowsmith, 3:505.

14. Euripides, "Medea," in *Complete Greek Tragedies*, trans. Rex Warner, 3:73; "Heracles," in *Complete Greek Tragedies*, trans. William Arrowsmith, 3:293.

15. Demosthenes, *Against Aristocrates*, trans. J. H. Vines (Cambridge, Mass.: Harvard Univ. Press, 1955), 206.

16. Euripides, "Orestes," in *Complete Greek Tragedies*, trans. William Arrowsmith, 4:250.

17. *The Philosophy of Epicurus*, trans. George C. Trodach (Evanston, Ill.: Northwestern Univ. Press, 1963); "Leading Doctrines," 201; "Letter to Menoeceus," 179; "Aphorisms," 206.

18. Jacob Burckhardt, *The Civilization of the Renaissance in Italy*, trans. S. G. C. Middlemore (New York: Random House, 1954), 100.

19. J. G. A. Pocock, *The Machiavellian Moment* (Princeton, N.J.: Princeton Univ. Press, 1975), 202.

20. Niccolo Machiavelli, *Discourses*, trans. Christine E. Detmold (New York: Scribner, 1950), 41; Machiavelli, *The Prince*, trans. Robert M. Adams (New York: Norton, 1950), chap. 18, 50–51.

21. Michel de Montaigne, "Apology for Raymond Sebond," in *Complete Works*, trans. Donald M. Frame (Stanford, Calif.: Stanford Univ. Press, 1957), 318–457.

22. Alan MacFarlane, *The Origins of English Individualism* (New York: Cambridge Univ. Press, 1978), 80–102; James Q. Wilson, *The Moral Sense* (New York: Free Press, 1993), 200–207.

23. Thomas Hobbes, "Leviathan," in *Complete Works* (London: Routledge/ Thoemmes Press, 1994), chap. 17, 156; *De Cive* (Oxford: Oxford Univ. Press, 1983), preface.

24. Hobbes, "Leviathan," chap. 6, 41; chap. 13, 113.

25. Hobbes, "Leviathan," chap. 13, 110; chap. 16, 158.

26. J.B. Schneewind, *The Invention of Autonomy* (Cambridge: Cambridge Univ. Press, 1998), 97.

27. Hobbes, "Leviathan," chap. 16, 41. Peter Berkowitz, *Virtue and the Making of Modern Liberalism* (Princeton, N.J.: Princeton Univ. Press, 1999), 40–73, argues that Hobbes's system requires virtue to produce the clarity of mind needed to grasp the human situation, to motivate subjects to keep their bargain with the sovereign once they have agreed to it, and to motivate the sovereign to benevolence. What Berkowitz actually reveals, I think, are inconsistencies in Hobbes's thought—some of which were pointed out by John Locke.

28. Trenchard and Gordon quoted in Bernard Bailyn, *Origins of American Politics* (New York: Knopf, 1976), 41; Sir William Blackstone, *Commentaries on the Law of England* (London: Strahan and Woodfall, 1791), introduction, section 2; Turgot quoted in Robert Nisbet, *History of the Idea of Progress* (New York: Basic, 1980), 180.

29. Roger Chartier, "Forms of Privatization," in *A History of Private Life* (Cambridge, Mass.: Harvard Univ. Press, 1989), 3:165.

30. Quoted in Taylor, *Self*, 325.

31. Jerry Z. Muller, "Adam Smith as Social Policy Analyst," paper presented at American Enterprise Institute conference on Religion and Economics, Washington, D.C., 17 December 1992.

32. Adam Smith, *The Theory of Moral Sentiments* (Oxford: Clarendon Press, 1976), 1.

33. Adam Smith, *An Inquiry into the Nature and Causes of the Wealth of Nations* (Oxford: Clarendon Press, 1976), book 1, chap. 2, 26; chap. 10, 145.

34. Smith, *An Inquiry*, book 4, chap. 2, 456.

35. Sade quoted in Taylor, *Self*, 336; Michel Foucault, *Madness and Civilization*, trans. Richard Howard (New York: Random House, 1978), 210.

36. Stirner quoted in Bernard Williams, *Ethics and the Limits of Philosophy* (Cambridge, Mass.: Harvard Univ. Press, 1985), 62.

37. Friedrich Nietzsche, *Thus Spoke Zarathustra*, trans. W. Kaufmann (New York: Viking, 1966), 20, 35.

38. Friedrich A. von Hayek, *The Constitution of Liberty* (Chicago: Univ. of Chicago Press, 1960), 303.

39. Milton Friedman, *Capitalism and Freedom* (Chicago: Univ. of Chicago Press, 1962), 2, 133.

40. Friedman, *Capitalism and Freedom*, 119.

41. Robert Nozick, *Anarchy, State, and Utopia* (New York: Basic 1974), 458.

42. Nozick, *Anarchy, State, and Utopia*, 185. A compressed version of the sepa-

rated Robinson Crusoe parable was presented by Milton Friedman in *Capitalism and Freedom*, 165.

43. Herbert Marcuse, *Eros and Civilization* (New York: Vintage, 1962), 205; Jerry Rubin, *Do It! Scenarios of the Revolution* (New York: Simon & Schuster, 1970), 98; Sartre quoted in Noel O'Sullivan, *Conservatism* (London: J. M. Dent & Sons, 1976), 130.

44. MacIntyre, *Whose Justice?* 339; Ronald Dworkin, *Taking Rights Seriously* (Cambridge, Mass.: Harvard Univ. Press, 1977), 269; Alan E. Guskin (president, Antioch College), "The Rules of Antioch," *Washington Post*, 10 November 1993; John Rawls, *A Theory of Justice* (Cambridge, Mass.: Harvard Univ. Press, 1971), 13.

45. C. B. MacPherson, *The Political Theory of Possessive Individualism* (Oxford: Oxford Univ. Press, 1962), 1–4; Charles A. Reich, *The Greening of America* (New York: Random House, 1970), 205; Ernest Mandel, *Marxist Economic Theory* (London: Merlin, 1968), 668; Marcuse, *Eros*, 138.

46. Herbert Marcuse, *One-Dimensional Man* (Boston: Beacon Press, 1964), 2.

47. "Youth Say TV Shapes Values," *Washington Post*, 27 February 1995.

48. Kevin Merida and Richard Leiby, "When Death Imitates Art," *Washington Post*, 22 April 1999.

49. Martha Bayles, *Hole in Our Soul: The Loss of Beauty and Meaning in American Popular Music* (New York: Free Press, 1994), 12; "Pop Culture and Drugs," *Wall Street Journal*, 26 July 1995.

50. Peter Levine, *Nietzsche and the Modern Crisis in the Humanities* (Albany: State Univ. of New York Press, 1995), 174; Still quoted in Robert Hughes, *The Shock of the New* (New York: Knopf, 1995), 316; Foucault, *Madness*, 282; Robert W. Corrigan, *Masterpieces of the Modern German Theatre* (New York: Collier, 1967), 222.

51. Popper quoted in Richard Bernstein, *Beyond Objectivism and Relativism* (Philadelphia: Univ. of Pennsylvania Press, 1983), 4.

52. Horkheimer quoted in Jurgen Habermas, *The Theory of Communicative Action*, trans. Thomas McCarthy (Boston: Beacon Press, 1984), 349.

53. Jean Bethke Elshtain, *Augustine and the Limits of Politics* (Notre Dame, Ind.: Univ. of Notre Dame Press, 1995), 84.

54. Michel Foucault, "Nietzsche, Genealogy, History," in *Language, Counter-Memory, Practice*, ed. Donald F. Bouchaud (Ithaca, N.Y.: Cornell Univ. Press, 1971), 153.

CHAPTER 3

1. Aristotle, "Politics," in *Complete Works*, trans. Benjamin Jowett, ed. Jonathan Barnes (Princeton, N.J.: Princeton Univ. Press, 1984), book 1, chap. 2, 1253A29; Charles Darwin, *The Descent of Man, and Selection in Relation to Sex* (Princeton, N.J.: Princeton Univ. Press, 1981), chap. 31.

2. James Q. Wilson, *The Moral Sense* (New York: Free Press, 1993), 49, 139.

3. Clifford Geertz, *The Interpretation of Cultures* (New York: Basic, 1973), 49;

Jurgen Habermas, *The Theory of Communicative Action*, trans. Thomas McCarthy (Boston, Mass.: Beacon Press, 1984), 1:325–326, 2:259; Alasdair MacIntyre, *After Virtue: A Study in Moral Theory* (Notre Dame, Ind.: Univ. of Notre Dame Press, 1981).

4. Peter J. Wilson, *Man, the Promising Primate* (New Haven, Conn.: Yale Univ. Press, 1980), 45–69; E. R. Service, *Origins of the State and Civilization: The Process of Cultural Evolution* (New York: Norton, 1975), 1.

5. M. D. Sahlins, *Tribesmen* (Englewood Cliffs, N.J.: Prentice-Hall, 1968), 2.

6. Peter Farb, *Man's Rise to Civilization* (New York: Dutton, 1968), 137; Service, *Origins*, 16.

7. William H. McNeill, *The Rise of the West: A History of the Human Community* (Chicago, Ill.: Univ. of Chicago Press, 1963), 43. The name Menes comes to us from the third-century BC Egyptian historian Manetho. Modern scholars generally identify him with the ruler Narmer.

8. John Keegan, *A History of Warfare*, (New York: Knopf, 1993), 122; J. M. Roberts, *The Pelican History of the World* (London: Pelican, 1987), 51.

9. Franz Oppenheimer, *The State*, trans. John Gitterman (New York: Free Life, 1975).

10. Samuel Noah Kramer, *Sumerian Mythology* (Westport, Conn.: Greenwood Press, 1972), 4; *The Letters and Inscriptions of Hammurabi*, trans. L. W. King (London: Luzac, 1900).

11. "Shu King," in *The World's Great Scriptures*, trans. James Legge, ed. Lewis Browne (New York: Macmillan, 1946), 213.

12. *The Mahabharata*, trans. B. Van Nooten (Berkeley: Univ. of California Press, 1973), 75.

13. Werner Jaeger, *Paideia: The Ideals of Greek Culture* (New York: Oxford Univ. Press, 1945), 1:83.

14. Plato, "Phaedo," in *Collected Dialogues*, trans. Hugh Tredennick, ed. Edith Hamilton and Huntingdon Cairns (New York: Pantheon, 1961), 65–66.

15. Plato, *The Republic*, trans. Benjamin Jowett (New York: Scribner's, 1928), book 4, 431C6.

16. Plato, *The Republic*, book 8, 558C3; book 5, 473C10.

17. Plato, *The Republic*, book 2, 372A2; book 4, 441A3.

18. Plato, *The Republic*, book 3, 416D4; book 5, 460B1.

19. Plato, *The Republic*, book 2, 377B12; book 3, 389B7, 414B10.

20. Plato, "Laws," in *Collected Dialogues*, trans. A. E. Taylor, 942C; Noel O'Sullivan, *Conservatism* (London: J. M. Dent & Sons, 1976), 69.

21. Jaeger, *Paideia*, 2:297.

22. Keegan, *Warfare*, 268–269.

23. John King Fairbank, *China: A New History* (Cambridge, Mass.: Harvard Univ. Press, 1992), 29.

24. Fairbank, *China*, 63.

25. "Shu King," in *World's Great Scriptures*, ed. Browne, 212.

26. "Li-Ki," in *World's Great Scriptures*, trans. James Legge, 227; Max Weber, *The Sociology of Religion*, trans. Ephraim Fischoff (Boston, Mass.: Beacon Press, 1963); Fairbank, *China*, 19.

27. *The Wisdom of Confucius,* trans. Lin Yutang (New York: Random House, 1938), 116; James Legge, *The Life and Teachings of Confucius* (London, 1895), 67.

28. Confucius, "Analects," in *World's Great Scriptures,* trans. William Jennings, 236.

29. Samuel P. Huntington, *The Clash of Civilizations and the Remaking of World Order* (New York: Simon & Schuster, 1996), 225.

30. Fairbank, *China,* 138, 181.

31. Fairbank, *China,* 324.

32. Kishore Mahbubani, "The United States: 'Go East, Young Man,' " *The Washington Quarterly* (Spring 1994).

33. Thomas Metzger, "Continuity between Modern and Pre-modern China," in *Ideas Across Cultures,* ed. P. A. Cohen and M. Goldman (Cambridge, Mass.: Harvard Univ. Press, 1990).

34. Jean-Jacques Rousseau, "On Social Contract of Principles of Political Right," in *Rousseau's Political Writings,* trans. Julia Conaway Bondanella (New York: Norton, 1988), book 1, chap. 1, 92.

35. Charles W. Hendel, *Citizen of Geneva: Selections from the Letters of Jean-Jacques Rousseau* (Oxford: Oxford Univ. Press, 1937), 208.

36. Rousseau, *Emile,* trans. Barbara Foxley (London: Dent, 1911), 56; Rousseau, *Social Contract,* book 1, chap. 1, 85.

37. Rousseau, "Discourse on the Origin and Foundations of Inequality among Men," in *Political Writings,* trans J. C. Bondanella, 34; Crane Brinton, *The Shaping of the Modern Mind* (New York: Prentice-Hall, 1950), 126.

38. Rousseau, *Social Contract,* book 1, chap. 6, 93.

39. Rousseau, *Social Contract,* book 2, chap. 3, 101.

40. Rousseau, *Social Contract,* book 1, chap. 7, 95.

41. Rousseau, *Social Contract,* book 4, chap. 8, 166–71.

42. Rousseau, *Social Contract,* book 4, chap. 8, 172. With characteristic inconsistency, Rousseau had earlier acknowledged that what he calls "the religion of the citizen," which sounds very much like his idea of civil religion, is "also evil," because "it makes a people sanguinary and intolerant to such a degree that they breathe nothing but massacre and murder, and believe they perform a sacred action in killing every person who will not bow to their gods." Perhaps he meant to distinguish between a religion glorifying the old unreformed state, and one upholding the state after introduction of rule by the general will, but this distinction is not made clear. At some level, Rousseau was no doubt a sincere Christian. At times, notably in his attacks on Voltaire, his protestations of religious faith could rival St. Paul, but in *The Social Contract,* his most systematic political work, he explicitly describes Christianity as not only irrelevant but actually subversive to social health.

43. Lynn Hunt, "The Unstable Boundaries of the French Revolution," in *A History of Private Life,* ed. Michelle Perot, trans. Arthur Goldhammer (Cambridge, Mass.: Harvard Univ. Press, 1990), 29; Simon Schama, *Citizens: A Chronicle of the French Revolution* (New York: Random House, 1990), 579–580.

44. Schama, *Citizens,* 734, 787.

45. Michael Harrington, *Socialism* (New York: Saturday Review Press, 1970), 24; Schama, *Citizens,* 484; James Hastings Nichols, *Democracy and the Churches* (Philadelphia, Penn.: Westminster Press, 1951), 43.

46. Hunt, "Unstable Boundaries," 29; Schama, *Citizens*, 858.

47. Georg Wilhelm Friedrich Hegel, *The Phenomenology of Mind*, trans. J. B. Baillie (London: Allen & Unwin, 1966), 473; Hegel, *The Philosophy of Right*, trans. T. M. Knox (London: Oxford Univ. Press, 1952), no. 257; Hegel, *The Philosophy of History*, trans. J. Sibree (New York: Colonial Press, 1900), 47.

48. Hegel, *Phenomenology of Mind*, 497; Hegel, *Philosophy of Right*, no. 324.

49. Hegel, *Selections,* ed. J. Lowenberg, quoted in Karl R. Popper, *The Open Society and Its Enemies* (Princeton, N.J.: Princeton Univ. Press, 1950), 241, 238.

50. Hegel, *Selections*, 227.

51. Friedrich Nietzsche, *Thus Spoke Zarathustra*, trans. Walter Kaufmann (New York: Viking, 1966), 48; Nietzsche, "Thoughts on the Philosophy of Morals" in *Ethical Theories*, trans. W. Hagen and U. Mahlendorf, ed. A. I. Melden (Englewood Cliffs, N.J.: Prentice-Hall, 1967), 441; Nietzsche, *Zarathustra*, 41.

52. Keegan, *Warfare*, 358.

53. Gordon A. Craig, *Germany: 1866–1945* (New York: Oxford Univ. Press, 1978), 415.

54. Karl Marx, "A Contribution to the Critique of Political Economy," in *Essential Writings,* ed. Frederic L. Bender (New York: Harper & Row, 1972), 161.

55. Marx with Friedrich Engels, "The German Ideology," in *Essential Writings*, 197.

56. Marx with Friedrich Engels, "The German Ideology," 176.

57. Marx, "Political Right versus Human Emancipation," in *Essential Writings*, 58, 66; "Critique of the Gotha Program," in *Essential Writings*, 281.

58. Marx, "The Poverty of Philosophy," in *Essential Writings*, 239; Marx with Engels, "Communist Manifesto," in *Essential Writings,* 258–259.

59. Marx, "Address of the Central Council to the Communist League," in *Essential Writings*, 267; Critique of Gotha, 272.

60. Plekhanov quoted in Melvin Lasky, *Utopia and Revolution* (Chicago, Ill.: Univ. of Chicago Press, 1976), 112; Lenin quoted in Albert Camus, *The Rebel* (New York: Knopf, 1954), 196.

61. Stalin quoted in Harrington, *Socialism*, 174.

62. Harrington, *Socialism*, 175.

CHAPTER 4

1. *The Mahabharata*, trans. Barend Van Nooten (Berkeley: University of California Press, 1973), 64.

2. Bronislaw Malinowski, *Magic, Science and Religion* (New York: Doubleday, 1954), 28–29.

3. Max Weber, *The Sociology of Religion*, trans. Ephraim Fischord (Boston, Mass.: Beacon Press, 1963), 1.

4. Joseph Campbell, *The Masks of God: Primitive Mythology* (New York: Viking, 1959), 61–78.

5. Alexis de Tocqueville, *Democracy in America* (New York: Vintage, 1945), 1:320.

6. Sir Leonard Woolley, *The Beginnings of Civilization* (New York: New American Library,) 459–477; John King Fairbank, *China: A New History* (Cambridge, Mass.: Harvard Univ. Press, 1992), 34; Kwasi Wiredu, "The Akan Worldview," paper presented at Woodrow Wilson International Center for Scholars, Washington, D.C., 19 May 1985.

7. Walter Burkert, *Creation of the Sacred: Tracks of Biology in Early Religion* (Cambridge, Mass.: Harvard Univ. Press, 1996), 33.

8. Emile Durkheim, *The Elementary Forms of Religious Life* (Glencoe, Ill.: Free Press, 1947); Patricia Crone, "The Tribe and the State," in *States in History*, ed. John A. Hall (Oxford: Basil Blackwell, 1980), 63; A. R. Radcliffe Brown, *The Andaman Islanders* (London: Cambridge Univ. Press, 1933), 233.

9. William James, *The Varieties of Religious Experience* (New York: New American Library, 1958), 61.

10. *American Indian Myths and Legends*, ed. Richard Erdoes and Alfonso Ortiz (New York: Pantheon, 1984); Mircea Eliade, *The Myth of the Eternal Return*, trans. Willard R. Trask (New York: Pantheon, 1954), 97; John Calvin, *Institutes of the Christian Religion*, trans. John Allen (Philadelphia, Penn.: Westminster Press, 1936), 1:54.

11. Eliade, *Myth*, 5.

12. Campbell, *Primitive Mythology*, 68, 321; Robert Graves, *The White Goddess: A Historical Grammar of Poetic Myth* (New York: Creative Age Press, 1948), 44–54.

13. Campbell, *Primitive Mythology*, 449.

14. Ecclesiastes, 1:4–5, 9; 3:15.

15. Thales quoted in Aristotle, "de Anima," in *Complete Works*, trans. J. A. Smith, ed. Jonathan Barnes (Princeton, N.J.: Princeton Univ. Press, 1984), book 1, 1:5, 411A7.

16. Heraclitus, *Fragments*, trans. G. T. W. Patrick (Chicago, Ill.: Argonaut, 1969), 36, 57, 61, 93–99.

17. Parmenides, *Fragments*, trans. A. H. Coxone (Wolfeboro, N.H.: Van Gorcum, 1986), 8, 60.

18. Plato, "Phaedo," in *Collected Dialogues*, trans. Hugh Tredennick, ed. Edith Hamilton and Huntingdon Cairns (New York: Pantheon, 1961), 65C5; "Phaedrus," in *Collected Dialogues*, trans. R. Hackforth, 247C3.

19. Robert B. Todd, "Monism and Immanence: The Foundations of Stoic Physics," in *The Stoics*, ed. John M. Rist (Berkeley: Univ. of California Press, 1978), 137–160; Marcus Aurelius, *Meditations,* trans. George Long (New York: P. F. Collier, 1909), book 4, 40, 219.

20. Marcus Aurelius, Meditations, 2, 11, 202; "Diogenes Laertes," in *Hellenistic Philosophers*, ed. A. A. Long and D. N. Smedley (Cambridge: Cambridge Univ. Press, 1987), 7:23.

21. Benedict de Spinoza, "Short Treatise on God, Man, and His Well Being," in *Collected Works*, trans. Edwin Curley (Princeton, N.J.: Princeton Univ. Press, 1985), 66.

22. Benedict de Spinoza, "Ethics," in *Collected Works*, prop. 18, 428; prop. 33, 436.

23. Spinoza, "Ethics," part 4, prop. 50, 331.

24. Klaus K. Klostermaier, *Mythologies and Philosophies of Salvation in the Theistic Tradition of India* (Waterloo, Ontario: Wilfrid Laurier Univ. Press, 1984), 6; *Hymns of the Rig Veda*, trans. Ralph T. H. Griffiths (Benares: E. J. Lazarus & Co., 1896), book 3, 48; book 10, 125.

25. Sri Aurobindo, quoted in Klaus K. Klostermaier, *A Survey of Hinduism* (Albany: State Univ. of New York Press, 1994), 278.

26. Nancy Wilson Ross, *Three Ways of Asian Wisdom* (New York: Simon and Schuster, 1966), 15; Sir Monier Monier-Williams, *Hinduism* (Calcutta: Susil Gupta Ltd., 1877).

27. "The Upanishads," in *Sacred Books of the East,* trans. F. Max Muller (New York: Dover, 1962), part 2, Second Mundaka, 37.

28. *Bhagavad Gita*, trans. Sir Edwin Arnold (Los Angeles, Calif.: Self-Realization Fellowship, 1981), chap. 7.

29. *Bhagavad Gita*, chap. 2.

30. *The Mahabharata,* 30; James, *Religious Experience*, 280.

31. Campbell, *The Masks of God*, 302.

32. Klostermaier, *Hinduism*, 50–52; Max Stackhouse, *Creeds, Society, and Human Rights* (Grand Rapids, Mich.: Eerdmans, 1984), 207.

33. Klostermaier, *Hinduism*, 52.

34. *Bhagavad Gita*, chap. 2.

35. Ross, *Three Ways*, 29.

36. D. S. Sarma, *Hinduism Through the Ages* (Bombay: Bharatiya Vidya Bhavan, 1958); Mahatma Gandhi, quoted in Stackhouse, *Creeds*, 253.

37. Robert Bellah, *Beyond Belief: Essays on Religion in a Post-Industrial Society* (New York: Harper & Row, 1970), 23.

38. Ross, *Three Ways*, 81.

39. "Discourse on the Foundations of the Kingdom of Righteousness," in *The Sacred Books and Early Literature of the East,* trans. T. W. Rhys Davids, ed. Charles Horne (New York: Parke, Austin, and Lipscott, 1917), 10:42.

40. "Discourse on the Foundations," 42.

41. "Discourse on the Foundations," 82.

42. Richard Storry, *A History of Modern Japan* (Baltimore, Md.: Penguin, 1960), 42.

43. Ross, *Three Ways*, 47–48.

44. Weber, *Sociology of Religion*, 147; Louis Dupre, "Spiritual Life in a Secular Age," *Daedalus* (Winter, 1982), 26.

45. Ernst Troeltsch, *Christian Thought* (London: Univ. of London Press, 1923), 137.

46. T. S. Eliot, "Burnt Norton," in *The Complete Poems and Plays* (New York: Harcourt, Brace, 1952), 117.

47. Alfred North Whitehead, quoted in Robert Hughes, *The Shock of the New* (New York: Knopf, 1995), 52; Robert Oppenheimer, quoted in Ross, *Three Ways*, 55; Julian Barbour, *End of Time: The Next Revolution in Physics* (New York: Oxford Univ. Press, 1999).

48. Rosemary Radford Reuther, *Sexism and God-Talk* (Boston, Mass.: Beacon Press, 1983), 48.

CHAPTER 5

1. Karl Barth, *The Epistle to the Romans*, trans. Edwyn C. Hoskyns (Oxford: Oxford Univ. Press, 1968), 28.

2. Robert L. Wilken, "Pagan Criticism of Christianity: Greek Religion and Christian Faith," in *Early Christian Literature and the Classical Intellectual Tradition* (Paris: Editions Beauchesne, 1979), 117–134.

3. E. O. Service, *Origins of the State and Civilization: The Process of Cultural Evolution* (New York: Norton, 1975), 207–230.

4. Peter Brown, *The Body and Society* (New York: Columbia Univ. Press, 1988), 43.

5. Peter Farb, *Man's Rise to Civilization* (New York: Dutton, 1968), 182.

6. Patricia Crone, "The Temple and the State," in *States in History*, ed. John A. Hall (Oxford: Basil Blackwell, 1986), 63.

7. Northrop Frye, *The Great Code: The Bible and Literature* (New York: Harcourt Brace Jovanovich, 1982), 90.

8. Sir Leonard Woolley, *The Beginning of Civilization* (New York: New American Library, 1963), 459–477; John Keegan, *A History of Warfare* (New York: Knopf, 1993), 130; Frye, *Great Code*, 88.

9. Woolley, *Civilization*, 172–173.

10. "Hymns of the One God," in *Development of Religion and Thought in Ancient Egypt*, trans. J. H. Breasted (New York: Scribner, 1912), 326.

11. Woolley, *Civilization*, 472.

12. Woolley, *Civilization*, 475.

13. Genesis 17:7–8.

14. Genesis 22:18.

15. Exodus 20:3–17.

16. Joseph Klausner, The Messianic Idea in Israel (New York: Macmillan, 1955); Wayne A. Meeks, *The Origins of Christian Morality* (New Haven, Conn.: Yale Univ. Press, 1993), 122; Joseph Campbell, *The Masks of God: Primitive Mythology* (New York: Viking, 1959), 291.

17. Mircea Eliade, *The Myth of the Eternal Return*, trans. Willard P. Trask (New York: Pantheon, 1954), 104; Meeks, *Origins*, 191.

18. Meeks, *Origins*, 166.

19. Psalms 137:5–6.

20. Some scholars argue much earlier.

21. "The Venidad," in *The Sacred Books of the East*, trans. James Darmester (Oxford: Clarendon Press, 1895), vol. 4, chap. 4, 1, 3B.

22. "The Gathas," in *Early Zoroastrianism*, trans. J. H. Moulton (London: Allen & Unwin, 1913), yasna 13.

23. Like most legendary events in history, the Masada story has recently incurred substantial scholarly skepticism. See Nachaman Ben-Yuda, *The Masada Myth* (Madison: Univ. of Wisconsin Press, 1995).

24. John 18:14.

25. Matthew 12:25, 30; John 10:16.

26. Matthew 25:35–40.

27. Matthew 24:36; Mark 13:32.

28. Robin Lane Fox, *Pagans and Christians* (New York: Knopf, 1986), 420.

29. Richard E. Rubenstein, *When Jesus Became God* (New York: Harcourt Brace, 1999).

30. Tertullian, *Prescription Against Heretics*, chaps. 7, 11, 16, quoted in Elaine Pagels, *The Origins of Satan* (New York: Random House, 1995), 164.

31. Jaroslav Pelikan, *Jesus through the Centuries: His Place in the History of Culture* (New Haven, Conn.: Yale Univ. Press, 1985), 64.

32. Fox, *Pagans*, 556; Pagels, *Satan*, 146.

33. Brown, *Body and Society*, 341–365; Neil B. McLynn, *Ambrose of Milan: Church and Court in a Christian Capital* (Berkeley: Univ. of California Press, 1995).

34. Brown, *Body and Society*, 347.

35. Khalil Bin Sayeed, *Western Dominance and Political Islam: Challenge and Response* (Albany: State Univ. of New York Press, 1994), 1; Khomeini quoted in Sayeed, *Western Dominance*, 142.

36. Fourth *Surrah*.

37. Fourth *Surrah*; Andrew Rippin, *Muslims: Their Religious Beliefs and Practices* (London: Routledge, 1990), 1:19.

38. Bernard Lewis, *The Middle East: A Brief History of the Last 2,000 Years* (New York: Simon & Schuster, 1995), 56.

39. Lewis, *Middle East*, 73.

40. Lewis, *Middle East*, 117–28.

41. William Cantwell Smith, quoted in George Weigel, "Waiting for Augustine: Islam and the West," *American Purpose*, November 1992, 69.

42. Samuel P. Huntington, *The Clash of Civilizations and the Remaking of World Order* (New York: Simon & Schuster, 1997), 109.

43. John Esposito, quoted in Weigel, "Islam and the West," 69.

44. Sayeed, *Political Islam*, 131–153.

45. Weigel, "Islam and the West," 72.

46. Thomas Cahill, *How the Irish Saved Civilization* (New York: Doubleday, 1995).

47. Johan Huizinga, *The Waning of the Middle Ages* (New York: Doubleday, 1954), 9.

48. Ernst Troeltsch, *Social Teachings of the Christian Churches*, trans. Olive Wyon (New York: Macmillan, 1931), 1:203.

49. Lewis, *Middle East*, 134.

50. Thomas G. Sanders, *Protestant Concepts of Church and State* (New York: Holt, Rinehart, and Winston, 1964), 26–31; John Calvin, *Institutes of the Christian Religion*, trans. John Allen (Philadelphia, Penn.: Westminster Press, 1936), 2:775–779; Ralph C. Hancock, *Calvin and the Foundations of Modern Politics* (Ithaca, N.Y.: Cornell Univ. Press, 1989), 63; David Little, *Religion, Order, and Law* (New York: Harper & Row, 1969), 96–97.

51. James Hastings Nichols, *Democracy and the Churches* (Philadelphia, Penn.: Westminster Press, 1951), 48.

52. John Courtney Murray, *The Problem of Religious Freedom* (Westminster, Md.: Newman Press, 1965), 17–31; James Hennesey, *American Catholics* (New

York: Oxford Univ. Press, 1981), 309–311; John Tracy Ellis, *American Catholicism* (Chicago, Ill.: Univ. of Chicago Press, 1969), 240.

53. Christian Smith, *American Evangelicalism* (Chicago, Ill.: Univ. of Chicago Press, 1998), 180.

54. James Davidson Hunter, "Fundamentalism in Its Global Contours," in *The Fundamentalist Phenomenon* (Grand Rapids, Mich.: Eerdmans, 1990), 59.

55. Francis Fukuyama, *The End of History and the Last Man* (New York: Avon, 1992).

56. Sayeed, *Political Islam*, 144.

CHAPTER 6

1. Max Weber, *The Sociology of Religion*, trans. Ephraim Fischoff (Boston: Beacon Press, 1963), 151; Karl Mannheim, *Ideology and Utopia* (New York: Harcourt Brace, 1936), 259; Martin Heidegger, *Being and Time*, trans. John Macquarrie and Edward Robinson (Oxford: Basil Blackwell, 1962), 377.

2. Simon Schama, *Citizens: A Chronicle of the French Revolution* (New York: Random House, 1990), 149; Friedrich Nietzsche, *The Will to Power*, trans. Walter Kaufmann with R. J. Hollingdale (New York: Random House, 1967), 617.

3. Peter Farb, *Man's Rise to Civilization* (New York: Dutton, 1968), 182; Wayne A. Meeks, *The Origins of Christian Morality* (New Haven, Conn.: Yale Univ. Press, 1993), 113; Joseph Campbell, *The Masks of God: Primitive Mythology* (New York: Viking, 1959), 231.

4. Giovanni Filoramo, *A History of Gnosticism*, trans. Anthony Alcock (Oxford: Basil Blackwell, 1990), 24–27.

5. Friedrich Nietzsche, *The Birth of Tragedy*, trans. Walter Kaufmann (New York: Random House, 1967), 22.

6. Nietzsche, *Birth of Tragedy*, 10.

7. Ezekiel 37:1–14; Song of Solomon 1:15; 4:5–6.

8. Matthew 1:48–50; 18:3; 9:17; Luke 18:29.

9. Matthew 6:24–34.

10. Acts 3:1–9.

11. John 1:1–14; 3:1–8.

12. John 1:1–5; 2:15.

13. Wayne A. Meeks, *The Moral World of the First Christians* (Philadelphia, Penn.: Westminster Press, 1986), 104–108.

14. Peter Brown, *The Body and Society* (New York: Columbia Univ. Press, 1988), 223–224.

15. Brown, *Body and Society*, 332–333.

16. Elaine Pagels, *The Origins of Satan* (New York: Random House, 1995), 167.

17. Pagels, *Satan*, 17; Meeks, *Christian Morality*, 52–55, Pagels, *Satan*, 65–74.

18. Meeks, *Christian Morality*, 56–57; Pagels, *Satan*, 166–168; Brown, *Body and Society*, 106–113.

19. Filoramo, *Gnosticism*, 176–177; Brown, *Body and Society*, 114–117.

20. Filoramo, *Gnosticism*, 67–72.

21. Filoramo, *Gnosticism*, 130, 173; Brown, *Body and Society*, 124–125.

22. Filoramo, *Gnosticism*, 106–121.

23. Johan Huizinga, *The Waning of the Middle Ages* (New York: Doubleday, 1954), 220–225.

24. Huizinga, *Waning of the Middle Ages*, 194.

25. Orlando Patterson, *Freedom* (New York: Basic, 1991), 396–401.

26. Patterson, *Freedom*, 40.

27. Thomas G. Sanders, *Protestant Concepts of Church and State* (New York: Holt, Rinehart, and Winston, 1964), 82.

28. Perry Miller, *The New England Mind: From Colony to Province* (Cambridge, Mass.: Harvard Univ. Press, 1953), 59, 128.

29. A. O. Lovejoy, *The Great Chain of Being* (Cambridge, Mass.: Harvard Univ. Press, 1936), 293; Charles Taylor, *Sources of the Self: The Making of the Modern Identity* (Cambridge, Mass.: Harvard Univ. Press, 1989), 373.

30. Rousseau's letter to D'Alembert, 1758, quoted in *A History of Private Life*, ed. Roger Chartier (Cambridge, Mass.: Harvard Univ. Press, 1989), 3:376.

31. Soren Kierkegaard, *Fear and Trembling*, trans. Francis Golffing (Garden City, N.Y.: Doubleday, 1956), 69.

32. Samuel Taylor Coleridge, *Biographa Literaria*, chapter 13, quoted in *Poets of the English Language*, ed. W. H. Auden and Norman Holmes Pearson (New York: Viking, 1950), 4:15.

33. *Poets of the English Language*, ed. Auden and Pearson, 4:xiii–xviii.

34. Scott Burnham, *Beethoven Hero* (Princeton, N.J.: Princeton Univ. Press, 1995).

35. Friedrich Nietzsche, "Thoughts on the Philosophy of Morals," in *Ethical Theories*, trans. Fred Hagen and Ursula Mahlendorf, ed. A. I. Melden (Englewood Cliffs, N.J.: Prentice-Hall, 1967), 442.

36. Nietzsche, *Thus Spoke Zarathustra*, trans. Walter Kaufmann (New York: Viking, 1996), 34, 44; Peter Levine, *Nietzsche and the Modern Crisis of the Humanities* (Albany: State Univ. of New York Press, 1995), xv.

37. Nietzsche, *Will to Power*, 602; Nietzsche, *Zarathustra*, 26–27.

38. Nietzsche, *Zarathustra*, 48, 52.

39. Levine, *Nietzsche*, xii–xv, 82–85.

40. Nietzsche, *Birth of Tragedy*, 109.

41. Nietzsche, *Zarathustra*, 67, 100, 327.

42. Nietzsche, *Zarathustra*, 12; Levine, *Nietzsche*, xiv.

43. Stefan Zweig, quoted in the introduction in Nietzsche, *Zarathustra*, xiii.

44. Walter Kaufmann, introduction to Neitzsche, *Zarathustra*, xiv.

45. S. Petrement, quoted by Filoramo, *Gnosticism*, xviii; Herman Hesse, *Steppenwolf*, trans. Basil Creighton (New York: Holt, Rinehart and Winston, 1957), 266–267.

46. Wassily Kandinsky quoted in Martha Bayles, *Hole in Our Soul* (New York: Free Press, 1994), 329.

47. John Updike, "On 'The Portrait of a Lady,'" *New York Review of Books*, 46 (2 December 1999), 22.

48. Bayles, *Soul*, 12.

49. Melvin Lasky, *Utopia and Revolution* (Chicago, Ill.: Univ. of Chicago Press, 1976), 602, 150.

50. Herbert Marcuse, *Eros and Civilization* (New York: Vintage, 1962), 130, 205; Wilhelm Reich, *The Mass Psychology of Fascism* (New York: Farrar, Straus, and Giroux, 1970), 29, 55.

CHAPTER 7

1. When I first wrote on this subject in the middle of the 1980s, the term secular humanism had acquired a somewhat pejorative connotation from its employment by right-wing publicists to bash scientific materialism, and I preferred a more neutral term. Secular humanism has since pretty much passed into the general language, used by advocates and more or less neutral commentators as well as adversaries. But I have grown accustomed to civil humanism, and prefer its ring, so will continue generally to use it, occasionally substituting secular humanism when that fits better in the context.

2. Thucydides, *The Peloponnesian War,* trans. Benjamin Jowett (Oxford: Clarendon Press, 1881), 35–46.

3. Plato, "Apology," in *The Dialogues of Plato,* trans. Benjamin Jowett (Oxford: Clarendon Press, 1892), 38E.

4. Harvey Mansfield, Jr., *Taming the Prince* (New York: Free Press, 1989), 122.

5. Aristotle, *Eudemian Ethics,* trans. J. Solomon, in *Complete Works,* ed. Jonathan Barnes (Princeton, N.J.: Princeton Univ. Press, 1984), vol. 2, book 1, chaps. 12–14, 1244–48. Anthony Kenny, *Aristotle on the Perfect Life* (Oxford: Clarendon Press, 1992), 96; Aristotle, *Politics,* trans. Benjamin Jowett, in *Complete Works,* vol. 2, book 7, chap. 14, 1332A39.

6. Aristotle, *Politics,* book 7, chap. 15, 1334B13.

7. Aristotle, *Politics,* book 1, chap. 2, 1253A2.

8. Aristotle, *Nicomachean Ethics,* trans. W. D. Ross, in *Complete Works,* vol. 2, book 2, chap. 6, 1106B15.

9. Aristotle, *Nicomachean Ethics.*

10. Aristotle, *Politics,* book 2, chap. 11, 1282A14.

11. Aristotle, *Politics,* book 4, chap. 11, 1275B35; book 1, chap. 8, 1309C8; book 2, chap. 9, 1280A11.

12. Aristotle, *Politics,* book 2, chap. 3, 1261B34; chap. 5, 1263A36.

13. Alasdair MacIntyre, *After Virtue: A Study in Moral Theory* (Notre Dame, Ind.: Univ. of Notre Dame Press, 1981).

14. Aristotle, *Nicomachean Ethics,* books 8 and 9, particularly book 8, chaps. 12–13. For a contrary view on Aristotle as a moral foundation for citizenship, see Kenny, *Aristotle,* 43–55.

15. John Keegan, *A History of Warfare* (New York: Knopf, 1993), 264–266.

16. Lily Ross Taylor, *Party Politics in the Age of Caesar* (Berkeley: Univ. of California Press, 1949), 2.

17. Taylor, *Party Politics,* 4–5.

18. Augustus, *Res gestae divi Augusti*, trans. P. A. Brunt and J. M. Moore (Oxford: Oxford Univ. Press, 1967), 1:19.

19. Edward Gibbon, *The History of the Decline and Fall of the Roman Empire*, ed. David Womersley (London: Penguin Press, 1994), 1:70.

20. Orlando Patterson, *Freedom* (New York: Basic, 1991), 271.

21. Marcus Aurelius, *Meditations*, trans. George Long (New York: P.F. Collier, 1909), 4:4.

22. Cicero, *De Republica*, trans. Clinton Walker Keyes (Cambridge, Mass.: Harvard Univ. Press, 1970), 1:xxxiv, 79; Marcus Aurelius, *Meditations*, book 11, 18.

23. Anthony Black, "Christianity and Republicanism: From St. Cyprian to Rousseau," *American Political Science Review*, 19, no. 3, September 1997, 651.

24. John Addington Symonds, *The Renaissance in Italy* (London: Smith, Elder, 1900), 1:1–24.

25. Charles Taylor, *Sources of the Self: The Making of the Modern Identity* (Cambridge, Mass.: Harvard Univ. Press, 1989), 200–201.

26. Jacob Burckhardt, *The Civilization of the Renaissance in Italy*, trans. S. G. C. Middlemore (New York: Random House, 1954), 226; Kenneth Clark, *Civilisation* (New York: Harper & Row, 1969), 108.

27. J. G. A. Pocock, *The Machiavellian Moment* (Princeton, N.J.: Princeton Univ. Press, 1975), 88; Burckhardt, *Renaissance in Italy*.

28. Clark, *Civilisation*, 101.

29. Pocock, *Machiavellian Moment*, 88; Hans Baron, "Franciscan Poverty and Civic Wealth in Humanistic Thought," *Speculum* 13, January 1938, 18–24.

30. Pocock, *Machiavellian Moment*, 85.

31. Reinhold Niebuhr, *The Nature and Destiny of Man: A Christian Interpretation* (New York: Scribner's, 1941), 1:150; H. R. Trevor-Roper, *The Crisis of the Seventeenth Century: Religion, the Reformation and Social Change* (New York: Harper & Row, 1968), 24–26.

32. Evidence for John Shakespeare's attachment to Catholicism is based on a document discovered in Stratford in 1757. Some scholars believe that this document, which has since been lost, may have been a forgery, but the circumstantial case for its authenticity is at least suggestive. See Samuel Schoenbaum, *William Shakespeare: A Compact Documentary Life* (Oxford: Oxford Univ. Press, 1977).

33. T. S. Eliot, *Selected Essays* (New York: Harcourt, Brace, 1950), 125.

34. Harold Bloom, *Shakespeare: The Invention of the Human* (New York: Penguin Putnam, 1998).

CHAPTER 8

1. J. B. Schneewind, *The Invention of Autonomy* (Cambridge: Cambridge Univ. Press, 1998), 8, among others, doubts that there was an "Enlightenment project," in the sense of showing "that morality had no need of religion because it had its own, wholly rational, foundations." It is true that many Enlightenment writers, including Voltaire and Paine, were reluctant to abandon all ties with theistic religion. But Schneewind's book provides plenty of evidence that the main thrust of the En-

lightenment was to establish a basis for morality independent of traditional religion. See, for example, his discussions of Hume, 354–377; the French *philosophes,* 413–419; and Bentham, 419–424. See also Jose Casanova, *Public Religions in the Modern World* (Chicago, Ill.: Univ. of Chicago Press, 1994), 19–38.

2. J. G. A. Pocock, *The Machiavellian Moment* (Princeton, N.J.: Princeton Univ. Press, 1975), 461; Louis Dupre, "Spiritual Life in a Secular Age," *Deadalus* 3, no. 1, winter 1982, 21; Henry F. May, *The Enlightenment in America* (New York: Oxford Univ. Press, 1976), xiv; Ernst Cassirer, *The Myth of the State* (New Haven, Conn.: Yale Univ. Press, 1946), 229.

3. May, *Enlightenment,* 17.

4. Peter Gay, *The Enlightenment: The Science of Freedom* (New York: Norton, 1977), 526–527.

5. Diderot quoted in Charles Taylor, *Sources of the Self: The Making of the Modern Identity* (Cambridge, Mass.: Harvard Univ. Press, 1989), 329; Voltaire quoted in J. B. Bury, *The Idea of Progress* (New York: Macmillan, 1955), 149.

6. Taylor, *Self,* 341.

7. J. B. Schneewind argues, however: "The claim that the main effort of the moral philosophy of the eighteenth century was to secularize morality simply does not stand up. . . . Indeed, if I were forced to identify something or other as 'the Enlightenment project' for morality, I should say that it was the effort to limit God's control over earthly life while keeping him essential to morality." Schneewind, *Invention of Autonomy,* 8.

8. Immanuel Kant, *Critique of Pure Reason,* trans. Paul Guyer and Allen W. Wood (Cambridge: Cambridge Univ. Press, 1998), A595/B623, 65.

9. Kant, *Critique of Judgement,* trans. Werner S. Pluhar (Indianapolis, Ind.: Hackett Publishing Co. 1987), 450, 340.

10. David Hume, *A Treatise of Human Nature* (Oxford: Clarendon Press, 1978), book 3, part 1, 454–476; Alasdair MacIntyre, *Whose Justice? Which Rationality?* (Notre Dame, Ind.: Univ. of Notre Dame Press, 1988), 286–289.

11. Immanuel Kant, "Groundwork of the Metaphysics of Morals," in *Practical Philosophy,* trans. Mary J. Gregor (Cambridge: Cambridge Univ. Press, 1996), 4:421, 73; Kant, *Critique of Judgment,* 451, 340–341.

12. Schneewind, *Autonomy,* 524–525.

13. Kant, "Metaphysic of Morals," 4:429, 80.

14. Schneewind, *Autonomy,* 544–545.

15. Kant, "Critique of Practical Reason," in *Practical Philosophy,* trans. Mary J. Gregor, 5:86, 209.

16. Jeremy Bentham, *An Introduction to the Principles of Morals and Legislation* (Oxford: Clarendon Press, 1996), chap. 1, 4,12.

17. Bentham, *Introduction to the Principles,* chap. 2, 14, 27.

18. John Rawls, *A Theory of Justice* (Cambridge, Mass.: Harvard Univ. Press, 1971), 14.

19. Michael Sandel, "Morality and the Liberal Ideal" in *Justice and Economic Distribution,* eds. J. Arthur and W. H. Shaw (Englewood Cliffs, N.J.: Prentice Hall, 1978), 245.

20. John Stuart Mill, "On Liberty," in *Utlitarianism, Liberty, and Representative*

Government (New York: Dutton, 1951), chap. 1, 97; Mill, *Utilitarianism,* chap. 2, 12.

21. Mill, "On Liberty," chap. 1, 95.

22. Mill, "On Liberty," 96; chap. 3, 152.

23. Mill, "On Liberty," chap. 1, 99.

24. John Stuart Mill, "Theism," in *Essays on Ethics, Religion, and Society,* ed. J. M. Robson (Toronto: Univ. of Toronto Press, 1969), pt. 5, 429–489; Mill, "On Liberty," chap. 2, 143–152.

25. John Stuart Mill, "Thoughts on Parliamentary Reform," in *Essays on Politics and Society,* ed. J. M. Robson (Toronto: Univ. of Toronto Press, 1977), 474–475.

26. Isaiah Berlin, quoted in Peter Berkowitz, *Virtue and the Making of Modern Liberalism* (Princeton, N.J.: Princeton Univ. Press, 1999), 148.

27. William James, *Pragmatism: A New Name for Old Ways of Thinking* (New York: Longmans, Green, 1907); John Dewey, *Human Nature and Conduct* (New York: Henry Holt, 1922).

28. Richard Rorty, *Contingency, Irony, and Solidarity* (Cambridge: Cambridge Univ. Press, 1989).

29. William James, *The Varieties of Religious Experience* (New York: New American Library, 1958), 391.

30. John Dewey, *The Public and Its Problems* (Chicago, Ill.: Gateway Books, 1946), 87; John Dewey, *Reconstruction in Philosophy* (Boston: Beacon Press, 1948), 209; John Dewey, "Philosophers of Freedom," in *The Later Works,* ed. Jo Ann Boydston (Carbondale: Southern Illinois Univ. Press, 1984), 3:108.

31. Dewey, *Public and Its Problems,* 145; Dewey, "A New World in the Making"; Dewey, *Later Works,* 3:223; John Dewey, *Liberalism and Social Action* (New York: Putnam, 1935), 70–73; John Dewey, *Freedom and Culture* (New York: Putnam, 1939), 101–102. Dewey's changing views on the Soviet Union are discussed by James H. Nichols, Jr., "Pragmatism and the U.S. Constitution," in *Confronting the Constitution,* ed. Allan Bloom (Washington, D.C.: AEI Press, 1990), 387.

32. Dewey, *Reconstruction in Philosophy,* 177; Dewey, *Human Nature,* 307.

33. Rorty, *Contingency,* xiv.

34. Rorty, *Contingency,* 45.

35. Rorty, *Contingency,* 97, 54 (FN 8).

36. Rorty, *Contingency,* 196.

37. Rorty, *Contingency,* xv.

38. Rawls, *Justice,* 11–13.

39. Rawls, *Justice,* 302.

40. Rawls, *Justice,* 75–83, 100–101.

41. Rawls, *Justice,* 78.

42. Rawls, *Justice,* 12.

43. Daniel Bell, *The Coming of Post-Industrial Society* (New York: Basic, 1973), 419; Michael Sandel, *Liberalism and the Limits of Justice* (New York: Cambridge Univ. Press, 1982), 132.

44. Rawls, *Justice,* 30–31, 395–399, 446–452.

45. Rawls, *Justice,* 11; John Rawls, *Political Liberalism* (New York: Columbia Univ. Press, 1993), 10.

46. Rawls, *Political Liberalism*, 10–11.

47. Robert Nozick, *Anarchy, State, and Utopia* (New York: Basic, 1974).

48. Barber prefers the term "civil society" to "communitarianism," finding a smack of what I call absolutism in the latter; but his arguments and strategies reflect those of the secular communitarians.

49. Nicholas Greenwood Onuf, *The Republican Legacy in International Thought* (Cambridge: Cambridge Univ. Press, 1998), 109. For examples of secular communitarianism, see Amitai Etzioni, *The New Golden Rule: Community and Morality in a Democratic Society* (New York: Basic Books, 1996); Alan Wolfe, *One Nation, After All* (New York: Viking, 1998); and Benjamin R. Barber, *A Place for Us* (New York: Hill and Wang, 1998). Civil religion was first introduced into current discourse by Robert Bellah in *Beyond Belief* (New York: Harper & Row, 1970), 168–189.

50. Edward O. Wilson, *On Human Nature* (Cambridge, Mass.: Harvard Univ. Pres, 1978); Lawrence Kohlberg, *The Philosophy of Moral Development* (New York: Harper & Row, 1981); Eric A. Posner, *Law and Social Norms* (Cambridge, Mass.: Harvard Univ. Press, 2000).

51. James Q. Wilson, *The Moral Sense* (New York: Free Press, 1993), 250.

52. Hume, *Treatise of Human Nature,* book 3, part 1, 454–476; Karlis Racevskis, *Modernity's Pretenses* (Albany: State University of New York Press, 1998), 31.

53. Alfred North Whitehead, *Adventures of Ideas* (New York: Macmillan, 1933), 159.

54. B. A. Ackerman, *Social Justice and the Liberal State* (New Haven, Conn.: Yale Univ. Press, 1980), 368; Bernard Williams, *Shame and Necessity* (Berkeley: Univ. of California Press, 1933), 166.

55. Ernst Troeltsch, *Christian Thought* (London: Univ. of London Press, 1923), 108.

CHAPTER 9

1. "The Books of Mencius," in *The World's Great Scriptures*, trans. Charles A. Wong, ed. Lewis Browne (New York: Macmillan, 1961), 265.

2. Northrop Frye, *The Great Code: The Bible and Literature* (New York: Harcourt, Brace, Jovanovich, 1982), 69.

3. Genesis 2, 3.

4. Genesis 4:1–17; 9:8–17.

5. Genesis 18:19; Psalm 23.

6. Wayne A. Meeks, *The Moral World of the First Christians* (Philadelphia, Penn.: Westminster Press, 1986), 101; Germain Grisez, *Beyond the New Theism: A Philosophy of Religion* (Notre Dame, Ind.: Univ. of Notre Dame Press, 1975), 227; James Q. Wilson, *The Moral Sense* (New York: Free Press, 1993), 212.

7. William L. Langer, "Infanticide: A Historical Survey," *History of Childhood Quarterly*, 1974, 1:353–366.

8. Amos 5:11; Isaiah 10:1–2; Micah 6:12; Jeremiah 12:4.

9. Isaiah 1:18.

10. Isaiah 40:30–31, 61:1; Robert Benne, *The Ethic of Democratic Capitalism* (Philadelphia, Penn.: Fortress Press, 1981), 35.

11. Job 1, 2.

12. Job 13:15.

13. Job 38.

14. Job 42:2–3.

15. Job 42:7.

16. Hillel, quoted in Will Durant, *Caesar and Christ* (New York: Simon and Schuster, 1944), 539.

17. Jacob Neusner, *Ancient Judaism* (Atlanta, Ga.: Scholars Press, 1993), 3–55.

18. Neusner, *Judaism: The Evidence of the Mishnah* (Chicago, Ill.: Univ. of Chicago Press, 1981), 270–283; "Babylonian Talmud" in *The Jewish Political Tradition*, ed. Michael Walzer, Menachem Lorberbaum, and Noam Zohar (New Haven, Conn.: Yale Univ. Press, 2000), 258

19. "Rabbis and Sages," selections in *Jewish Political Tradition*, 244–306; Maimonides quoted in Oswald Spengler, *Decline of the West* (New York: Knopf, 1926), 2:295.

20. Leviticus 25:10.

21. "Fragments of Xenophanes" in *Selections from Early Greek Philosophy*, ed. Milton C. Nahm (New York: Crofts, 1947), 1:109.

22. Werner Jaeger, *Paideia: The Ideals of Greek Culture* (New York: Oxford Univ. Press, 1943), 2:296.

23. Plato, "Phaedo," in *Dialogues of Plato*, trans. Benjamin Jowett (Oxford: Clarendon Press, 1892), 80A; Plato, "Timaues," in *Dialogues of Plato*, trans. Benjamin Jowett (Oxford: Clarendon Press, 1892) 28C; Plato, "Laws," *Dialogues of Plato*, trans. Benjamin Jowett (Oxford: Clarendon Press, 1892), book 10, 907A.

24. Aeschylus, "Agamemnon," in *Complete Greek Tragedies*, trans. Richard Lattimore, ed. David Greene and Richard Lattimore (Chicago, Ill.: Univ. Chicago Press, 1958), 1:78.

25. Sophocles, "Oedipus the King," in *Complete Greek Tragedies*, trans. David Greene, 2:76.

26. Euripides, "Medea," in *Complete Greek Tragedies*, trans. Rex Warner, 3:63.

27. Aeschylus, "The Eumenides," in *Complete Greek Tragedies*, trans. Richard Lattimore, 1:170.

28. Aeschylus, "Eumenides," 160, 153.

29. Aeschylus, "The Persians," in *Complete Greek Tragedies*, trans. Seth G. Bernardete, 1:249.

30. Aeschylus, "Prometheus Bound," in *Complete Greek Tragedies*, trans. David Greene, 1:351.

31. Sophocles, "Oedipus at Colonus," in *Complete Greek Tragedies*, trans. Robert Fitzgerald, 2:112.

32. Alasdair MacIntyre, *Whose Justice? Which Rationality?* (Notre Dame, Ind.: Univ. of Notre Dame Press, 1988), 58.

33. Sophocles, "Antigone," in *Complete Greek Tragedies*, trans. Elizabeth Wyckoff, 182.

34. Sophocles, "Antigone," 161.

35. Sophocles, "Antigone," 201.

36. Bernard M. N. Knox, *Oedipus at Thebes* (New Haven, Conn.: Yale Univ. Press, 1957), 63.

37. Sophocles, "Oedipus the King," 47.

38. Sophocles, "Oedipus the King," 69.

39. Sophocles, "Oedipus at Colonus," 148.

40. Euripides, "The Trojan Women," in *Complete Greek Tragedies*, trans. Richard Lattimore, 3:630.

41. Jaroslav Pelikan, *Jesus Through the Centuries: His Place in the History of Culture* (New Haven, Conn.: Yale Univ. Press, 1985), 233.

42. Matthew 4:1–11.

43. Matthew 19:29–30, 19:6; Mark 2:27; Matthew 5:17–18, 19:24, 25:14–30, 5:39, 10:34.

44. For a thoughtful presentation of the case for the Jesus Seminar approach, see John Dominic Crossan, *The Birth of Christianity* (New York: HarperCollins, 1998).

45. Matthew 22:37–40.

46. John 13:34.

47. Ernst Troeltsch, *The Social Teachings of the Christian Churches*, trans. Olive Wyon (New York: Macmillan, 1931), 1:55.

48. Galatians 3:28.

49. Matthew 22:15–22.

50. Charles Taylor, *Sources of the Self* (Cambridge, Mass.: Harvard Univ. Press, 1989), 218–219.

51. C. H. Dodd, *The Founder of Christianity* (New York: Macmillan, 1970), 28.

52. Pelikan, *Jesus*, 1.

CHAPTER 10

1. F. R. Leavis, *The Great Tradition* (London: Chatto & Windus, 1955), 7–9.

2. Romans 12:2; Tertullian, *Apology*, 28, quoted in Elaine Pagels, *The Origin of Satan* (New York: Random House, 1995), 147; Origen, *Contra Celsum*, 1.1, quoted in Pagels, *Satan*, 147.

3. Anthony Black, "Christianity and Republicanism: From St. Cyprian to Rousseau," *American Political Science Review*, no. 3, September 1997, 91:649.

4. Augustine, *Confessions*, trans. Henry Chadwick (New York: Oxford Univ. Press, 1991) book 8, vii, 17, 145.

5. Judith Herrin, *The Formation of Christendom* (Oxford: Basil Blackwell, 1987), 102.

6. William J. Bouwsma, *A Usable Past: Essays in European Cultural History* (Berkeley: Univ. of California Press, 1990), 26.

7. Augustine, *City of God*, 4: 4, 112.

8. Augustine, *de moribus ecclesiae catholicae*, 1.30.63, quoted in Peter Brown, *The Body and Society* (New York: Columbia Univ. Press, 1988), 364.

9. Reinhold Niebuhr, *The Nature and Destiny of Man: A Christian Interpretation* (New York: Scribner 1941), 1:138.

10. Charles Taylor, *Sources of the Self* (Cambridge, Mass.: Harvard Univ. Press, 1989), 130–133.

11. Augustine, *City of God,* 5:10, 157.

12. Bouwsma, *Usable Past,* 26; Jean Bethke Elshtain, *Augustine and the Limits of Politics* (Notre Dame, Ind.: Univ. of Notre Dame Press, 1995), 101–105.

13. Augustine, *City of God,* 14:28, 447; Elshtain, *Augustine,* 89–112.

14. Augustine, *City of God,* 19:12, 687–690.

15. Bouwsma, *Usable Past,* 27.

16. Brown, *Body and Society,* 425; Augustine, "Enarrant in Psalmum," in *Augustine of Hippo,* trans. Mary T. Clark (New York: Paulist Press, 1984), quoted in Brown, *Body and Society,* 427.

17. Thomas Aquinas, "Summa Theologiae," in *St. Thomas Aquinas on Politics and Ethics* 2, trans. and ed. Paul E. Sigmund, (New York: Norton, 1988), First Part, 94.4, 51; 91.1, 46; 95.1, 53.

18. Aquinas, "De Regimine Principium," in *Politics and Ethics,* trans. Sigmund, 4, 28.

19. Aquinas, "Summa" 2, First Part, 95.2, 53.

20. Aquinas, "Summa," 97.2, 57; Dino Bigongiari, *The Political Ideas of St. Thomas Aquinas* (Riverside, N.J.: Hafner, 1953), xxiii; Aquinas, "Summa" 1, 92.1, 38.

21. Aquinas, "De Regimine," 2, 17–18; 6, 23.

22. Quoted in Bigongiari, *Political Ideas,* xxxiv.

23. Aquinas, "Summa" 2, First Part, 90.3, 45; 105.1, 58–59.

24. Black, "Christianity and Republicanism," 651.

25. John Courtney Murray, *We Hold These Truths* (New York: Sheed and Ward, 1960), 117; MacIntyre, *Whose Justice?,* 200.

26. Sigmund, *Politics and Ethics,* xvi.

27. Martin Luther, "On Christian Liberty," quoted by Reinhold Niebuhr, *The Nature and Destiny of Man* (New York: Scribner, 1943), 2:186; *The Martin Luther Christmas Book,* ed. Roland H. Bainton (Philadelphia, Penn.: Westminster Press, 1948), 38.

28. Luther, "On Trade and Usury," in *Works,* ed. Walther I. Brandt (Philadelphia: Muhlenberg Press, 1962), vol. 45, trans. Charles M. Jacobs, 245–310; H. Richard Niebuhr, *Christ and Culture* (New York: Harper, 1951), 177.

29. Ernst Troeltsch, *The Social Teachings of the Christian Churches,* trans. Olive Wyon (New York: Macmillan, 1931), 2:541; Roy Pascal, *The Social Basis of the German Reformation: Martin Luther and His Times* (New York: Augustus Kelley, 1971), 146, 187; Luther, "Against the Robbing and Murdering Hordes," trans. Charles M. Jacobs, in *Works* (Philadelphia: Fortress Press, 1967), vol. 46, 53.

30. Karl Holl, *What Did Luther Understand by Religion?* (Philadelphia, Penn.: Fortress Press, 1977), 105–108; John M. Headley, *Luther's View of Church History* (New Haven, Conn.: Yale Univ. Press, 1963), 2–10.

31. Hugh T. Kerr, *A Compend of Luther's Theology* (Philadelphia, Penn.: Westminster Press, 1966), 147.

32. Max Weber, "Religious Rejections of the World," in *From Max Weber,* trans. H. H. Green and C. W. Mills (New York: Oxford Univ. Press, 1958), 342.

33. John Calvin, *Institutes of the Christian Religion*, trans. John Allen (Philadelphia, Penn.: Westminster Press, 1936), vol. 1, book 3, ix, 1, 778, 220; David Little, *Religion, Order, and Law* (New York: Harper & Row, 1969), 40.

34. Calvin, *Institutes*, vol. 1, book 1, xiii-xiv, 70–98; Ephesians 1:4–5.

35. Calvin, *Institutes*, vol. 2, book 4, xx, 2, 772; Ralph C. Hancock, *Calvin and the Foundations of Modern Politics* (Ithaca, N.Y.: Cornell Univ. Press, 1989), 166.

36. Calvin, *Institutes*, vol. 2, book 4, xx, 3, 772–773; Troeltsch, *Social Teachings*, 2:620.

37. Calvin, *Institutes*, vol. 2, book 4, xx, 25, 798; Michael Walzer, *The Revolution of the Saints* (Cambridge, Mass.: Harvard Univ. Press, 1965).

38. Calvin, *Institutes*, vol. 2, book 4, xx, 31, 304; 32, 804.

39. Calvin, *Institutes*, book 4, xx, 8, 778; Sheldon Wolin, *Politics and Vision: Continuity and Innovation in Western Political Thought* (Boston: Little Brown, Boston, 1960), 176.

40. Calvin, *Institutes*, vol. 1, book 4, iii, 15, 330; Hancock, *Calvin and Foundations*, 49.

41. Little, *Religion*, 127.

42. Little, *Religion*, 57–65.

43. The most famous are, of course, Max Weber, *The Protestant Ethic and the Spirit of Capitalism* (1905), and R. H. Tawney, *Religion and the Rise of Capitalism* (1926). See also H. R. Trevor-Roper, *The Crisis of the Seventeenth Century: Religion, the Reformation and Social Change* (New York: Harper and Row, 1968).

44. Romans 15:1–2.

45. Troeltsch, *Social Teachings*, 2:589.

46. Troeltsch, *Social Teachings*, 2:663.

47. William Bradford, *Of Plymouth Plantation* (New York: Knopf, 1970).

48. Quoted in James Hastings Nichols, *Democracy and the Churches* (Philadelphia, Penn.: Westminster Press, 1951), 29.

49. Simon Schama, *Rembrandt's Eyes* (Knopf, New York, 1999), 497.

50. John Butt, *Johann Sebastian Bach: The Learned Musician* (Norton, New York, 2000).

CHAPTER 11

1. Thomas G. Saunders, *Protestant Concepts of Church and State* (New York: Holt, Rinehart and Winston, 1964), 243; Martin E. Marty, *Righteous Empire: The Protestant Experience in America* (New York: Dial, 1970), 265.

2. Perry Miller, *Jonathan Edwards* (New York: Greenwood Press, 1949), 11; John Coolidge, *The Pauline Renaissance in England* (Oxford: Clarendon Press, 1970), 69; George Armstrong Kelley, "Politics and the American Religious Consciousness," *Deadalus* 3, Winter 1982, 132.

3. Mark DeWolfe Howe, *The Garden and the Wilderness: Religion and Government in American Constitutional History* (Chicago, Ill.: Univ. of Chicago Press, 1965); Irwin H. Polishook, *A Controversy in New and Old England* (Englewood Cliffs, N.J.: Prentice-Hall, 1967), 34.

4. Albert C. Applegarth, *Quakers in Pennsylvania* (Baltimore, Md.: Johns Hopkins Press, 1892), 40.

5. Sydney E. Ahlstrom, *A Religious History of the American People* (New York: Doubleday, 1975), 1:169; T. J. Curry, *First Freedoms*, 218; Henry May, *The Enlightenment in America* (New York: Oxford Univ. Press, 1976), 45–46; Barry Alan Shain, *The Myth of American Individualism* (Princeton, N.J.: Princeton Univ. Press, 1994), 193.

6. Shain, American Individualism, 132; Catherine L. Albanese, *Sons of the Fathers: The Civil Religion of the American Revolution* (Philadelphia, Penn.: Temple Univ. Press, 1976), 194; John Adams, "Letter to Thomas Jefferson," in *Adams-Jefferson Letters,* 339–340, quoted in Shain, *American Individualism*, 196.

7. Paul F. Boller Jr., *George Washington and Religion* (Dallas, Tex.: SMU Press, 1963); "Washington's Farewell Address" in *Annals of America* (Chicago, Ill.: Encyclopedia Britannica, 1968), 3:612.

8. Anson Phelps Stokes, *Church and State in the United States* (New York: Harper, 1950), 1:512; Robert N. Bellah and Phillip E. Hammond, *Varieties of Civil Religion* (New York: Harper and Row, 1980), 17.

9. James Madison, *Papers* (Chicago, Ill.: Univ. of Chicago Press, 1973), 8:299–300; Walter Berns, *The First Amendment and the Future of American Democracy* (New York: Basic, 1970), 205.

10. Stokes, *Church and State*, 1:338–339; Robert N. Bellah, "Civil Religion in America," *Deadalus* 96, Winter 1967, 7–8.

11. G. Adolf Koch, *Republican Religion: The American Revolution and the Cult of Reason* (New York: Holt, 1933), 38–50; May, *Enlightenment*, 174–175.

12. Bernard Bailyn, *The Ideological Origins of the American Revolution* (Cambridge, Mass.: Harvard Univ. Press, 1967), 23–25; Charles F. Mullettt, "Classical Influences on the American Revolution," *Classical Journal* 35 (1939–1940), 93–94.

13. Bailyn, *Ideological Origins*, 24–26; Donald H. Meyer, *The Democratic Enlightenment* (New York: Putnam, 1976), 118; Shain, *American Individualism*, ix–xx.

14. John Locke, *Second Treatise on Government* in *Two Treatises on Government* (Cambridge: Cambridge Univ. Press, 1970), chap. 5, 25, 304.

15. John Locke, *An Essay Concerning Human Understanding*, ed. Peter H. Nidditch (Oxford: Clarendon Press, 1979), book 2, chap. 1, 2; book 4, chap. 9, 2; chap. 10, 2.

16. John Locke, *The Reasonableness of Christianity* (Palo Alto, Calif.: Stanford Univ. Press, 1958), 57–59.

17. Locke, *Second Treatise*, chap. 5, 35, 310.

18. Locke, *Second Treatise*, chap. 5, 27, 305.

19. Locke, *Second Treatise*, chap. 5, 27, 306; 31, 308; 46, 318.

20. Locke, *Second Treatise*, chap. 7, 88, 342; 90, 344; chap. 11, 138, 379.

21. Locke, *Second Treatise*, chap. 6, 54, 322.

22. Locke, *Second Treatise*, chap. 8, 96, 350.

23. John Locke, *A Letter Concerning Toleration* (Oxford: Clarendon Press, 1979).

24. Locke, *A Letter Concerning Toleration*.

25. See, for example, Garry Wills, *Inventing America: Jefferson's Declaration of Independence* (Garden City, N.Y.: Doubleday, 1978).

26. Francis Hutcheson, *A System of Moral Philosophy* 2, ix, 2, quoted in Alasdair MacIntyre, *Whose Justice? Which Rationality?* (Notre Dame, Ind.: Univ. of Notre Dame Press, 1988), 274.

27. James Bryce, *The American Commonwealth* (Chicago, Ill.: Sergel, 1891), 1:299; Glen Tinder, "At the End of Pragmatism," *First Things* 56, October 1995; *The Federalist* (New York: Modern Library, 1937), 232, 237.

28. *Annals of Congress of the United States* (Washington, D.C.: Gales and Seaton, 1834), 1:370; Berns, *First Amendment*, 7–8.

29. Jefferson, during his presidency in 1802, wrote in response to an inquiry from the Baptists at Danbury, Connecticut: "I contemplate with sovereign reverence that act of the whole American people [the First Amendment] building a wall of separation between church and state."

30. Lawrence M. Friedman, "The Conflict Over Constitutional Legitimacy," in *The Abortion Dispute and the American System*, ed. Gilbert Y. Steiner (Washington, D.C.: Brookings, 1983), 20–21.

31. *Annals of Congress*, 1:729–730.

32. The term "benevolent neutrality" was used in a somewhat narrower sense by Chief Justice Warren Burger in his decision for the Court in the case of *Walz v. Tax Commission*, 397 U.S. 669 (1969), approving tax exemptions for religious bodies.

33. The establishment clause was first found to cover the states in *Cantwell v. Connecticut*, 310 U.S. 296 (1940), but was not actually applied to state law until Justice Hugo Black's epoch-making decision in *Everson v. Board of Education*, 330 U.S. 15 (1946). Prayer and Bible reading in the public schools were ruled unconstitutional in *Engel v. Vitale*, 370 U.S. 425 (1961), and *Abington School District v. Schempp*, 374 U.S. 222 (1962).

34. Alexis de Tocqueville, *Democracy in America* (New York: Vintage, 1945), 1:316.

CHAPTER 12

1. "How Are We Doing?" *Public Perspective* 8 (Storrs, Conn.: Roper Center, October 1997), no. 6, 19.

2. "Americans Rate Their Society," *Public Perspective* 8 (February, 1997), no. 2, 22.

3. "Americans Rate Their Society."

4. "The State of the Church, 2000," *Berna Research Online*, 21 March 2000; Christian Smith, *American Evangelicalism: Embattled and Thriving* (Chicago, Ill.: Univ. of Chicago Press, 1998), 219.

5. Robert N. Bellah, et al., *Habits of the Heart* (Berkeley: Univ. of California Press, 1985), 221; Robert Wuthnow, "Science and the Sacred," in *The Struggle for America's Soul* (Grand Rapids, Mich.: Eerdmans, 1998), 143–144; Robert S. Lichter, Stanley Rothman, and Linda S. Lichter, *The Media Elite* (Bethesda, Md.: Adler and Adler, 1986).

6. "How Are We Doing?" (October 1997), 3; George H. Gallup Jr., and James

Castelli, *The People's Religion: American Faith in the 90s* (New York: Macmillan, 1989), 21.

7. "Americans Rate Their Society," (February 1997), 10; Everett C. Ladd, "Everyday Life: How Are We Doing?" *Public Perspective* 10 (April 1999), no. 3, 1; Peter Berkowitz, *Virtue and the Making of Modern Liberalism* (Princeton, N.J.: Princeton Univ. Press, 1999), 26.

8. John Rawls, *A Theory of Justice* (Cambridge, Mass.: Harvard Univ. Press, 1971), 508.

9. Samuel P. Huntington, *The Clash of Civilizations and the Remaking of World Order* (New York: Simon & Schuster, 1996), 305.

10. *Statistical Abstract of the World*, third edition, ed. Annmarie Muth (Detroit, Mich.: Gale, 1997); "Crime-busting," *The Economist*, 1 November 1997.

11. John Finnis, *Natural Law and Natural Rights* (Oxford: Clarendon Press, 1980), 397.

12. For example, Isaiah 2:2–4, Jeremiah 22:3, Micah 4:3–4, Matthew 5:44–45, Mark 7:1–16, Luke 2:30–32, I Corinthians 12:4–13, and Galatians 2:14, 3:28.

13. Joseph A. Califano Jr., "A Weapon in the War on Drugs," *Washington Post*, 10 October 1998; John J. DiIulio Jr., "Supporting Black Churches," *Brookings Review* (Spring 1999), 43; David B. Larson and Byron R. Johnson, "Religion: The Forgotten Factor in Cutting Youth Crime" (New York: Manhattan Institute, 1999), 12.

14. Daniel P. Moloney, " 'Saving' the Poor," *First Things*, May 1999, 42; Amy L. Sherman, *Restorers of Hope* (Wheaton, Ill.: Crossway Books, 1997), 217.

15. Charles L. Glenn, *The Ambiguous Embrace* (Princeton, N.J.: Princeton Univ. Press, 2000), 62–73.

16. Glenn, *Ambiguous Embrace*, 241–256; Stephen V. Monsma, *Positive Neutrality* (Westport, Conn.: Greenwood Press, 1993), 257–258; Glenn C. Loury, "Professors and the Poor: Discussion at a Poverty Conference," in *One by One from the Inside Out: Essays and Reviews on Race and Responsibility in America* (New York: Free Press, 1995), 213, cited by Glenn, *Ambiguous Embrace*, 35.

17. Guenter Lewy, *Why America Needs Religion: Secular Modernity and Its Discontents* (Grand Rapids, Mich.: Eerdmans, 1996), 87–115; T. David Evans, et al., "Religion and Crime Reexamined," *Criminology* 33 (1955), 195–224; John Cochran and Ronald Akers, "Beyond Hellfire," *Journal of Research in Crime and Delinquency* 26 (1989), 221; Barry A. Kosmin, *The National Survey of Religious Identification: 1989–90* (New York: City University of New York, 1991), 5; *The Connecticut Mutual Life Report on American Values in the 1980s: The Impact of Belief* (New York: Research and Forecasts, 1981), 66; Lewy, *Why America Needs Religion*, 125.

18. Proverbs 29:18.

19. Isaiah 28:7.

20. Karl Barth, *Community, State, and Church* (Garden City, N.Y.: Doubleday, 1960), 80.

21. Albert R. Hunt, "The Religious Right Is About Politics, Not Faith," *Wall Street Journal*, 20 August 1998.

22. In my own experience at the grassroots level, as a volunteer worker at a church-based shelter and advocacy chairman for a coalition of churches and syna-

gogues operating social service programs for the poor in a suburban county outside Washington, D.C., I have found that religious groups can constructively engage on some public policy issues, but also can be tempted to give unconsidered backing, without independent research, to measures on complicated subjects that at least require careful study.

23. Stanley Hauerwas, *The Peaceable Kingdom: A Primer of Christian Ethics* (Notre Dame, Ind.: Univ. of Notre Dame Press, 1983), 100; John Paul II quoted by Robert A. Sirico, "The Bishops' Big Economic Tent," *Wall Street Journal*, 10 December 1996.

24. *Board of Education v. Mergens*, 496 U.S. 226 (1990).

25. *Jackson v. Benson* [Case No. 98–376], 1998.

26. *Santa Fe Independent School District v. Doe* [Case No. 99–62], 2000.

27. Stephen V. Monsma, *When Sacred and Secular Mix* (Lanham, Md.: Rowman & Littlefield, 1996), 73.

28. Glenn, *Ambiguous Embrace*, 107–109.

29. Robert Wuthnow, "Tocqueville's Question Reconsidered: Voluntarism and Public Discourse in Advanced Industrial Societies," in *Between States and Markets: The Voluntary Sector in Comparative Perspective*, ed. Robert Wuthnow (Princeton, N.J.: Princeton Univ. Press, 1991), 291.

30. Monsma, *Positive Neutrality*, 258.

31. Glenn, *Charitable Choice*, 99.

32. See, for example, Steven Weinberg, "A Designer Universe?" *New York Review of Books*, 21 October 1999, 46.

33. H. Richard Niebuhr, *The Kingdom of God in America* (New York: Harper, 1937), 12.

Index

truth, 36
Tudor monarchy, 148–49
Turgot, Anne-Robert-Jacques, 19
Tutankhamen, 83
Twain, Mark, 122
Two Treatises on Government (Locke), 222

Umayyads, 95
umma, 95
Unitarians, 101
United States, 172–73; Bill of Rights, 215, 219, 225–26; and classical models, 220–21; founders, 218–20; fundamentalism, 103, 105; and religion, 215–18; religious liberty, 225–28; tolerance, 216–17, 223–24
universal law, 202
universalism, 49, 142–43, 193
University of Paris, 202
University of Virginia, 220
Upanishads, 67, 69
Uthman, 95
utilitarianism, 16, 159–63

Vaisyas, 69, 72–73
Valentinus, 114
Valla, Lorenzo, 145
value systems, 6–8; single source, 230–32
values, 2–6, 229–30
van Noorten, Bernard, 56
Varhamana (Mahavira), 71
Vasari, Giorgio, 146
Vedas, 66, 67
veil of ignorance, 167, 168, 169
Vendidad, 86
Venus of Lespurges, 60
Vermeer, Jan, 65
Vietnam War, 129–31, 167
Virgil, 140
virtue, 137–38, 146
Vishnu, 66
Visigoths, 196

Voltaire, 21, 154–56, 231
voting, and general will, 44–45

Wagner, Richard, 125
war, 48, 50, 94–95, 140, 201
warrior people, 38
Washington, George, 21, 218–19, 246
Weber, Max, 17, 57, 73, 107, 208
Weigel, George, 97
Welfare Reform Act, 244
Wesley, John, 209–10, 211
Whigs, 19
The White Goddess (Graves), 60
Whitehead, Alfred North, 75–76, 172
Wilde, Oscar, 23
Wilken, Robert, 80
will, 199, 200, 209
William of Ockham, 100
Williams, Bernard, 173
Williams, Roger, 216, 223
Wilson, Edward O., 10, 32, 171
Wilson, James Q., 32, 171
Winthrop, John, 119, 216
Wiredu, Kwasi, 58
Wittgenstein, Ludwig, 166
women, 138; and religion, 76, 109, 114–15
Woodstock Nation, 130
Woolley, Leonard, 58, 81, 82–83
Wordsworth, William, 121, 122, 132
world spirit, 47, 52
World War II, 50–51, 75–76
Wuthnow, Robert, 244

Xenophanes, 182
Xia dynasty, 38–39

Yahweh, 83
yin and yang, 39
Yohanah ben Zakkai, 181

Zealots, 88
Zen Buddhism, 73
Zeno, 64
Zoroastrianism, 85–86, 196
Zweig, Stefan, 126
Zwingli, Ulrich, 118

About the Author

A. James Reichley is Senior Fellow at the Public Policy Institute at George-town University.